WISCONSIN'S BEST
BEER GUIDE

A Travel Companion
THIRD EDITION

by Kevin Revolinski

Holt, Michigan 48842

Wisconsin's Best Beer Guide, 3rd edition
by Kevin Revolinski

Copyright © 2015 Kevin Revolinski

Thunder Bay Press
Holt, Michigan 48842
www.thunderbaypressmi.com

First edition June 2010
Second edition November 2012
Third edition September 2015

19   18   17   16   15   1   2   3   4   5

ISBN: 978-1-933272-55-9
Library of Congress Control Number: 2015941262

Photographs by Preamtip Satasuk except where credited.
Book and cover design by Julie Taylor.

Printed in the United States of America

Note: Prices, special offers, hours, availability, etc. listed in this guide are
subject to change.

For Grandpa Louie

He told me this joke once and I said I'd put it in the next edition of this book...

Two guys sitting at the bar. One guy sips his beer and makes a face. "I think there's something in my beer." His buddy tells him, "Well, why don't you send it to a lab to be tested." So he does. About a week later he gets a letter. "What's it say?" asks his friend. "Says here I should rest that horse for two weeks and it should be fine."

TABLE OF CONTENTS

PREFACE

In 2006 I wrote my first version of this book finding a brewing scene that included just over 60 breweries. By the first edition of the newly titled *Wisconsin's Best Beer Guide* in 2010, there were over 70. For the second edition we rolled up over 90. Now in just two years that number has leapt over 130, and the numbers of craft beer bars, growler fills/liquor stores, and restaurants with a couple dozen craft beers on draft have increased as well, making the "Stumbling Distance" suggestions for each brewery richer and more difficult to choose.

The Wisconsin reputation for beer is well known. In September 2011 when the *Today Show* came to Green Bay to broadcast live from Lambeau Field on the opening day of NFL football, I was invited on to line up a few samples for Al Roker at 8 AM. Beer for breakfast? Sure, why not? And a bit of cheese and bratwurst on the side that day.

More and more people aren't interested in just drinking any old thing. There is an increased expectation of quality and a call to support your local businesses. More and more, the average beer drinker is taking a good long look at the local beers. Craft beer perhaps intimidates some drinkers who aren't accustomed to a few of the bolder styles or who have gotten used to the "lawnmower" beers of summer. There is no question that people's palates are getting more sophisticated. Just note the most popular beers listed for each of the breweries. Back in 2006 it was strictly the pilsners or whatever had "Light" tacked on at the end of the beer name. That's not always the case anymore, and even in cases where it is, other styles are creeping up on these. Many breweries see their Scotch ales, stouts, and Belgian-style brews taking the lead. More than anything, the hopheads are putting the India Pale Ales out in front. Barrel-aging has become expected for at least special occasion releases, and sours are getting a surprising amount of attention.

Yes, a few breweries went under or changed hands since the last edition, but Wisconsin still has a net gain of a couple dozen, and there are more to come. Here's a tip of the hat to the ones who closed their doors.

American Sky Beer
Cheddarheads
Das Bierhaus
Hydro Street Brewing

Randy's Funhunter's became 841 Brewhouse
Stonefly Brewing became Company Brewing

I put a few breweries in this edition that weren't open when we went to print but would be a month or three after that. I wanted to make sure this book would be up-to-date for as long as possible after its release. Just be sure to phone first or check a website if you're making a long pils-grimage. This is a static guidebook (until the next edition) and changes can happen overnight. Two of the breweries that closed did so while I was looking at final edits.

Drive safely and don't drive at all when you've had too much. The mission here is to have fun exploring while trying new brews and revisiting favorites. Go enjoy the great brews Wisconsin has to offer and stop at a few other cool places along the way. Lift a pint and let the pils-grimage begin!

DRINK WISCONSINBLY

Wisconsin: It's not just a state, it's a lifestyle—a mindset—and it's a drinking style. Richard Lorbach of Waukesha came up with this perfect expression, and he's been selling t-shirts ever since. Sure, it starts with a t-shirt, but pretty soon you know you want to  collect the pint glass, shot glass, mug, flask, can cooler, bottle openers, magnets, and then for the advanced level of Wisconsin love, perhaps the Drink Wisconsinbly neon sign.

Tailgate Wisconsinbly and Fish Wisconsinbly are also options as is a pink breast cancer-themed Fight Wisconsinbly shirt. So get out there and show everyone how you drink.

Wisconsin retailers such as ShopKo, Kohl's, Mill's Fleet Farm, The University Book Store and several others (plus a few Minnesota retailers with Wisconsin-envy) are carrying Drink Wisconsinbly products or you can order online directly from the website. www.drinkwisconsinbly.com Use the special code BEERGUIDE for 10% off your order.

INTRODUCTION

We live in "God's Country" with water from when the earth was pure, when glaciers melted and left artesian wells that would create the foundation of a land of lagers, an empire of ales, where Schlitz made Milwaukee famous, Pabst got blue ribbons, and Miller called its beer "champagne" and put its name on that time when we just needed a good brewsky. (It's Miller time!) Even our baseball team is the Brewers. This is a Beer State where *kraeusening* is tantamount to breathing and a brewed beverage is something akin to a fine French wine or Scotch whiskey. We are only considered Cheeseheads because Beerheads seemed inappropriate for prime-time television—what with the kids watching and all—and frankly the cheese wedge was simply easier to balance than a beer mug when they designed the hats—not to mention spillage.

At one time before the Dark Ages of 1919 to 1933 (Prohibition), Wisconsin had a brewer at practically every crossroads with farmers doing their own little operations and bigger bottle works setting up in town. You couldn't swing a cat without hitting one. When consumption of our veritable holy water became a mortal and legal sin, many were the breweries that went beer belly up. The larger ones survived, a few got by on root beer and soda (Pabst survived with cheese), and for this we can lift a pint. Miller, Pabst, Schlitz, G. Heileman, Blatz—the list of Hall of Famers is long in Wisconsin, but we live in a new golden age. Since the late 1980s, we have witnessed a rise in the number of local breweries. Places that love beer for beer's sake. Places that aren't necessarily looking to send a keg to a tavern in Hoboken, New Jersey, or a million cases to a liquor store in L.A. Point Beer always claimed, "When you're out of Point, you're out of town." Nowadays, they might be getting a little more distance on shipping, but they have a good... er... point: many of Wisconsin's beers are personal, and unless you take your glass outside the screen door behind the bar, you won't find some of these brews beyond a good dart toss from the tap handle. Many of us Wisconsinites are fortunate to have someone looking out for us with a handcrafted lager or ale. Who in this state should not have their own personal hometown beer? (My condolences to those who don't, but don't worry—this book can help you adopt.) Designate a driver (or pack your sleeping bag in the trunk), turn the page, and set off on a *pils*-grimage to the breweries of Wisconsin.

BUT I DON'T LIKE BEER

You'll hear it time and time again when you ask a brewer—pro or homebrewer—why they got into brewing. Many of them will tell you they were dissatisfied with what was on the market back before the advent of the modern craft beer revolution. Maybe they took a trip to Germany. Maybe they were inspired by another homebrewer. But in the end, regardless of that original motivation, it becomes a passion for quality beer. I have to admit it took me a long time to come to beer. If you had offered me a beer in college, I would likely have gone the choosy beggar path and asked if you had any vodka or rum instead. I really didn't even like beer. I can already hear the collective gasp of horror, but let me explain: beer was social lubricant, something you sipped at with friends at a cookout, bought for the cute woman at the other end of the bar, or beer-bonged on occasion. I didn't like the taste so much and—oh the humanity—often didn't even finish them. I killed many a houseplant at parties and have gotten hordes of bees drunk at picnics with the remains of a bottle of Something-or-Other Light.

But consider this: what better person to send around on a beer discovery journey than the person who knew absolutely nothing? I'd be learning from scratch and whatever I found would be useful for a beginning beer drinker or at least commiserating confirmation for the connoisseur. And since Wisconsin is my home state, there was more than a little pride involved as well, like I might be introducing my family to friends or fellow travelers.

It wasn't until craft beer that I became a Born Again Beer Drinker. Beer experts already know, and commercial beer drinkers might be leery of the fact, that outside of the mass-produced impersonal brews, beers are as different as people. They have tremendous character, and the people who dedicate their lives to brewing are characters as well. Traveling to visit a brewery—what I like to call a *pils*-grimage—is as much about appreciating the subtleties and variations of beer as it is about taking a peek into local communities and beer's place in them. Part of what makes Wisconsin great, and what makes brewing great, is that even the little guy can get in on the action. All respects to the giants of the mass-market beer industry, but how cool is it to walk into a local place and see the brewmaster standing at the bar sharing suds with the guy next door?

This book is a compilation of all the places that brew their own beer commercially in Wisconsin. That means from the megabrewer

MillerCoors all the way down to the little nanobrewery Mines Creek Brewery in Spring Valley. The list changes often as pubs close and others pounce on the used equipment and open up elsewhere. Since the first book *The Wisconsin Beer Guide: A Travel Companion* in 2007, through these three editions of *Wisconsin's Best Beer Guide*, the numbers have been growing faster and faster, and we are now in triple digits.

Using the very latest cutting edge state-of-the-art rocket-science-level technology, I established the locations of all of the breweries in the state. OK, actually it was a Sharpie and a free Wisconsin highway map paid for with tax dollars and available at www.travelwisconsin.com or 800-432-8747. I sat down with the list and divided the state into six zones. Each of those zones is listed in the Where's the Beer At? section and shows the brewtowns alphabetically. If you already know the name of the brewery

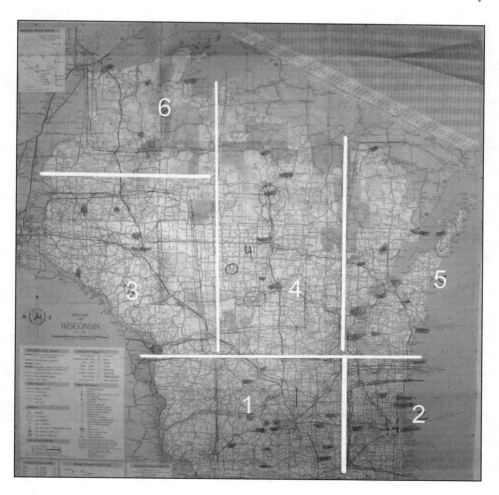

you are seeking, look for it in the cross referenced lists at the beginning of Where's the Beer At? The center brewery of each zone is generally no more than an hour's drive from any of the surrounding breweries in that same zone. Make sense? Worked for me!

And do I still hate beer? Not on your life! Just characterless beer maybe. I am a convert. I gained about ten pounds from my research the first time around and chose to write *60 Hikes Madison* right after that to wear it off. You may notice *Best Easy Day Hikes Milwaukee* appeared on the market at the same time the second book was released. And this one? Well, let's just say I need to write another hiking book. I call it the guidebook-writing weight-control program. Results may vary.

WHAT IS BEER?

Beer is produced by fermenting some sort of starch product. In many cases this is barley, wheat, oats, or rye, but even corn, rice, potatoes, and certain starchy roots in Africa have been used. In parts of Latin America, corn is chewed, spit out, and left to ferment and become a sort of corn beer called *chicha*. I've tried it… *before* my traveling companion told me about the chewing process. We are no longer on speaking terms. Don't expect MillerCoors to be rolling it out in mass quantities very soon. And since you don't hear anyone advertising "brewed from the finest Senegalese cassava roots" you can guess barley is still the primary grain of choice. (If you've tasted some of those commercial non-Wisconsin beers though, you've gotta wonder.) There's no distilling for beer—that would make it some kind of liquor, and it's not strictly sugars or fruit juices—which is where your wine comes from.

THE HISTORY OF BEER

MANNA FROM HEAVEN

Yes, beer is pure brewed right here in "God's country" (Wisconsin, or so claimed G. Heileman's Old Style Beer), but it wasn't always so. Egyptians loved it long before; Sumerians wrote down recipes for it on stone tablets, and you can imagine the drunken bar brawls over at the Viking lodge. Beer dates way back beyond 5000 BC, which is before *writing* even. (I think Ernest Hemingway, F. Scott Fitzgerald, and many other writers have also put the one before the other.)

The word itself comes to us by way of Middle English *ber,* from Old English *bEor* which goes to show you just how difficult life must have been without spellchecker. The English version surely comes from *bior* which was Old High German which became Old Low German by the end of a serious night of drinking.

BEER IN WISCONSIN

In 1998, I traveled to Czech Republic to see a bit of the land my forefathers left behind for the sake of Wisconsin. I landed in Frankfurt, Germany, (cheaper flight!) and with a rental car drove to Prague. Remember the movie *Stripes* with Bill Murray? His character said this about getting into Czechoslovakia: "It's like going into Wisconsin—you drive in, you drive out." Well, it is. In fact, as I bundled up in a jacket and faced an unseasonably cold June in Plzen, this is pretty much what struck me. My great-grandparents had packed up all they had into small trunks or had a big garage sale perhaps, left behind everyone they knew on this earth—friends, family, perhaps a few creditors—spent much of their remaining money on ocean liner tickets, braved the long and sometimes dangerous Atlantic crossing, had their names misspelled at Ellis Island* and went overland halfway across a continent to settle in the same damn place they left behind. Seriously. Change the highway signs to English and set up some road construction detours and I may as well have been driving down County Trunk C outside of Stevens Point. But these immigrants' absurd

---

* 'Hey Bucko?'—one of the family surnames had an unfortunate pronunciation with the English spelling so we had to add the 'h' after the 'c' (Buchko) to get everyone to pronounce it right, otherwise anyone addressing us felt they were potentially getting a little surly. Fuggetabout 'Lajcak,' many of us just let people say it as they will.

notions of improving their lots worked to our benefit: conditions were perfect here for making the same great German, Belgian, Czech, etc. beers of Northern Europe—and so they did.

The brewing equation in Wisconsin goes like this:

Immigrants

+

cold (frozen tundra)

+

water (unfrozen tundra)

+

grain (that flat sort of boring part near my hometown)

+

happy hour

=

beer!

Or even more simply:

Cold thirsty immigrant farmers = beer.

BEER TERRITORY

How serious were the European settlers about beer? Consider this: Wisconsin became a state in 1848. 1856 was the first kindergarten. The first brewery? 1835 in Mineral Point founded by John Phillips. The Welsh, coming to work in the lead mines, really started things off. Milwaukee's first brewery was Milwaukee Brewery (never would have thought of *that* name), founded in 1840. Despite our reputation for lagers, this brewery was doing English-style ales and porters. The name changed to Lake Brewery (interestingly we have Lakefront and Milwaukee Brewing Co. again these days), but the locals knew it by the surname of one of the founders: Owens' Brewery. The competition in town led Milwaukee to be the great brew city that it is. They had almost *fifty* breweries only twenty years later. And of course the state itself also blossomed with breweries. Most of this was due to the massive German immigration. *Prosit!* (A German toast to your health. Sometimes also *prost!*)

PROHIBITION

Just before the ratification of the 18th Amendment in 1919, people were as bitter as an IPA on mega-hops about the Germans, what with the World War and all, and of course it was the German-Americans running most of the breweries in Wisconsin! So we had some beer hate on the brew. A: Americans hate Germans. B: Germans make beer. C: Americans hate… now wait a minute! Why can't we all just get along? But the Prohibitionists had been on the boil already since the middle of the nineteenth century for religious and social motivations.

So the fat lady was singing you might say, but not in Wisconsin. Thirty-two states already had Prohibition in their state constitutions—Wisconsin was one of sixteen that did not.

In 1917 Congress passed a resolution to shut down sales, transportation, and production of all forms of alcohol. States signed off on it and the amendment went into effect on July 1, 1919. If you were looking for loopholes, the Volstead Act in October defined alcoholic beverages as containing over one-half percent of alcohol. So do the math here. At best, you'd need about NINE BEERS to drink the equivalent amount of alcohol as a normal picnic beer! Even the most ambitious drinkers weren't going to be getting a buzz.

Beer was one of the top industries in the state and it had just been banned.

The best way to make something attractive? Prohibit it. This also goes a long way to making it profitable on the black market. Stories of Al Capone and bootleggers and the mob in Chicago are widely known. But Wisconsin played the backyard to this story. Capone had his hangouts in

SO I MARRIED AN AXE-PROHIBITIONIST: CARRIE A. NATION

Imagine a six-foot, 175-pound teetotaler woman with an axe and an attitude. And you thought *your* marriage was rough. Once married to an alcoholic, Carrie A. Nation went on a rage against alcohol in the 1890s and until her death in 1911. Often joined by a chorus of hymn-singing women, she is known for marching into taverns and busting up the place with a hatchet. A resident of then dry-state Kansas, she wandered up to Wisconsin on occasion to lecture us. If you find yourself passing through Fond du Lac sometime (Zone 5), stop by J.D. Finnagan's Tavern and you'll find the "Historic Schmidt Sample Room, Scene Of The Famous Carrie Nation Hatchet Swinging Episode, July 18, 1902" where she smashed up a bottle of whiskey offered as a peace gesture by someone she was arguing with. The fighting words? "Every German in Wisconsin should be blown up with dynamite." Now *that's* harsh.

the Northwoods, and there are old escape tunnels he allegedly employed below Shipwrecked Brewpub in Door County. Something as crazy as outlawing beer was doomed to fail, and when Prohibition was repealed by the Twenty-first Amendment in 1933, there was much celebration. Miller sent a case to President Roosevelt. Many communities such as Cross Plains even had parades (see Esser's Cross Plains Brewing).

Not long after, the University of Wisconsin-Madison decided to serve beer on campus. This just seems normal to a Wisconsinite, but apparently there are a lot of colleges that still do not. What's *that* all about? Wisconsin even has a university named for beer: UW-Stout. OK, that's just coincidence actually, but I like the idea.

PHOTOGRAPHS COURTESY OF ESSER'S CROSS PLAINS BREWERY

BEER COMMERCIALS

Advertising wasn't a big deal right away. Who needed an ad to know where the brewery was across the street? As breweries got bigger and started shipping over distances (Milwaukee's population in the nineteenth century was too small to drink all the beer, and so they shipped to Chicago), there was a rise in beer propaganda. It started with newspapers, of course, and then on into the radio age. When the beloved radio show *Amos 'n' Andy* went to TV in 1951, Milwaukee's Blatz Beer was the sponsor.

Thanks to all the advertising, the names of Wisconsin's old beers are widely known. Think of Schlitz, "the beer that made Milwaukee famous." Laverne and Shirley worked at the fictional Milwaukee equivalent "Schotz" brewery. "Schlemiel! Schlimazel! Hasenpfeffer* Incorporated!" Old Style was "pure brewed in God's country" with waters from when the earth was pure (over in La Crosse at G. Heileman Brewing). Pabst Blue Ribbon: "PBR me ASAP." Old Milwaukee which "tastes as great as its name" boasted in their ads, "It doesn't get any better than this." Always an ad with some guys fishing in Alaska or eating crawdads in the bayou or whatever and the voiceover about New Orleans or someplace and Milwaukee being a thousand miles apart and it didn't make any difference to these guys who knew good beer. I wasn't really convinced that people would go so far out of their way for an Old Mil until I saw it appeared to be the import of choice in Panama when I lived there in 2003! "Welcome to Miller Time" "when it's time to relax, one beer stands clear" (the champagne of beers). And of course the "Tastes great, less filling" debates of Miller Lite. My favorite Lite commercial was the one with Bob Uecker, voice of the Milwaukee Brewers baseball team, being moved from his seat by an usher to the worst bleacher seat—"I must be in front row!" Classic.

Well, despite surviving the dry years on soda or near beer (or in the case of Pabst, cheese!), most of the breweries hit hard times by the late 60s, and some even crawled into the 70s before giving up the ghost. Rhinelander, Marshfield, Oshkosh, Rahr Green Bay, Potosi, Fauerbach—all these breweries bit the dust. One of the survival strategies of the big guys was to buy up the labels of the sinking ships and thus acquire the loyalists who went with them. So, for example, places like Point continued to brew Chief Oshkosh, and for years Joseph Huber Brewing (now Minhas Craft Brewery) produced Rhinelander and Augsburger.

A handful of the giants made it a bit further through the troubled times.

---

*   Hasenpfeffer is a traditional German stew made from marinated rabbit.

Schlitz, once America's largest brewer, made it to the 80s (still at number three in size) when Stroh's of Detroit bought them out. G. Heileman did some label buying (they bought Blatz in 1969) and then was passed around itself in the late 80s and early 90s until it was bought by Pabst in 1999. When all Heileman's breweries were shut down, City Brewery took over the original La Crosse facilities and kept the previous brewmaster. Now City Brewery does a pretty sizeable business with contract brews. They even repainted the famous World's Largest Six Pack grain silos. Pabst closed in Milwaukee in 1996 and the last of its breweries shut its doors in

RETRO BEER: SCHLITZ RETURNS!

Jos. Schlitz Brewing was a powerhouse which started when Mr. Schlitz took over the 1849 brewery of August Krug. Schlitz beer was a huge success and became known as "the beer that made Milwaukee famous." Schlitz dominated the market for years (and waited on hold throughout Prohibition), but then a strike at the brewery tripped them up. A certain St. Louis brewery stepped in and has dominated since. Schlitz suffered when the reins were no longer kept in the family. The thirst for expansion may have outweighed the thirst for good beer and in pushing to brew faster, the quality went down.

The beer got flat and to try to compensate, an additive was used to help produce a head. As that additive aged, it solidified! Schlitz became a bit like peanut butter—do you prefer creamy or chunky style? That didn't go over too well, and by 1981 the owners stopped brewing and sold off the brand to Stroh's in Detroit. Now Pabst Brewing, also a former Milwaukee brewer which now contracts breweries to make its namesake Blue Ribbon Beer and several other old-school brews, owns the Schlitz brand.

In 2008 Pabst brought the old legend back. They spent some time going over old brewery notes and interviewing the former brewers to come up with what they believe to be the old-school top-notch recipe: The Classic 60's Formula. Fans seem to agree. Schlitz is back in bottles and tap lines all around Wisconsin. Here's the craziness of mass-market beer: Schlitz is owned by Pabst but brewed by MillerCoors (formerly Miller) at a non-Wisconsin brewery facility. Hats off to them all for bringing back a nostalgic beer, but it sure would be nice if it came home to be brewed. Crack open a 16-oz (used to be 24) Tall Boy and take yourself back to the 1960s.

2001. The offices moved to Texas, Chicago, then California, but now they are opening a small brewery in an old church within their former brewing complex in Milwaukee! They own the labels for a variety of old Wisconsin beers including Old Style, Special Export, Old Milwaukee, and Schlitz, but now they contract brew, many of them at Miller.

Who's left standing after all this? It's hard to say and depends on one's definition. Miller, of course, remains but has been bought and merged a couple times and is now MillerCoors in the United States. Point Brewery still lives, and though Leinenkugel was bought by Miller, they still operate independently and retain their classic integrity. Gray's Brewing in Janesville is an old timer as well, but Prohibition switched them to a successful line of sodas, and it wasn't until the 90s that they started producing beer again.

Even as a few old-school brewers lay there bleeding, a few fresh upstarts were putting down roots and starting a trend that continues to grow and gives this book a reason for being. Randy Sprecher was working at Pabst when the blade of downsizing swept through. With a bit of inspiration, a modest sum of capital, and a whole lot of used equipment, Sprecher founded a "microbrewery" in 1985, the first in the state since Prohibition. Of the original small breweries to start up in the 80s, Capital Brewery (1986) and Lakefront (1987) are still up and running, and continuing to grow in popularity.

The history of Wisconsin brewing continues as we speak, with new brewpubs opening every year and a few unfortunates falling by the wayside. But you can play your part in making history: support your local brewers!

WHEN FARM BREWERIES WERE KING

One of the most overlooked breweries in your typical history of brewing is the farm brewery. OK, perhaps you get the image of Old Farmer Braun brewing up a batch of bad brewsky in the kitchen sink, but such is certainly not the case. On farms all across the state, from the 1830s to the 1860s, the good stuff was being made. These brewers—primarily German immigrants—knew their craft. Wisconsin had just become a state in 1848, and a revolution in the same year over in Germany was driving some people to seek a better life. And what's a better life without beer, pray tell?

Location was key. To brew, farmers needed a property with an artesian well, and since they were all lager brewers, they needed a freezable water source—such as a stream that could be dammed—for the ice needed to keep the beer below 40 degrees while it fermented (though most brewing was simply done in the winter when air conditioning was already amply provided).

Don't compare the farm breweries to sly moonshiners or bootleggers; these were legitimate businesses and tax records for many of them still exist. The German brewers adhered to the strict German Purity Law. Doing it all yourself, from the crops to the stein, was by no means a simple job. The farmers grew all their ingredients—hops and barley—and then needed to malt the grain. This part of the process took up about three-quarters of the facility. The actual brewing, in fact, took a much smaller portion of the space and labor. It was done typically in open top, iron brew kettles over an open wood flame. Imagine sweating over a smoky fire and then crossing the yard through a Wisconsin subzero winter to get to the 40-degree beer cellar. Lager was called Summer Beer, and if the temperature was too high in the cellars either the fermentation would blow up the kegs or the beer itself would spoil. Ice blocks and straw, however, could last long into the summer. Ever wonder why your grandparents referred to the freezer portion of your refrigerator as the ice box? The same method was at work on a smaller scale in homes.

By the end of the 1870s, most farm brewers were already out of business. Better transportation and the discovery of pasteurization meant that city brewers could ship beer farther without spoilage. Some of them had chemists on staff. Advertising made a contribution as well. And then, of course, there was just plain competitive big business strategies—the big city guys could come into town and court the saloons by offering whatever the saloons needed—new set of tables? Chairs? Maybe a new roof? Plus they could just drop prices to drive off the local competition. Then dairy farming went big and farmers saw better money (the cities didn't do so well raising milk herds).

Few are the remains of the farm breweries today; most of the structures have been worked into other more modern buildings or simply dismantled completely. These were pretty big operations in little townships and in rural sites (and the locations of remains are often still out in the country). Roman arches that mark old lagering cellars can still be found here and there. Most were never recorded in history books, so it takes an expert to identify them. Wayne Kroll of Fort Atkinson is one such person dedicated to the preservation of the record and has spent a lot of time searching them out. To date he has confirmed 150, but there are surely more. Wayne

PHOTOGRAPH COURTESY OF WAYNE KROLL

estimates there were once 25–30 farm breweries in the average county, one in nearly every township. Production was probably 100 to 300 barrels per year.

Some of the city breweries started as farm operations. Fred Miller was initially rural, though he bought some of his ingredients so was not quite a true farm brewery. And yes, nowadays Dave's Brew Farm operates in a wind-powered barn, and Sand Creek was founded in a farm shed, but these modern brewers aren't farm breweries in the strictest sense either.

Want to know more? Check out *Wisconsin's Frontier Farm Breweries* by Wayne Kroll, self-published. Order it from the Wisconsin Historical Society in Madison or Wayne Kroll himself at W3016 Green Isle Drive, Fort Atkinson, WI 53538, kroll@centurytel.net.

HOPS

Pioneers in Wisconsin found their new home to be an agricultural haven, and in the middle of the nineteenth century many farmers had success growing wheat. After that market peaked for them and prices dropped, many moved on to dairy farming which contributed to a great cheese industry and our future reputation as cheeseheads. Others found another crop that was in high demand locally and paying big prices: hops.

The first hops in Wisconsin were planted at what is now Wollersheim Winery near Prairie du Sac. Prior to the Civil War, much of the nation's hops were being grown in the east, but problems with a destructive pest, the hop louse, took their toll. Wisconsin, um, "hopped on the bandwagon," and by the end of the 1860s the crop had grown to over fifty times its yield at the beginning of that decade. Sauk County led the state and was one of the top growing regions in the United States. Much of the hops got on the rails in Kilbourn City and was shipped to other parts of the country. (Kilbourn City became Wisconsin Dells, and you can still find some local hops in Wisconsin Dells Brewing's Kilbourn Hop Ale.)

A blight, however, in 1882 put the smackdown on Wisconsin hops. That, combined with dropping hop prices, was the end of hoppy times, and the industry eventually found itself backed into a corner of sorts in the Washington State region.

A recent hop shortage in 2008 had brewers extremely concerned about where they could get hops in a timely manner and without breaking open piggy banks to afford them. The hops availability has gotten better, but the scare has inspired more and more Wisconsin growers to look at growing them. Brewers, however, have committed to buy what the farmers grow. Hops are a sensitive plant, and the risks—from pests to rainfall to blight—are numerous. But hops, I mean, *hopes* are high that this is a slight return to the heyday of Wisconsin hops.

INGREDIENTS

Hops
Malt
Water
Yeast
Other

THE DIVINE PROCESS

The first step in brewing beer is *MASHING*, and for this you need a malted grain, such as barley, and it needs to be coarsely ground. In Wisconsin we are fortunate to have our very own source of malt in Chilton (see Briess later in the book and check out the malting process). The brewer will add hot water to the malt to get the natural enzymes in the grain to start converting the starches into the sugars necessary for fermentation. Think of your bowl of sugared breakfast cereal growing soggy and then making the milk sweet. It's kind of like that, only different.

The next step is *SPARGING* when water ("from when the earth was pure") is flushed through the mash to get a sweet liquid we call *WORT*, which in all caps looks like a great alternative radio station we have in our capital, Madison. See? I told you we're all about beer here. The wort is sent to the brew kettle and filtered to remove the barley husks and spent grain.

Wort then needs to be boiled to kill off any unwanted microcritters and to get rid of some of the excess water. This generally goes on for about an hour and a half. It is at this stage that any other flavoring ingredients are generally added, including hops.

Once this is all done, the fermentation is ready to begin. A brewer once told me, "People don't make beer, yeast does." Yes, yeast is the magical little element that monks referred to as "God is Good" when they were making their liquid bread in the monasteries. If you wanted to grab a brewsky in the Middle Ages (and believe me you didn't want to drink the water), the best place to stop was the local monastery. The monks made beer, the travelers spent money, the church got along. Everyone happy. How the church ended up with Bingo instead of beer we may never know. Bummer.

Yeast eats sugars like the little fat boy in *Willie Wonka and the Chocolate Factory,* and as we all know from a long afternoon of drinking and stuffing our faces, what goes in must come out. As Kurt Vonnegut once put it and as unpleasant as it may seem, beer is yeast excrement: alcohol and a little bit of gas. Reminds me of a night of Keystone Light, actually.

ALES VS. LAGERS

There are two basic kinds of beer: ales and lagers. It's all about yeast's preferences. Some yeasts like it on top; some prefer to be on bottom. Up until now, yeasts have not been more creative in their brewing positions, but we can always fantasize.

Ale yeasts like it on top and will ferment at higher temperatures (60–70 °F) and so are quicker finishers (1–3 weeks) than lagers. Usually ales are sweeter and have a fuller body, which really starts to take this sexual allusion to extremes.

Lagers, on the other hand, use yeasts that settle in at the bottom to do their work and prefer cooler temps of about 40–55 °F. They take 1–3 months to ferment. Lagers tend to be lighter and drier than ales and are the most common beers, often easier to get along with for the average drinker and they don't mind if you leave the seat up. (In fact, you may as well, you'll be coming back a few times before the night is done.) For lager we can thank the Bavarians who—when they found that cold temperatures could control runaway wild yeasts in the warm summer ale batches—moved them to the Alps. The name lager comes from the German "to store."

Wisconsin, being the frozen tundra that it is in the wintertime, was ideal for this type of beer, and we have the German immigrant population to credit for getting things started here. Oh, they'll tell you that it was because of our cold water, winter, and great farmland, but then I have to ask myself: how could they have chosen any other place when we count

---

WHAT ARE IBUs?

Compounds in hops are what bring bitterness to your beer. IBU stands for International Bittering Units and gives beer drinkers something else to say about how bitter a beer is besides "really really" or "very very very" or "just a bit." Brewers use a spectrophotometer which measures how light passes through or reflects off a solution and thus determine the chemistry of their beer. This system offers an objective scientific accounting of a beer's bitterness, which, of course, is harder to otherwise pin down with our subjective tongues. The higher the number, the greater the actual (not *perceived* necessarily) bitterness. However, this number may not always predict your own experience of the beer. A beer with a lot of malt and a higher IBU of 60, for example, might not taste to you as bitter as a pint of bitters made with less malt and rated at 30 IBU. There is a limit to how much of the bittering compounds are actually soluble, so one cannot simply add hops infinitely and go screaming toward 100s of IBUs. (Heaven knows, because someone would have done it by now!) Plus, there's a limit to how much your tongue can even perceive. Debate goes on about what those limits are but pretty much after about 110 IBUs you are likely near the limit.

Germantown, Berlin, *New* Berlin, and Kohler among our communities? It's like we knew they were coming! Did you know there are also two Pilsens in Wisconsin? My grandfather, in fact, was a Pilsner and made a point of supporting pilsners quite well over the years.

Ale is the first real beer that was made and it was sort of a mutation of another alcoholic drink called *mead.* This was made with fermented honey. Remember the mead halls when you read *Beowulf* in high school? OK, I didn't read it either, but the Cliffs Notes mentioned it some. This is the sweet and potent concoction that put the happy in the Vikings as they raped, pillaged, and plundered. Someone added a bit of hops, and later some malt, and the hybrid *brackett* evolved. You can still find both of these here in Wisconsin (see White Winter Winery in Iron River) along with the ales and lagers. We don't discriminate like that. Equal opportunity drinkers we are.

THESE ARE NOT YOUR MALTED MILKBALLS

Malting is a process of taking a grain, such as barley or wheat, getting it to start germinating, and then drying it quickly to cut off that process. I like to call this *germinus interruptus,* but then I like to make a lot of words up, so take that with a grain of barley.

So the malting process is 1: get grain (seeds) wet; 2: let it get started; 3: roast it in a kiln until dried. And here's where the specialty malts come in. You can roast the malted grains to different shades, a bit like coffee beans, and you can even *smoke* the stuff for a real twist on flavor (check out Rauchbier). I mean like you smoke bacon, not like you smoke tobacco— don't get any ideas.

Why is barley the most common grain? It has a high amount of those enzymes for beer. So although corn, wheat, rye, and even rice can be used, you'll see that barley is the king of the malts. If you have gluten troubles, this is bad news because barley has it, but fear not—Wisconsin to the rescue. Check out Lakefront Brewery's gluten-free brew made with yet another grain called sorghum.

I know you're wondering, because I was too: What about malted milk balls? There *is* a connection, in fact. William Horlick of Racine, Wisconsin, sought to create a food for infants that was both nutritious and easy to digest. He mixed wheat extract and malted barley with powdered milk to form malted milk. Walgreen's Drugstores almost immediately started selling malted milkshakes, and *Voila!* another great Wisconsin idea entered the world.

WHAT'S HOPPENIN', HOP STUFF?

So why the hops? It's a plant for cryin' out loud; do you really want *salad* in your beer?? Actually, without refrigeration beer didn't keep all too well. The medieval monks discovered that hops had preservative properties. The sun never set on the British Empire which meant it never set on the beer either. So the Brits hopped the ale hard to get it all the way to India and thus India Pale Ale was born. (No, the color is not really pale, but compare it to a porter or a stout, and the name makes sense.)

The point in the process when you put the hops in makes all the difference, and generally it goes in the boil. Boil it an hour and it's bitter; half an hour and it's less bitter with a touch of the flavor and aroma; toward the end of the boil and you lose the bitter and end up with just the aroma and flavor, making it highly "drinkable." (You will hear people describing beer as very "drinkable," and it would seem to me that this was a given. Apparently not.) There is another way to get the hoppiness you want. Dry hopping—which sounds a lot like what some of yous kids was doin' in the backseat of the car—is actually adding the hops after the wort has cooled,

---

REINHEITSGEBOT!

Gezundtheit! Actually, it's not a Bavarian sneezing; it's the German Purity Law. Want to know how serious the Germans were about beer? By *law* dating back to 1516, beer had to be made using only these three ingredients: barley, hops, and water. (The law later added yeast to the ingredient list once Louis Pasteur explained to the world the role of the little sugar-eating microorganisms in the process.) But this meant you wheat or rye or oat lovers were out of luck. Barbarians! Bootleggers! Outcasts! Why so harsh on the alternative grains? Because these grains were necessary for breads and these were times of famines and the like. Fortunately, times got better and we have the wide variety of ales and lagers that we see today. Nevertheless, the Germans came to Wisconsin quite serious about beer (see Farm Breweries). In the end, the law was used more to control competitors and corner a market—so much for its pure intentions.

There's more to beer quality than a list of ingredients anyway; it's the *purity* of those ingredients that makes all the difference. It's also the time, patience, and care of the brewer that lifts the brew to a higher level. Am I talking about craft brewing here? I most certainly am!

say, in the fermenter, or more commonly in the keg.

But let me tell you this, when I first sipped a beer I only stared blankly at brewers when they asked me, "Now, do ya taste the hops in this one?" How was I to know? I mean, if someone from Papua New Guinea says, "Do you get that little hint of grub worm in that beer?" I really have nothing to go on. Before touring or on your brew tour, if you aren't already hops-wise, ask someone if you can have a whiff of some. I did, and suddenly the heavens parted and Divine Knowledge was to me thus imparted. I could then identify that aroma more accurately, and I have to confess I'm still not sure I taste it in those mass market beers.

THERE'S SOMETHING FUNNY IN MY BEER

So you know about the German Purity Law and the limits on what goes into a beer, but obviously there is a whole range of stuff out there that thumbs its nose at boundaries. Some of this is a good thing, some of it not so much. These beyond-the-basics ingredients are called *adjuncts*.

Let's talk about the type of adjunct that ought to make you suspicious and will elicit a curse or look of horror from a beer snob. In this sense an adjunct is a source of starch used to beef up the sugars available for fermentation. It is an ingredient, commonly rice or corn, used to cut costs by being a substitute for the more expensive barley. Pale lagers on the mass market production line commonly do this. It doesn't affect the flavor and often cuts back on the body and mouth feel of the brew, which is why if you drink a mass market beer and then compare it to the same style (but *without* adjuncts) from a craft brewer you will taste a significant difference.

You may hear beer snobs use the word adjunct when ripping on the mass produced non-handcrafted brews, but there are other ingredients which are also adjuncts that we can't knock so much.

Wheat, rye, corn, wild rice, oats, sorghum, honey—many are the options that don't just serve to save a buck or two on the batch ingredients but rather bring something to the beer. Maybe a longer lasting head, a silkier mouth feel, or a sweeter taste. And in the case of a wheat beer, can one really call wheat an adjunct? Most would say no. Word dicers will say yes. Whatever.

Fruits and spices are also friendly adjuncts. Think of cherry, orange, or pumpkin flavors in certain brews, or spices such as coriander in Belgian wit beers, ginger, nutmeg, or even cayenne pepper like Valkyrie Brewing's Hot Chocolate Stout or the Great Dane's Tri-Pepper Pils. Brewers can add chocolate, milk sugar, or even coffee as in the case of Lakefront's

Fuel Café Stout or Stone Cellar's Caffeinator Doppelbock. I had mint in a stout from South Shore. Furthermore puts black pepper in their IPA. By German Purity Law, of course, this is a big no-no, but there's nothing wrong with pushing the envelope a bit for some new tastes. It's not cutting corners, but rather creating new avenues.

Are you gluten-sensitive? Well, bummer for you, beer has that. But an alternative grain called sorghum does not, and Lakefront is making beer with it, and ALT Brew in Madison makes nothing but gluten-free beers. Adjunct? I'd say not. Point Brewery took a Specialty Ale gold at the 1991

BARRELS OF FUN

Remember pull tops[*], those little throwaway raindrop-shaped openers from beer cans that you used to cut your foot on at the beach? Prior to the pull tops and the modern apparatus that thankfully stays attached, some cans needed an opener like you'd use for a tin can of condensed milk. Thus some great collectibles in the beer can world are the first pull-top cans which boasted No Opener Needed (Pabst was one). There were also cone-tops, cans that opened like a bottle with a cap and had heads like the Tin Man. But before all this, and before the advent of the aluminum kegs, there were wooden barrels. The cooper—the guy who tended them—was almost as important as the brewer. He had to choose the right wood and get a tight fit in a world without duct tape and crazy glue. Imagine! Gone, you might say, are *those* days. But not so! Some of the craft brewers still age some of their beers in wood. Especially popular are the recycled bourbon barrels which give that whiskey aroma to the beer, but now rum, rye, wine and even tequila barrels are being used. Look for a barrel-aged brew at your local brewery and see what all the buzz is about.

[*]   Point Brewery was the last brewery to use pull tabs.

Great American Beer Festival for its Spud Premier Beer—made with the starch from Wisconsin potatoes!

GREEN BEER

It may sound like I'm talking about St. Patrick's Day, but this is about local brewers doing their part to work toward a cleaner, energy-efficient future while keeping us well stocked in suds. One of the first brewers to go "green" was Central Waters Brewing Company. They have solar panels heating water, providing power, and saving them money. The system pays for itself in roughly seven years and the savings over the lifetime of it are enormous. Dave's BrewFarm has some wind and solar power going as well, and the Grumpy Troll in Mt. Horeb installed solar panels at the beginning of 2010. Milwaukee Brewing Company uses vegetable oil from the Milwaukee Ale House to heat their boiler thus reducing fuel consumption, repurposing the old oil, and reducing bad exhaust gases.

Having a grain silo eliminates the need for bags of malt. Heat exchangers recapture the heat of cooling wort. Cooling water can be used to clean the tanks. In fact, New Glarus Brewery's expanded brewhouse uses the heat from a previous brew by pumping the wort into another tank and bringing in the next.

Using recycled equipment is another method of minimizing a brewery's impact on the environment. So many have used old dairy equipment in the past, but many more have purchased another brewer's systems.

Keeping the ingredients local is another great contributor to Wisconsin's economy that also cuts down on the energy required to bring grains in from far away. Capital Brewery made a buzz when they worked with growers on Washington Island to get the wheat for their Island Wheat beer. It was a shot in the arm for a struggling industry, and other brewers around the state—Lakefront Brewery and South Shore Brewery to name a couple—have followed suit. South Shore now grows all its own grain. Lakefront makes a beer brewed with *all* ingredients produced within 100 miles of the brewery. The recent hops shortages have inspired more growers to invest in hops production and cooperatives.

Not only are more and more brewers using local ingredients, but many more are also recycling the spent grain, sending it out to area farmers as feed for farm animals. As Bo Belanger of South Shore says, "Essentially we're paying the farmer to grow his own feed. I just borrow it for a moment for the sugars."

The latest trend has been in packaging: the aluminum can. Milwaukee

THE MAN BEHIND THE BARRELS

When Wisconsinite Tom Griffin tasted his first whiskey-barrel-aged beer, it was a life changing event. It was at a beer festival in Milwaukee and it had been brought in from someone out of state. So there was no way he could pick it up on a regular basis. But if he could get it locally… So he had an idea: convince brewers in the neighborhood to start making it as well. "Great idea, Tom, but we can't get barrels." "What if I can get the barrels for you?" This was the beginning of something special.

Tom had a background in biochemistry and had worked building bio-reactors. What's that? "Basically it looks like a giant stainless steel pressurized coffee pot that costs $25,000 to $250,000 depending on the size and bells and whistles," he says. "Bio-reactor" is a system that degrades contaminants in groundwater and soil with microorganisms which can be used as pharmaceuticals or food flavorings. I like the coffee pot answer better.

Tom's "coffee pot" work had taken him to Kentucky, a land of whiskey, and he knew where he could get the used barrels that would lend their unique character to an aging beer. He had no idea just how well his idea and efforts were going to be received. Soon he was delivering the barrels to more than 90% of the breweries across the entire country that wanted them. Now it may be down to a lot less than that, but nevertheless, this is a man the brewers call friend and his basement is stocked with the delicious "thank yous" of brewers.

Most of the old barrels have been used for 10 to 15 years. He took some to Tyranena Brewing Co. that are as old as 25 years. (Older than some of the drinkers of the beer!) Most of the barrels held whisky, rye or brandy. Tom is always looking for new types of barrels to expand the palette of flavors. It's up to the brewers, of course, to see what can be done with them.

How long does a beer have to wait? Tom suggests one month of aging per alcohol percentage point. So seven months for a 7% alcohol beer. The beer takes on some of the bourbon flavors but also develops a relationship with the charred wood. "You have to get to that stuff, and that takes time. You can't just pour it in and pour it out." Just like wine, beer can mellow and age, and some beers might be best drunk fresh, while others just keep getting better over time.

If you are drinking a barrel-aged brew, odds are Tom had something to do with it. He makes various road trips throughout the year, sometimes sleeping in his car or in a brewhouse. Tom holds the record for most showers taken with a brewery hose. Cheers to the barrel guy!

Brewing Co. still does bottles but has greatly increased their use of cans. The lighter weight saves energy and money on shipping/transportation, and aluminum doesn't let the beer-spoiling light in like glass. Plus it's easier to recycle.

And let's not forget, if you are drinking at your local brewpub, there's a bottle or can that was never needed. Pack a growler for carry-out purposes!

SOUR ALES

Throw out what you think you know about keeping your brewing equipment all squeaky clean so as not to spoil a brew. Yes, that is extremely important for brewing typical beers, but it's a rule that gets a little bending when making a sour ale. This is not a beer gone wrong but an actual style of beer that is gaining in popularity in the US and so is worth noting here.

Most commonly associated with Belgium (lambics or Flanders red ales), sour ales are intentionally allowed to go "bad." And by bad, we mean good. Wild yeasts and/or bacteria are purposely introduced to the beer to give it a sour or tart acidity.

Fruit can be added for a secondary fermentation, but many sours use bacteria such as Lactobacillus or Pediococcus, or a special yeast, such as "Brett" (Brettanomyces), which occurs in nature on fruit skins. Brewing such a beer can be challenging in that by introducing these wilder elements into the brewhouse, a brewer increases the risk of infecting other beers that aren't intended to be soured. When done well, this is a unique beer experience, another alternative for those who claim they don't like any kind of beer, and maybe a crossover for those wine drinkers.

TASTING YOUR BEER

Back in the days of youth I suppose savoring the taste of your beer meant you belched after pouring it down your throat. Since you have evolved to drinking craft beers, you may take a bit more time to savor it. Here are a few pointers for savoring the stuff:

Sniff it for aromas. Remember your nose works with your tongue to make you taste things. Kids plug their noses to eat liver for a reason! Get a bit of that beer in your sniffer before you sip by swirling it around in your glass to raise that aroma like you would with wine.

OK, now sip it. Swirl it a bit around on your tongue. Gargling is generally frowned upon, however. Is it watery or does it have a bit of body to it? Squish it against the roof of your mouth with your tongue to appreciate the "mouth feel."

Swallow! Wine tasters can spit it out during a tasting but beer has a finish that you can only get at the back of the tongue where the taste receptors for bitterness are. The most graceful option is to swallow. (Remember what I said about gargling!)

Everyone's tastes are different, of course, and some may prefer a bitter IPA to a sweet Belgian tripel, but the test of a good beer is that bittersweet balance. Now if you want to be good at this tasting business, you need to practice. I know, I know, oh the humanity of it all! But you can suffer all this drinking if it really matters to you. Repeat the process with various craft brews and you will start to see how different all the beers are. Is this one too bitter? Too malty? Is the hops aroma strong, fair to middlin', barely noticeable? Hints of chocolate? Coffee? Caramel? Is it citrusy? Creamy? Crisp? Even smoky? (See "rauch beer" in the glossary.)

Is that *butterscotch* I'm tasting?!?

Shouldn't be! Beware of diacetyl! This natural byproduct of yeast is actually used in artificial butter flavoring. At low levels diacetyl gives a slippery mouth feel to the brew. A bit more and the butterscotch flavor starts to appear. Brewers need to leave the yeast a couple days or so after the end of fermentation and it will reabsorb the flavor-spoiling agent. The warmer temp of ale brewing makes this happen faster.

Here's something that will sound crazy: a good beer will even taste good when it has gone warm in your glass. (Some will even taste better!) Now try THAT with your crappy picnic beer!

BEER ENGINES AND NITRO

On your exploration of the brewpubs you may find a beer engine. No, I'm not talking about an alternative motor for your car that runs on brewsky. The beer engine looks suspiciously like a tap handle, but not exactly. Normally, beer is under pressure from carbon dioxide—or air you pumped into the keg at a party—which pushes your pint out at the tap. Now this can affect your beer, of course. Air will eventually skunkify it (which is why pubs aren't using it; at a party you will probably finish the keg in one go, so it doesn't matter anyway), and too much CO_2 increases the carbonation of the brew, sometimes beyond what is desirable. There are a couple of tricks that can avoid all this.

The beer engine is one. It is a piston-operated pump that literally pulls the beer up from the barrel or holding tanks. So when it looks like the barkeep is out at the water pump in an old western, he or she is actually using a beer engine. When you use this, the beer gets a cascading

SOME FOOD WITH YOUR BEER

PAIRING AND PALATES *with Lucy Saunders*

Think about your taste buds and what you savor: the five elements of taste—salty, sweet, bitter, sour and savory umami—are foremost. Pour a glass of beer and ponder its possible pairings.

But start with sniff, not a sip. In tasting beer, often aromatics can suggest herbs, spices or other ingredients that might make a bridge for a potential food pairing.

Hops can be piney and resinous—which suggests rosemary or juniper berries. Citrusy hops meld well with tropical flavors such as mango or lemons and limes.

Witbiers brewed with coriander and orange zest bring out the best in seafood and many salads. Malty, bready notes suggest caramelized flavors and meld well with rind-washed cheeses. Peppery, high ABV brews will extend the heat of chiles and spicy foods. Yeasty dark ales balance the acidity in dark chocolate.

Since everyone's palate and threshold of sensitivity differs, know how to approach a pairing.

I interviewed Chef Jonathan Zearfoss, a professor at the Culinary Institute of America, about pairing tips. "The standard approach to flavors is to complement, contrast, or create a third new flavor through the synergy of flavor," he says.

For example, Zearfoss read a menu description of a rauchbier that suggested pairing it with smoked foods. "I had the rauchbier with a lentil salad made with smoked bacon and a vinaigrette. On my palate, the acidity of the vinegar cut through the smoke. But my friend, who was eating a pasta with cream sauce, found that the smoky taste coated her palate and became cloying."

"The taste memory is composed of the synergy between the drink and the food," says Zearfoss, "and that's especially true with beer since it has a definite aftertaste." Texture elements in beer—carbonation, residual yeast—also contribute to flavor.

When tasting a beer that's new to you, try sampling both bottled and draft versions of the same beer. Fresh beer tastes best, and be sure you know what the brewer wanted the beer to taste like.

There's a delightful weaving of the experience of drinking beer: your sensations, your palate and overall enjoyment. With literally hundreds of beer styles from which to choose, allow experimentation and sampling beyond your usual preferences. It's an adventure you can enjoy in Wisconsin. Cheers!

© 2012, 2015 Lucy Saunders

Lucy Saunders *is the author of five cookbooks and has written about craft beer and food for more than 20 years. One of my favorites of her books is* Grilling With Beer *and her most recent is* Dinner In the Beer Garden. *For more tips on beer and food pairing, plus free recipes, follow her @lucybeercook*

foam going in the glass (very cool and hypnotic, really) and a meringue-like head. Look for the tap with the long curved swan-neck spout that delivers the beer right against the bottom of the glass to make that special effect.

In Ireland, the Guinness people came up with an alternative to the barkeep arm wrestling the pump handle. They put the beer "under nitro." This was not some sort of IRA terrorist plan (talk about hitting the Irish where it hurts!), it meant nitrogen. Unlike CO_2, nitrogen does not affect the natural carbonation of the beer and yet it still provides the pressure to get the brew up the lines and into your glass. You'll mostly see Irish-style stouts coming out this way, though a few exceptions are out there, such as the Great Dane's Devil's Lake Red Lager, O'so's Rusty Red and Hinterland's Pale Ale.

PRESERVING YOUR BEER

You probably know enough to cool your beer before you drink it, but remember that many craft brews are not pasteurized. Yes, hops are a natural preservative, but let's face it, we are not sailing round the Cape of Good Hope to India eating hardtack and hoping for the best for the ale. This is fine beer, like fine wine, and deserves some tender loving care.

If during your brewery travels you pick up a growler, put that thing on ice! If you don't refrigerate unpasteurized beer, you are getting it at less than its best and perhaps eventually at its worst. Basically, anything above 75 degrees may begin to produce some off flavors. Excepting bottle-conditioned live yeast beers, beers degrade over time; they get old. The higher the temperature, the faster that process goes. (A beer in a hot room for a week will taste perhaps twice as old as one kept at normal room temperature.) If you are picking up brew on a longer road trip, take a cooler along or bring it inside to your hotel room. The longer you leave good beer exposed to light and heat, the more likely the taste will deteriorate until you have the infamous beer of Pepé Le Pew.

That said, beer is not milk, so don't freak out if the temperature is a little high for a short while or if it is being re-cooled a few times. The hot trunk coming back from the liquor store? Not a big deal. A week in the trunk on vacation in July? Don't do it.

BREW YOUR OWN

OK, I know what you're thinking: if so many of these brewmasters started in their basements, why can't I? Well, truth is, you can!

Check your local yellow pages under BEER to find a place near you that sells what you need.

MAP YOUR CAPS

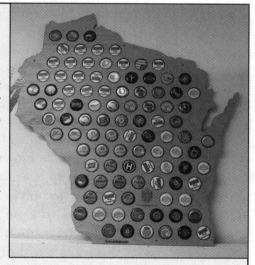

I confess: I was a collector of many things as a child. Beer cans (of course), stamps, coins, rocks, baseball cards (and basketball, football and Star Wars), and much more, including bottle caps. Laugh all you want, but now collecting bottle caps is a thing, thanks to a couple of engineers in Madison, Wisconsin.

These cool wooden cutouts of the State of Wisconsin are riddled with holes perfectly sized so you can wedge the cap off your Wisconsin beer to record it for posterity. There are other states and even a USA version.

Jasper Darley, a six year old, started collecting. He had just a plastic bag to hold them, until his dad Jesse, used a laser to burn out the holes. (You gotta admit: a dad who has access to a laser is pretty cool.) Jesse's co-worker Steve Latham pointed out this was brilliant and that everyone would want them, and so they started producing the cap-maps for mass consumption. Get one and get started. Check their website to see where they are being sold in your state.

beercapmaps.com

Facebook.com/beercapmaps

LOUIS PASTEUR CHANGED BEER FOREVER

Well, and milk too, I suppose. But really, which one is more important? Louis demonstrated that there wasn't any sort of magic mumbo jumbo going on in the brewing process and that, actually, fermentation was brought about by microorganisms (that'd be the yeast). Prior to this the theory was spontaneous generation, that things just happened, but he figured out it was airborne yeasts that got into the brew kettles. The alcohol, of course, comes as a byproduct as the little buggers went about eating the sugar. (Author Kurt Vonnegut once described alcohol as "yeast excrement," but that's kind of a gross thought, so let's forget it.)

It wasn't just yeast getting in there—there were other little critters messing up things and making people sick or simply skunking up the beer. Solution? Pasteurize it. (Notice the name is from Louis. I'm just pointing it out in case you are four or five beers in on that case you bought already.) Pasteurization was heating the liquid (milk, beer, etc.) and killing off the nasty bits that would eventually spoil the beverage (or worst case, such as with milk, make the drinker quite sick!).

A basic single-stage brew kit includes a 6.5 gallon plastic bucket with a lid and fermentation lock, a siphoning tube, bottle brush, handheld bottle capper and caps, and hopefully, instructions. You then need a recipe pack and about 50 returnable-style bottles (not twist-offs). (Grolsch bottles with the ceramic stopper also work great; you only need to buy new rubber rings for the seal.) The kit starts around $50.

A two-stage kit throws in a hydrometer, thermometer and a 5-gallon glass "carboy" where the brew from the bucket goes to complete fermentation. Now you can watch it like an aquarium. Don't put any fish in it though.

Ingredient kits have all you need for a certain recipe. Simple light ales might start around $25 while an IPA with oak chips can get up around $50. Each makes about 50 bottles of beer. In many cases you are using malt extracts thus skipping the grinding of grain in the wort-making process. As you go deeper into the art you will likely want to do this yourself as well.

If your future brewpub patrons are really slow drinkers or Mormons, this basic kit will do you fine. That said, the pros are by no means always using the state-of-the-art equipment either. Remember Egyptians and Sumerians were already making beer over 5000 years ago and they didn't even have toilet paper yet. Um… my point is, big brewers might have the funds to get the fancy copper brew kettles made in Bavaria and a microbiology lab, while others, like the guys at Central Waters at least got their start with used equipment that had other original purposes. Old dairy tanks are popular. And Appleton Beer Factory actually welded their own tanks. Talk about hardcore.

Before you get all excited about naming your beers and what the sign on the pub is going to look like, consider Tom Porter's thoughts on the challenges of starting a brewery.

ON STARTING A BREWERY: TOM PORTER

If you want to start a brewery, use somebody else's money. Because you can go big to start, big enough to make it a profitable minimum, and then if it goes belly up you just tell them, "Sorry, guys, I did the best I could!" I'm on the hook for it, win or lose. It *does* give you tremendous impetus to not fail. There's no doubt about it. "Hey, you gotta make good beer." That's a given. There's nobody out there making really crummy beer anymore, they all went belly up and we all bought their used equipment. It's a given that the beer is pretty darn good. Yeah, there are different interpretations of style, but it's really all about costs.

I could be in the muffler business, or I could be in the hub cap business; I could be making paper clips for chrissakes, as long as the paper clip quality is as good as everybody else's, it doesn't matter. The reality is you better be darn good on cost control and you better know business, and I didn't. I was an engineer. Engineers sit way in back of a great big company. Someone else goes and sells it, someone else decides if there is profit in it. By the time the paper ever gets to your desk, it's a done deal. I went from the engineering business to having to *do* the business, the books, the capital decisions, the sales... *inventory* control. All those things: debt amortization, accounting... ggarrggh, accounting? Man! I never went to accounting classes. I got out of those thinking they were like the plague to me. "A credit is a debit until it's paid?!?" *What?!?*

My accounting system that started out when I started this brewery is I had a bucket of money. And every time I get some more I put it in the bucket. And when I need it, I take it out of the bucket. When the bucket's empty I got to stop taking money out until I get some more to put in. Well, that system still works here, but

CANS VS. BOTTLES

Because you couldn't spend your entire life at the saloon—though many have tried—we developed methods of taking some brew home with us. Growlers and the like worked fine but didn't last long. Bottling was the best method back in the late 19th century. But canning beer was in the works, at least in research, even before Prohibition. But that dark space between the 18th and 21st Amendments put cans on hold. Beer reacts with steel, so to prevent that American Can Co. developed a can liner. G. Krueger Brewing of New Jersey became the first to use the "Keglined" cans in 1935, and from that point forward, cans grew to take over the market. Continental Can Co. gave us the "cone top" that same year, a can with a tapered top capped like a bottle. Milwaukee brewer Jos. Schlitz Brewing is allegedly the first brewery to use them (though some argue La Crosse's G. Heileman Brewing beat them to it). Rice Lake Brewing of Wisconsin was the last.

But most cans were flat-topped cylinders. Initially, one needed a pointed can opener (a "church key") to puncture the top to get at the beer. Then the pull tab arrived, invented by Ermal Fraze in 1959, and this was big news. You can still find old Pabst steel cans touting "No opener needed!" A prized can for collectors. After a couple decades of cutting our feet on those tabs at the beach, the Sta-Tab came into favor—the little lever we still use today that stays with the can—unless you are collecting them for the Ronald McDonald House. As the craft brewing age came upon us, bottles became the favored packaging. Beer tastes better from glass, we said. The bottles are sexier, we believed. In a bar brawl one couldn't break a can and cut someone.

Pragmatism, however, is bringing back the cans—both in 12- and 16-oz sizes—and it all makes good sense. No returns or deposits. Easy to recycle. Easier to stack and thus easier to ship and store. Lighter, quick to cool, and not so fragile like glass. Plus, it keeps the beer-damaging light out completely. We still may think it tastes different, but that's why you should always pour your beer into the proper glassware anyway.

there's a WHOLE—SERIES—OF BUCKETS now! There's literally *dozens* of buckets. It gets hard to remember which one do I put it into and which one do I take it out of. And sometimes you don't notice one's empty. So business and accounting—that's really been my learning curve. I went from going "What's a balance sheet?" to a profit and loss statement, and now I work off cash flow statements and sometimes I split them up. I want to know where the push and pull is of my cash flow, because that's really what makes a good businessman. And I'm learning this because I HAVE to. And it has had NOTHING to do with making good beer. The good beer part is a given. You've gotta have it. If you don't have it, don't even think about it. But having that is not enough. I have a lot of people here coming through the door on tours and such saying, "I'm thinking of starting a brewpub. Gees, I make really good homebrew." And I say, "That's a really good first step." But the second through fortieth steps are... how are your plumbing skills? How're your carpentry skills? Can you pour concrete? Can you weld? And then can you balance a balance sheet every thirty days?

BARLEY'S ANGELS

Few things are more irritating than the notion that women somehow don't like beer. Testament to the nonsense of that idea is an organization called Barley's Angels (barleysangels.org). An international network of local chapters—100 chapters in 7 countries—Barley's Angels unites women around the world who appreciate good beer. They host events, both for fun and education, such as beer and food/chocolate pairings or cooking with beer discussions, and they organize beer outings. Bringing women together over beers is their mission as is helping breweries, beer bars, and restaurants grow their beer-wise female client base. Join a chapter or start one if there's not one near you. Follow them on Twitter @barleysangelsor and Facebook. com/barleysangels.org. There are two chapters currently in Wisconsin:

Barley's Angels – Milwaukee
Contact: Erin Anderson
Email: barleysangelsmke@gmail.com
Info: https://www.facebook.com/barleysangelsMKE
Meeting schedule: Monthly
Meeting location: Roving

Barley's Angels – Lakeshore Chapter
Contact: Carrie Stuckmann
Email: BarleysAngelsLakeshore@gmail.com
Info: https://www.facebook.com/MoJoSheboygan
Meeting schedule: Monthly
Meeting location: MoJo, 1235 Pennsylvania Avenue, Sheboygan WI 53081

Where's The Beer At?

(INTRO TO THE LISTINGS)

The listings for all the commercial brewers in Wisconsin are divided here into the six zones I mentioned before. Each section has a map of that portion of the state with the brewtowns marked. Within each zone the communities are listed in alphabetical order with the brewpubs and breweries below the town heading. Watch for a few extra non-brewing but brewing related attractions and other interesting bits you can read during your journey.

HOW TO USE THE LISTINGS:

OK, this isn't rocket science but let's go over a brief summary of the finer points of the listings.

Brewmaster or Head Brewer: So you know who to ask brewing questions.

Number of Beers: This may indicate the number of different brews in a year and/or the number of beers on tap.

Staple Beers: Always on tap.

Rotating Beers: Like roulette only with beer, the beers that may come and go, often seasonal brews, series beers, or in some cases one-offs that are listed here only to show the breadth of their brewing styles. Mention of casks, barrel-aging or other specialties might be here as well.

Best Time to Go: Be aware that opening hours, happy hours, or trivia nights, etc. here listed may change, especially seasonally. Best to call or check websites to be sure.

Samples and **Tours**: Prices (and tour times) may change from what you see here.

Got food? A recent law change does allow **brewery** taprooms to get approval to serve food, though most probably still don't. In that case, most are likely "food friendly," meaning you can order delivery or bring your own grub into the taproom. **Brewpubs** by legal definition serve food and may offer a full bar and other brewerys' beers.

Directions: For those without a GPS, these written directions should indicate the nearest major highway and specific driving directions and distances. Sometimes bus and metro lines/stops are also shown in italics, as are nearby trails and paths for cyclists.

Special Offer: *This is NOT a guarantee. The brewer reserves the right to rescind this offer at any time and for any reason.* This is something the management of the place you're visiting suggested they'd give to a patron who comes in and gets **this book** signed on the signature line of that particular brewer in the back of the book. This is a **one-time bonus** and the signature cancels it out. You must have a complete book, and photocopies or print-outs don't count. I didn't charge them and they didn't charge me; it's out of the goodness of their hearts, so take it as such and don't get all goofy on them if the keychain turns out to be a bumper sticker or supplies have run out or the bartender that night didn't get the memo about how the offer works. And if they are offering a discount on a beer, it is assumed that it is the brewer's own beer, not Bud Light or some such stuff or that fancy import you've been wishing would go on special. Legal drinking age still applies, of course. Not all brewers are participating, and that will be noted on each brewer's page.

Stumbling Distance: Two or three cool things near the brewery that are very local, very beery, very Minnesotan, or just plain cool. Some may be more of a short car ride away. If you really *are* stumbling, get a designated driver for those.

And that's about it, the rest should be self-explanatory. Enjoy the ride! Last one all the way through the breweries is a rotten egg. Or a skunk beer.

LISTINGS BY BREWER

LISTINGS BY BREWTOWN

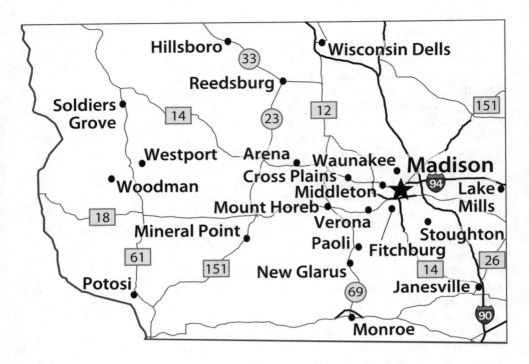

ZONE 1

Arena: Lake Louie Brewing
Cross Plains: Cross Plains Brewery
Fitchburg: Great Dane Pub and Brewery
Hillsboro: Hillsboro Brewing Co.
Janesville: Gray's Brewing Co.
Janesville: Rock County Brewing Co.
Lake Mills: Tyranena Brewing Co.
Madison: Ale Asylum
Madison: ALT Brew
Madison: Funk Factory Geurzeria
Madison: Furthermore Beer
Madison: Granite City Food and Brewery
Madison: Great Dane Pub and Brewery
Madison: Great Dane Pub and Brewery—Hilldale
Madison: House of Brews
Madison: Karben4 Brewing
Madison: Next Door Brewing Co.
Madison: One Barrel Brewing
Madison: Rockhound Brewing Co.
Madison: Vintage Brewing Company
Middleton: Capital Brewery
Mineral Point: Brewery Creek Brewpub
Monroe: Minhas Craft Brewery
Mount Horeb: Grumpy Troll Brew Pub
New Glarus: New Glarus Brewing Co.
Paoli: The Hop Garden Tap Room
Potosi: Potosi Brewing Co.
Reedsburg: Corner Pub
Soldiers Grove: Driftless Brewing Co.
Stoughton: Viking Brew Pub
Verona: Gray's Tied House
Verona: Hop Haus Brewing Co.
Verona: Wisconsin Brewing Co.
Waunakee: Octopi Brewing Co. (3rd Sign Brewing)
Westport: Parched Eagle Brewpub
Wisconsin Dells: Wisconsin Dells Brewing Co. (Moosejaw Pizza)
Wisconsin Dells: Port Huron Brewing Co.
Woodman: Woodman Brewery (Whistle Stop Restaurant)

Lake Louie Brewing

Founded: 2000
Brewmaster: Tom Porter
Address: 7556 Pine Road • Arena, WI 53503
Phone: 608-753-2675
Website: www.lakelouie.com
Annual Production: 6,000 bbls
Number of Beers: 13–15

Staple Beers:
- » Arena Premium Pale Ale
- » Golden Booty Cream Ale (formerly Coon Rock Cream Ale)
- » Kiss the Lips IPA
- » Tommy's Porter
- » Warped Speed Scotch Ale

Rotating Beers:
- » 10-81 IPA (session IPA)
- » Impulse Drive (session Warped Speed)
- » Louie's Reserve (a limited batch of Scotch Ale with higher alcohol, see story below)
- » Milk Stout
- » Mosquito Beach
- » Mr. Mephisto's Imperial Stout (I get goosebumps even typing it)
- » Prairie Moon Belgian Farmhouse Wit (with blood orange)
- » The Twins (Maibock)
- » **Dark Shadows Series:**
  - » Nudge Nudge (English mild brown ale)
  - » Maple Surple (brown ale w/maple syrup)
  - » Milk Stout (made with Meister Cheese lactose)
- » **Hop-A-Louie Series:**
  - » Blue Peter (Dortmunder style)
  - » Bunny Green Toe (IPA)
  - » Grade 10 (IPA)

Most Popular Brew: Warped Speed Scotch Ale

Brewmaster's Fave: "The next one we haven't made yet."

Tours? One Saturday a month at noon and 1:15 PM. Check the website and email a reservation via the online form. Tours are free, include samples, and fill fast. Kids will be given an espresso and a free kitten. Allegedly.

Where can you buy it? Lake Louie beer can be found statewide in bottled six-packs (four-packs for specialty brews) and as tap accounts in various bars some of which are listed on the website. If your local pub doesn't have it, request it.

Special Offer: Not participating. Tours and samples are already free!

Directions: From US Hwy 14 go north on Oak Street in Arena. Turn left where it ends and becomes Elizabeth St/Pine Dr. Follow this until it too takes a right angle turn to the right. Just about 1000 feet past this on the right you will see the Porter mail box and the driveway to the brewery.

The Beer Buzz: Another engineer gone brewing, founder/owner Tom Porter quit his job, cashed in the 401K, and made his garage into a brewery. "I figured I'd fail, but fail small and recover." Not so much. He brewed it all himself, produced about 200 gallons every two weeks, and then did all the deliveries as well. And it caught on. Tom used to get his parents in to pack boxes sometimes. They once had a waiting list for wannabe customers. Limited releases would sell out in less than two days, and it wasn't uncommon to see serious fans following the delivery truck on release dates. They no longer have to deliver their own beer, and a brewery expansion has helped them keep ahead of demand—just barely. It's popular stuff.

Tom bought the original brewing system from a microbrewery that gave up its ghost in Eugene, Oregon. It took four semi-trucks to get it to Wisconsin. The brewery is on twenty acres Tom got from his uncle. The name comes from the pond there where he and some friends used to go skinny dipping when they were in high school. Uncle Louie would come and chase them out of his "lake."

Louie's Reserve, for those in the know, is Liquid Reefer as it was dubbed when Tom tried the first batch out on the locals. They changed the name so as not to antagonize the ATF, what with them brewing in the middle of the woods and all! They have three series of beers with rotating brews throughout the year: Dark Shadow Series, Hop-A-Louie Series and the Session Series which includes Golden Booty, 10-81, and Impulse Drive, all under 5% abv. 10-81 is the police code for a breathalyzer test.

Want to do what Tom did? Read his "On Starting a Brewery" in the History of Beer section.

Stumbling Distance: Get your cheese curd fix at *Arena Cheese* (arenacheese. com, 300 US Hwy 14, 608-753-2501), the place with the big mouse out front. There's a window into the production area so you can watch.

ESSER'S CROSS PLAINS BREWERY

Founded: 1863
Brewer: Sand Creek Brewery
Address: 2109 Hickory Street • Cross Plains, WI 53528
Phone: 608-798-3911
Website: www.essersbest.com
Number of beers: 3

Staple Beers:
- » CROSS PLAINS SPECIAL (lighter pilsner)
- » ESSER'S BEST (hearty lager, caramel color)
- » ANNIVERSARY ALE (amber ale)

Tours? By appointment only.

Samples: Yes

Best time to go: Not during Badger football home game days!

Where can you buy it? In area stores and bars throughout Wisconsin.

Got food? Go to Main Street for restaurants.

Special Offer: Bring your book for a signature and get a free sample and an Esser's Best patch.

Directions: Come into Cross Plains on US Hwy 14 (Main Street) and turn north on Hickory Street and they're right there on your left.

The Beer Buzz: George Esser came all the way from Cologne, Germany, in 1852 and started brewing beer for us in 1863, beating out his buddy Heinrich Leinenkugel to get a brewery started in Cross Plains. Esser's Best was brewed until 1910 when the Essers gave up brewing in favor of being a distributor. Six generations later, the family has taken the recipe from George's German diary and is producing the original with the help of the Sand Creek Brewery. The "brewery" has a collection of cool odds and ends from the old-school brewing days as well as an old hack (horse-drawn carriage) that they pull out for special events. Cross Plains threw one helluva parade in '33 when Prohibition ended and the Essers were part of the 75 year anniversary in 2008. They threw another big party and parade in 2013 to celebrate 80 years of legal beer. This is one of the oldest family businesses in the USA with the 5th and 6th generations running the show now. Great stories here, and Wayne and Larry love to chat it up, but be sure to make an appointment.

Stumbling Distance: Check out *Coach's Club* (1200 Main St, 608-413-0400) which uses Esser's Best to beer batter some fish for an excellent Friday night fish fry. *Main Street Lanes* (1721 Main St., 608-798-4900) offers great burgers and sandwiches. Nearby Black Earth Creek offers some world class trout fishing. The Table Bluff and Cross Plains Segments of *The Ice Age National Scenic Trail* (iceagetrail.org, 2110 Main St, 800-227-0046) is just outside of town and the Ice Age Trail Alliance's office is in Cross Plains. Pack some beer for the hike! (See my book *60 Hikes Within 60 Miles of Madison*!)

The Great Dane Pub and Brewery

Founded: 2002
Brewmaster: Pat Keller
Address: 2980 Cahill Main • Fitchburg, WI 53711
Phone: 608-442-9000
Website: www.greatdanepub.com
Annual Production: 1,400 bbls
Number of Beers: 12 taps

Staple Beers:

» Crop Circle Wheat
» Jon Stoner's Oatmeal Stout
» Landmark Lite Lager
» Old Glory American Pale Ale
» Stone of Scone Scotch Ale
» Verruckte Stadt German Pils

Rotating Beers:

» Amber Lager *(summer)*
» Bock
» Doppelbock *(winter)*
» Foxy Brown
» Maibock *(spring)*
» Oktoberfest

Most Popular Brew: Crop Circle Wheat

Brewmaster's Fave: Maibock

Tours? By chance or appointment but always welcomed.

Samples? Yes, a sip to decide, dontcha know, or sampler platters of four beers for about $6.50 (add 2 more for $2.50).

Best Time to Go: Happy hour is 4–6 weekdays and offers beer discounts.

Where can you buy it? On-site growlers, pub kegs, and half barrels (with 24-hour notice), but see their other locations near Hilldale Mall (also a brewpub), at the airport, an east side location, and the original downtown Madison location. The Duck Blind at Madison Mallards Northwoods-League baseball games is fueled by 4 specially brewed Great Dane beers. For something farther afield, find the Dane in Wausau, WI. 100+ tap accounts around the state and now some cans in distribution.

Got food? Yes, a full menu of soups, salads, burgers, and entrees. The bratburger (created on a dare) is an original with bacon on a pretzel bun. Beer, brat, and cheese soup is Wisconsin in a bowl. Beer bread is standard, fish and chips available, and a load of other great dishes. Friday night pilsner-battered fish fry!

Special Offer: A free 10-oz beer!

Directions: From the Beltline Hwy 12/14/18/151, go south just over 1 mile on Fish Hatchery Road and the brewpub is in the complex to the right, across from the fish hatchery.

The Beer Buzz: You can change the scenery, but the beer remains the same. With a few beers unique to this location, this Dane is a nice option for those who don't want to go all the way downtown for their great beer. In the upper level of a strip mall across from the Fish Hatchery on Fish Hatchery Road just south of Madison, this place draws more of the after-work crowd and families on the weekends.

Inside you'll find dark hardwood floors around a horseshoe-shaped bar in a high-ceiling room with a large projection screen TV. (Packer and Badger games!) To the right along the wall under glass is the brewhouse on both the first floor and mezzanine, and copper brew kettles greet you by the door. The rooftop terrace is partly canopied in case of summer sprinkles and has a bar of its own. The mezzanine with four pool tables and shuffleboard rests over a quieter dining area with spacious booths and windows looking out over the parking lot toward the greenery of the Fish Hatchery across the road. Brewmaster Pat did a career in the Coast Guard, and when that ended a friend told him, "Find something you do for free and get them to pay you for it." It was serendipity: his resume arrived at the Dane downtown the same day someone quit. "Can there be a better job? I love the immediate reaction of the people in the pub. It's pretty much my life."

From the parking lot out front you will see the sign on the pub upstairs, but look to the left (if you're facing it) for the white grain silo and a black arrow to find the outdoor stairs up the hill to get in. There is an access road behind the mall and ramp parking if you want to avoid the steps. Smoking is allowed out on the patio.

Free WiFi. Facebook.com/greatdanefitchburg and Twitter @greatdanepub

Stumbling Distance: *Liliana's* (www.lilianasrestaurant.com, 2951 Triverton Pike, 608-442-4444) is a New Orleans-themed fine-dining restaurant with a stellar wine list, all of which are available by the glass. *Yahara Bay Distillery* (3118 Kingsley Way, Madison, 608-275-1050, yaharabay.com) produces craft whiskey, gin, vodka, rum, brandies and creative liqueurs. They also operate an art gallery onsite, but are only open very limited hours. Go Thursday evenings for open house for a cash bar and free tours and tastings. Behind the scenes distillery tours (about $7) must be booked on the website.

Hillsboro Brewing Co.

Founded: February 2012
Brewmaster: Snapper Verbsky
Address: 815 Water Ave •
Hillsboro, WI 54634
Phone: 608-489-7486
Web Site: hillsborobrewingcompany.com
Annual Production: 240 barrels
Number of Beers: 14 taps, 5 of them house beers

Staple Beers:
- » Joe Beer (porter)
- » Hillsboro Pale Ale

Rotating Beers:
- » Hillsboro Lager
- » Honey Ale (local honey, in August)
- » Oktoberfest
- » Sap (brewed with 100% maple sap in place of water)
- » Shandy

Most Popular Brew: Joe Beer

Brewmaster's Fave: Hillsboro Pale Ale

Tours? Yes, by chance or by appointment.

Samples: Yes, flight of 4 five-oz pours for about $6.

Best Time to Go: Brewpub is open Tue–Sun 11am–10pm. Closed Sundays from Nov 15–Apr 15. Watch website or call for weekend taproom hours at the brewery once it opens.

Where can you buy it? Only here on tap and to go in growlers, but soon also in the taproom at the separate brewery down the street.

Got food? Yes, a full pub menu with salads, appetizers, sandwiches, and square pizza on a housemade crust (GF available). Friday night fish tacos are a big hit. Text GOTJOE to 36000 for daily lunch specials

Special Offer: Your first Hillsboro beer is free when you get your book signed.

Directions: State Highways 33, 80, and 82 come into downtown Hillsboro from either direction and become Water Ave. Look for the brewpub at the corner of Water and Mill St. The brewery will be a couple blocks east at the corner of Water and Garden St.

The Beer Buzz: Snapper and Kim Verbsky operate this popular brewpub in Hillsboro, and you can expect to be surrounded mostly by locals. Snapper's family has been local for 5 generations. He turned down a college wrestling opportunity to stay in Hillsboro and go into business with his father Joe, a carpenter. Thus you can see where the restoration talent came from. Joe was a homebrewer, and for a full year he worked on a beer recipe to get it just how he wanted it. He had always thought of having a brewery, and when he perfected that beer in 2012, he was ecstatic. Sadly, just days later, Joe died in a car accident. It was a devastating loss, but Snapper keeps his father's memory and beer alive in that Joe Beer you're drinking.

Snapper has a talent for restoring old buildings, and the brewpub was one of them. Back in 1906 it was a general store, but over the years it served a variety of purposes, including a shoe store. You can still see the old sign here on the wall as well as the old wood floor, tongue-in-groove ceiling, and brick walls. The concrete top bar has old shed siding on it as does the front of the building. The brewery name is a historical one as you can see from the old Hillsboro Brewery's beer cases and photos. There's plenty of room at the bar, as well as tall tables and booths. Two TVs pipe in sports.

When Snapper started brewing for the public, he headed over to Corner Pub in Reedsburg where brewer/owner Pete shared his equipment with him. As the demand grew, Snapper knew he needed his own set up. In 2015 he remodeled a tavern down the street at 1001 Water Ave. to make a brewery for a new 7-barrel system. The hours for the taproom there may be limited, but check with the bar or website. *Trivia note:* the last four digits of the phone number spell PIVO, Czech for beer.

Free WiFi. Facebook/hillsborobrewingcompany

Stumbling Distance: *The Cheese Store & More* (186 Madison St, 608-489-2651) has Wisconsin cheese, ice cream, and a lunch menu. If you need a place to crash, a good option is *Hotel Hillsboro* (1235 Water Ave, 608-433-2807, hotelhillsboro.com). This is the Driftless Area, the land untouched by the last glaciers, so the driving around here can be quite scenic. *Wildcat Mountain State Park* (E 13660 WI-33, Ontario, WI, 608-337-4775, dnr.wi.gov) is an excellent place to camp and the *Kickapoo River* zigzagging past it is popular with paddlers (see my book *Paddling Wisconsin*).

Gray Brewing Co.

Founded: 1856
Brewmaster: Fred Gray
Address: 2424 W Court Street • Janesville, WI 53548
Phone: 608-754-5150
Website: www.graybrewing.com
Annual Production: 3,500 bbls
Number of Beers: 9 or so

Staple Beers:
- » Black Rose Black Ale
- » Busted Knuckle Irish-Style Ale
- » Honey Ale
- » Oatmeal Stout
- » Rathskeller Amber Ale (draft only)
- » Rock Hard Red (malternative)

Rotating Beers:
- » Bully Porter
- » Wisco Wheat

Most Popular Brew: Busted Knuckle or Oatmeal

Brewmaster's Fave: Oatmeal Stout

Tours? No.

Samples? At future tasting room or Gray's Tied House.

Best Time to Go: Watch for planned tasting room.

Where can you buy it? Available in 6-pack bottles in Wisconsin, Illinois, and Pennsylvania as well as on tap at Gray's Tied House in Verona.

The Beer Buzz: Founded by Irish immigrant Joshua Gray in 1856, this was the first all-ale brewery in Wisconsin, and Fred is the fifth generation of the Gray family to operate it. Only 15% of the production is actually beer, the rest is some very popular sodas—especially the root beer. Soda is what carried the brewery through Prohibition and the Grays stuck with it until the plant was burnt down by arson in 1992. When they decided to press on, it was with the plan of their forefathers: beer and soda. The malt beverage is the raspberry-flavored Rock Hard Red. The lobby has a nice collection of breweriana and there's a gift shop. Gray's Tied House in Verona is a great brewpub showcasing Gray's beers.

Rock County Brewing Co.

Opening: Early 2016!
Address: 10 North Parker Drive • Janesville, WI 53545
Web Site: www.RockCountyBrewing.com
Annual Production: 200–250 barrels
Number of Beers: 8–10 on tap

Beers:
» Several staples and many rotating brews

Tours? Yes

Samples: Yes

Best Time to Go: Open Thu–Fri 4–9PM, Sat 12–10PM. Check website!

Where can you buy it? Here on tap and in growlers/howlers to go.

Got food? No, but food friendly and possible food trucks.

Special Offer: A free sample of Rock County beer.

Directions: US 51 follows Parker Dr a bit through town. On the east side of the Rock River Bridge (US 51) at Centerway and Parker, go south on Parker to the corner of Milwaukee St and the brewery is on the left.

The Beer Buzz: When his employer downsized and he lost his job, founder/ brewer John Rocco turned to beer. In order to continue homebrewing during leaner times, he started buying and selling brew supplies in 2009. By 2012, he opened Farmhouse Brewing Supply (3000 Milton Ave, Ste 109, 608-305-HOPS, FarmhouseBrewingSupply.com). John and two of his three partners, Andrew Walker and Ed Sundstedt, brew as a team. A fourth, Antoni Canzian, still lives in Pennsylvania.

Located in a restored 1900 Carriage Factory building, the brewery has a 3-bbl system on a budget—cobbled together from old dairy equipment and new brite tanks. They will settle on some staples and may brew a lot of IPAs but plan to explore styles a lot.

Free WiFi. Find them on Facebook and Twitter

Stumbling Distance: *Frankie's Supper Club* (12 S Main St, 608-352-7411) is your place for nicer dining (plus fish fry) though it is not a supper club in the traditional sense.

Tyranena Brewing Co.

Founded: November 1998
Brewmaster: Rob Larson
Address: 1025 Owen Street • Lake Mills, WI 53551
Phone: 920-648-8699
Website: www.tyranena.com
Annual Production: 4,500 bbls
Number of Beers: 6 year-round, 6 seasonal, a variety of specialties

Staple Beers:
- » Bitter Woman IPA
- » Chief Blackhawk Porter
- » Headless Man Amber Alt
- » Rocky's Revenge (bourbon-barrel aged brown ale)
- » Stone Tepee Pale Ale
- » Three Beaches Honey Blonde

Seasonal & Specialty Beers:
- » Down 'n Dirty Chocolate Oatmeal Stout
- » Fargo Brothers Hefeweizen
- » Gemuetlichkeit Oktoberfest
- » Painted Ladies Pumpkin Spice Ale
- » Scurvy IPA with Orange Peel
- » Sheep Shagger Scotch Ale

"Brewers Gone Wild!" is a series of limited batches of "big, bold or ballsy beers." Past brews include: Who's Your Daddy? Bourbon Barrel-Aged Imperial Porter, Bitter Woman from Hell Extra IPA, Carnal Knowledge Double Oatmeal Stout, Fatal Attraction Imperial Black IPA, HopWhore Imperial IPA, Spank Me Baby! Barley Wine-Style Ale, The Devil Made Me Do It! Imperial Oatmeal Coffee Porter, Benji's Smoked Imperial Porter Brewed with Chipotle Pepper.

Most Popular Brew: Bitter Woman IPA

Brewmaster's Fave: Bitter Woman IPA

Tours? Yes, free tours *most* Saturdays at 2 and 3:30PM, but check the website for exact dates/times.

Samples? No, but you can buy some in the tasting room. Occasionally there is a fun beer only available on tap here.

Best Time to Go: Off season hours for the tasting room are usually Wed–Thu 4:30–10PM, Fri 3–11PM, Sat 12PM–11PM, Sun 12PM–8PM. In summer, they usually open Mon–Tue 4:30–10PM, but check to be sure. Live music every Saturday and in summer on Fridays as well.

Where can you buy it? Here on tap and to go in growlers, and distributed in bottles all over Wisconsin and in goodly portions of Minnesota, Indiana, and the Greater Chicago area.

Got food? No, but you can carry-in or have it delivered from area restaurants. (No outside beverages though! That'd be rude and insensitive.)

Special Offer: Not participating

Directions: From the 259 Exit on I-94 head south towards Lake Mills and take the first left (east) at Tyranena Park Road (Cty Hwy V). The first right after Cty Hwy A is Owen St.

The Beer Buzz: What does Brewmaster Rob love about this job? "At the end of the day, sitting down to a beer that I brewed." When Rob left his previous job, he had to sign a 5-year non-competitive agreement which essentially meant he was bound for a career change. Life's little curveball worked to the benefit of the rest of us because Rob decided to open this brewery. It takes its name from a native name for the nearby lake. Settlers came up with the inventive moniker Rock Lake for the rocks along the shore and Lake Mills for the town's grist mill. For a while in the 1870s, the town tried out the name Tyranena but it was soon changed back, perhaps for spelling difficulties. Rob's favorite legend of the origin of the name is that it was given to the Ho Chunk tribe by a "foreign tribe" that had lived there before them. Could it have been the same pyramidal mound-building tribe of Aztalan down the road? Who knows?

The tasting room is decorated with historical photos of Lake Mills and offers glassware, apparel, and samples for purchase. There's a beer garden in summer and even a gas grill that patrons can use.

Facebook.com/tyranena and Twitter @tyranena

Stumbling Distance: *Aztalan Inn* (920-648-3206, W6630 Hwy B at Cty Hwy Q) is a local favorite for Friday fish fries. *Hering's Sand Bar* (920-648-3227, 345 Sandy Beach Rd) is only open in the summer but also offers the fish fry as well as cheese curds, with outdoor seating and a view of the sunset. Locally loved and arguably dangerous are the "sliders," yummy greasy burgers at the *American Legion Post 67 Hamburger Stand* (133 N Main St, only in summer—locals freeze them for winter). Rinse the arteries with some Tyranena products afterward[*]. First Saturday in October is the *Tyranena Oktoberfest Bike Ride* at the brewery, with food, live music, and… well, you know—beer.

---

[*]   Not actual medical advice, consult a heart specialist and don't sue me.

MORE BEER COMING

Bent Kettle Brewing (bentkettle.com), founded by an eye doctor who traded in his eyeglasses for beer glasses, is already contract brewing at House of Brews in Madison, but is seeking a taproom in the Fort Atkinson area. They are already on tap in a few area locations and sell growlers via Lewis Station Winery in Lake Mills.

ALE ASYLUM

Founded: May 2006
Brewmaster: Dean Coffey
Address: 2002 Pankratz Street • Madison, WI 53704
Phone: 608-663-3926
Website: www.aleasylum.com
Annual Production: 20,000 bbls and rising
Number of Beers: up to 20 on tap; almost as many in distribution

Staple Beers:

- » AMBERGEDDON AMBER ALE
- » BEDLAM! (IPA)
- » DEMENTO (Session Pale Ale)
- » HOPALICIOUS (American Pale Ale)
- » MADTOWN NUTBROWN ALE
- » UNSHADOWED (German Hefeweizen)

Rotating Beers:

- » BALLISTIC IPA
- » BIG SLICK STOUT
- » DIABLO BELGA (Belgian-style Dubbel)
- » HIGH COUP IPA
- » KINK (Belgian-style Abbey)
- » MERCY (Belgian-style Grand Cru)
- » PANTHEON (Imperial Brown Ale)
- » SATISFACTION JACKSIN (Double IPA)
- » SUBCULTCHA IPA
- » TRIPEL NOVA (Belgian-style Tripel)
- » VELVETEEN HABIT IPA

Taproom Only:

- » CONTORTER PORTER (English Porter)
- » GOLD DIGGER BLONDE ALE
- » STICKY MCDOOGLE (Scotch Ale)
- » …plus occasional one-offs or test batches

Most Popular Brew: Hopalicious

Brewmaster's Fave: "I can't choose one of my children above the others. That'd be rude!"

Tours? They offer six on-the-hour tours every Sunday between 12:00–5:00. This 30–45 minute trip around the brewery is $5 (cash only) and includes a free pint of your choice plus a special sampling. See also Hop Head Tours!

Samples? Yes, sips to help decide and flights.

Best Time to Go: Friday nights are busiest. Open Mon–Thu 11AM–midnight; Fri–Sat 11AM–2:30PM, Sun 11AM–10PM.

Where can you buy it? On tap here and in growlers, six-packs, twelve packs (bottles and cans) and cases to go. Six-packs, twelve-packs (bottles and cans), cases and kegs are available from Wisconsin and Illinois craft-beer retailers. On tap and in bottles in many Wisconsin bars.

Got food? Fresh-made pizza, sandwiches, salads, and limited light fare. Fish tacos are legendary when offered.

Special Offer: A free beer during your signature visit.

Directions: From Hwy 151/East Washington Ave, take First Street north a block to where it ends at Packers Avenue. Go right here and follow it to International Lane, the road to the airport. You'll see the brewery on the corner on your right, but you'll need to go down International to the next right (Anderson St) to get to Pankratz, your next right.

The Beer Buzz: Located just west of Dane County Regional Airport (Truax Field) is one of Madison's hottest contributors to the art of brewing. On how he started homebrewing, Brewmaster Dean offers this about his college days: "I was too poor to buy good beer and too proud to drink cheap beer." So he took matters into his own brew kit. He made a name for himself during his ten years at the now defunct Angelic Brewpub, and when he broke out on his own Dean was without limits. "Some places have strict rules about what remains on tap. I just want to play." *Fermented In Sanity* is the motto here. The name Ale Asylum acknowledges this as a refuge to pursue the art of beer. All beers are unfiltered and unpasteurized.

From the get-go Ale Asylum was a hit and growth came rapidly. Hopalicious and Madtown Nutbrown have become staples at area bars. In August 2012 they completed construction of this 45,000 square-foot production brewery, and their annual production capacity jumped from their current 11,000 barrels/year to a maximum capacity of 50,000 barrels/year. To ensure they wouldn't have to move again, the brewery is designed to expand an additional 85,000 square feet. Expect more seasonals with longer run times. Their previous digs in an old industrial office space (now *Karben4 Brewing*) was too cramped for their growing business and had to be manipulated to be a brewery; this place is specifically designed for it, straight out of the brain of Dean Coffey.

The taproom area has a long bar and high ceilings, and a mezzanine level with a smaller bar and lounge furniture (via steps in back near the restrooms). A separate dining area has booths and tables. A large patio area and a rooftop deck are outside.

Free WiFi. ATM onsite. Facebook.com/aleasylum

Stumbling Distance: Just north on Packers Ave is *Smoky Jon's Championship BBQ* (smokyjons.com, 2310 Packers Ave, 608-249-7427), an award-winning carry-out or casual sit-down joint. The other direction out on East Washington will take you to *The Malt House* (2609 E Washington Ave, 608-204-6258, malthousetavern.com). One of Madison's finest beer bars, it is owned by a beer judge. A great place to catch a live band is *The Crystal Corner* (www.thecrystalcornerbar.com, 1302 Williamson St, 608-256-2953). They also run 19 beers on tap including such Wisconsin greats as Capital, New Glarus, Point, Leinie's and… Old Style? They still make that?? *Karben4 Brewing* is 5 minutes east on the other side of the airport. This lies within Madison's Beermuda Triangle.

BREW & VIEW

Beer pairs well with a lot of things, not the least of which is film. **The Majestic Theatre** in Madison (around the corner from **The Great Dane Pub and Brewery**) is typically a live music venue but also hosts DJs and theme parties. The theme here (besides beer) is cinematic gems. The Brew and View tradition started with the classic *The Big Lebowski*, which makes a return from time to time. Other classics? *Office Space, Dazed and Confused, This is Spinal Tap*—you get the idea. Watch for these events!

115 King Street | majesticmadison.com | 608-255-0901

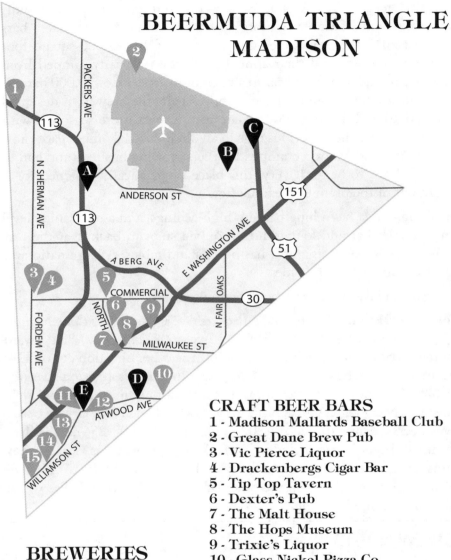

BEERMUDA TRIANGLE
MADISON

CRAFT BEER BARS
1 - Madison Mallards Baseball Club
2 - Great Dane Brew Pub
3 - Vic Pierce Liquor
4 - Drackenbergs Cigar Bar
5 - Tip Top Tavern
6 - Dexter's Pub
7 - The Malt House
8 - The Hops Museum
9 - Trixie's Liquor
10 - Glass Nickel Pizza Co
11 - Alchemy
12 - Tex Tubb's Taco Palace
13 - Mickey's Tavern
14 - Gib's Bar
15 - Star Liquor

BREWERIES
A - Ale Asylum
B - ALT Brew
C - Karben4 Brewing
D - Next Door
E - One Barrel Brewing

THE BEERMUDA TRIANGLE: MADISON

Call it synchronicity. Sometimes great things congregate together and there's no explaining why. For a community under 250,000 people, Madison and the surrounding area have a nice variety of breweries and craft beer bars, and the standard for restaurants has even changed remarkably over the year. There is a notable clustering of beervanic bliss on the east side that forms what many of us are calling the Beermuda Triangle. And much like its punny namesake, once you go in you may not ever come out again.

Breweries located in the triangle are *Ale Asylum*, *ALT Brew*, *Karben4*, *Next Door* and *One Barrel Brewing*.

Craft Beer Bars are as follows:

Alchemy Cafe
1980 Atwood Ave, 608-204-7644, alchemycafe.net
Excellent gastropub food with a well-curated tap list.

Dexter's Pub
301 North St, 608-244-3535, dexterspubmadison.com
Arguably the city's best fish fry, excellent bar menu, garlic chili fries to die for/from, and 24 changing craft taps and frequent tap takeovers.

Drackenbergs Cigar Bar
605 North Sherman Ave, 608-513-2596, drackenbergs.com
A near northside bar with craft beer taps and smoking onsite.

Gib's Bar
1380 Williamson St, gibs.bar
A converted house with lounge seating, craft cocktails, and several craft beer taps.

Glass Nickel Pizza Co
2916 Atwood Ave, 608-245-0880, glassnickelpizza.com
Often voted the best pie in town, the Nickel's great tap lineup is often overlooked.

Great Dane Brew Pub & Brewery
4000 International Lane, greatdanepub.com
While they don't brew here, this pub inside security is your last (or first) Madison craft beer at the airport.

The Hops Museum
2617 East Washington Ave, 608-618-3746, thehopsmuseum.org
Learn about hops, history, and more at this free museum next door to
The Malt House. Watch for events.

Madison Mallards at Warner Park
2920 North Sherman, 608-246-4277, mallardsbaseball.com
Several beer stations, including the all you can drink/eat Duck Blind.

The Malt House
2609 East Washington Ave, 608-204-6258, malthousetavern.com
Best selection of beer in town, owned and operated by a beer judge and
four-time president of Madison Homebrewer's and Taster's Guild.

Mickey's Tavern
1524 Williamson St, 608-251-9964
A Madison classic with great bar food, a notable brunch, and several
great taps.

Star Liquor
1209 Williamson St, 608-255-8041, starliquor.com
Known for frequent free tastings, the neighborhood liquor store has a
great selection of beer.

Tex Tubb's Taco Palace
2009 Atwood Ave, 608-242-1800, textubbstacos.com
Popular for Tex-Mex, this restaurant has a good craft beer list and
often hosts releases and events.

Tip Top Tavern
601 North St, 608-241-5515, thetiptoptavern.com
Recently redone with a nicer menu, the tavern also serves craft beer.

Trixie's Liquor
2929 East Washington Ave, 608-442-5347, trixiesliquor.com
An excellent selection and knowledgeable staff.

Vic Pierce Liquor
609 North Sherman Ave, 608-244-4147
The north side's best bet for craft beer to go.

ALT BREW

Founded: 2012 (Brewery opened 2015)
Brewmaster: Trevor Easton
Address: 1808 Wright Street • Madison, WI 53704
Phone: 608-352-3373
Web Site: www.altbrew.com
Annual Production: 100 barrels
Number of Beers: 3

Staple Beers:
  » COPPERHEAD COPPER ALE
  » FARMHOUSE ALE
  » HOLLYWOOD NIGHTS BLONDE IPA

Rotating Beers:
  » BELGIAN TRIPEL
  » plus various seasonals

Most Popular Brew: All 3 staples selling about even.

Samples: Yes, sample flights available.

Brewmaster's Fave: On a hot summer day? Farmhouse. Hanging with friends? Hollywood Nights.

Best Time to Go: Open Fri–Sat noon–late. Check the website for certainty.

Where can you buy it? Here on tap and to go in growlers. A few local draft accounts and in stores in bombers throughout Madison. Find their beer on a map on their website.

Got food? Yes, light snacks and possibly some local food carts. Food friendly in the taproom, but of course nothing with gluten allowed in the brewing area.

Tours? Yes, by chance or by appointment.

Special Offer: A buy your first pint of Alt Brew, get one free during your signature visit.

Directions: From Stoughton Rd/US 51 just north of Washington Ave, head north one block to Anderson St. Turn left, and take the next right on Wright St. Pass Madison College and turn into the lot of the next long building on the left. You will find the brewery here.

The Beer Buzz: Necessity is the mother of fermentation. Trevor started as a homebrewer in college, and after he got married, his wife Maureen was diagnosed with celiac disease. Beer would make her sick. He couldn't brew at home either, because it would contaminate their kitchen. So he became determined to make gluten-free homebrew. The first six months he says were really bad, but he started to work things out with these alternative grains and it started to improve. After two years, they realized that if they hosted a party, they'd actually move through their own beer faster than anything else. People seemed to like it a lot. As public knowledge about celiac has grown, so has the demand for gluten-free products, and they saw this as a unique business opportunity. They were living in Chicago at the time, but both were originally East Siders in Madison. They put together a business plan, moved back to Madison, and met with Page Buchanan at House of Brews. Page tried the beer and recommended Trevor brew there. Trevor and Maureen got legal approvals as Greenview Brewing in 2013 and took over a space at House of Brews. Though this was technically an alternating proprietorship, the equipment was exclusive to avoid contamination. In 2014, they had beer on the market.

All their ingredients are gluten-free not gluten-removed. Trevor uses sorghum, rice, millet, honey, teff, and buckwheat, and works with a couple of gluten-free malters. Great care needs to be taken to avoid contact with malted barley or wheat or rye. They adopted the name Greenview, the name of their street when they were in Chicago, but changed the brand name to ALT. The new name fit as Trevor uses the alt bier style as a base for a clean, well-balanced beer, and alt also suggests their alternative ingredients. The couple opened a simple taproom and brewery in fall of 2015 with the same one-barrel system they had been using at House of Brews. With the move they hope to start expanding their market reach, which will mean a larger system sometime soon.

Free WiFi. Facebook/altbrew and Twitter @AltBrew

Stumbling Distance: This location is just off the bike path near Madison College (MATC) and block and a half from *Karben4 Brewing*. Try some alternative food: the award-winning Venezuelan eatery *La Taguara* (3502 E Washington Ave, 608-721-9100, lataguara-madison.com) lets you order online for dine-in or carryout. *Ale Asylum* is minutes away on the west side of the airport and *House of Brews* is 10 minutes south on Stoughton Rd. This is inside Madison's Beermuda Triangle.

PHOTOS COURTESY OF ALT BREW

FUNK FACTORY GEUZERIA

Founded: 2015
Blender: Levi Funk
Address: 1604 Gilson Street • Madison, WI 53715
Web Site: www.funkfactorygeuzeria.com
Annual Production: 150 barrels

Lambic-style Beers:
  » DOOR KRIEK (sour cherries from Door County)
  » THE FOX AND THE GRAPES (with Foch grapes)
  » FRAMROOD (with raspberries)

Best Time to Go: Special events (see below)

Tours? By appointment only

The Beer Buzz: Lambic, a style generally associated with Belgium, is a beer made from spontaneous fermentation—in other words, wild yeasts and bacteria native to the place they are brewed. They are aged in wood barrels where they pick up their most significant microorganisms. Of the 80 or so little critters in there, the most important are the yeasts Saccharomyces cerevisiae, Saccharomyces pastorianus and Brettanomyces bruxellensis. Lambic is a sour beer with a varying tartness, and the style has been catching on in the US. Brewers may add fruit (fruited lambic), as is the case in a *kriek* (sour cherry) lambic. Not a surprise in a state known for its Door County cherries. Another style of beer, known as *geuze*, is created when two lambics are blended. An older lambic—aged

2–3 years—and a "young" lambic that is only about a year old.

This is the funk that Levi Funk (actual name) has going on here, and people are eager to get their hands on a bottle. Already released are some of the fruited lambics (above) he made with O'so Brewing, but the geuze will require more time. Previously he drove to O'so to collaborate and left the barrels in their large space. In 2014, however, he found a warehouse on Madison's south side that had sat empty, slowly decaying for 30 years. With the help of his wife Amanda, a talented remodeling designer, they turned a dismal place into a brighter one that now is home to pyramids of barrels. He gets his wort from O'so and other brewers and will be blending

geuze which will eventually be sold in corked and caged 750 ml bottles. For now, watch this space for occasional special events, but eventually this will also be a tasting room. Summer of 2017 should see the release of the geuze, but you will see more fruited lambics before then.

Spelled either geuze or gueuze, the pronunciation is varied and elusive. Belgians have more than one language in the region, so that accounts for some of the differences. I've heard just plain gooz here in the States, but it sounds to me more like geh-ooz, with the two syllables themselves blending nicely like two lambics. In documentaries from Belgium in Flemish (Belgian Dutch), it sounds more like GH(y)ER-zuh, with the tricky-sounding Dutch g. Good luck with that. Just point at the bottle.

Facebook/funkfactorygeuzeria and Twitter @FFGeuzeria

FURTHERMORE BEER

Founded: June 9 (*my birthday too!*), 2006
Brewmaster: Aran Madden
Website: www.furthermorebeer.com
Annual Production: 1,800 bbls
Number of Beers: 8 and more to come

Beers:
- » FATTY BOOMBALATTY (Belgian white)
- » PROPER (light-bodied English-style ale specially brewed for American Players Theatre)
- » KNOT STOCK (APA with fresh black pepper)
- » FALLEN APPLE (fall seasonal, fresh pressed cider blended with cream ale)
- » FLOATING FIRE (rye and smoked malt with hibiscus)
- » OSCURA (summer seasonal, Mexican lager with coffee)
- » THREE FEET DEEP STOUT (winter seasonal with peat-smoked malt)
- » VIKING AFTERNOON (spring seasonal, Session IPA)

Most Popular Brew: Fatty Boombalatty

Brewmaster's Fave: "Knot Stock is the one-of-a-kind beer that gave me confidence to start my own brewing. Fallen Apple is a fun alternative to the usual harvest beers."

Where can you buy it? Primarily in southern Wisconsin (Madison, Milwaukee), plus Twin Cities liquor stores and scattered parts of Minnesota, and the Chicagoland area. (Check the website for an updated map.)

The Beer Buzz: Here's a popular craft beer that hasn't got a home, really. There is no taproom or brewhouse for you to visit, though you should have no problem finding it on tap and in stores. Brewer/founder Aran started homebrewing in 1993, went to the American Brewers Guild, and then took his first job in 1997 at a microbrewery in Pittsburgh. Any new brewer sees the failure of another microbrewery as an opportunity: used equipment. But Aran saw it as a lesson. He didn't want to jump in so deep, so fast, and risk failure. So initially Furthermore started contract brewing at Sand Creek in Black River Falls and evaluating site options in Spring Green. And as their production grew, the idea of buying some stainless seemed furthermore away. As of now, the current model is working so well, they figure, why change it?

Aran's Knot Stock is a bit unusual perhaps, but he insists on being different. "For us to make just another amber it's like who cares? There are a lot of beers out there—you may as well make it exciting. Don't give me the same old same old." The name Furthermore alludes to that, going beyond what's out there. If any of the recipe ingredients sound a little unusual, a taste will likely make you a believer. Check the website periodically to see if they've found a home yet. Meanwhile, get thee to a liquor store or local pub. Also, watch their website because Furthermore is on the road a lot making appearances at a variety of tastings and special events.

BEER JELLY FOR YOUR BEER BELLY

Some call her Chef K, others The Pickle Lady, but to me Kimberly Clark Anderson is the Beer Jelly Lady. She's already doing quite well online and at markets with her unique pickles and preserves—including Mexican sour gherkins, Moroccan-spiced pickled asparagus, pickled Brussels sprouts, blueberry balsamic jam, strawberry lavender, red currant with cardamom. Plus Gussie Mary pickled asparagus and carrots cut for cocktails. And her Chili Hot Chow Chow may be the next Sriracha sauce. But then she had a genius idea: beer jelly.

She was prepping for Fermentation Fest (fermentationfest.com) one October and did a tasting with a brewer to learn a bit about pairing. She had maybe one too many, and when she got home she thought, "I can make jelly out of anything, why not beer?" The stuff is great on crackers, toast, and a variety of other combos (which are listed on each label). She's tried every variety of beer. "Not all beer works, but put great beer in, get great jelly out." Flavors include Smoked Porter, Oatmeal Stout, Scotch Ale, APA, Oktoberfest, Cherry beer, Tangerine IPA, and Bourbon barrel aged beers. Nearly all of it is Wisconsin beer, including some Chocolate Stout from Badger State Brewing and Black Bavarian from Sprecher. Available in 4-oz jars. Check her website to order or see where she's selling.

www.chefkclark.com

Granite City Food and Brewery

Founded: 2006
Brewmaster: Cory O'Neel in Iowa
Address: 72 West Towne Mall • Madison, WI 53719
Phone: 608-829-0700
Website: www.gcfb.net
Annual Production: 700 bbls
Number of Beers: 5 regular styles + seasonal beers and brewer's choice selections

Staple Beers:
  » Batch 1000 Double IPA
  » Broad Axe Stout
  » Brother Benedict's Bock
  » Duke of Wellington IPA
  » Northern Light Lager

Most Popular Brew: Northern Light or Bock

Brewmaster's Fave: The IPA and specialty beers

Tours? Yes, by request.

Samples? A tray for about $4.95 for eight 4-oz samples. Also try a "2-Pull," the Northern Light/Bock blend, invented by pub patrons.

Best Time to Go: Open daily: Mon–Thu 11AM–12AM, Fri–Sat 11AM–1AM, Sun 9AM–10PM. While someone else is hitting the mall hard. Happy hour is 3–6PM and 9PM–close Mon–Fri, and noon–5PM Sat–Sun.

Where can you buy it? Growlers on site (or any of the other 34 Granite City locations in 14 states)!

Got food? Yes, flatbread pizzas, soups and salads, seafood, pasta, burgers, steaks and monthly specials. There are also a gluten-free and kids' menus.

Special Offer: Not participating.

Directions: To get here get off the "Beltline" (Hwy 12-18) at Gammon Rd exit and head north. The first traffic light marks the West Towne Mall entrance on the left and Granite City is a stand-alone building right there.

The Beer Buzz: This brewpub franchise was first founded in 1999 in St. Cloud, Minnesota, but has since expanded throughout the Midwest. Part of their ease of expansion was streamlining the brewing process and eliminating some of the need for equipment at each location. One of the co-founders was a bit of a legend in the craft brewing scene in the Twin Cities: Bill Burdick was the guy behind Sherlock's Home Restaurant Pub and Brewery, which made a lasting impression on brewers and beer drinkers during its run from 1989 to 2002. At Granite City, Burdick developed a process they called Fermentus Interruptus™. The wort is actually prepared in their central brewing facility—a brewhouse in Ellsworth, Iowa—and then shipped to each location where it is fermented. The result is consistent staple beers and less investment in multiple brewhouses. The Granite City name comes from the 19th century industry that built St. Cloud: quarrying granite.

The interior is upscale casual and done up with stonework to honor the name. A display kitchen allows you to see the food prep just as the glass window shows the brewing facility. The menu pairs beers with particular items. There are a few TVs about the place, but it's not a sports bar per se. For anyone who has been dragged to the mall to shop, this is a perfect escape. The brewpub offers an excellent mug club as well as gift cards. Daily specials are a good reason to check the website and Tuesdays and Thursdays offer $6.50 refills on their growlers! (That's an absurdly great deal.) Free WiFi.

Stumbling Distance: *Capital Brewery* is just north of here in Middleton and *Vintage Brewing Co.* is one exit east off the Beltline Highway. For a superb liquor store to take some Wisconsin beer home, go south on Gammon Road to *Woodman's* grocery store. You can find a ton of craft beers plus a section that allows you to build your own six-pack.

The Great Dane Pub and Brewery

Founded: November 1994
Brewmaster: Michael Fay
Address: 123 E Doty Street • Madison, WI 53703
Phone: 608-284-0000
Website: www.greatdanepub.com
Annual Production: 2,700 bbls
Number of Beers: 17 on tap plus a couple casks

Staple Beers:
» Black Earth Porter
» Crop Circle Wheat Ale
» Devil's Lake Red Lager (on nitro)
» Emerald Isle Stout
» Landmark Lite
» Old Glory APA
» Peck's Pilsner
» Potter's Run IPA
» Stone of Scone Scotch Ale
» Verrückte Stadt German Pils

Rotating Beers:
» Barleywine
» Furious River IPA
» John Jacob Jingle Heimer Schmidt Dunkel-Doppel-Hefe-Weizenbock (ask them to say it for you really fast)
» A couple Belgian Brews throughout the year
» Fruit Beers in summer
» Always 1–2 Gravity Casks
» Irish Ale around St. Patty's
» Oktoberfest
» Spiced Holiday Ale
» ... and loads of others

Most Popular Brew: Crop Circle Wheat

Brewmaster's Fave: Verrückte Stadt German Pils

Tours? By appointment only.

Samples? Yes, a sip to decide, dontcha know, or sampler platters of four beers for about $6.50 (add 2 more for $2.50).

Best Time to Go: Happy hour 4–6 PM Mon–Fri plus free popcorn. When the university is in session, the place hops on weekends (and even when it's not). Sunday brunch is nice too.

Where can you buy it? On-site growlers and crowlers (fill-on-demand 32-oz cans), pub kegs, and half barrels (with 24-hour notice), but see their other locations at Hilldale and in Fitchburg (also brewpubs), at the airport, and the latest Great Dane East Side location. The Duck Blind at Madison Mallards Northwoods-League baseball games is fueled by four specially brewed Great Dane beers. For something farther afield, find the Dane in Wausau, WI. 100+ tap accounts around the state and now some cans in distribution.

Got food? Yes, and it's very popular for lunch and dinner. Full menu of soups, salads, burgers, entrees and more. The bratburger (created on a dare) is an original with bacon on a pretzel bun. Beer, brat and cheese soup is Wisconsin in a bowl. Beer bread is standard, fish and chips available, and a load of other great dishes. Friday night pilsner-battered fish fry!

Special Offer: A 10-oz beer and all the coasters you can eat.

Directions: Head for the Capitol and follow the Capitol Loop (two streets out from the Capitol) along Doty Street where it meets King and Webster St. The Dane is on the corner. Street parking is metered until 6 PM or park in the ramp on the opposite end of the same block.

The Beer Buzz: The Great Dane has been around long enough to be a landmark in itself just off the Capitol Square in Madison, but its home is also the former Fess Hotel, built in the 1850s with an addition in 1883 and remodeled in 1901. The opening of the Dane by college buddies Rob LoBreglio and Eliot Butler saw some more remodeling in 1994, and it is now a lively joint with music, a pool hall, and three bars. You'll spot the big neon Brewpub sign as you come up the hill. The Rathskeller (the basement bar) was once a stable for horses and keeps the original stone walls. Outside dining is a seasonal bonus in the beer garden where hops climb the bricks on the backside of the building. There are also some tales of spirits of the nonalcohol kind, perhaps former guests of the Fess.

All the character of the historic building and the awesome menu aside, the beer is the crowning centerpiece of this place. On the way to the restrooms downstairs, you can pass the tanks where this magical stuff works its way up to the bars through a tangling system of tap lines referred to as The Matrix. The Red Lager is run through a Guinness tap (under nitrogen) which gives it that cascading foam head which can hypnotize you to drink more beer. This is brewmaster Rob LoBreglio's pride and joy. Expect innovative ideas from this bunch, always with an insistence on quality. The Dane now also sells Eliot Butler's Scotch Ale jerky as well as beer soap. "It'll get you clean but not necessarily sober."

Free WiFi. Facebook.com/greatdanedowntown and Twitter @GreatDanePub

Trivia note: Right across the street is a sign marking the site of Madison's first public house: Peck's Cabin.

Stumbling Distance: *The Old Fashioned* (www.theoldfashioned.com, 23 N Pinckney St, 608-310-4545), highly recommended, offers an all-Wisconsin menu and 52 taps of Wisconsin beers plus a truckload in bottles. The menu is 100% Wisconsin style, with beer-cheese soup, brats, the state cocktail, and the best curds in town. The *Wisconsin State Capitol* (www. wisconsin.gov, 608-266-0382) is one block from here and a definite must-see with daily free tours and a 6th floor observation deck and museum. The square itself hosts a variety of events throughout the year, but especially a Saturday morning *Farmers' Market* (exclusively local produce, cheese, meats, and other products) and Wednesday evening *Concerts on the Square* or *Jazz at 5* in summer. Down the hill from the Dane are *Come Back In* (508 E Wilson St, 608-258-8619) and *Essen Haus* (514 E Wilson, 608-255-4674), connected at the hip: one is quite tavern with 24 craft taps plus bottles, the other is quite German, with German tap beers, glass boots, and often a polka band. Free peanuts and popcorn at both. *Bos Meadery* (849 E Washington Ave, 608-628-3792, bosmeadery.com) has a tasting room serving their meads and offering tours, open Thu–Sat evenings. *Old Sugar Distillery* (931 E Main St, 608-260-0812, oldsugardistillery.com) produces craft rum, ouzo, whiskey and honey liqueur and serves cocktails in their tasting room Thu–Sat with a limited snack/appetizer menu. Free tastes and tours.

BEER GALORE: STATE STREET

State Street connects the Capitol with the University of Wisconsin. Primarily a pedestrian zone (buses, bikes, and delivery are allowed), it is the heart of downtown. Overture Center for the Arts (overturecenter.org) is here with two main performance halls, art museums and rooftop dining, and across the street is The Orpheum for concerts. Restaurants, bars, shops, and sidewalk cafes run the length. And it is also a canyon of craft beer. Highlights from the Capitol to the university's lakeside include:

Cooper's Tavern (20 W Mifflin St, 608-256-1600, thecooperstavern.com) just on the square, has a nice selection of craft beers with some Belgians.

Capital Tap Haus Tavern (107 State St, 608-310-1010, capitaltaphaus.com) is like a tied house for Capital's beers and does a good fish fry.

Mr. Brew's Taphouse (305 W Johnson St, 608-819-6841, mrbrewstaphouse.com) keeps 72 on tap.

Brickhouse BBQ (408 W Gorham St, 608-257-7675, thebrickhousebbq.com) pours 40 draft beers, has abundant seating, and a rooftop terrace with a Capitol view.

HopCat (222 W Gorham St, 608-807-1361, hopcat.com/Madison), the Grand Rapids-based beer bar, has a whopping 130 beers on tap, plus food and a rooftop terrace.

Paul's Club (204 State St, 608-257-5250, facebook.com/PaulsClub), a Madison classic, a bar with a fake tree in the middle, is now a newer bar with a fake tree—plus a 24-tap lineup.

Vintage Brewing's sister restaurant (529 University Ave, 608-250-0700, vintage-madison.com) serves their beers and more just off State Street.

State Street Brats (603 State St, 608-255-5544, statestreetbrats.com) not huge on craft, but the brat scene, sports TV, and patio deserve a nod.

Last but not least, the **Rathskeller** and outdoor *Terrace* at the *UW Memorial Union* (800 Langdon St, 608-265-3000, union.wisc.edu) are the very heart of the community and ideal in the summer. Watch the sunset and hear free live music while drinking an impressive assortment of Wisconsin and other craft beers by the glass or in plastic pitchers on the shores of Lake Mendota. You no longer need to be a Union member to purchase beer. In winter, the music continues but indoors. Also served is outdoor grilled food (burgers, brats) and the famous Babcock ice cream. Out-of-staters should at least taste Blue Moon, a very Wisconsin ice cream flavor.

THE GREAT DANE PUB AND BREWERY (HILLDALE)

Founded: 2006
Head Brewer: Nate Zukas
Address: 357 Price Place • Madison, WI 53705 (Hilldale Mall on Midvale Blvd.)
Phone: 608-661-9400
Website: www.greatdanepub.com
Annual Production: 3,000 bbls
Number of Beers: 15 on tap, 1 cider, 2 beer engines

Staple Beers:
- » Black Earth Porter
- » Crop Circle Wheat
- » Emerald Isle Stout
- » Hopsconsin
- » Imperial IPA
- » Landmark Lite Lager
- » Old Glory American Pale Ale
- » Peck's Pilsner
- » Stone of Scone Scotch Ale
- » Verruckte Stadt German Pils

Rotating Beers:
- » Amber Lager (summer)
- » Barleywine
- » Bock
- » Doppelbock (winter)
- » JOHN JACOB JINGLE HEIMER SCHMIDT DUNKEL-DOPPEL-HEFE-WEIZENBOCK (ask them to say it for you really fast)
- » Maibock (spring)
- » Mudluscious Imperial Stout
- » Oktoberfest
- » Pine Marten Red Ale
- » Siam Strong Pale Ale
- » Tangerine Dream (dry-hopped doppel-hefe-weizenbock)

Most Popular Brew: Imperial IPA

Brewer's Fave: "Impossible to pick one."

Tours? By chance or appointment but always welcomed.

Samples? Yes, a sip to decide, dontcha know, or sampler platters of four beers for about $6.50 (add 2 more for $2.50).

Best Time to Go: Happy hour is 4–6PM and offers beer discounts

Where can you buy it? On-site growlers, pub kegs, and half barrels (with 24-hour notice), but see their other locations in Fitchburg (also a brewpub), at the airport, an east side location, and the original downtown brewpub. The Duck Blind at Madison Mallards Northwoods-League baseball games is fueled by 4 specially brewed Great Dane beers. All beer for the airport and ballpark is produced here and a bit extra shores up production in Fitchburg as well. For something farther afield, find the Dane in Wausau, WI. 100+ tap accounts around the state and now some cans in distribution.

Got food? Yes, a full menu of soups, salads, burgers, and entrees. The bratburger (created on a dare) is an original with bacon on a pretzel bun. Beer, brat and cheese soup is Wisconsin in a bowl. Beer bread is standard, fish and chips available, and a load of other great dishes. Friday night pilsner-battered fish fry!

Special Offer: A free 10-oz beer!

Directions: From the Beltline Highway (12/14/18/151) go north on Midvale Blvd until just before University Avenue and turn left at Heather Crest (or come south one long block south of University Avenue and turn right). The Dane is on the left corner at the next cross street right before the Hilldale Mall building.

The Beer Buzz: This brewpub was a challenge to an outdated brewing law in Wisconsin that didn't allow a brewer producing over 4,000 barrels each year to have more than two brewing locations. When the Hilldale location opened its doors in 2006 it could not serve its own brews and for a while got by on featuring other Wisconsin beers. When the law finally changed in 2007, the expected varieties of Dane brews started flowing. Brewer Eric took over here, leaving Michael in charge at the downtown location. Nate was assistant for 3 years before taking the lead in 2012. They've expanded internally here and, with the help of a mobile canning unit, are distributing in cans starting with Verruckte Stadt and Hopsconsin Red Ale.

Abundant table seating for diners is complemented by booths in the bar area as well as tall tables and a long narrow bar-table with stools down the middle of the room in front of the bar itself. The near west side location has been a huge success, and an expansion in 2009 opened up more seating including a mezzanine section and added room for pool tables, shuffleboard and foosball. Lots of big TVs pipe in sports from around the world. The Dane equation for its multiple locations can be expressed thus: similar enough that you can count on all of them for good beer and good times, different enough that you want to visit them all. Parking is on the street or in a nearby free ramp. The stout's name mud-luscious comes from a puddle-wonderful poem by e.e. cummings i think.

Stumbling Distance: Nearby are fabulous eateries: *Café Porta Alba* (cafeportaalba.com, 608-441-0202) with some true Italian wood-fired oven pizza, some of Madison's best sushi at *Sushi Muramoto* (muramoto.biz, 608-441-1090), and the tequila bar and southwestern restaurant *Pasqual's* (pasquals.net, 608-663-8226). Right down the row in front of Hilldale Mall. Inside the mall complex is the new *Café Hollander*, a Madison version of Milwaukee's well known Europub with a long list of Belgian beers.

House Of Brews

Founded: 2011
Brewmaster: Page Buchanan
Address: 4539 Helegesen Drive • Madison, WI 53718
Phone: 608-347-7243
Website: www.houseofbrewsmadison.com
Annual Production: up to 960 bbls
Number of Beers: 6 on tap

Staple Beers:
  » A-Frame Amber
  » Observatory Pale Ale
  » Standing Stone Scotch Ale

Rotating Beers:
  » Bungalow Rye Esb
  » Citadel IPA
  » Gazebo Wheat (summer)
  » Mausoleum Black IPA
  » Pagoda IPA
  » Prairie Rye (spring/summer)
  » Snug Stout
  » Various IPAs showcasing specific hops
  » A variety of barrel-aged brews and various test brews along the way of others...

Most Popular Brew: Standing Stone Scotch Ale

Brewmaster's Fave: Prairie Rye

Tours? Yes, available on request. See also Hop Head Tours!

Samples? Yes.

Best Time to Go: The taproom is open Tue–Fri 3:30–9:30PM, Sat 2–9:30PM.

Where can you buy it? On tap here and in growlers, bombers, and kegs to go. Bombers are in area stores and find it on tap locally as well.

Got food? Only some free popcorn, but carry-in is encouraged and there are a few menus around to order delivery.

Special Offer: A free glass of Page's beer.

Directions: Take Stoughton Road (US 51) south from East Washington Ave (or north from the Beltline Hwy) and go east at Buckeye Road. The next right is a frontage version of Stoughton Road that takes a couple turns before running parallel to US 51. Turn left on Helgesen Dr and the brewery will be on your right halfway down the block.

The Beer Buzz: Page Buchanan is the owner/head brewer of this little brewery tucked into an industrial neighborhood. While he had been brewing at home for almost 18 years, he hadn't decided to go commercial until he lost his job as a labor rep in 2009. By mid-2010 he was building his facility, and selling from his first batch on September 1, 2011 (to the awesome Madison beer bar The Malt House). Now about 80% of his beer is contract brewed for others. He may have 5–7 clients each year and the situation varies: a brand-launching, supplemental brewing for small brewers struggling to keep up with demand, or full-on production for a brewing company with no equipment yet. And in this case it can be pure contract brewing or an alternating proprietorship arrangement, wherein the outside brewer "owns" that equipment while they are using it, thus paying their own beer taxes and such. Brewers such as *MobCraft Beer* and *Alt Brew* (formerly *Greenview Brewing*) got themselves going in this manner, and current contract brew *Bent Kettle Brewing* hopes to do the same. *One Barrel Brewing* purchased fermenters and keeps them here to help keep up with their supplemented production. *Dead Bird Brewing* is a contract startup by one of Page's assistant brewers.

Page's brewhouse has some hand-me-down equipment from *O'so Brewery* in Plover (after first passing through Falls Brewing and Pioneer Brewing), *Lake Louie's* of Arena, and *Central Waters* of Amherst. The taproom is small, with just a few tables made out of old barrels, and feels a bit like what it was—some office space at the front of the facility. There's a TV, a jukebox, and a cooler with bombers for sale.

Page has a couple other things going on here. The first is a CSB, Community Supported Brewery. Much like a CSA arrangement with a farmer for a weekly basket of produce, but in this case a supply of beer. Member numbers are about 30, and he still accepts new applicants. He also hopes to offer a few smaller brew kettles for a "brew on premises" program for aspiring brewers. "I want to be inclusive, reaching out to the community in different ways, working with local chefs," says Buchanan. In cooperation with local restaurants, he comes up with specialty brews for their menus.

Stumbling Distance: *Habanero's Mexican Grill* (2229 S Stoughton Rd, 608-223-9222, habanerosmg.com) is close by and very popular. The drive to *The Great Dane Eastside* location isn't long from here (876 Jupiter Dr, 608-467-1231). The liquor store at *Woodman's* grocery just off of US 51/Stoughton Rd at Milwaukee St has a killer assortment of Wisconsin microbrews if you want to put together some chilled souvenirs from your trip to town. *Karben4 Brewing* is 10 minutes north on Stoughton Rd.

BASEBALL AND A BEEYAH HEEYAH! (A BEER HERE!)

It's our national pastime, the perfect way to enjoy a summer afternoon—nostalgic, exciting, and as American as apple pie and American Idol. Beer, I mean. And it goes great with baseball, too. Wisconsin's professional baseball team is of course the Milwaukee Brewers (brewers.mlb.com) and they play in Miller Park. That's as beery as it gets. Don't be surprised to see some Wisconsin craft beers there as well. New Glarus Brewing's Spotted Cow is a given, plus local brewers such as Lakefront and Milwaukee Brewing Co., plus Leinie's and Point. A few "imports" such as Bell's, Sierra Nevada, and New Belgium are also on tap.

Part of the Summer Collegiate Baseball's Northwoods League, the Madison Mallards (www.mallardsbaseball.com) at Warner Park on North Sherman Avenue offer games that are a lot of fun but don't pinch the wallet so much as the majors do. The ballpark has several beer stands with Wisconsin and other craft beers in the lineup. The Duck Blind, a great beer garden serviced by The Great Dane, provides all you can eat and drink in the Duck Blind and nearly 20 beers are on tap including Great Dane brews and others.

Up in Appleton, Stone Cellar is brewing Rattler Brau (their Scotch-style ale) for the Wisconsin Timber Rattlers, a Class A minor league team of the Midwest League affiliated with the Milwaukee Brewers.

Be careful as you pass the next cup down the bleacher row. Nobody likes a spiller.

KARBEN4 BREWING

Founded: September 2012
Brewmaster: Ryan Koga
Address: 3698 Kinsman Blvd • Madison, WI 53704
Phone: 608-241-4812
Website: www.karben4.com
Annual Production: 12,000 barrels
Number of Beers: up to 10 on tap

Staple Beers:
- » BLOCK PARTY AMBER ALE
- » FANTASY FACTORY IPA
- » LADY LUCK IRISH RED
- » NIGHTCALL SMOKED PORTER
- » TOKYO SAUNA PALE ALE
- » UNDERCOVER SESSION ALE

Rotating Beers:
- » CHAMPAGNE TORTOISE ENGLISH MILD
- » DRAGON FLUTE IPA
- » IDIOT FARM DOUBLE IPA
- » SILK SCORPION BLACK IPA
- » plus other seasonals and various barrel-aged beers

Most Popular Brew: Fantasy Factory

Brewmaster's Fave: Depends on his mood.

Tours? Yes, free tours at 1PM on Saturdays. See also Hop Head Tours!

Samples: Yes, sample pours for $2 each

Best Time to Go: Open Mon–Wed 11AM–10PM, Thu–Sat 11AM–12AM, Sun 11AM–10PM. Watch Facebook for beer release parties. See also The Dilly Dally Beer Fest in September when the brewery hosts a Madison-only brew festival.

Where can you buy it? On tap here and in growlers to go. Distributed in 6-pack (and occasional 4-pack) bottles and draft accounts in the Madison, Milwaukee areas.

Got food? Yes, a list of "Boards" with cheese and sausage, chips and dip sorts of things, plus soups, sandwiches, salads and flatbreads. Sunday brunch has its own menu 11AM–4PM. Most of the food is locally sourced. There is a full bar.

Special Offer: Buy your first Karben4 pour, get one free during your signature visit.

Directions: Take US Hwy 151 on Madison's east side (E Washington Ave) and turn north on Hwy 51/Stoughton Rd. At the cross street Kinsman where there's a McDonald's on the right, go left and it is the first driveway on the right. *Karben4 is also on the #6 bus line.*

The Beer Buzz: Nature abhors a vacuum, they say. As soon as Ale Asylum moved out of this place to their new big brewery, Karben4 moved right in, even keeping some of the previous brewers' equipment. Ryan went to school for pre-med so has a background in biology, chemistry, and psychology. But life took a malty turn when he moved to Montana for a grad program in sports medicine. Another guy in his program was a brewer and needed some bottling help, and Ryan took on the job for rent money. He wasn't into beer, didn't homebrew, but when he popped open an oatmeal stout on the line, he had his A-ha! moment and was hooked. "All beer experiences should be like this," he says. He finished school and picked up more responsibilities at the brewery and was soon co-brewer. Then the other guy left.

What's the best part about brewing? "The people you meet in the tap room." He met his wife at the brewery in Montana, as well as his best friend, doctor, mechanic… "You get to meet a lot of cool people." Yes, beer brings us together. Originally from Appleton, he made the move back to Wisconsin at just the right time to take over the old Ale Asylum digs. Growth and success came pretty fast.

Geeks Brewing Co. was the original name idea. Ryan has the passion of a beer geek and believes the name ought to reflect that, thus the sci-fi sounding name. In terms of brewing style, he loves the varieties of malt out there. While he's fine with a hoppy brew (and his Fantasy Factory is killing it with 70% of their distribution), he really likes looking at beer from the malt angle. He also likes to do a lot of research into a beer style and reads the culinary and cultural history of a place to influence his recipes.

The taproom has polished concrete floors, high industrial ceilings, and a gray interior contrasted by some very colorful paintings—each one inspired by each beer—by artist Tom Kowalke. A long bar bends around the kitchen and various tables and tall tables fill the room. Three 70-inch TVs that come on for the Packers/Badgers and other big events. A nice outdoor patio/beer garden is under a trellis. Plus their darts, music playing, and plenty of merchandise behind the bar.

Free WiFi. Facebook.com/Karben4 and on Twitter @Karben4

Stumbling Distance: *Dexter's* (www.dexterspubmadison.com, 301 North St, 608-244-3535) is a stellar neighborhood bar and grill with superb burgers, unbelievable garlic-chili fries and loads more, plus a rotating menu of top-notch microbrews. Dexter's lies at one corner of the *Beermuda Triangle* (see One Barrel Brewing's Stumbling Distance). Straight south on Stoughton Road/US 51 takes you to *House of Brews* in 10 minutes. *Ale Asylum* is 5 minutes west on the other side of the airport.

Next Door Brewing Co.

Founded: January 2013
Head Brewer: Bryan Kreiter
Address: 2439 Atwood Ave • Madison, WI 53704
Phone: 608-729-3683
Web Site: www.nextdoorbrewing.com
Annual Production: 425 barrels (plus some contract brewing)
Number of Beers: 11 on tap; 30 beers per year

Staple Beers:
» Bascom Blonde
» Kaleidospoke Pale Ale (formerly East Side Pale Ale)
» Four Lakes Saison
» Iron Brigade Stout
» Luminous IPA
» Rocket's Red

Rotating Beers:
» Belgian IPA
» Gose
» Ice Cutter Double IPA
» Imperial Rye Stout
» Mutha Pucka (sour blonde with pineapple)
» Plumptuous Scotch Ale
» …mostly ales, some fruit infusions and oak/barrel aging, and occasional firkins

Most Popular Brew: East Side Pale Ale

Samples: Yes, build your own flights with 4-oz pours for $2–3 each (depending on abv)

Brewer's Fave: Plumptuous

Best Time to Go: Mon 4–10PM, Tue 11AM–10PM, Wed–Thu 11AM–11PM, Fri–Sat 11–12AM, Sun 11AM–9PM (Sunday brunch specials 11AM–3PM). Happy hour runs Mon 4–9, Tue–Thu 4–7PM, and Fri 3–6PM, with different specials each night. Monday night bring in some vinyl to play and get a discount on a beer.

Where can you buy it? Here on tap in pints and half-pints and to go in growlers, and occasional limited 22-oz bombers onsite and soon six-pack 12-oz bottles in local distribution.

Got food? Yes, a menu of sliders, croquettes, small plates (including curds and poutine), soups/salads, and burgers/sandwiches. Friday fish fry.

Tours? Yes, by chance or by appointment. See also Hop Head Tours.

Special Offer: A free half pint of Next Door beer during your signature visit.

Directions: Follow Williamson Street east and it becomes Eastwood, then Atwood. The brewery is on the right. (From East Washington, head south on 1st St and take a left on Eastwood.)

Cyclists: not far off the Capital City Trail

The Beer Buzz: Started two months after opened. One owner born and raised in WI and wanted to open brewpub and two others had same mission and hooked up on a website. Business dating?

Set in a former appliance repair shop, Next Door Brewing happened when Keith Symonds, a Wisconsin native with a mission to start a brewpub, found Aric Dieter and Pepper Stebbins, who had the same ambition. They built out this neighborhood location and for a while Keith did the brewing. Bryan grew up on farm in Iowa and spent 13 years working for The Nature Conservancy. He got into homebrewing, and as a volunteer working his butt off, helped some friends start a brewery in Mississippi. He moved to Madison, took a brewing tech course at Siebel Institute, and started here as an assistant before stepping up to head brewer in May 2014. (*Trivia note*: Dan Sherman, the head brewer at One Barrel down the street, officiated Bryan and his wife's wedding in 2015.)

They run a three-barrel electric brew system and have 36 barrels of fermentation capacity. For the present, they are doing some contract brewing, in addition to the beer made onsite, as a stepping stone to a future expansion. The dining area offers tables, half-booths and big communal tables (made from wood salvaged from the old Point Brewery malt silos). The bar area has an L-shaped bar and some tall tables, and a counter along the wall looking through glass into the brewery. A few TVs come out during major sporting events.

East Side Pale Ale has been a real winner for them and as they moved toward distributing it, they changed the name to Kaleidospoke to avoid trademark confusions.

Free WiFi. Facebook/NextDoorBrewing and Twitter @NextDoorBrewing

Stumbling Distance: *Stalzy's Deli* (2701 Atwood Ave, 608-249-7806, stalzysdeli.com) is right across the street and does great sandwiches. *Bunky's Café* (2425 Atwood Ave, 608-204-7004, bunkyscafe.net) is a long-time favorite with Mediterranean/Italian fare. *Harmony Bar & Grill* (2201 Atwood Ave, 608-249-4333, harmonybarandgrill.com) is a real tavern with good grub (especially their pizza) and a short but decent tap list.

One Barrel Brewing

Founded: July 2012
Brewmaster: Dan Sherman
Address: 2001 Atwood Ave.
        Madison, WI 53704
Phone: 608-630-9286
Website: www.onebarrelbrewing.com
Annual Production: 1,000 bbls
Number of Beers: 8 on tap (with some guests)

Staple Beers:
  » Bilbo Baggins Black IPA
  » Commuter Kölsch
  » Penguin Pale Ale
  » #2 Strong Ale

Rotating Beers:
  » Breakfast Beer Oatmeal Stout
  » Emperor Penguin
  » Hopticity Jones IPA
  » Sour beers and many other come-and-go brews, plus guest taps from other Wisconsin brewers

Most Popular Brew: Penguin Pale Ale

Brewmaster's Fave: Hopticity Jones

Tours? Yes, randomly and if you ask politely, but the tour can be done from the bar stool. See also Hop Head Tours!

Samples? Yes, flights of four 5-oz pours for about $10.

Best Time to Go: Open Mon–Wed 4–11pm, Thu 4pm–1am, Fri 3:30pm–1am, Sat 12pm–1am, Sun 12pm–11pm. Thursday is Commuter Night when you can get a beer discount if you came on bike (just show your helmet).

Where can you buy it? Here on tap and to go in growlers, plus several dozen tap accounts in Madison.

Got food? Yes, various pre-made foods from local vendors, meat and cheese boards with Wisconsin cheeses and Underground Meats, Fraboni's pizzas, and Batch Bakehouse soft pretzels, for example. Or just carry in—it's OK!

Special Offer: A hug or the best high five you'll ever get, plus $1 off your first One Barrel beer when you get your book signed!

Directions: From East Washington Ave (US Highway 151) go south on S. 2nd Street and then go right on Winnebago Street a half block to where it intersects Atwood Avenue. It's right there at this intersection on the corner, known as Schenk's Corners.

Cyclists: not far off the Capital City Trail

The Beer Buzz: As might be apparent in the name, this little brewery brews the hard way, one barrel (two half-barrels, 31 gallons, see the index if you're measure-curious) at a time. Peter Gentry was born and raised in this neighborhood, Schenk's Corners, as was his father. This is as local as you get. Gentry thought he was buying his father a brewing kit back in 2004 when he picked one up from the Wine and Hop Shop in Madison. But it turned out Peter loved it more. He brewed for friends at first but won the Grumpy Troll brewing challenge in 2008. From there he went

on to a national competition and in 2010 his #2 Strong Ale got honorable mention in the US Beer Tasting Championship. He quit his day job in 2011 to plan this brewery, which opened not long after. They brew like mad to keep up with demand and added two 20-barrel fermenters offsite. They also have a sour program in the basement, so you can expect a monthly release that will go fast.

Set in an old brick building that was once a cooper's shop (barrel maker, how appropriate!) and then a grocer's in the early 1900s, the brewpub has hardwood floors and exposed brick walls. Track lighting is left over from its previous occupation as an art gallery. The brew system is glassed in at the back of the bar. They brew 4 or 5 one-barrel batches per week, so you can expect something new every time you stop in. They've got board games, a jackalope on the wall, and a large-screen TV, which is only unveiled for special games.

Free WiFi. Facebook.com/OneBarrelBrewing

Stumbling Distance: This is Schenk's Corners, the heart of one of Madison's old neighborhoods, and there are a number of places to eat around here. *Tex Tubb's Taco Palace* (608-242-1800, textubbstacos.com) is next door and serves Tex-Mex and hosts the occasional beer event. Great tap lists await at *Alchemy Café* (across the intersection, 608-204-7644, alchemycafe.net), *Dexter's Pub & Grill* (301 North St, 608-244-3535, dexterspubmadison.com), and *The Malt House* (2609 E Washington Ave, 608-204-6258, malthousetavern.com). The *Barrymore Theatre* is also a stone's throw down Atwood Ave offering great live music of local, national, and international acclaim. *Next Door Brewing* is minutes away east on Atwood Ave.

One Barrel also touches on the *Beermuda Triangle* (see Beermuda Triangle text box).

Rockhound Brewing Co.

Opening Date: January, 2016
Brewmaster: Nate Warnke
Address: 444 South Park Street • Madison, WI 53715
Phone: _____
Web Site: www.rockhoundbrewing.com
Annual Production: 500 barrels
Number of Beers: up to 16 on tap (some guests)

Staple Beers:
- » Balanced Rock Rye
- » Greenbush Pale Ale
- » Ice Shanty Bock
- » Outcrop Oatmeal Ale

Rotating Beers:
- » Plowshare Farmhouse Ale
- » Grandpa's Lager
- » Grinder
- » Midnight Harvest (Belgian-style multi-grain ale)
- » Mosquito Bite IPA
- » Shot Rock Scotch Ale

Most Popular Brew: Too soon to tell.

Samples: Yes, flights available.

Brewmaster's Fave: Balanced Rock Rye

Best Time to Go: Open Sun, Tue–Thu 11AM–11PM, Fri–Sat 11AM–1AM. Closed Mondays. Check the website to be sure.

Where can you buy it? Here on tap and to go in growlers.

Got food? Yes, a full menu of upscale pub food, including appetizers, soups and salads, sandwiches and more.

Tours? Yes, by chance or by appointment.

Special Offer: Buy your first pint of Rockhound beer, get 1 free during your signature visit.

Directions: US 151 passes right through Madison on several connecting streets. From where West Washington meets Park Street, go one block south on Park St and it is on the corner of Park and Drake in a multi-story building with retail at street level.

The Beer Buzz: Rockhound is an old-fashioned term for a geologist or rock collector, which is owner/brewer Nate Warnke's academic training: a geology degree. What does one do with such a degree? Make beer, of course.

Nate got into homebrewing ten years before opening this place because his wife Tracy wanted to try it. They took it on as a hobby, and she found she preferred to be the taste tester, a role she takes quite seriously. Under pressure from Tracy, Nate decided to go pro late in 2013, but it took about two years to bring his brewpub to fruition.

He lives in this neighborhood, so already had a preference for this location, plus it has the benefit of being close to downtown and on a major street that brings a lot of traffic in and out each day. Park Street has been an "under-served" neighborhood and he sees good things coming here. When a new building with street-level retail started going up on Lane Bakery's former site, he knew this was the place.

He has 4,000 square feet, half of which is the restaurant with booths, tables, and a u-shaped bar. He operates a 5-barrel system in the next room. When asked how he'd describe his brewing philosophy, he thought a moment and replied, "Balanced." Nothing super hoppy or super malty.

Free WiFi. Mug Club. Facebook/rockhoundbrewing,
Twitter @rockhoundbrew and Instagram @rockhoundbrewing

Stumbling Distance: *Henry Vilas Zoo* (702 S Randall Ave, 608-258-9490, vilaszoo.org) is free and nearby, as is the 1,260-acre, trail-filled *UW Arboretum* (608) 263-7888, arboretum.wisc.edu) along Lake Wingra. *Taqueria Guadelajara* (1033 S Park St, 608-250-1824, lataqueriaguadalajara.com) serves the best Mexican in town. *The Mason Lounge* (416 S Park St, 608-255-7777) is a very laid back, neighborhood bar with 15+ craft beers on draft served in Mason jars. For some excellent Peruvian cuisine, including ceviche, go to *Inka Heritage* (602 S Park St, 608-310-4282, inkaheritagerestaurant.com). *OSS* (910 Regent St, 608-709-1000) serves its own varied sausages, plus curds and craft beers. Next to that is the classic *Greenbush Bar* (914 Regent St, 608-257-2874, greenbushbar.net) with old-school thin-crust Sicilian pizza in a basement location with Christmas lights.

Vintage Brewing Co.

Founded: December 2009
Brewmaster: Scott Manning
Address: 674 S Whitney Way • Madison, WI 53711
Phone: 608-204-2739
Website: vintagebrewingco.com
Annual Production: 1,600 bbls
Number of Beers: 18–25 house beers on tap at a time

Staple Beers:
- » Dedication Abbey Dubbel
- » McLovin Irish Red Ale
- » Scaredy Cat Oatmeal Stout
- » Weiss-Blau Weissbier
- » Woodshed Oaked IPA

Rotating Beers:
- » Better Off Red
- » Bee's Knees
- » Derby Girl ESB
- » Hickory Chicory Bock
- » Jinja Ninja
- » Joulupukki
- » Mach Schnell Pilsner
- » Maltiplicity
- » Maximilian Stout
- » Oktoberfest
- » Palindrome Pale Ale
- » Pumpkin Disorderly
- » Rochambeau
- » Square Pig
- » Thirty Point Bock
- » Tippy Toboggan
- » Toy Boat IPA
- » Trepidation
- » Whippoorwill Wit
- » ... and more (80+ Beers)

Most Popular Brew: Woodshed Oaked IPA.

Brewmaster's Faves: Rochambeau, Maltiplicity, and Palindrome.

Tours? Free, but by advance appointment only.

Samples? Yes, a complimentary "skosh," to try before you buy, or full 5-oz tasters ranging from $2-4 each, or available in flights.

Best Time to Go: Open for lunch and dinner daily 11AM–close. Monday Happy Hour: discounted select VBC pints! "Thirsty Thursday" VBC and guest draft beer discounts. In season, the patio opens up for dining and drinking in the sun.

Where can you buy it? Served here or at sister pubs Vintage Spirits & Grill, 529 University Ave, Madison, and Woodshed Ale House, 101

Jackson St, Sauk City, plus on tap at finer bars/restaurants in Madison, Milwaukee and Racine areas.

Got food? The menu offers made-to-order, from-scratch dishes and the chef favors local ingredients with modern twists. They offer their own fine beers but also an assortment of other great brews making this a great foodie and, um, beery? destination.

Special Offer: For each previously unsigned book newly signed by the brewmaster (or another owner/manager if brewmaster is unavailable), guest is entitled to $2 off regular-priced growler fills (valid on up to 4 growlers) OR 10% off regular price Vintage Brewing Company merchandise (max merchandise discount $8.00). Valid signature visit only. Some restrictions may apply.

Directions: From Hwy 12-14 (the Beltline) take the Whitney Way exit heading north. Cross Odana Road (the traffic lights one block away from the highway overpass) and take the next left into the parking lot of the Whitney Square strip mall. Vintage is in a stand-alone building in the lot.

The Beer Buzz: Vintage Spirits and Grill already had good success over on University Avenue with its retro style and convivial spirit. So when JT Whitney's Brewpub closed its doors in 2009 and this location remained vacant, the family-based partnership at Vintage decided it was time not just to serve great beer but to brew it as well. Vintage aims for some class without snobbery combining a plush lounge atmosphere with some old-school brewery décor.

Scott was born and raised in Wisconsin and graduated from the University of Wisconsin-Madison. From 1997 on, his professional brewing took him out west to places in AZ, CA and NV. His brother Bryan and cousin Trent had been secretly plotting a brewpub for years with the aim of luring Scott back to the Beer State. The nefarious plan worked and Scott has happily become his own boss and brewmaster for their family business.

Stumbling Distance: Just south of Madison off Hwy 151 is *Bavaria Sausage* (www.bavariasausage.com, 6317 Nesbitt Rd, 800-733-6695) which sells a wide variety of German and other sausages (a lot of it made in-house) and much more. Fresh cheese curds are delivered here on Thursday afternoons and Friday mornings. Do mini-golf, a year-round driving range, a par 3, a climbing wall, or batting cages interest you at all? Go across the highway from here to *Vitense Golfland* (www.vitense.com, 5501 Schroeder Road, 608-271-1411).

CAPITAL BREWERY

Opened: April 17, 1986
Brewmaster: Ashley Kinart
Address: 7734 Terrace Ave • Middleton, WI 53562
Phone: 608-836-7100
Website: www.capitalbrewery.com
Annual Production: 28,000 bbls and climbing
Number of Beers: 24+ annually

Staple Beers:
- CAPITAL PILSNER
- DARK VOYAGE (Black IPA)
- GHOST SHIP (White IPA)
- GRATEFUL RED (Red IPA)
- ISLAND WHEAT ALE
- MUNICH DARK
- MUTINY IPA
- SUPPER CLUB (Classic lager)
- U.S. PALE ALE
- WISCONSIN AMBER

Rotating Beers:
- LAKE HOUSE (Helles lager)
- MAIBOCK (Spring)
- OKTOBERFEST (Aug–Oct)
- WINTER SKÅL (Nov–Jan)

Limited: (4-packs)
- AUTUMNAL FIRE
- BLONDE DOPPELBOCK
- DARK DOPPELBOCK
- FISHIN' IN THE DARK

Bombers:
- ETERNAL FLAME (imperial stout)
- JOBU (rum-barrel aged brown ale)
- PUMKINATAUR
- ... and Brewer's choice!

Most Popular Brew: Wisconsin Amber (but Supper Club commands the beer garden).

Tours? Yes. Tuesdays, Fridays, Saturdays and Sundays—check the website for the current schedule. Reservations recommended. $7 includes the tour, 4 samples or 1 pint of their beer, and a pint glass to take home. Private tours available. See also Hop Head Tours!

Samples? Yes, flights are available.

Best Time to Go: The Bier Garten is open from May to October (weather willing) Tue–Thu 4–9PM, Fri 3–10PM, Sat 12–9PM, Sun 12–5PM with live music on Fridays. Check online for shorter winter hours. Bundle up for *Bockfest* in the Bier Garten the last Saturday of February, when the brewery releases their Maibock and Blonde Doppelbock. When the Bier Garten otherwise closes for winter, head inside for the Bier Stube to keep on drinking. Watch also for Stark Beer Fest in March, with 12+ breweries serving strong ales and sours, and Burgers & Brews at the end of May.

Where can you buy it? Here on tap and in growlers to go. Bottles—four-packs, six-packs, and 22-oz bombers—as well as in cans for the staple beers. Lake House and Amber are in 16-oz cans. Their distribution is all over Wisconsin with a growing presence in Minnesota, Iowa, and Illinois.

Got food? No, but food vendors come on Tue, Thu, and Fri evenings in season.

Special Offer: $1 off your first pint of Capital beer when you get your book signed.

Directions: Best way to get here is from the West Beltline (Hwy 12/14 on the west side of Madison metro area). Take Exit 252, go east on Greenway Blvd to a three-way stop and go left (north) on High Point Rd just three blocks to Terrace Ave and the brewery is there on the corner.

The Beer Buzz: Capital is one of the elder statesmen of Wisconsin's breweries and for a long time it was known mostly as a lager specialist. In recent years, they have produced a line-up that expands convincingly into ales as well.

Their Island Wheat marked a return to being more dependent on local suppliers. Most of the wheat comes from Washington Island off the tip of the Door County Peninsula. Keep an eye open for limited releases known as Capital Square Series. These come in four-pack bottles and include Dark Doppelbock, Autumnal Fire, and Fishin' in the Dark.

Ashley is a UW-Madison graduate with a BS in Biology. She previously was an assistant beer manager at The Old Fashioned, the popular Madison restaurant with the finest all-Wisconsin beer list around. She has an International Brewing Diploma from the Siebel Institute of Technology at the Doemens Academy in Munch, Germany, and served as assistant brewer for two years before taking over the lead here. (She is one of three female head brewers in the state—see also Wisconsin Dells Brewing and Thirsty Pagan Brewpub).

The brewhouse holds two 1955 Huppman copper kettles. Be sure to see the trophy case sagging from the wall near the gift shop to appreciate how many awards these brews have won. Check out their website for flavor profiles of their beers. In the summer, the Bier Garten has dozens of picnic tables and a stage for live music. It is quite popular with the after-work crowd, and now has a waterproof tent at the center.

Free WiFi. ATM onsite. Facebook.com/CapBrew, Twitter @capbrew and Instagram @capitalbrewery

Stumbling Distance: Just a short walk away is *The Village Green* (7508 Hubbard Ave, 608-831-9962) a homey restaurant featuring one of Madison area's best Friday fish fries. Try the grilled summer sausage and Capital on tap. Several modern places offer upscale pub food and well-chosen tap lists, such as *The Freehouse Pub* (1902 Parmenter St, 608-831-5000) and *Craftsman Table & Tap* (6712 Frank Lloyd Wright Ave, 608-836-3988). *Mr. Brew's Taphouse* (610 Junction Rd, Madison, 608-824-9600, mrbrewstaphouse.com) has a fine 40 on tap and great happy hour deals. *The Club Tavern* (1915 Branch St, 608-836-3773) has been around over 100 years. Live music, volleyball, great food. The Moose Burger is my fave. Look for crazily cheap beer the first day in the year that the temperature goes over 70. Make a reservation with *Betty Lou Cruises* (bettyloucruises.com, 608-246-3138) to eat Ian's Pizza and drink Capital on Lake Monona. *Sprecher's Restaurant & Pub* (sprecherspub.com, 1262 John Q Hammons Dr, 608-203-6545) is an independent restaurant exclusively serving Sprecher's beer.

Brewery Creek Brewpub

Founded: June 1998
Brewmaster: Jeffrey Donaghue
Address: 23 Commerce Street • Mineral Point, WI 53565
Phone: 608-987-3298
Website: www.brewerycreek.com
Annual Production: 500 bbls
Number of Beers: At least 4 but up to 8 on tap at any one time

Staple Beers:
» Altbier
» Amber Ale
» Cream Ale
» Golden Ale
» Hefeweizen
» Schwarzbier
» ...basically one light, one dark and a couple in between

Rotating Beers:
» Dark Wheat Doppelbock
» London Porter
» Shandy
» Stout

Most Popular Brew: Whatever's lightest

Brewmaster's Fave: The most recent. "Imagine you had gallons of beer in your home. It wouldn't take long for you to look forward to the next one."

Tours? By appointment or by chance if he is not busy.

Samples? Yes.

Best Time to Go: Hours are seasonal so double check. Summer Jun–Oct 23 11:30–8 PM Tue–Thu, until 8:30 Fri–Sat, and til 3 PM on Sun. Closed Mondays. In winter only open Thu–Sat hours, but odds are you will have the place to yourself. This is not a late-night place because that would disturb the B&B guests upstairs. Come for a pleasant afternoon or early evening.

Where can you buy it? Here on tap in 12- and 16-oz pours and in growlers to go.

Got food? Definitely! Very homemade meals (the owners live on site). A veggie burger with a reputation all the way back to Madison. Belgian fries, homemade sauces and desserts, and a Friday fish fry (cod). Burgers are made with hormone-free beef. Don't miss the Brewery burger! Housemade root beer as well.

Special Offer: Not participating.

The Beer Buzz: The first commercial brewery was built here by John Phillips in 1835 on Brewery Creek just behind the modern brewpub. Mineral Point had two more breweries thereafter: Garden City, until Prohibition came, and Terrill's Brewery. The latter was renamed "Tornado Brewery" after it was destroyed by one in 1878. It changed names once again, and ended its brewing days as Mineral Springs Brewery in the 60s. You can still see the old building on Shake Rag Street. Brewmaster Jeffrey has been a homebrewer since 1967, and when he and his wife decided they needed a change, they moved here from Minneapolis and found an 1854 warehouse with no heating, wiring, insulation or even interior walls. It was no small feat to turn this place into the charming restaurant, brewery, and guesthouse we see today. If you plan to stay the night in one of the brewpub's guest rooms (recommended), be sure to call for a reservation, but they don't take dinner reservations.

Stumbling Distance: *Mineral Point* (www.mineralpoint.com) is loaded with art galleries, and *"Gallery Nights,"* when the stores stay open a bit later, might be a good time to come to town. *Hook's Cheese Co.* (320 Commerce St, 608-987-3259, hookscheese.com) is only open weekdays until 2PM but is world famous. Get your bleu cheese, cheddar and curds on your way through. If they are closed try the convenience store across the street—they carry Hook's products. History buffs will enjoy *Pendarvis* (www.wisconsinhistory.org/pendarvis, 608-987-2122) a Cornish miners' colony with guides in costume. Not a history buff? Visit the brewpub for a few pints first. Also, see Biking for Beer in the back of the book. *Bob's Bitchin' BBQ* (167 N Iowa St, Dodgeville, 608-930-2227, bobsbitchinbbq. com) is just down the highway in Dodgeville and has people driving hours for their BBQ. The tap list doesn't disappoint either.

The Grumpy Troll Brew Pub

Founded: 2000
Brewmaster: Mark Knoebl
Address: 105 South Second Street • Mount Horeb, WI 53572
Phone: 608-437-2739
Website: www.thegrumpytroll.com
Annual Production: 600+ bbls
Number of Beers: up to 12 on tap

Staple Beers:
» Captain Fred American Lager (named after Captain Pabst)
» Erik the Red
» Hoppa Loppa IPA
» Maggie Imperial IPA
» Spetsnaz Stout
» Trailside Wheat

Rotating Beers: (30+)
» A & J IIPA
» Amnesia Baltic Porter
» Dragon Ship Wit
» Grumpy Crik Pale Ale
» Keller Brau
» Liberty Pole Pale Ale
» Monk (Belgian golden strong)
» Norski Nut Brown
» Norwegian Wood
» Ol' Eagle's Summer Porter
» Sunflower Farmhouse Ale
» Troll's Gold Lager
» Trollfest
» Wee Curly Scottish Ale

Most Popular Brew: Captain Fred, Hoppa Loppa IPA, and Maggie Imperial IPA

Brewmaster's Fave: Trailside Wheat

Tours? By appointment or check website for dates. See also Hop Head Tours!

Samples: Four-ounce samplers are $1.25 each, or get all 12 on a tray.

Best Time To Go: Open daily at 11AM. Happy hours run from 4–6PM Sun–Wed and Thu–close when pints and 11-oz pours are discounted. Packers games are always a blast.

Where can you buy it? Only here on tap and in growlers to go and several bottled in 22-oz bombers.

Got food? Yes, in the pub, full lunch and dinner menus. Burgers with local beef, cheese curds and bar fare, but also plenty of great soups, sandwiches, salads, dinner entrees and a Friday fish fry. Check out the beer related items: beer-battered fish, Erik the Red Brats, and beer cheese soup! *Their pizzeria (608-437-2741)* on the second floor is a big hit and open Mon–Thu 4–9PM, Fri 4–10PM, Sat 11–10PM, Sun 11–8PM. They also brew their own root beer.

Special Offer: A free 11-oz glass of house beer when you get your book signed.

Directions: Take Business Hwy 18/151 through downtown to 2nd Street. Go south at the stop light and it is at one block down on the left (east) side of 2nd St.

The Beer Buzz: Hard to imagine what makes this troll grumpy with such fine beer on hand. Originally a creamery when it was built in 1916, the building is said to be haunted. The pub name comes from this little town's Scandinavian-inherited obsession with trolls, and you will see plenty of troll-related stuff around town. Brewer Mark has been brewing over 20 years and was already known around town for his great homebrewing (he won Midwest Homebrewer of the Year once) and commercial brewing at various area breweries (New Glarus, City Brewery and Sand Creek). Mark is also a graduate of the Siebel Institute.

Since 2006, the Grumpy Troll has been steadily winning awards for their beers: from prestigious international, national and regional contests including the World Beer Cup, United States Beer Tasting Championship and Beverage Tasters Institute. Check out the walls in the main bar area to see the accolades. In 2008, Rate Beer listed the Grumpy Troll #40 out of 50 best brewpubs in the world.

Each spring they host a local competition among homebrewers and the winner is invited in to brew the winning recipe which will then appear on tap. Upstairs you can enjoy video games, pool, and darts—the English kind with the metal tips, so pace yourself on those beers or wear Kevlar. In season, enjoy some outdoor dining and drinking in the beer garden.

In 2010, the Grumpy Troll made the leap to serving some "green" beer. No, it's not a St Patty's thing. I mean solar panels on the roof generate the electricity for the brewpub. Pick up some Grumpy Troll paraphernalia, including handmade ceramic mugs and Grumpy wear.

Free WiFi. Facebook.com/grumpytrollbrew and Twitter @GrumpyTrollBrew

Stumbling Distance: *Tyrol Basin* (www.tyrolbasin.com, 608-437-4135) is a collection of short runs for skiers and snowboarders just down the road. Just a bit farther west on Highway 151 is *Blue Mound State Park* (4350 Mounds Park Rd., Blue Mounds, 608-437-5711) with a couple of scenic overlook towers, swimming and wading pools, and miles of hiking (or skiing) and mountain biking. Take a one-hour tour of the geological wonder that is *Cave of the Mounds* (2975 Cave of the Mounds Rd, Blue Mounds, 608-437-3038 caveofthemounds.com). Check out Mt. Horeb Summer Frolic in early June or the Art Fair in July. The *Thirsty Troll Brew Fest* is held every September at Grundahl Park. *Fisher King Winery* (102 W Main St, 608-437-6020, fisherkingwinery.com) has a tasting room and some live music.

PHOTO COURTESY THE GRUMPY TROLL

MINHAS CRAFT BREWERY

Founded: 1845/2006
Brewmaster: Jim Beyer
Address: 1208 14th (Brewery) Ave • Monroe, WI 53566
Phone: 608-325-3191
Website: www.minhasbrewery.com
Annual Production: 300,000+ bbls
Number of Beers: 25 plus contract brews

Staple Beers:
- » 1845 PILS
- » AXEHEAD MALT LIQUOR
- » BOXER APPLE ALE
- » BOXER GLUTEN FREE BEER
- » BOXER ICE
- » BOXER LAGER
- » BOXER LIGHT
- » CLEAR CREEK ICE
- » HUBER BOCK
- » HUBER PREMIUM
- » MOUNTAIN CREST
- » SWISS AMBER

Lazy Mutt Beers:
- » LAZY MUTT DOUBLE IPA
- » LAZY MUTT FARMHOUSE ALE
- » LAZY MUTT SO CAL IPA
- » LAZY MUTT TRADITIONAL IPA

Lazy Mutt Seasonals:
- » ALCOHOLIC GINGER BEER
- » CHOCOLATE CHERRY
- » GLUTEN FREE BEER
- » HAZELNUT DARK
- » HEFEWEIZEN
- » OKTOBERFEST
- » PUMPKIN ALE
- » SHANDY
- » WET HOPPED IPA
- » WINTER BOCK
- » …plus several contract brews.

Most Popular Brew: Boxer Lager

Brewmaster's Fave: Huber Bock

Tours? Tours run 45–60 minutes and are offered Mon at 11AM, Tues–Thu at 1PM, Fri 1PM and 3PM, Sat 11AM, 1PM, 3PM, and Sun 1PM and 3PM. Make a reservation for large groups (12 or more). The price is $10 per person for ages 12 and up and includes a gift pack containing 4 bottles of beer, 1 Blumers Soda and a branded sampler glass. Call 1-800-BEER-205 to reserve a tour.

Samples? Yes! (and Blumers sodas too. Blueberry Cream is my favorite!)

Best Time to Go: See tour times.

Where can you buy it? Minhas products are in 16 states as far east as New York, as far west as Nevada, and north into Canada, with the core market being the Midwest.

Special Offer: A free pint glass when you get your book signed.

Directions: If you are coming from the west on Hwy 11 take West 8th Street heading east (right) until 14th Ave then go right (south). From the east take Hwy 59 (6th Street) west to 15th Ave, turn left (south) to 12th St then hop a block right (west) to 14th Ave and take a left (south) to the brewery a block away. Coming in on 81 you will hit 8th Street and follow the rest of the Hwy 11-from-west directions. Hwy 69 will hit 6th St—from there use the from-the-east directions. It's not as bad is it sounds; Monroe is a nice grid and streets are numbered: Streets run east-west, Avenues north-south. If lost, come on, men, the ladies won't mind if you stop for directions for a change.

The Beer Buzz: This is the oldest continuously running brewery in Wisconsin (older even than the state itself!) and the second oldest in the US. As of 2014 it is the tenth largest brewery in the nation based on beer sales volume. One of my first beer memories was a dusty case of Huber Beer empties which sat in our root cellar for much of the 1970s when I was a child. There's a fifty-cent deposit we can never get back! This is that case's birthplace. The brewery switched hands a few times and was known as The Blumer Brewery (now the name of the gourmet sodas produced here) when Bavarian-born Joseph Huber began working here in 1923. The company survived Prohibition with a non-alcoholic beer, Golden Glow, and in the end Huber organized an employee stock buyout which saved the brewery. In 1947, the brewery took his name. In 1960, it started producing Berghoff for a restaurant of the same name in Chicago. Former Pabst executives bought the company from Fred Huber in 1985, and some bad corporate shenanigans led to the near closing of the brewery and the Augsburger label being sold off to Stroh's (Stevens Point Brewery has since picked it up and we can drink it once again). Fred Huber bought the brewery back and with the help of the success of Berghoff beers and some other contract brewing the brewery stayed alive. In 2006, Huber was bought by Canadian entrepreneur Ravinder Minhas and took on its new name. The beer continues to flow and Lazy Mutt, Boxer, and Huber Bock are the flagship brews. Huber Bock still wins awards.

Stumbling Distance: Green County is cheese country. Founded in 1931, *Baumgartner's Cheese Store & Tavern* (1023 16th Ave, 608-325-6157), on the historic central square, is Wisconsin's oldest cheese store and a must-see. They serve local beer with their sandwiches. You are definitely in Wisconsin. This is one of the only places you will ever find a limburger and onion sandwich. Feeling bold and invincible? Just ask for a sample of the stuff. There are those who love it. The local welcome center is also the *National Historic Cheesemaking Museum* (2108 6th Ave, 608-325-4636, nationalhistoriccheesemakingcenter.org), worth seeing and more area info is on hand. Chalet Cheese Cooperative (N4858 Cty Rd N, 608-325-4343) does tours for 4 or more people and sells cheese on site. Tours are personal and free; best between 8 and 11 AM, but not on Sunday or Wednesday. *Turner Hall* (www.turnerhallofmonroe.org, 1217 17th Ave, 608-325-3461) is a 1938 Swiss Emmental-style chalet, and represents the strong Swiss heritage of the town. Pop in for some local and traditional food in a real rathskeller. *Alp and Dell Cheese* (657 Second St, 608-328-3355, alpanddellcheese.com) is a great cheese outlet and corporate home to *Roth Kase USA* (emmirothusa.com).

New Glarus Brewing Co.

Founded: June 1993
Brewmaster: Dan Carey
Address: Hilltop Brewery, 2400 State Hwy 69 • New Glarus, WI 53574
Phone: 608-527-5850
Website: www.newglarusbrewing.com
Annual Production: 190,000 bbls
Number of Beers: 6 on tap at the brewery; 7 year round, 3–5 seasonals, 2–3 Thumbprint beers each year

Staple Beers:
- » Fat Squirrel
- » Moon Man
- » Raspberry Tart
- » Scream IPA
- » Spotted Cow
- » Two Women
- » Wisconsin Belgian Red

Rotating Beers:
- » Back Forty Bock
- » Black Top
- » Cabin Fever Honey Bock
- » Crack'd Wheat
- » Dancing Man Wheat
- » Enigma
- » Oud Bruin
- » Road Slush Oatmeal Stout
- » Serendipity
- » Staghorn Octoberfest
- » Stone Soup
- » Totally Naked

…but this list itself rotates each year! So many beers: Uff-da Bock, Hop Hearty Ale (IPA), Hometown Blonde Pilsner, Norsky (maibock), Solstice (hefeweizen), Coffee Stout, Snowshoe Ale (copper ale), Yokel (unfiltered lager), Copper Kettle (dunkelweiss), Apple Ale, the list can and does go on! Watch for R&D beers and the "Thumbprint" series (see below in The Beer Buzz). Check the website for current beers.

Most Popular Brew: Spotted Cow

Brewmaster's Fave: "I don't have a favorite beer. That's like asking a parent which is his favorite child! Secondly, beer is a food and I never limit myself to one food. I enjoy everything from an American Style Lager (like our Totally Naked) to a sour brown ale (like ours) and everything in between. When I travel, I NEVER drink beer from the big brewers. Fresh, locally brewed beer is the way to go! One must be willing to experiment."

Tours? Yes, a free self-guided audio tour with handheld coded listening devices is available daily from 10–4 at the Hilltop Brewery. The original Riverside facility is closed to the public. However, "hard-hat tours," which include visits to both the Hilltop and Riverside breweries, are still available on Fridays at 1:00 PM for $30 and require reservations. These are led by a brewery ambassador and end with a beer and cheese tasting. They book up long in advance! These tour times may expand, so check the website.

Samples? Three 3-oz samples and a souvenir glass for about $8. Pints are also available with the purchase of a pint glass designed by Deb (look for the little Wisconsin in the bottom). Some specialty beers are on draft here.

Best Time to Go: Open daily from 10–4.

Where can you buy it? On tap here in the Courtyard and Tasting Room. Distributed in 4-pack and 6-pack bottles, 750 ml bottles, and cases *only in Wisconsin*. Packaged sales on site in the Beer Depot, including bottles, cases, and barrels. Spotted Cow is pretty popular on tap throughout the state as well. Single bottles of R&D (Randy and Dan) beers are available on occasion only at the brewery, and watch for special release dates when folks line up here to wait.

Got food? No, but there are packaged Wisconsin cheeses in the gift shop. You can bring in your own food in the outdoor courtyard only.

Special Offer: An undefined highly prized trinket when you get your book signed.

Directions: Head south of New Glarus on Highway 69 and watch for the entry on the left. You will see the brewhouse up on the hill but the road goes east first and then comes up the backside of the hill to give you that going-through-the-country-to-visit-a-farmhouse feel. (Intentional!) The Riverside facility (*not open to the public*) is at the north end of town where Highway 69 meets County Highway W.

The Beer Buzz: There are, of course, brewers with multiple brewery locations, but this one has two in the same little Wisconsin town. Deborah Carey is the first woman to be the original founder of a brewery in the US. She is a native of our dear state of Wisconsin and an entrepreneur extraordinaire. Add her husband Dan, a superb brewmaster, and there really is no way they could have failed. Dan did his apprenticeship in Bavaria, studied at the Seibel Institute in Chicago, and earned the Master Brewer diploma from the Institute of Brewing in London. His beer and

HORSING AROUND

In season, the New Glarus Brewery delivers beer the old fashioned way: by horse and wagon. At 1PM on Fridays, you'll hear hooves clopping on pavement as two beautiful big draft horses trot up with some New Glarus delivery staff riding behind them. They follow a route through town, delivering some fresh cases before heading back to the brewery.

their brewery have awards all over the place. Dan used to install brewery equipment and several of the Wisconsin microbrewers have a story or two about him. His work at Anheuser-Busch pushed him to do his own thing, and we can all be thankful that Deborah made that possible. The original "Riverside" facility is a story itself with its 1962 vintage Huppmann brewery rescued from oblivion in Selb, Germany, purchased for a ridiculously low price, and hauled halfway round the world to find its new home in a Swiss town in a beer state.

In June 2009, the Careys opened their $20 million expanded brewing facility on a hilltop at the south end of town. This is now where the big work goes on but the Riverside brewery still does smaller specialty batches and all of the sour beers, which Dan has been making since the 80s. Herein is a very large coolship, a wide, shallow open tank where hot wort strains down from the copper brew tanks and cools. Steam from this condenses on the natural timber ceiling and drips back in. The wort rests for 3–4 days with open windows which allow the wild yeasts to lend their touch to the sour brews.

Expansion continues at the Hilltop. The Careys value their employees and have made brewery improvements that ease the demands of some of the physical work. After all, the employees own the brewery. The hospitality center underwent more design upgrades in 2012 and a look of historic ruins graces the hilltop in and around the outdoor Courtyard, which features a clocktower with musical bells, a fountain, and old brewhouse

controls turned into a rinse station for your glass. From the courtyard, stone, ruins and picnic tables are scattered about the hill, offering many places to enjoy a beer with a view.

Spotted Cow has become a Wisconsin standard, found at even the least craft-inclined taverns in the middle of nowhere. Check out Dan's "Thumbprint" series of small, very limited (and typically one-off) batches of beers that he is let loose on. Smoked Rye Bock, Sour Brown Ale, Cherry Stout are some of the past creations. Look for the bottles with the red foil tops. These may never repeat, so if you miss one of these adventurous brews, you may be sorry! The R&D (Randy and Dan) beers are only available at the brewery. (Randy Thiel is the Laboratory Manager.)

Stumbling Distance: New Glarus (www.swisstown.com) has a strong Swiss heritage and you can see it in the style of the buildings and the abundance of fondue. For the best Swiss dining, try either *Glarner Stube* (518 1st St, 608-527-2216, glarnerstube.com) or *New Glarus Hotel Restaurant* (www.newglarushotel.com, 100 6ᵗʰ Ave, 800-727-9477) for fondue and much more. *New Glarus Primrose Winery* (226 2nd St, 608-527-5053, daily May–Dec; Thurs–Mon Jan–Apr) offers free tastings. *Puempel's Olde Tavern* (www.puempels.com, 18 6th Ave, 608-527-2045) is an old (1893) classic tavern with folk art murals and the original back bar and ice box. New Glarus beer is on tap! Stop in at *Ruef's Meat Market* (538 1st St, 608-527-2554, ruefsmeatmarket.com) either for some great meats to carry home (wieners, bratwurst, and other sausages) or Landjaeger a sort of Swiss jerky to nibble on immediately. *Edelweiss Cheese Shop* (529 First St, 608-636-2155, edelweisscheeseshop.com) features the award-winning creations of Bruce Workman plus a fine selection of other great cheeses and single bottles of craft beer.

THE HOP GARDEN TAP ROOM

Opened: April 2015
Brewers: Rich Joseph
Address: 6818 Canal Street • Paoli, WI 53508
Hop Yard: N8668 County Road D • Belleville, WI 53508
Phone: 608-516-9649
Web Site: www.thehopgarden.net
Annual Production: 250 barrels
Number of Beers: 6 taps (3 guest taps)

Beers:
  » Farmstead Ale
  » Nuggetopia IPA
  » Sunset Imperial Amber
  » Wisconsin Festiv Ale

Most Popular Brew: Nuggetopia IPA

Samples: Yes, four 5-oz for $6

Brewer's Fave: Nuggetopia IPA, but Festiv Ale in summer.

Best Time to Go: Open Tue–Thu 3–8PM, Fri–Sat noon–8PM, Sun noon–5PM. Closed Mondays. Frequent live music. Double check hours on the website in winter.

Where can you buy it? Here on tap by the pint and pitchers, and in growlers, bombers to go. The bombers are distributed to major groceries and liquor stores in the Madison area and parts of southern Wisconsin.

Got food? A few snacks for sale. Food friendly. Carry in from Paoli Bread & Brat Haus or have Sugar River Pizza delivered.

Tours? Nothing here to tour, but you can visit the hop farm in nearby Belleville.

Special Offer: $1 off your first pint of Hop Garden beer during your signature visit (as well as anyone in your group at the time)!

Directions: Coming into Paoli on WI 69 from the north/west, turn left on Paoli Rd. From County Road PB from Verona, turn right on Paoli Rd. When you come to the center of Paoli at Range Road, go north. Go right at the next street (Canal St) and the road runs 100 feet right into the parking area of the taproom.

The Beer Buzz: Rich has been growing hops since 2009. He started on his father-in-law's property near Oconomowoc, which is now a 2-acre hop garden. He started looking for a farm closer to where they live in Belleville, and found exactly what he was hoping for.

By 2013 he was selling hops to the Wisconsin Hops Exchange and working with a lot of brewers statewide. He was looking for other business opportunities, and a few brewers suggested he jump from his homebrew habit to commercial brewing. He developed some recipes and took them to Page Buchanan at House of Brews in Madison and worked out a contract brewing arrangement. In January 2015, bombers of Hop Garden brews became available.

Rich wanted to open a taproom at the farm, but zoning restrictions prevented it. Paoli was nearby and it gets a lot of traffic for the art scene and its place in a popular rural bicyclist area. In the center of town is an old mill from the early 1800s which has been remodeled, and at the time the back space was open. So he signed a lease and created the little taproom with an upstairs room for events as well. The doors open up to some seating right outside. His Beer Garden is the entire adjacent green space and as long as there isn't a wedding in progress, you can go all the way to the banks of the Sugar River where it cuts through Paoli. Part of a canal still remains, where the mill used to draw water from the river, send it through

the turbine, and dump it back to the river. A big turbine remains in the basement but isn't viewable to the public at this time. Rich aims to create a farm to glass experience, and this is a family operation, with everyone lending a hand at the hop farm or the taproom.

Free WiFi. Mug Club. Facebook/thehopgardenwi and Twitter @wihops

Pronunciation guide: Paoli = Pay-OH-lie

Visiting the hop farm: You can drive by the hop farm 10 miles south of the taproom (N8668 County Rd D, Belleville, 608-516-9649) just to have a look. Tours and open house dates are scheduled in August, so watch the website for specific dates. Harvest is the first part of September (done by machine), but there are also pick your own hops events.

Stumbling Distance: *Paoli Bread & Brat Haus* (608-845-8087, paoli-breadandbrathaus.com) occupies the front of the building and serves soups, sandwiches (brisket, pulled pork, tilapia, brat, etc.), bakery and desserts even here in the taproom until about 4–5PM. *Sugar River Pizza* (1019 River St # 5, Belleville, 608-424-6777, sugarriverpizza.com) delivers. *Paoli Cheese* (6890 Paoli Rd, Paoli, 608-845-7031, paolicheese.com) right in front of the old mill building on the main street has quite an assortment to take home or to the taproom.

Potosi Brewing Company

Founded: First in 1852, again in 2008
Brewmaster: Steve McCoy
Address: 209 South Main St • Potosi, WI 53820
Phone: 608-763-4002
Website: www.potosibrewery.com
Annual Production: 8,000 bbls
Number of Beers: 13 on tap, 20–25 per year

Staple Beers:
- » Good Old Potosi Beer
- » Potosi Czech-Style Pilsner
- » Potosi Cave Ale
- » Snake Hollow IPA
- » (also Potosi Root Beer)

Rotating Beers:
- » Fiddler Oatmeal Stout
- » Gandy Dancer Porter
- » Helles Bock
- » Holiday Beer
- » Hopsmith Imperial IPA
- » Ice Breaker (barrel-aged Baltic Porter)
- » Miner's Dopplebock
- » Oktoberfest
- » Potosi Barrel-Aged Belgian Quad (22-oz bombers only)
- » Potosi Light
- » Potosi Slugger (barrel-aged Oatmeal Stout)
- » Rye Saison
- » Stingy-ER Jack (barrel-aged Pumpkin Ale)
- » Stingy Jack Pumpkin Ale
- » Scotch Ale
- » St. Thomas Belgian Abbey
- » Steamboat Shandy
- » Tangerine IPA (also in 16-oz cans)
- » Wee Stein Wit (Belgian)
- » White IPA
- » Various limited editions, barrel-aged beers and sours on the way

Brewmaster's Fave: Snake Hollow IPA

Tours? Yes, call or check website for current brewery tour schedule. Remember the ABA National Brewery Museum™ is here too: open 10:30AM–9PM with a $5 entry fee for self-guided tours ($3 for seniors, free for kids).

Samples? Yes, a flight of six 5-oz beers is about $8.

Best Time to Go: The restaurant is open daily (in season) from 11AM–9PM, museums from 10:30AM–4PM 10:30AM–5PM Fri Sat. Double check hours in the off season; some days they may be closed. Look for live music on Saturdays in the beer garden. Fall colors around here are awesome, especially on the Great River Road.

Where can you buy it? Here on tap and in growlers and bottles to go, and it is distributed statewide and in parts of IL and IA with eyes on MN.

Got food? Yes, great brewpub fare such as burgers, cheese curds, steaks, chicken, ribs. Check out the beer cheese soup with Cave Ale, smoked Wisconsin Gouda, and roasted red peppers, the Cave Ale-boiled bratwurst, and the Friday fish fry.

Special Offer: A free pint of their beer when you get your book signed.

Directions: Come into Potosi on Hwy 133 from the west or east. Coming from the east the brewery is on the right side of the road to the west side of Potosi across from the giant cone-top beer can. Hard to miss. If coming from Platteville consider taking County Rd O which is more direct but curvy and scenic.

The Beer Buzz: Potosi is home to the world's largest cone-top beer can. The town also has the longest Main Street in the world and it goes right past the old 1852 brewery building which is home to the ABA National Brewery Museum. But what's a brewery museum without beer? Steve Zuidema of the former Front Street Brewery in Davenport, Iowa, started the brewing again at Potosi, then Steve Buszka (formerly Bell's, O'so) took over. Finally, Steve McCoy took the reins in 2013. (Third Steve is a charm?) Steve McCoy has long been a craft beer fan and homebrewer. He studied biology at UW- La Crosse and went into food and beverage work after graduation. He spent time as lab tech in dairy, then worked at City Brewery in the lab for a year and in production brewing for 5 years before landing here.

In the beginning, Potosi brought back versions of the traditional Potosi brews—Good Old Potosi, for one—but now the lineup includes a wide assortment of ales and some lagers. Potosi Brewery also makes its own root beer with Wisconsin honey, so if beer is not your thing, there's something else to sample on a brewery tour.

In making beer, the quality is, of course, in the ingredients, and the first matter is the water. Many of the breweries of old were built around or on top of artesian wells and natural springs. Potosi is no exception. The water still rushes out of the ground into the old brewery pond behind the beer

garden. The flow is so overwhelming that years ago it would get into the brewhouse and collect in puddles on the floor. Remodeling included an overflow pipe which diverts some of the spring water, and you can see it rushing beneath a piece of plate glass in the brewpub floor. Potosians Gary David, his son Tyler, and his father Marvin—three generations of woodworkers—created the beautiful handcrafted bar. The tables around the room are made with the cypress of the old fermentation tanks. As the brewery ad once asked, "Have you had your Good Old Potosi today?"

When the brewery started distributing, they needed to brew larger batches at Stevens Point Brewery under an alternating proprietorship agreement, but in fall of 2013 they began repurposing an industrial building next to the brewery. In April 2015 they opened a 24,000 sq ft production brewery, with a 40-barrel brewhouse, 120-bbl fermenters, and bottling and canning lines, plus a large barrel-aging cooler. They are still using the old system at the brewpub where they make many specialty beers (Helles Bock, Schwarzbier, White IPA, Rye Saison, etc.) typically only available over the bar. They've also started a Belgian sour program using the old lagering caves you see when you walk in the front doors of the old brewery.

The Potosi Foundation, run by a board of elected volunteers, is the sole owner of the brewery, and is actually a 501(c)(3), making this the nation's first not-for-profit brewery. All profits go to charity.

Free Wifi. Facebook.com/PotosiBrewery.

Stumbling Distance: Hardly much of a stumble, but right inside the same structure is the *National Brewery Museum* and the *Great River Road Interpretive Center*. For a roadside attraction, check out the *Dickeyville Grotto* (www.dickeyvillegrotto.com, 305 W Main St, Dickeyville, 608-568-3119) a collection of shrines both religious and patriotic built by a priest in the 1920s using stone, mortar and all sorts of eye catching little objects. Watch Potosi for the annual Catfish Festival in August, the Potosi Brewfest the 4th Saturday of August, and the Potosi Bicycle Tour in September. *Whispering Bluff Winery* (196 S Main St, 608-763-2468, facebook.com/whisperingbluffswinery) is right across the street. Staying the night? *Potosi Inn* (102 N Main St, 608-763-2269, potosiinn.com) and *Pine Point Lodge* (219 S Main St, 608-763-2767, pinepointlodgepotosi. com) will do nicely.

Head up the Great River Road to La Crosse for more beer. It's a two-hour drive but worth taking your time for the scenery.

THE GREAT RIVER ROAD

A National Scenic Byway, it runs parallel along the Mississippi River offering a pretty incredible slice of American life and natural views to wear out your camera. Wisconsin's portion stretches 250 miles and passes through 33 towns. It also comes with a free downloadable audio tour (wigrr.com). Much of the land along the route is protected natural areas and the bluffs are beautiful from above and below. Birdwatchers love this area as it is a flyway for migratory species and eagle sightings are basically a given. Local produce, cheese, family restaurants and taverns, B&Bs, wineries and more lie along this route. Boat tours, camping and paddling opportunities (see my book *Paddling Wisconsin*) are also abundant. Check the Wisconsin Great River Road website (wigrr.com, 800-658-9424) for maps, podcasts and more to plan your journey, and visit the Great River Road Interpretive Center at the Potosi Brewery/National Brewery Museum.

THE NATIONAL BREWERY MUSEUM™

Like any good Wisconsin boy, I collected beer cans when I was young. It was a veritable rite of passage to acquire all the Schmidt cans with their varying pictures, and a must for any collection was the Pabst Blue Ribbon beer can with the dawn-of-the-pull-tab message, "No Opener Needed." You were a hero in my neighborhood if you found one of the old bottle-can hybrids first introduced to the market by Milwaukee's Jos. Schlitz Brewing known as a cone-top. Potosi Wisconsin offers the opportunity to see the World's Largest Cone-top, in fact, but more importantly Potosi is also home to the National Brewery Museum.

The Potosi Brewery opened in 1852 and made a long run until 1972. The brewery that once produced Good Old Potosi lay in ruins and by the 1990s trees were growing through the roof, but locals had a plan to revive some of the town's heritage. What if they restored the old brewery and started brewing again. Better yet, what if that restored building was a tourist attraction?

Just so happens that the American Breweriana Association wanted a museum location to display the amazing collections of their members. Breweriana—collectible beer memorabilia and not a bad name for your first-born daughter I might add—ranges from cans and tap handles to beer signs and rare lithographs. Where would such a brewing tribute make its home? Milwaukee? Nope. St. Louis? No way. How about Potosi, Wisconsin, population 711?

How did that happen? Well, Potosi threw their bid in and the ABA made the rounds in 2004 to hear the proposals and see the sites. Remember the forest through the roof of the old brewery? It seemed as if their chances were slim indeed, but after the ABA members sneaked a peek at the building, the next day they said Yes. The reason for that was the brand-spanking new firehouse. They believed that if little Potosi could provide such a facility for their volunteer fire department and rescue squad, they could redo the brewery.

What's to see here? A vintage Pabst lithograph print worth $15,000. Rare character steins from the 1920s and 30s—even some of Mickey Mouse and Donald Duck—tap handles, serving trays, clocks, calendars, posters and even oil paintings fill the rooms. Watch vintage beer commercials and documentaries about the brewing process on a few video monitors. Another room holds a research library with information on nearly all of the American breweries that ever existed. On the ground floor is a transportation museum and an interactive interpretive center for Wisconsin's segment of the Great River Road Scenic Byway (a really lovely roadtrip all by itself with local beer both here and up in La Crosse). An old lagering cave is viewable behind a glass wall, and a gift shop offers all sorts of Wisconsin paraphernalia and a selection of locally produced cheeses, wines, syrup, honey, and beer.

I highly recommend a visit, and when you are done, have a meal and a Potosi beer in the brewpub!

Entry to the Great River Road Interpretive Center and Transportation Museum is free. The brewery museum charges $5 (free for 17 and under, $3 for 60+). (www.potosibrewery.com, 608-763-4002, 209 S. Main St., Potosi)

Directions: Potosi is located on the edge of the Mississippi River in the southwestern corner of Wisconsin on the Great River Road Scenic Byway (www.wigreatriverroad.org). Come into Potosi on Hwy 133 from the west or east. Coming from the east the museum is on the right side of the road to the west side of Potosi across from the giant cone-top beer can.

Double your fun and visit Potosi during its annual catfish festival, the second full weekend in August, when more than 2,300 pounds of fish are fried.

Corner Pub

Founded: 1996
Brewmaster: Pete Peterson
Address: 100 Main Street • Reedsburg, WI 53959
Phone: 608-524-8989
Email: cornerpb@mwt.net
Annual Production: up to 100 bbls
Number of Beers: 7 or 8 on tap at a time

Staple Beers:
- » APA
- » Bourbon Scotch Ale
- » Cream Ale
- » Milk Stout
- » Porter
- » Red Dot India Pale Ale
- » Smoked Porter

Rotating Beers:
- » Bock (winter)
- » Brown Ale
- » Dill Pickle (an APA with dill and garlic)
- » Dry Stout
- » IPL
- » Mint APA
- » Oktoberfest (fall)
- » Old Gold Lager
- » Saison
- » Weiss (summer)

Most Popular Brew: Porter or Red Dot IPA

Brewmaster's Fave: Red Dot IPA

Tours? By chance.

Samples? Nope.

Best Time to Go: Open daily 10AM–11PM (Sun 11–11). Piano music on Friday nights during dinner, and piano luncheon on Tuesdays. Butter Festival in June recognizes Reedsburg as one of the world's largest producers. Come for Fermentation Fest in October.

Where can you buy it? Right here, or fill up a growler to go.

Got food? Good hearty pub fare. Blackened burgers are not something you see often, and all burgers are fresh hand patties. Deep-fried local curds are in the house! Fish fry every Wednesday and Friday.

Special Offer: Not participating.

Directions: Hwys 33 and 23 run right through town as Main St. Corner Pub is on the corner (oddly enough) at the first block of E Main St.

The Beer Buzz: This little two-barrel brewhouse is what micro-brewing is all about—local beer, handcrafted, nothing glitzy or overdone. A small-town humility and a product worth some pride. Pete started homebrewing with a buddy of his in 1995 and moved it into his EndeHouse Brewery and Restaurant in 1996. In 2002, Pete brought his brewing into the

FERMENTATION FEST

Art, food, ideas and the people who love them gather at Fermentation Fest. It's not just beer, but all things fermented—pickles, wine, sauerkraut, sourdough, cheese, soy sauce—are celebrated and discussed here. Put on by the *Wormfarm Institute* (wormfarminstitute.org) and scheduled across two weekends in October, the fest offers classes, seminars, tastings, products for sale, and entertainment. Additionally, art is on the scene: the DTour is a 50-mile self-guided route (drivable or bikable) "through scenic working lands" to see temporary art installations, Roadside Culture Stands, Pasture Performances, and more. fermentationfest.com current location. He enjoys the modest production, and this is as unpretentious a place as you'll find. Local pastries and muffins are for sale by the door. Sports banners hang from the ceiling, and four TVs pipe in the important games. Live music is hosted occasionally on a small stage. The popcorn at the bar is free and comes with the caveat: "Can't always guarantee freshness." Food's good, people are friendly, and the beer is quite fine as well. In 2008 some regional flooding swamped the brewhouse, and for a while the equipment was out on the sidewalk and beer was on hold. They got through it. Check out the mural on the side of the building dedicated to the history of hops growing in the area. If you like a little smokiness to your beer, do NOT miss Pete's Smoked Porter—one of my personal favorites.

Stumbling Distance: Just a couple blocks away is the start of the state's "400" bike trail which connects up to the *Elroy-Sparta Trail*. Check out the Beer, Boats and Bikes section for a pedaling-for-beer idea. Reedsburg is famous for its antiques shops, and there are several in town. *Wisconsin Dells* is not far down the road and *Devil's Lake State Park* is definitely not to be missed with its rocky outcroppings from where the glacier stopped in the last Ice Age. Fall colors are notable there. Over 60 varieties of cheese—including fresh curds—are waiting to be eaten twelve minutes northwest of Reedsburg at *Carr Valley Cheese Co.* in nearby LaValle (www. carrvalleycheese.com, S3797 Cty Hwy G, LaValle, 608-986-2781). Over 100 awards have been taken worldwide by this little cheesemaker.

Driftless Brewing Co.

Founded: 2013
Head Brewer: Chris Balistreri
Address: 102 Sunbeam Blvd. W • Soldiers Grove, WI 54655
Phone: 608-624-5577
Web Site: www.driftlessbrewing.com
Annual Production: 120 barrels
Number of Beers: 10–12 on tap (with guests)

Staple Beers:
  » Solar Town (Stout)
  » Dirt (Brown Ale)
  » The Local Buzz (Golden Honey Ale)
  » Kick-Axe (Pale Ale)
  » Rolling Ground (IPA)

Rotating Beers:
  » BMW² (Double Pale Ale)
  » Mt. Sterling (Cascadian Ale)
  » Metamorphosis Seasonal Series
  » Various Belgian style ales

Most Popular Brew: Depends on the venue; each has a niche.

Brewmaster's Fave: Changes all the time, but IPAs, if pushed.

Tours? By appointment only.

Samples: Yes, flights in the taproom.

Best Time to Go: Best to check the Facebook page or call for hours.

Where can you buy it? Here on tap and in 22-oz bombers and growlers to go, and distributed here in the Driftless Area nearby.

Got food? Yes, but there's no kitchen, so it will be limited offerings such as cheese and meat plates, Amish pretzels. It's food friendly, so you can order locally off menus onsite or bring your own.

Special Offer: Buy your first beer in the taproom and get one free beer of equal value when you get your book signed.

Directions: US 61 runs north-south through town. At the southern end of town look for Driftless Brewing Company on the west side of the Highway. Turn in here and park. The brewery has the tall white-paneled peaked passive solar roof.

The Beer Buzz: This project had been kicking around in Chris' mind since the late 80s. He'd go to keg parties, pay the cover, and still bring his own beer (Augsburger or some imports). He followed the craft beer movement closely in its early years and fired up his first brew kettle in 1988. In 2011 Chris took the Master Brewers Association of America's brewing course at UW-Madison.

Chris and co-founder Michael Varnes-Epstein started brewing in a dairy barn in Excelsior, Wisconsin, in the middle of the middle of nowhere. Being deeply connected to the land and the area, they took on the name given to this corner of the state, the Driftless Area. They were licensed and ready to go in January 2013, brewing a 20-gallon batch and hand-bottling it to be sold at the Viroqua Co-op. They delivered 10 cases on a Friday and by Monday they got a call: We need more! Six months later they needed to expand and relocated to Soldiers Grove, where they were joined by Cynthia Olmstead and Scott Noe to help with all aspects of the expansion and running the brewery.

Soldier Grove itself had relocated back in 1981 when it was washed away from its original site by a flooding Kickapoo River. The new town became the first "solar village" with buildings all over town built with passive solar. The brewery is the former grocery store, which had been empty for eight years, and you can see the oddly towering peaked roof made to absorb heat even in winter. They bought it in March 2014, and sold their first deliveries on the fourth of July that year.

Initially they brewed using well water from Michael's farm, hauled here in 55-gallon barrels on brew days. They use Wisconsin hops in all brews. In late 2015 they are expanding to a 15-barrel brewhouse and adding a taproom with a long bar with a view of the open brewery behind it, plus some tables and chairs, and a dartboard. Outdoor seating is at a few picnic tables.

Free WiFi. Mug club. Facebook/DriftlessBrewingCompany

Stumbling Distance: *The Old Oak Inn Bed & Breakfast* (500 Church St, 608-624-5217, theoldoakinn.net) is an impressive Victorian home, a perfect place to stay during your visit to the area. It also has a great Friday fish fry and other specially scheduled public dining. See *Roadtripping the Driftless Area*.

One hour to La Crosse from here for *Pearl Street Brewery* and *Turtle Stack Brewery*.

ROADTRIPPING THE DRIFTLESS AREA

The Driftless Area is that southwestern corner of Wisconsin that shows deep river valleys and no glacial debris or "drift" thanks to having been spared the grinding of the glaciers in the last glacial period of the Ice Age (125,000–12,000 years ago). Consequently, there are no lakes but lots of hills and winding roads, making it generally a very scenic place to do a road trip. Fall colors are a given but also watch for various festivals. Here's just a short list of events and local products you should check out if you've come all the way to **Driftless Brewing** in Soldiers Grove:

Gays Mills Folk Festival (gaysmillsfolkfest.org) is Mothers' Day weekend in May.

Soldier Grove Dairy Days (soldiersgrove.com) is a June festival.

Driftless Area Art Festival (driftlessareaartfestival.com) is in Soldiers Grove the third weekend in September, gathering a vast area of regional artists.

Gays Mills Apple Festival (gaysmills.org) is the last full weekend in September.

The Kickapoo River runs through the area on its famously serpentine course to the Wisconsin River, and offers some great paddling, typically farther upriver between Ontario (40 min from Soldiers Grove) and La Farge (25 min) through the *Kickapoo Valley Reserve*. (See my book *Paddling Wisconsin*)

The Driftless Angler (106 S Main St, Viroqua, 608-637-8779, driftlessangler.com) supplies and guides fly-fishers and has lodging options.

Mt. Sterling Co-op Creamery (505 Diagonal St, Mt Sterling, 608-734-3151, buymtsterlinggoatcheese.com, Mon–Fri 8AM–4PM) is the local goat cheese producer and gets raves (and awards).

Westby Cooperative Creamery (401 South Main Street, Westby, 800-492-9282, westbycreamery.com)

Organic Valley (507 West Main Street, La Farge, 608-625-2602, organicvalley.coop) produces some very fine dairy products and more, and operates a retail store Mon–Sat in La Farge.

Wisco Pop (wiscopopsoda.com) is the local soda pop made in Viroqua and distributed in the area and as far as Madison.

Kickapoo Coffee (608-637-2022, kickapoocoffee.com) is a Viroqua coffee roaster whose beans are available wholesale and served at select coffee shops.

For an abundance of information about Wisconsin's Driftless Area, go to driftlesswisconsin.com

Viking Brew Pub

Founded: 2014

Brewmaster: David Worth

Address: 211 East Main Street • Stoughton, WI

Phone: 608-719-5041

Web Site: www.vikingbrewpub.com

Annual Production: 200+ barrels

Number of Beers: 12 taps (6–7 of their own beers)

Staple Beers:
- » Midnite Sun Cream Ale
- » Nordic Blonde
- » Soot in My Eye (Black IPA)

Rotating Beers: (examples)
- » Viking Blodappelsin Saison
- » Viking Kaos (Belgian strong ale)

Most Popular Brew: Nordic Blonde.

Samples: Yes, 4-oz pours for about $1.50 or 4 for $5

Best Time to Go: Open Mon, Wed–Fri 4–11pm, Sat 11am–12am, Sun 12pm–8pm. Closed Tuesdays.

Where can you buy it? On tap here and in growlers to go.

Got food? Yes, pub fare with appetizers, burger baskets, soups and salads, and a Friday fish fry (cod, perch, salmon, shrimp). Norwegian meatballs on Sat, and daily specials.

Tours? Yes, on request. Hop Head Tours from Madison comes here from time to time.

Special Offer: $1 off your first Viking beer during your signature visit.

Directions: US 51 passes right through downtown as Main St. 3 blocks east of the bridge over the river and on the south side of the street at the corner of Forrest St.

The Beer Buzz: If you were looking for a smoke-breathing Viking dragon ship—and who isn't?—this is the place to go. It's pretty much the first thing you see when you walk in: a magnificent oak bow with a dragon's head nearly up to the ceiling, blowing smoke on demand. Owners Vik ("Vike" not "Vick") and Lori Malling opened this brewpub in 2014 in the remodeled 19th-century Stoughton State Bank building and started as a beer bar with some contract brewing at Madison's House of Brews. By summer of 2015, they brought the brewing in-house. The 3.5-barrel brewhouse is visible from the bar, and they keep a pilot system in the basement to play with. Vik used to fly tanker aircraft for the Air Force, from Vietnam through the Gulf War and Kosovo, a career spanning 34 years. Vik developed the staple beer recipes but handed off brewing responsibilities to Brewer David who has been homebrewing since forever and has a satchel of awards for his efforts.

Vik and his father-in-law Duane Brickson used to go on regular pilsgrimage outings to nearby breweries. Duane off-handedly remarked that some day Stoughton would have one and they wouldn't have to drive so far. Inspired by the simple model of Madison's One Barrel Brewing, Duane, a talented master carpenter, sat down and drew up some plans for what they might build for various possible locations in Stoughton. What you see before you was hand built (and the dragon head was hand carved) by his son Mitchell, partly using century-old wood reclaimed from an old silo at Stevens Point Brewery. Smoke blows when the Packers or Badgers score. Metal worker Aaron Howard designed the Viking logo—or rather his 1993 sophomore year metal shop project was adopted by Vik and Lori. Aaron, now with a blacksmith shop in Madison, was happy to contribute it.

The bar area shows a lot of natural logs and wood, and along with the two-sided bar, offers booths and tables. Five TVs pipe in sports and the "upper" room (a couple steps up next door) even has a few couches ideal for a group during a big game.

Free WiFi. ATM onsite. Mug Club. Find them on Facebook.

Stumbling Distance: The gloriously remodeled *Stoughton Opera House* (381 E. Main St, 608-877-4400, stoughtonoperahouse.com) brings in some top-talent performers throughout the year. *Big Sky Restaurant* (176 E Main St, 608-205-6278) across the street has some high-class, outstanding gourmet food people come from out of town for. *Fahrenheit 364* (364 East Main St, 608-205-2763) is known for their cocktails. In summer, watch for *Gazebo Musikk* on Thursday nights, free concerts in Stoughton Rotary Park (401 E Main St, facebook.com/gazebomusikk).

Gray's Tied House

Founded: October 2006
Brewmaster: Fred Gray
Address: 950 Kimball Lane • Verona, WI 53593
Phone: 608-845-2337
Website: www.graystiedhouse.com
Number of Beers: 12

Staple Beers:
- » Bully Porter
- » Busted Knuckle Irish Ale
- » Gray's Light
- » Honey Ale
- » Oatmeal Stout
- » Rathskeller Amber
- » Rock Hard Red, a 'malternative'
- » Wisco Wit
- » …plus seasonals

Rotating Beers:
- » Coffee Stout
- » Maibock
- » Pale Ale
- » …and more

Most Popular Brew: Honey Ale or Rathskeller Amber

Brewmaster's Fave: Oatmeal Stout

Tours? Yes, on request and by appointment.

Samples? Yes, 8 sample pours for $15.

Best Time to Go: After work or Sat/Sun during big games. Open daily 11 to close with happy hour from 3–6 Mon–Thu. They offer a shuttle to UW Badger football games.

Where can you buy it? On tap or in growlers to go, plus bottles and cans of beers and sodas here and in distribution from their Janesville brewery.

Got food? Yes, a full menu with apps (brewschetta, deep-fried curds or pickles, etc.), soups/salads, burgers/sandwiches, pasta/steaks/entrees, and brick-oven pizzas. Plates ranging from $8–19.

Special Offer: A free pint when you get your book signed!

Directions: The brewpub/eatery is located just off of Hwy 151 at Verona. From Exit 79 take Old PB toward town and turn left onto Whalen Rd. It's behind the BP gas station.

The Beer Buzz: The Gray family has a long history of brewing, but it has only been recently that they have returned to beer after using soda to survive Prohibition. This restaurant and microbrewery was a new venture and has been very successful. The name is from a term used back when breweries had taverns that were obliged to sell only that brewery's beer. The 450-seat restaurant has a menu featuring a little bit of something from various regions of the U.S. including New England and New Orleans, and serves it up in a wood building with a Western touch to it. Right as you walk in you are met by a collection of breweriana from Gray's history. Two outdoor patios make up the beer garden which has portable heaters and a bonfire pit to extend the Wisconsin dine-outside season a bit. Expect acoustic guitar music inside and a fireplace lounge. Friday fish fry includes cod, walleye, and bluegill (beer battered and baked). The menu serves everyone from vegans to serious carnivores and includes beer cheese soup, a Reuben with amber ale sauce, hand-battered local cheese curds, and wood-fired oven pizzas. A private bar upstairs makes the Tied House a good place for parties, and the thirteen large-screen TVs bring in crowds on game days.

While the staple beers are shipped up here from the Janesville brewery, the specialty beers are brewed onsite. Free WiFi. Facebook.com/graystiedhouse

Stumbling Distance: Choco-holics won't want to skip *Candinas Chocolatier* (www.candinas.com, 2435 Old PB, Verona, 800-845-1554, Mon–Sat 10–5) where Swiss-trained Markus Candinas makes divine assortments that have been nationally recognized. *Edelweiss Cheese Shop* (edelweisscheeseshop.com, 202 W Verona Ave, 608-845-9005, open daily) sells the master work of the master cheesemaker from Monroe, Bruce Workman, plus other cheese, local beers, and wines. Just farther up the road toward Madison is *Bavaria Sausage Inc.* (www.bavariasausage. com, 6317 Nesbitt Rd, Fitchburg 53719, 608-271-1295, Mon–Fri 8–5, Sat 8–1) which makes a whole variety of outstanding sausages and sells over 100 different cheeses, including fresh cheese curds. From Hwy 151 just south of Madison turn west on Cty Hwy PD and a quick left onto Nesbitt Road heading south. See Gray's Tied House in the Biking for Beer section at the back of the book as well.

Hop Haus Brewing Co.

Opened: June 24, 2015
Brewmaster: Phil Hoechst
Address: 231 South Main St. • Verona, WI 53593
Phone: 608-497-3165
Web Site: www.hophausbrewing.com
Annual Production: 250 barrels
Number of Beers: up to 12 on tap

Beers:
- » Belgian Dubbel
- » Belgian IPA
- » Deuce Deuce Porter
- » Imperial Red IPA
- » IPA
- » Kölsch
- » Pale Ale
- » Scotch Ale
- » Wildcat Amber Ale

Most Popular Brew: Too soon to tell.

Brewmaster's Fave: IPAs

Tours? Yes, check the website for the future schedule or call for an appointment.

Samples: Yes, five 5-oz pours for about $9.

Best Time to Go: Open Mon–Thu 4–10PM, Fri 3–10PM, Sat 12–10PM, Sun 12–5PM. Double check on the website, especially during football season.

Where can you buy it? Only here on tap and in growlers and "baby" growlers to go.

Got food? Yes, some snacks plus local favorites: Fraboni's pizzas, Curt's Gourmet Popcorn, Batch Bakehouse soft pretzels, and Landjager from Bavaria Sausage Haus. See the website for a schedule for food carts. Also, food friendly.

Special Offer: $1 off your first pint of house beer during your signature visit.

Directions: US 18/151 runs south of Verona. Whether you take Exit 81 from the east nearer Madison or Exit 76 coming from the west, it will put you on Verona Ave which passes right through town. Take it to Main St/ County Road M and turn south.

The Beer Buzz: Owners Phil and Sara Hoechst opened this little brewery in downtown Verona. Looking for German beer? Well, Phil was *born* in Germany. Granted, he grew up here in Verona. He came to Wisconsin as a child when his father took a job at University of Wisconsin. Both Phil and Sara graduated from UW, but moved to Denver where Phil took up homebrewing. They had their first son and moved back to Verona to raise a family. They decided to open a brewery and developed a 5-year plan in 2012, which turned out to be a 2.5-year plan. When they started looking for a space, this former Cousin's Subs/Chocolate Shoppe ice cream parlor opened up and suddenly everything just fell into place.

Phil runs a 3-barrel system you can see through the windows of the taproom and his brewing gravitates toward IPAs and Belgians. Along with the staple beers, expect frequent one-offs. Large storefront windows let in a lot of light, and the bar and one wall incorporate reclaimed barn wood. A mix of regular and tall tables spread throughout the room and there are three TVs, some board games, and occasional live music. The amber ale is named for Verona's high school team mascot. Parking is off-street. Watch for a possible shuttle bus planned for Badger games in Madison.

Free WiFi. Facebook/Hop-Haus-Brewing-Company and
Twitter @Hophausbrewing

Stumbling Distance: *Tuvalu Coffeehouse & Gallery* (300 S Main St #101, 608-845-6800, tuvalucoffeehouse.com) also offers live music in the evenings. *AJ's Pizzeria* (300 S Main St, 608-497-1303, ajsverona.com) delivers to the taproom. Back toward Madison is *Quivey's Grove* (6261 Nesbitt Rd, Madison, 608-273-4900, quiveysgrove.com) for fine dining in a former mansion and *Bavaria Sausage* (6317 Nesbitt Rd, Fitchburg, 608-845-6691, bavariansausage.com) offers great German-style products, and not just sausages either. The brewery is right off the *Military Ridge State Trail* if you are a cyclist (trail pass required). See the Biking For Beer section of the book.

WISCONSIN BREWING CO.

Founded: November 1, 2013
Brewmaster: Kirby Nelson
Address: 1079 American Way • Verona, WI
Phone: 608-848-1079
Website: www.wisconsinbrewingcompany.com
Annual Production: 12,000 bbls
Number of Beers: 12 on tap here; 6 year round and several more limited/seasonal releases in distribution

Staple Beers:
> » 001 GOLDEN AMBER LAGER
> » 002 YANKEE BUZZARD AMERICAN IPA
> » 003 CHOCOLATE LAB PORTER
> » 008 OL' RELIABLE MUNICH-STYLE LAGER
> » 013 PSYCHOPATH INTENSE PALE ALE
> » 015 INAUGURAL RED LAGER

Rotating Beers:
IN AND OUT SERIES:
> » 004 SESSION IPA
> » 005 BIG SWEET LIFE MAIBOCK
> » 007 BETRAY ALE INDIA PALE PALE BOCK
> » 006 PORTER JOE COFFEE-INFUSED PORTER
> » 009 BLEEDING HEART DEEP AMBER SAISON
> » 011 ZENITH SAISON
> » 014 WISKATOR DOPPELBOCK
> » 016 BLISTER IN THE SUN (wit + IPA + lager)
> » … also expect some barrel-aging

Most Popular Brew: Inaugural Red

Brewmaster's Fave: Zenith

Tours? Yes, free tours. Check the online calendar and sign up or just walk-in and ask a bartender. See also Hop Head Tours!

Samples? Yes, flights of 5-oz pours: 4 for $6 or The Dog Bone: 12 for $16.

Best Time to Go: Taproom open Tue–Thu 3–9PM, Fri 1–11PM, Sat 11AM–11PM, Sun 11AM–9PM. Closed Mondays. Any time that backyard patio is open. Watch for live music events.

Where can you buy it? Here on tap and in growlers, 6-packs, or cases to go. Distributed throughout Wisconsin and Chicagoland.

Got food? Only some gourmet snacks for purchase, but it is food friendly and local menus are on hand. Food trucks often show up on Fridays in season.

Special Offer: A free pint of their beer when you get your book signed.

Directions: From US-151 take exit 79 and go south on County Highway PB. American Way is the second left (east) and the brewery is on your left here in Verona Technology Park.

The Beer Buzz: Wisconsin Brewing Company (WBC) may be a relatively new brewery, but founders Carl Nolen, Mark Nolen, and brewmaster Kirby Nelson have over 70 years of combined experience in the brewing industry. So WBC isn't your typical startup brewery. Through private investors, the founders raised the capital needed to build a 24,000 square-foot facility on five acres of land on the southern edge of Verona. The 80-barrel brewhouse is visible through two walls of windows in the taproom. A gift shop opens off to the side. The expansive backyard patio has its own bar and abundant seating with picnic tables, a fire pit, and plantation chairs (many cut in the shape of Wisconsin) overlooking an idyllic nine-acre pond surrounded by young willows. Thirsty hikers are going to like this: the *Ice Age National Scenic Trail* passes right by the brewery. Plus, the dog-friendly patio is popular with those visiting the popular nearby dog park at Prairie Moraine (1970 County Highway PB).

Wisconsin Brewing Company isn't just a name, it's the philosophy upon which the brewery was built. The German-engineered brewhouse was built in Hudson, WI. The water and fermentation tanks are made in Elroy,

WI. The pumps are made in Middleton, WI. The fiberglass decking comes from Milwaukee. And so on. Anything that couldn't be sourced from Wisconsin is American-made, including the apparel and trinkets in the gift shop. A stainless steel map of Wisconsin in the taproom shows many of the companies that had a hand in building the brewery.

Beer drinkers can also participate in the "Forward!" program and become a WBC insider. As a member of the Flight Crew, you are invited to the brewery to taste and give feedback on new recipes that Kirby & Co. brewed on Old Abe, the one-barrel pilot system. If it is decided that a trial beer is good enough for wider commercial production, Flight Crew members are invited to the brewery for a beer release party before it's available to the general public.

WBC is also collaborating with the Campus Craft Brewery, which is a part of the College of Agriculture and Life Sciences at the University of Wisconsin. The goal of the program is to give students an educational pathway into the craft brewing industry. May 2015 marked the first beer to come from the collaboration: Inaugural Red, an easy-drinking red lager. Six teams of three students each developed and brewed a recipe on a small brewhouse at the university. Then Judges Rob LoBreglio of the Great Dane Pub & Brewery, Dr. David Ryder of MillerCoors, and WBC Brewmaster Kirby selected a winner based on the stylistic parameters the students were given. Finally, the students came to WBC to brew the winning recipe on the full 80-barrel system. Inaugural Red is now available throughout the state (as well as on the UW campus) and enjoying tremendous popularity. And even better for the students (and craft beer lovers): every year the Campus Craft Brewery will create a new beer.

Free WiFi. Facebook.com/wisconsinbrewingcompany

Stumbling Distance: The Verona Segment of the *Ice Age Trail* starts at the Ice Age Junction site off County Highway PD, heads south through *Badger Prairie County Park*, passes under East Verona Avenue and ends in *Prairie Moraine County (Dog) Park* not far from the brewery. (Find this hike in detail in *60 Hikes Within 60 Miles of Madison*.) Also, the *Military Ridge Trail* isn't far away for bikers (See Biking for Beer in the back of the book). Choco-holics must visit *Candinas Chocolatier* (www.candinas. com, 2435 Old PB, Verona, 800-845-1554, Mon–Sat 10–5) where Swiss-trained Markus Candinas makes divine assortments that have been nationally recognized.

Octopi Brewing Co. (3rd Sign Brewing)

Founded: 2015
Head Brewer: Michael Krause
Address: 1131 Uniek Dr • Waunakee, WI 53597
Phone: _____
info@octopibrewing.com
Web Site: www.octopibrewing.com
Annual Production: 10–12,000 barrels (2,000–3,500 bbls for 3rd Sign brand)

Number of Beers: 14 taps (some guest brews), 2 nitro taps, and a beer engine for a weekly cask beer

Staple Beers:
> » Coffee Brown Ale
> » Cream Brown Ale
> » Forest IPA
> » Jungle IPA

Most Popular Brew: Too soon to tell.

Samples: Yes, sips for choosing and flights for sampling.

Brewer's Fave: Coffee Brown Ale

Best Time to Go: Taproom is open 4:30–10pm Mon–Fri to start. Watch the website for current hours.

Where can you buy it? Here on tap in 12-oz pours and growlers to go. Distribution in 4- and 6-pack 12-oz bottles and 22-oz bombers will start in Madison/Dane County and then in the Milwaukee market.

Got food? No, but food friendly and food trucks may park outside.

Tours? Yes, watch for a tour schedule online.

Special Offer: Buy your first 3rd Sign tap beer, get one free when you get your book signed.

Logo courtesy Octopi Brewing

Directions: From WI 19/113 on Waunakee's east side, go south on Hogan Rd. Turn right on Uniek Dr and the brewery is on your left.

The Beer Buzz: Founder Isaac Showaki is originally from Mexico and spent many years working on the business side of things with big breweries in Latin America. Outside work he had a hankering for craft beer, and when he moved to New York, he'd frequently visit his local bodega and pick up 6 or 7 new craft beers to try each time. Not enough. He rounded up investors and moved to Chicago to open the first Latin-American craft brewery in the US: Five Rabbit Cervecería. He hired Randy Mosier (author of *The Brewers Companion*) to create some recipes for him, and then he had them contract brewed. He quickly found he couldn't get the quality or quantity that he wanted for his brand. In one 18-month period, he needed to work with 8 different contract breweries. He decided if he ever opened another brewery, it'd be a contract brewery and he'd do it right. He left Five Rabbit in 2014, and here we are.

The name Octopi suggests the contract brewing having a hand in a lot of different brews, but their own brand of beer is 3rd Sign. In astrology, the third sign is Gemini, the Twins, and this relates to their brewing plan: They will choose a style and then brew two different takes on that style to show how much variation can happen within that single style.

A lot of young breweries lack the resources or capacity to grow, and Octopi aims to be a one-stop solution for small breweries or startups. Before opening, they had sold out their capacity for their first year. He chose Wisconsin because of the abundance of ingredients in the area, and Waunakee because of all the places he visited, this city asked, "What can we do to bring you here?" They were impressively supportive.

The 50-barrel Esau & Hueber brewhouse is German-made and fully automated to minimize the risk of human error. A GEA Westfalia centrifuge cuts down on fermentation times. A 30-head filler German bottling line is also onsite kicking out 150 bottles per minute. The 70-person taproom has windows into brewery operations. The bar, tables, and cold storage room are built with reclaimed wood from Chicago—Navy Pier, to be exact. There's a TV for special events and a small patio outside for seasonable weather.

Free WiFi. Find them on Facebook and Twitter @octopibrew

Stumbling Distance: *Doughboy's Pizza* (246 N Century Ave, 608-850-4960) has thin and hand-tossed pies and delivers. *Lucky's Bar and Grille* (1008 Quinn Dr, 608-850-5825, luckysbarandgrille.com) has good bar food, 24 beers on tap, and 33 TVs for the Packers and much more.

PARCHED EAGLE BREWPUB

Founded: 2015
Head Brewer: Jim Goronson
Address: 5440 Willow Rd. Suite 112 • Westport, WI 53597
Phone: 608-204-9192
Web Site: www.parchedeagle.com
Annual Production: 150 barrels
Number of Beers: 5–6 on tap; plus a couple guests

Staple Beers:
  » CRANE ALE APA
  » HOP-BEARER AMERICAN IPA
  » JANETHAN ROBUST PORTER
  » PARCHED EAGLE GOLDEN ALE
  » VERILY BELGIAN TRAPPIST DUBBEL

Rotating Beers:
  » ALFERD (black rye imperial saison)
  » BROOKIE'S SOUR BROWN (Flanders brown ale)
  » DECEMBERFEST (Munich dunkel)
  » DREAMLAND (witbier)
  » DUROK (saison)
  » GRAINNE'S SPECIAL BITTER (ESB)
  » HARPY (American strong ale)
  » HOMIE (American barleywine)
  » MANIAC (Baltic porter)
  » OKTOBERFEST
  » PEGBOY PILS (German pilsner)
  » SEÑOR SMOKE (Scotch ale)
  » STELLA (Belgian dark strong ale)
  » SWEETNESS (imperial sweet stout)
  » UTOPIAN IMPERIAL IPA
  » THE WEAKLING (Belgian tripel)

Most Popular Brew: Hop Bearers

Brewmaster's Fave: Hop Bearer

Tours? Yes, by chance.

Samples: Yes, sample flights of four 5-oz pours for about $6. An extra $1 for five.

Best Time to Go: Open Wed–Thu 3–11PM, Fri 3PM–12AM, Sat 12PM–12AM, Sun 12PM–8PM. Closed Mon–Tue.

Where can you buy it? Here on tap and in growlers to go.

Got food? Yes, a few sandwiches plus Bavarian pretzels and cheese and sausage platters.

Special Offer: $2 off your first pint of Parched Eagle beer when you get your book signed.

Directions: County Road M comes directly here from Middleton. Out of Madison, take WI 113/Northport Dr north, cross the Yahara River, and turn left at the lights on CR M. Watch for a turn lane through the grassy median and turn left on Willow Road. Pass the gas station there and turn right into a parking lot across the front of a strip of shops. The brewery is about in the middle.

The Beer Buzz: Even some people in Madison aren't going to know Westport by name, but it is a community on the north side of Lake Mendota near where the Yahara River enters the lake. Addresses may read Waunakee, but this is indeed Westport, and while the little community may not get proper respect, it does have a proper brewpub.

President and Head Brewer Jim was 29 when his parents gave him a Mr. Beer kit back in 1995. He loved craft beer already and here was an economical method of acquiring it. Encouraged by House of Brew's Page Buchanan, Jim went all grain and was soon hell bent on opening a brewpub. He attended Siebel Institute's World Brewing Academy and is a certified

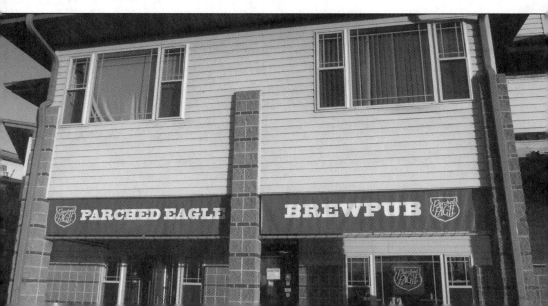

beer judge. Page continued to advise and encourage him until Jim finally partnered up with Tom Christie, another craft beer fan and mead maker, to open this brewpub. The name came up when Jim previously thought to open this in Sauk Prairie, a place famous for eagle watching. The name stuck, out of pure awesomeness.

The taproom features a short bar with some crazy cool metal tap handles (eagle talons clutching a crystal marble), some tall tables, and a second room with more tables. A parking lot is right out front along this line of shops with some outdoor seating on a patio between the sidewalk and the lot.

Free WiFi. Mug Club. Facebook/parchedeagle and Twitter @Parchedeagle

Stumbling Distance: In that gas station next door is some pretty good Greek fast food from *Athens Gyros* (5420 Willow Rd, Waunakee, 608-249-6720, athensgyros.com). *Mariner's Inn* (5339 Lighthouse Bay Dr, Madison, 608-246-3120, marinersmadison.com) inside the nearby marina to the east has been around since 1966 for some old-fashioned and supper club sort of dining.

Port Huron Brewing Co.

Founded: 2011
Brewmaster: Tanner Brethorst
Address: 805 Business Park Road •
Wisconsin Dells, WI 53965
Phone: 608-253-0340
Website: www.porthuronbeer.com
Annual Production: 500 bbls
Number of Beers: 6+ on tap; 7 in distribution

Staple Beers:
- » Alt Bier
- » Hefeweizen
- » Honey Blonde
- » Porter

Rotating Beers:
- » Bock
- » IPA
- » Kölsch
- » Oatmeal Stout
- » Oktoberfest
- » Pale Ale
- » Smoked Maibock

Most Popular Brew: Honey Blonde

Brewmaster's Fave: "The one in my hand! I like 'em all!"

Tours? Yes, scheduled on Fri and Sat. Call or check the website for times.

Samples: Yes, 4–6 beers in a flight for about $4–6

Best Time to Go: Taproom is open Friday 3–9, Saturday 2–9. Thursdays 4–9PM are added in summer.

Where can you buy it? Growlers and by the pint at the taproom. Bottled six-packs and draft accounts can be found in an increasing circle around The Dells, plus Madison and SW Wisconsin.

Got food? Free popcorn and pretzels. Also food friendly.

Special Offer: A free pint with your book signature.

Directions: From the center of the Dells take Broadway/Hwy 13 heading east. Where 13 heads north at a junction with Hwys 16 and 23, you continue straight east on Hwy 23 (still Broadway) and watch on your right for where Broadway breaks away from 23. Follow it and the next left is Business Park Road. The brewery is on your left.

The Beer Buzz: This is the first brewery in Columbia County since 1958! It starts with a running club. Tanner's father used to have a running and beer club. First the running, then drink a different Wisconsin beer every time. They eventually lost interest in the running part. Meanwhile, Tanner got a homebrew kit in college, and it compelled him to get a summer job at Tyranena Brewing in Lake Mills. "I was a sponge that summer, soaking up knowledge." He finished an Ag Business Management degree at UW-Madison and six months later he was at the Siebel Institute for the full course which included some time hitting breweries in Germany and Belgium. A week after completion, he landed a job at Lake Louie. The guy that used to be chased down the highway in the Lake Louie truck by people looking for limited release beers? That was him.

He then spent 3 years at Capital Brewery when his family decided it was time for an intervention. They came to him and suggested he open his own brewery. "It had been a running joke before," he says. Something talked about after a few beers. His father and uncles were dead serious and said if he drew up a solid plan, they would get behind it. Two years later he turned an ink plant in a Wisconsin Dells industrial park into a spacious brewery. Sit in the taproom and you look right into the brewery. Look for the awesome Flux Capacitor (you know? *Back to the Future?*) among the equipment; it's signed by Huey Lewis. The woodwork at the bar was done by his uncle. In fact, the brewery name itself is a reflection of a family ethic. His grandfather's 1917 Port Huron steam tractor still runs and is still in the family. As his grandfather once said, "There are two things you should never rush: a good story and quality built beer." Tanner also brews 10-gallon batches on a pilot system for taproom only. The taproom has one TV for Packers/Badgers/Brewers, music playing in the background, and board games and cribbage. Live music is getting more common, and a beer garden is planned for 2016.

Free WiFi. Facebook.com/PortHuron

Stumbling Distance: *Showboat Saloon* (showboatsaloon.com, 24 Broadway, 608-253-2628) has food, drinks, live entertainment, and Tanner's beers on tap. In fact, Broadway is the main drag in the Dells, a place to find a lot shops and restaurants and some historical buildings. Try *Ravina Bay Bar & Grill* (ravinabay.com, 231 E Durkee St, Lake Delton, 608-253-0433) overlooking Lake Delton if you're looking for a good old Friday fish fry. If you're a paddler, pick up my book *Paddling Wisconsin* and get on the Wisconsin River near here.

WISCONSIN DELLS BREWING CO.

Founded: 2002
Brewmaster: Jamie Martin
Address: 110 Wisconsin Dells Parkway South • Wisconsin Dells, WI 53965 (Moosejaw Pizza & Dells Brewing Co.)
Phone: 608-254-1122
Website: www.dellsmoosejaw.com
Annual Production: 1,400 bbls
Number of Beers: 25 annually, 10 on tap

Staple Beers:
- » APPLE ALE (year round only in distribution otherwise seasonal)
- » DELLS CLASSIC (Kölsch)
- » HAZEL'S NUT HOUSE ALE
- » HONEY ALE (brewed with pure Wisconsin honey)
- » KILBOURN HOP ALE (an APA with local hops!)
- » RELAXIN' RASPBERRY ALE
- » RUSTIC RED ALE

Rotating Beers:
- » BLONDE BOCK
- » DELLS PILSNER
- » MILK STOUT
- » OKTOBERFEST
- » PUMPKIN ALE
- » RED IPA
- » STAND ROCK BOCK
- » STRAWBERRY BITCH

Most Popular Brew: Hazel's Nut House Ale and Relaxin' Raspberry

Brewmaster's Fave: Oktoberfest or Pilsner

Tours? Yes, by appointment or by chance.

Samples: Yes, about $10 for 6, $14 for 10 (5-oz pours)

Best Time to Go: Open daily 11AM–12AM, but restaurant closes 10:30PM Sun–Thu, 11PM Fri–Sat. Watch for the Dells on Tap beer fest featuring 35+ brewers along with live entertainment the 3rd weekend in October.

Where can you buy it? On tap here and in growlers and bottles to go. Distribution of 6-pack bottles (4-packs for seasonals), mixed 12-packs,

16-oz cans in 4-packs, and craft sodas in 6- and 12-oz cans is mostly within a 20-mile radius of the Dells, but some product makes it as far south as Madison and even Beloit.

Got food? Oh yeah, their specialty is in their name! (Look for the giant moose sprawled on the roofs of their delivery cars.) They also have Beer Bread (Honey Ale) and Beer & Cheese soup (Honey Ale). Fantastic Friday Fish Fry. Check the website for printable coupons.

Special Offer: Not participating.

Directions: From I-90/94 take Exit 89 (Hwy 23) and go east and it will be on your right. Or from I-90/94 take Exit 92 (Wisconsin Dells Parkway) and head north and it will be on your left.

The Beer Buzz: This is not your typical tavern, and just walking in the front door ought to make you stop and simply take it in a bit. Designed like a giant backwoods lodge, the three-story, three-bar restaurant seats 500 and is laden with more game mounts than Hemingway could have shaken an elephant rifle at, including giant moose heads and chandeliers fashioned out of antlers. The name comes from Moosejaw, Canada, where, during Prohibition, Al Capone and his gang of "hooch" runners used tunnels to bring booze into the US. If the decor isn't enough to please your eye, the gleaming 15-barrel copper-clad brewhouse upstairs should be.

Jamie Martin is one of only three female head brewers in the state (see Thirsty Pagan in Superior and Capital Brewing in Middleton) and she's been around a good while now. It was her college professor in biotech who suggested she look into brewing beer. She is whipping out the suds and making a killer APA—actually a WPA, Wisconsin pale ale (Kilbourn) made with locally grown hops! This is a pretty large-scale operation for a brewpub, and Jamie keeps the copper tanks polished and purring. Two of her favorite beers were named after her two favorite people (her kids). The brewery started distributing in bottles in January 2014 and added cans in May 2014.

Stumbling Distance: 12 miles south of the Dells toward Baraboo is *The Barn* (WI-123 Trunk, Baraboo, 608-356-2161), one of the best selections of craft beer in the area and a great place to eat. It's inside a repurposed barn. *Wisconsin Dells* is the center of Wisconsin tourism and combines resort town with natural wonder. *Noah's Ark America's Largest Waterpark* (www.noahsarkwaterpark.com, 608-254-6351) and a whole assortment of water park attractions are huge in summer, and many hotels have *indoor* water parks that rival the outdoor brethren. *Original Wisconsin Ducks* (www.wisconsinducktours.com, 608-254-8751) uses reborn WWII amphibious craft to run tours of the river and its awesome landscape. Odd museums, souvenir shops, shows, parks, restaurants, and casinos—the Dells can fill its own guidebook. Grab a beer at *Moosejaw* while you decide where to start stumbling.

Woodman Brewery (Whistle Stop Restaurant)

Founded: October 2011
Brewmaster: Dennis Erb
Address: 401 Main Street • Woodman, WI 53827
Phone: 608-533-2200
Website: www.woodmanwi.com
Annual Production: 250 barrels
Number of Beers: 6 on tap, endless styles throughout the year

Rotating Beers: (many come and go all the time)

- » Arctic IPA (With Mint)
- » Black IPA
- » Coconut Wheat
- » Cola India Black Ale
- » Cranberry Crème Stout
- » Cupcake Ale
- » Irish Crème Stout
- » Jalapeño Blonde Ale
- » Mushroom Wheat (with Morels)
- » Rye Kölsch Bier
- » Tijuana Ale
- » Vanilla Bourbon Ale

Tours? No.

Samples: Yes

Best Time to Go: Open 7 days a week, from 9AM to close. Get there early on euchre nights.

Where can you buy it? You can mix and match a few bottles here and refill a growler. A few Madison outlets sell it such as Jenifer Street Market and, naturally, Woodman's Grocery Store (unrelated).

Got food? Yes, including pizzas, sweet potato fries, chicken, burgers, and homemade soups. Friday night fish fry as well as Taco Tuesdays.

Special Offer: A free sample platter of 4 beers.

Directions: Highway 133 passes right through town as Main Street. Go 10 minutes west of Boscobel and you're here. Watch for the Whistle Stop/

Woodman Brewery/US Post Office on the river side of the road (north).

The Beer Buzz: This little brewery is really pushing the envelope—in more ways than one. Not only is Dennis coming up with a wide variety of adventuresome recipes, but the Whistle Stop Restaurant building is also the local US Post Office (53827)!

The family business is run by mom Leslie, and the brewing is the duty of her son Dennis. He likes to think of this as the smallest brewery in Wisconsin with the largest selection; he brews in the bar's kitchen. The Erb family came here from Milwaukee in 2008 buying the tavern-restaurant.

Dennis may be the only bootlegger you ever meet. Before the paperwork went through for his brewery, he was giving away beer to locals in the bar to see what they thought. Someone with a grudge reported it, and he got a big fine and lost his equipment. The bar lost some liquor as well only because the paperwork proving its legal purchase wasn't on site. Lots of excitement for a little town, but luckily it ended up being a misdemeanor rather than a felony.

Dennis's father-in-law was a homebrewer, and so Dennis took it up as well. He had thought of being a mixologist but has found a similar creativity in his brewing as you can see from many of the recipes. He loves to explore.

Pints are incredibly cheap, so there is no best time to go get one. As they told me, "Every hour is happy hour." Whistle Stop has the look of your standard small town tavern, with darts and pool table, plenty of tables, a long looping bar and the token mounted buck. Plus you can mail a letter.

Stumbling Distance: The town is pretty small and this is about all that's going on here. The big attraction, however, is all around the place: the Great Outdoors. Hunting and fishing are popular, and hikers, bikers, and paddlers will find plenty to do. Boscobel is 10 minutes one way, *Wyalusing State Park* (608-996-2261) and the meeting of the Mississippi and Wisconsin Rivers are under a half hour the other. River fans should check *WI River Outings* (canoe-camping.com, 715 Wisconsin Ave, Boscobel, 608-375-5300) for paddling/camping options. No glass growlers allowed on the river though; find an alternative if you're thinking of packing beer! (See also my *Paddling Wisconsin* book.)

Check out *Tornado Brewing Co.* (N88 W16718 Appleton Ave, Menomonee Falls, 262-735-7328, Facebook.com/TornadoBrewing)—this is Woodman Brewery's Milwaukee-area taproom. They don't brew there, but his beer makes the trip if you can't get to Woodman.

41 45

43

West Bend

Grafton
Cedarburg

Glendale
Shorewood
Wauwatosa
Milwaukee

Oconomowoc

94

Delafield
Waukesha
Brookfield
Whitewater

St. Francis

Oak Creek

12

43

94

Kenosha

Lake Geneva

6

3   4   5

1   2

ZONE 2

Brookfield: Biloba Brewing Co.
Cedarburg: Silver Creek Brewing
Delafield: Delafield Brewhaus
Delafield: Water Street Brewery: Lake Country
Grafton: Water Street Brewery: Grafton
Kenosha: Public Craft Brewery
Kenosha: Rustic Road Brewing Co.
Lake Geneva: Geneva Lake Brewing Co.
Milwaukee (Shorewood): Big Bay Brewing Co.
Milwaukee: Brenner Brewing Co.
Milwaukee: Company Brewing
Milwaukee: District 14 Brewery (D14 Brewery)
Milwaukee: Horny Goat Brew Pub
Milwaukee: Lakefront Brewery
Milwaukee: Miller Brewing Co. (MillerCoors)
Milwaukee: Milwaukee Ale House
Milwaukee: Milwaukee Brewing Co./2nd Street Brewery
Milwaukee: MobCraft Beer
Milwaukee: Rock Bottom Restaurant and Brewery
Milwaukee (Glendale): Sprecher Brewery
Milwaukee: Tenth Street Brewery
Milwaukee: Urban Harvest Brewing Co.
Milwaukee: Water Street Brewery
Oak Creek: Water Street Brewery
Oconomowoc: Sweet Mullets Brewing
St. Francis: St. Francis Brewery and Restaurant
Waukesha: Fixture Brewing Co.
Wauwatosa: Big Head Brewing Co.
West Bend: Riverside Brewery and Restaurant
Whitewater: 841 Brewhouse
Whitewater: Second Salem Brewing Co.

Biloba Brewing Co.

Opened: April 2014
Brewers: Gordon Lane and Kristen Lane
Address: 18720 Pleasant St. • Brookfield, WI 53045
Phone: 262-309-5820
Web Site: www.bilobabrewing.com
Annual Production: 200 barrels
Number of Beers: 10 on tap

Possible Beers:

- » Biere de Mars
- » Biloba Blanc
- » Bitter Bitch IPA
- » Dark Side
- » Dunkel
- » Hefeweizen
- » Golden Ale
- » Rye of the Wort
- » Saison on Oak
- » Scottish Ale
- » Section 25
- » Smokin' Gramma
- » plus some barrel aging

Tours? No.

Samples: Yes, flights of all ten beers on a numbered platter.

Best Time to Go: Open Thu 5–9:30pm, Fri 5–10:30pm, Sat 1–6pm.

Where can you buy it? Here on tap and in growlers and some 22-oz bombers to go.

Got food? Not really, just water and sodas, and some Bavarian pretzels from Milwaukee Pretzel Co. Occasionally, caterers are here and food trucks on most Friday nights. Otherwise it is food friendly.

Special Offer: Not participating.

Directions: Take Brookfield Rd (south 1.2 miles from Capitol Dr or north 2.6 miles from Bluemound Rd) and then turn east on Pleasant St. The brewery shares a building on the left.

The Beer Buzz: This is a family affair, with Gordon and Jean Lane and their two daughters working together. Kristen and her father do the brewing. Her sister Kathryn Glomski runs the tasting room. Gordon has another pretty important connection to beer: he is president of Briess Malt in Chilton, provider of specialty grains since forever to much of the brewing industry here in Wisconsin and beyond.

They repurposed dairy equipment for some of the brewing, use an energy-efficient gas heater for the wort, and collected used furniture for the taproom. Spent grain, of course, goes to a local farmer. Their eco-minded approach got them recognition from Wisconsin Sustainable Business Council's Green Masters Program.

This is a community taproom, down a suburban side street, and likely busy

with locals coming to relax and chat. A few board games are on hand and there may be some background music. Photos of mug club members are on the wall. Clipboards hold the day's beer menu. When you walk in the front door, the brewhouse is to the left, but the taproom is to the right down a short hall. A small L-shaped bar occupies the far corner.

Free WiFi. Mug Club. Find them on Facebook, Twitter @BilobaBrewing and Instagram @bilobabrewing

Stumbling Distance: *Cafe Manna* (3815 N Brookfield Rd, 262-790-2340, cafemanna.com) serves vegetarian fare with local beer. Carnivores might prefer casual atmosphere and upscale food at *Mr. B's—A Bartolotta Steakhouse* (18380 W Capitol Dr, 262-790-7005, mrbssteakhouse.com). It's a wine place, not beer.

TORNADO BREWING CO.

Located north of Brookfield in Menomonee Falls, Tornado Brewing is not actually a brewery. Rather, it's the far-reaching taproom for Woodman Brewery, from Woodman, WI in Zone 1, situated along the Wisconsin River nearly 3 hours away. They have sidewalk seating in season, where you can text the bar inside to get your next round without getting up. All the crazy recipe brews Dennis Erb is known for but without the miles. Previously, this was located in Cudahy.

Tornado Brewing
N88 W16718 Appleton Ave | Menomonee Falls, WI 53051
262-735-7328 | Facebook.com/TornadoBrewing

Silver Creek Brewing Co.

Founded: 1999
Head Brewer: Kyle Ciske
Address: N57 W6172 Portland Road • Cedarburg, WI 53012
Phone: 262-375-4444
Website: www.silvercreekbrewing.com
Annual Production: 200 bbls
Number of Beers: 6–8 on tap of ours, 16 taps total

Staple Beers:

» Hefe-Weiss
» IPA
» Pacific Coast Lager (light)
» Porter (Baltic-style, more chocolate than coffee and 7.5% abv)
» Silver Creek Blonde Root Beer

Staple Beers:

» Imperial Mai-Bock (spring)
» Oktoberfest (fall)
» Session Ale
» Vintage Ale (winter)

Most Popular Brew: Pacific Coast Lager (but Weiss is pretty popular in summer, Porter in cooler weather).

Brewmaster's Fave: Porter or IPA, depends on his mood

Tours? Not exactly. All the brewing facilities are visible, but if he's around, he'll chat about brewing.

Samples? Yes, four beers and a blonde root beer plus one of the several guest taps. $11.50 for six 4-oz samplers.

Best Time to Go: Closed on Mondays. Open Tue–Fri 3pm–close, Sat noon–close, Sun noon–8pm. In summer it is nice to sit alongside the river and watch the ducks. Check the website for the live music schedule. Happy hour until 6pm Tue–Thu.

Where can you buy it? Originally only in growlers, but starting to distribute to local draft accounts.

Got food? Yes, snacks like cheese, bread rolls, and beef sticks. *Romano's Pizzeria* (262-375-9921) delivers here. Food friendly and local menus are on hand.

Special Offer: Buy a pint of their brew and get one free!

Directions: From I-43 take Exit 89 (Pioneer Rd). Go west to Washington Ave and take that north to Columbia Rd and go right (east). The first right before the bridge is Portland Rd and the Landmark Building.

The Beer Buzz: Cedarburg is only twenty minutes north of Milwaukee. Silver Creek is in the basement of the Landmark Building on the corner of

Portland and Columbia Roads in the historic downtown. In the mid-1800s, German and Irish immigrants built five dams and mills on Cedar Creek, and this one, built in 1855, was a flour mill. The pub entrance is around back down along the river where you will find outside seating. Inside you will pass the remnants of the water-powered mill and enter through a large wooden door. This place has the air of an old lagering cellar with its wood ceiling and the brick and stone walls. Photos of the old town adorn the place and a few TVs pipe in the news or sporting events. The brewing equipment is there for all to see, cordoned off from the rest of the bar. Some other Wisconsin beers are also on tap here.

Facebook.com/SilverCreekBrew and Twitter @SilverCreekBrew

Stumbling Distance: As an alternative to the grains, try the grapes at *Cedar Creek Winery* (www.cedarcreekwinery.com, N70 W6340 Bridge Rd, 800-827-8020). Housed in an 1860s woolen mill, the winery offers a 45-minute tour for $3 at 11:30 AM, 1:30 PM, and 3:30 PM. See the brewery offerings in nearby Grafton as well: *Water Street Brewery* and a Grafton version of *Milwaukee Ale House*.

Delafield Brewhaus

Founded: May 1999
Brewmaster: John Harrison
Address: 3832 Hillside Drive • Delafield, WI 53018
Phone: 262-646-7821
Website: www.delafield-brewhaus.com
Annual Production: 900 bbls
Number of Beers: 8–10 on tap, 12–15 per year

Staple Beers:
- » Delafield Amber
- » Dockside Ale (Kölsch)
- » Naga-Wicked Pale Ale
- » Pewaukee Porter
- » Sommerzeit Hefe Weizen

Rotating Beers:
- » 8 Malt Stout
- » Belgian Quad
- » Bengal Bay IPA (all Citra hops)
- » Einhorn Bock (gold medal in WBC)
- » Fruhlingzeit Maibock (spring; gold medal in WBC)
- » Fruit beers (year-round, different fruit ales: mango, raspberry, blueberry, strawberry)
- » Hop Harvest IPA (with Cascade hops grown in the beer garden)
- » Imperial IPA
- » Millennium Belgian-style Tripel
- » Oats and Barley Oatmeal Stout
- » Oktoberfest (fall)
- » Pilsner (summer)
- » Radlers (summer)
- » Whiskey barrel-aged beers (during holiday season)
- » Whiskey barrel-aged Imperial Rauchbier

Most Popular Brew: Delafield Amber then IPA

Brewmaster's Fave: Oktoberfest, Maibock, and Pilsner! Depends on the season.

Tours? No, but the brewing system is in the center of the room in the open. You can still watch.

Samples? Yes, about $7.50 for six 4-oz samples (or you can sample them all).

Best Time to Go: Happy hour is Monday, Wednesday, Friday 3–6PM. Live music on Saturday nights and a great Sunday breakfast buffet. Oktoberfest is on tap in September.

Where can you buy it? Here on tap and in growlers to go, plus ⅙, ¼ and ½ barrels. Half-liter bottles of staple beers for sale on site and in local liquor stores.

Got food? Yes, a full menu! John makes his own Beer-B-Q sauce and mustard, and you can buy bottles of it to take home. Fish fry on Fridays is Amber-battered, ribs come with the special Beer-B-Q sauce, and lunch and dinner have expansive menus. (If you have a party of 30 or more you can set up a beer dinner!)

Special Offer: A pint of John's beer or root beer.

Directions: If you take Exit 287 for Hwy 83 and go south there will be three traffic light-controlled intersections. The first is re-entry to 94, the second is Wal-Mart, and the third is Hillside Drive. Take it left (east) and follow it to the pub.

The Beer Buzz: Before brewing professionally, John was a homebrewer (he and friend Jim Olen of Milwaukee Ale House used to homebrew back in the day) and worked first in masonry and then as a branch manager for an outfit that sold fire safety equipment. "What's the best way to ruin a hobby?" he asks rhetorically. "If you don't love beer, how can you be in this business?" Originally, he founded Wisconsin Brewing Co. (not the new one in Verona) out of Wauwautosa in 1995, but when they were flooded out in '99—yet left high and dry by the insurance company—he opened this place overlooking I-94. He has total creative freedom and has put it to good use: he's made over 70 different beers since they opened! In 2000 Harrison won an award for Millennium Tripel at the World

Beer Championship, for Barley Wine at the GABF, and a huge trophy with Rhinelander beer labels all over it from the Master Brewers Association. Recent WBC awards included a silver for Hop Harvest IPA in 2014, as well as golds for his bock and maibock.

The first thing you see as you walk in under the high ceiling is the brewhouse which rises up behind a low wall like some kind of pipe organ, and John can be seen composing his brews out here in the open. He designed the brewing facility first and then built the building around it. "Brewery in your face" he calls it and shuns the idea of tanks behind glass somewhere over behind the kitchen next to the bathroom. A private collector with some investment in the brewhaus displays his outstanding collection of breweriana along the walls. The basement is a banquet room that can hold up to 200 and a mezzanine has even more seating and another bar. The two front corners of the bar are closed off into private booths inside of giant wooden lagering barrels from Milwaukee's Dunck Tank Works from the late 1800s. Another old tank has been fashioned into a wood-fired oven for the pizzas. In addition to the variety of beers, he makes root beer and also does a malt beverage (a "malternative") called Bomb Pop, which is blue and tastes a lot like a Fla-Vor-Ice of the same color. His IPAs are so popular, he had to purchase another fermenter and two more serving tanks to keep up with demand.

Stumbling Distance: If you are heading over to *Water Street Lake Country Brewpub* across the way, try this route: head east along the frontage road (Hillside Dr) to the first stop sign. Go left under I-94 overpass, take the first left on Golf Rd, and then follow that until the brewpub. Want some wine to go with your beer? *Lapham Peak* (www.laphampeakfriends.org, W329N846 Hwy C), part of the Kettle Moraine State Forest, is a great place for hiking or mountain biking, and it also has lighted cross country ski trails. A 45-foot observation tower gives the highest view in the county of this unique topography left behind by the glaciers of the last Ice Age and the *Ice Age National Scenic Trail* actually passes through the park. (See my book *Best Hikes Near Milwaukee*.)

WATER STREET LAKE COUNTRY BREWERY

Founded: 2000
Brewmaster: George Bluvas III
Address: 3191 Golf Road • Delafield, WI 53018
Phone: 262-646-7878
Website: www.waterstreetbrewery.com
Annual Production: 800 bbls
Number of Beers: 8–9 on tap

Staple Beers:
- » BAVARIAN WEISS
- » HONEY LAGER LIGHT
- » OLD WORLD OKTOBERFEST
- » PUNCH YOU IN THE EYE PA
- » RASPBERRY WEISS
- » VICTORY AMBER

Rotating Beers:
- » BELGIAN WIT
- » BLACK IPA
- » BLACK LAGER (Schwarzbier)
- » DOPPELBOCK
- » IMPERIAL STOUT
- » IRISH STOUT
- » SAISON
- » … and many more!

Most Popular Brew: Honey Lager Light/Old World Oktoberfest

Brewmaster's Fave: Pale Ale

Tours? Yes, but by appointment.

Samples? Yes, $8 gets you seven to nine 4-oz beers.

Best Time to Go: Summer offers outside seating next to a man-made pond in a strip mall parking lot. Lunch and dinner are busy! Best after 7PM if you just want a beer.

Where can you buy it? Growlers and tap accounts at sister restaurants: Louise's, Trinity, Harp, Black Rose, Solo Pizza—all in Milwaukee, and at Water Street Grafton and Oak Creek.

Got food? A full menu. Scotch eggs, beer-marinated Usinger bratwurst are total Wisconsin, the rest ranges from sandwiches to pasta, steak and seafood.

Special Offer: Not participating.

Directions: From I-94 take Exit 287 and go north on Hwy 83 to Golf Road. Take this to the right (east) and follow the gentle S-curve and you will see the brewpub on your left behind a small pond.

The Beer Buzz: Escape from the nearby shopping to a breweriana-laden brewpub. The copper brewhouse gleams behind glass and beer fans can marvel at a vast collection of cans and

tap handles as well as signs from the regional breweries of the past. Wood beams rise overhead to a central skylight above the bar. Brewmaster George does quadruple duty here and in the downtown Milwaukee location and others in Grafton and Oak Creek.

The building, a bit like a German hunting lodge or beer hall, was previously a different restaurant that couldn't make a go of it. Water Street knew they would have better luck and so with little alteration to the structure crammed in a brew system. (Not a microbrewery, but a microscopic brewery, says George).

Stumbling Distance: Looking for something frosty? You're in a good neighborhood. *Le Duc Frozen Custard Drive* (240 Summit Ave, Wales, WI, 262-968-2894) does it up the old-fashioned way in a 70's style outlet in Wales two miles away. Or if you want it Italian, get over to Waukesha's *Divino Gelato Café* (www.divinogelatocafe.com, 227 W Main St, Waukesha, 262-446-9490) for authentic ice cream Italiano and specialty drinks and soups. *Pewaukee Lake* is popular for swimmers. *Delafield Brewhaus* is right across the freeway.

Water Street Grafton Brewery

Founded: 2010
Brewmaster: George Bluvas III
Address: 2615 Washington Street • Grafton, WI 53024
Phone: 262-375-1402
Website: www.waterstreetbrewery.com
Annual Production: 800 bbls
Number of Beers: 8–9 on tap

Staple Beers:
  » Bavarian Weiss
  » Honey Lager Light
  » Old World Oktoberfest
  » Punch You in the Eye PA
  » Raspberry Weiss
  » Victory Amber

Rotating Beers:
  » Belgian Wit
  » Black IPA
  » Black Lager (Schwarzbier)
  » Doppelbock
  » Imperial Stout
  » Irish Stout
  » Saison
  » … and many more!

Most Popular Brew: Honey Lager Light/Oktoberfest

Brewmaster's Fave: Pale Ale

Tours? Yes, but by appointment.

Samples? Yes, $8 gets you seven to nine 4-oz beers.

Best Time to Go: Open daily at 11AM and popular for weekend brunches 10AM to 3PM.

Where can you buy it? Growlers on site and tap accounts at sister restaurants: Louise's, Trinity, Harp, Black Rose, Solo Pizza—all in Milwaukee, and the original Milwaukee location, and Water Street in Delafield and Oak Creek.

Got food? A full menu. Scotch eggs, beer-marinated Usinger bratwurst are total Wisconsin, the rest ranges from sandwiches to pasta, steak and seafood.

Special Offer: Not participating.

Directions: From the intersection of I-43 and Hwy 60 (Washington St), go east on Hwy 60 just a matter of feet and take the first street south which is still Washington St. The brewery will be on your right.

The Beer Buzz: Water Street, one of the oldest brewpubs in Milwaukee expanded first to Delafield and now north to Grafton with this third location (and a fourth in Oak Creek). The beers remain the same as Brewmaster George does quadruple duty here and in the Delafield, Oak Creek and downtown Milwaukee locations.

The restaurant, like the others, has breweriana on the walls. The main dining area is lined with booths and a high wood ceiling rises up past the surrounding mezzanine and its copper fermentation tanks. The large u-shaped bar sticks out from an impressive wood back bar. Like in Delafield this is a small brew system tucked inside. There is additional seating in another room. Outside you'll see wood siding that looks quite old school and the rising grain tank on the roof.

Stumbling Distance: *Milwaukee Ale-House* (ale-house.com, 1208 13th Ave, 262-375-2337) also has an outlet here in Grafton, and although they are not actually brewing there, you can get all the same Milwaukee Brewing Co. beers. If you are looking for some local foods and other products to take home, check out *Slow Pokes Local Food* (slowpokeslocalfood.com, 1229 12th Ave, 262-375-5522) for meats, cheeses, fermented foods, gluten-free items, and so much more.

Public Craft Brewing Co.

Founded: August 2012
Brewmaster: Matt Geary
Address: 716 58th Street • Kenosha, WI 53140
Phone: 262-652-2739
Website: www.publiccraftbrewing.com
Annual Production: 500 bbls
Number of Beers: 8–9 on tap; 18+ beers annually

Staple Beers:
  » Bone Dry Irish Stout Nitro
  » Hop In The Sack IPA
  » Ink Well Black IPA
  » K-Town Brown Ale
  » Perception Porter
  » Public Access Session IPA
  » Public Pale Ale

Rotating Beers:
  » Brain Baster English Bitter (nitro)
  » Getaway Wit
  » Handle Bar Blonde (summer)
  » Openbaar Saison
  » Sweet Colleen's Irish Red
  » Various special beers, one-offs such as Lucky Spile Maple Bock
  » A firkin every Friday

Most Popular Brew: Whatever's new (but K-Town Brown is consistent).

Brewmaster's Fave: Bone Dry Irish Stout

Tours? Yes, check the website for scheduled times.

Samples: Yes, usually flights of 8 plus root beer for about $15 (fewer beers possible).

Best Time to Go: Open daily: Mon–Fri 3:30–9pm, Sat 12–9pm, Sun 12–6pm.

Where can you buy it? Here on tap and in growlers and 22-oz bottles to go. Draft accounts in the area. Kenosha Racine Walworth Counties and into Milwaukee.

Got food? Nope. Food friendly. Menus onsite, possible food trucks outside, check Facebook.

Special Offer: A free pint of Matt's beer when you get your book signed.

Directions: From I-94 take Exit 342 and head east on 52nd St/Hwy 158 until Hwy 32/Sheridan Rd. Go right (south) six blocks and take a left on 58th St. The brewery is on the left in the next block.

The Beer Buzz: Built in the 1910s, this bowstring truss-roofed brick building was an auto shop (they found the old pits when digging the drains for the brewery) and spent some time as a grocery store before it was divided in half intended to be two smaller businesses. Brewer Matt didn't aim for this to be a bar. This is really a brewery. While there is a tap room, it's really a production facility. No TVs, no food. Basically, it's a place to come in, sample, and chat a bit.

Matt Geary has been homebrewing since college. When he felt general discontent with his career, that hobby started looking tempting. Everyone says "We should open a bar!" So Matt went to Siebel in Chicago for a beer course. Then he did a feasibility study and decided it would work. "'Holy cow!' I thought, 'I'm really doing this.'" Matt plans to brew British styles tending toward the mild beers which he feels are a little underrepresented.

Matt likes the social aspect of beer, and finds it encourages good discourse. The idea behind Public was that it was for everyone. Get people a place to

come together and talk and learn from each other and let the beer be at the hub of it, the common thread. The brewery also has what Matt calls The Public Library, a collection of resources on brewing that homebrewers are free to stop in and peruse. The brewery takes part in The Big Read (www. neabigread.org), a National Endowment for the Arts initiative each year by brewing a special beer. They did Old Poe Old Ale, a cask-conditioned ale (like cask of amontillado, get it?) in 2013, No Front Porches Smoked Imperial Red Ale for Farenheit 451 in 2014, and were working on something for To Kill a Mockingbird.

There are no TVs here; just come and hang out, have conversations. Matt's hoping to upgrade the brewhouse in 2016. Handle Bar Blonde features a tap handle made from a bike handle attached to a bike bell that rings with the pour.

Free WiFi. Facebook.com/deservingpublic and Twiter @PublicBrewing and Instagram@publicbrewing

Stumbling Distance: If you are looking for a Kenosha institution, don't miss *Frank's Diner* (franksdinerkenosha.com, 508 58th St, 262-657-1017) open for classic food from the wee hours to the wee hours. *Ashling on the Lough* (ashlingonthelough.com, 125 56th St, 262-653-0500) is an Irish pub/restaurant with a good UK beer selection and some of Public's brews as well. The two most important attractions out on the interstate are *The Brat Stop* (bratstop.com, 262-857-2011) and *Mars Cheese Castle* (marscheese.com, 262-859-2244).

Rustic Road Brewing Co.

Founded: June 22, 2012
Brewmaster: Greg York
Address: 510 56th Street • Kenosha, WI 53140
Phone: 262-320-7623
Website: www.rusticbrewing.com
Annual Production: 175 bbls
Number of Beers: 6 on tap

Staple Beers:
- » Hazelnut Harvest Ale
- » KPA (Kenosha Pale Ale)

Rotating Beers:
- » Accommodation Amber
- » Belgian Tripel
- » Cabin Up North Double Chocolate Milk Stout
- » Cerveza de Mayo
- » Oktobier
- » Queen Bee Belgian Strong Ale
- » Rustic Saison
- » Southport Wheat Bavarian Style
- » Springsback! Maibock
- » …a new beer each month plus a SMaSH beer series, quarterly seasonals and occasional lagers.

Most Popular Brew: Hazelnut Harvest Ale

Brewmaster's Fave: Belgian Tripel and Queen Bee

Tours? Yes, but you can see everything from the door. It's a nickel tour. (Actually it's free, so you've saved a nickel. Bonus!) Watch for brewing classes once a month in the colder season; come in and participate in the brewing of a batch from start to finish.

Samples: Yes, sample flights of six 4-oz beers (plus a root beer) for about $8.50.

Best Time to Go: The tap room has a full bar with some other Wisconsin craft beers available as well. Hours are Wed–Thu 5–10pm, Fri 4–1-ish, Sat noon–1-ish, Sun noon–6pm. Different drink specials each day and Happy Hour is Mon–Thu 5–7, Fri–Sat 4–7. Live music at least once a month.

Where can you buy it? Here on tap or in growlers to go. They also have about a dozen draft accounts in Kenosha and Racine Counties.

Got food? Just some small appetizers, simple snacks or cheese plates.

Special Offer: A free bumper sticker when you get your book signed.

The Beer Buzz: The idea started like many: one too many homebrews one night. Greg said, "One day when I retire, I will open a brewery." At that moment of beer talking, the idea was a big thing. It'll have a movie theatre, pool tables, a bowling alley… But unlike most of our similarly big ideas, Greg's became reality. In 2009, he had heard "one too many stories of a 35-year old crossing a finish line and dying," and he began contemplating how life doesn't always wait around for you. While he had to scale down the Big Idea—sorry, no bowling alley, folks—it became the Serious Idea.

In 1999 during his last year of college, Greg went in for halfsies on a brew kit with of buddy of his and started homebrewing (dormbrewing?). The first batch was great. In the second, the thermometer shattered in the brew kettle and they had to dump it. At the end of the year, Greg bought out the other half of the kit. Then he began to read everything he could and started going to conferences. The brew passion evolved and continued to grow. In 2010 he took Best In Category at the Wisconsin State Fair with a Summer Saison.

When he was ready, he put together a scaled-down vision of something manageable, something small and more artisanal. "There was once a brewery on every block, providing for the locals, and they'd come down with their bucket each day." The brewery is a repurposed office building that had been empty. He worked with the landlord to take an eyesore and make it a fabulous little place in the heart of the south downtown, next to the performing arts center. It has a coffee house sort of vibe. The name Rustic Road comes from the legislated preservation program begun in 1973 to save Wisconsin's scenic country roads. They've got a TV, a jukebox, board games, and some outdoor seating. Beers change often and Greg does a few special brews such as a donut beer for Mike's Chicken & Donuts (a cream ale with vanilla) and a collaboration with Public Brewing on a brew for Kenosha's Craft Beer Week in May.

Rustic Road's Maibock was originally named Helles Yeah. You may recognize that as Leinenkugel's trademarked name for their Munich Helles Lager. In these days of increasing legal bickering over trademarks, it is interesting to note that Greg produced his Helles Yeah first. When Leinenkugel's came up with the name and saw it had already been used, Dick Leinenkugel himself came down to ask Greg's permission. Class act.

Free WiFi. Mug club. Find them on Facebook.

Trivia note: Kenosha's first brewery, Muntzenberger Brewing, opened in 1847, a year before Wisconsin's statehood.

Stumbling Distance: *Captain Mike's Beer and Burger Bar* (mikelikesbeer. com, 5118 6th Ave, 262-658-2278) shouldn't be missed, a crazy-big beer list. *Wine Knot Bar & Bistro* (wine-knot.com, 5611 6th Ave, 262-653-9580) is a great restaurant across the street. And do check out the Kenosha Harbor Park and the Market—great for walking around. Sister establishment *Mike's Donuts & Chicken* (707 56th St, A., 262-764-9520)—or is it Chicken & Donuts?—is not to be missed. You can carry out to the breweries.

Geneva Lake Brewing Co.

Founded: February 1, 2012
Head Brewer: Pat McIntosh
Address: 750 Veterans Parkway, Suite 107 • Lake Geneva, WI 53147
Phone: 262-248-2539
Website: www.genevalakebrewingcompany.com
Annual Production: 1,000 bbls
Number of Beers: 8 on tap; 8 per year

Staple Beers:
- » Black Point Oatmeal Stout (22-oz bombers)
- » Boathouse Blonde
- » Cedar Point Amber Ale
- » Implosion Double IPA
- » No Wake IPA
- » Weekender Wheat (22-oz bombers)

Rotating Beers:
- » Imperial Cherry Stout (December)
- » Oktoberfest (September)
- » White River Pale Ale (summer)

Most Popular Brew: No Wake IPA

Brewer's Fave: Implosion Double IPA

Tours? By appointment or by chance.

Samples: Yes, three and six 5-oz pours.

Best Time to Go: The taproom is open Mon 11AM–3PM, Wed–Thu 3–7PM, Fri–Sat 11AM–8PM, Sun 11AM–3PM. Closed Tuesdays.

Where can you buy it? Here on tap and to go in growlers, cans and bombers. Distributed statewide in Wisconsin and McHenry, Lake, and Cook Counties in Illinois. Cedar Point, Boathouse Blonde, No Wake, and Implosion Double IPA are in 12-oz cans, while Oatmeal Stout, Weekender Wheat, Implosion, and Imperial Cherry Stout sell in 22-oz bombers.

Got food? No. Food friendly and menus onsite for delivery.

Special Offer: A pint glass.

Directions: From Hwy 120 outside Lake Geneva, take Exit 330A and head west toward town (still Hwy 120 South) and follow it again when it turns left on Edwards Blvd. Just over a half mile turn left onto E Townline Rd and left again onto the next street, Veteran's Parkway. It's in the two U-shaped buildings on your left.

The Beer Buzz: Pat McIntosh spent 28 years working the corporate end of the manufacturing industry, and when he retired early he was looking for a big change. His son Jonathan gave him a very good idea. You see, Lake Geneva is a tourist mecca (thus the Weekender Wheat name) and draws good traffic from Chicago. As Jonathan noted, most touristy areas have at least one craft brewery or brewpub, but Lake Geneva had none.

Pat and Jonathan had started homebrewing back in 2005 or so. It's a big leap from your basement to a production brewery, but they were up to the challenge. They both took some coursework, and Jonathan enrolled in the Siebel Institute in Chicago. With guidance from brewing consultant Tim Lenahan of Brew to Win, they got their first two recipes perfected, and then developed two more as they opened their facility in an industrial condo in town. The taproom soon followed. Pat took over the brewing by himself and now distribution crosses the state line to the south.

Geneva Lake is actually the second largest lake in Wisconsin, with 21 miles of shoreline and a widest point of 2.6 miles.

Facebook.com/GLBrewCo and Twitter @GenevaLakeBrew

Stumbling Distance: The lake is the main attraction, of course. A hiking trail follows the shoreline for 20+ miles (see my book *Best Hikes Near Milwaukee*). Pick up delicious local sausages/meats from *Lake Geneva Country Meats* (5907 WI-50, 262-248-3339, lakegenevacountrymeats. com). *Champs Sports Bar & Grill* (747 West Main St, 262-248-6008) is the biggest beer seller in town (Geneva Lake is on tap) and a perfect place to gather for the big games. *University of Chicago's Yerkes Observatory* (astro.uchicago.edu/yerkes, 373 W Geneva St, Williams Bay, 262-245-5555) is open every Saturday for free tours. *Chuck's Lakeshore Inn* (352 Lake St, Fontana, 262-275-3222) at the other end of the lake sits right on the water for some casual bar fare and good drinks.

MILWAUKEE

Wisconsin's largest city was once the nation's (and world's) largest manufacturing zone. It is the birthplace of Harley Davidson, the home of Happy Days, LaVerne & Shirley, and That 70s Show, and the site of Summerfest, the world's largest outdoor music festival. A strong influx of German immigrants in the nineteenth century brought with them the one thing Milwaukee is most associated with: beer.

This is the original Brew City—Beer Town, U.S.A. By the late 1860s, Germans were associated with the 48 or so breweries already up and running. The very first was Milwaukee Brewery—known locally as Owens' Brewery—which was built by three Welshmen in 1840 and brewed ales not lagers.

Many brewing giants emerged from the competition. What began as Best & Company in 1844 became Pabst Brewing Co. in 1889, going on to win the blue ribbon associated with its flagship beer. Valentine Blatz opened his brewery in 1851. Originally founded as a tavern brewery in 1849, the brewery of the beer that "made Milwaukee famous" would become Joseph Schlitz Brewery in 1858, two years after its former bookkeeper bought the works from the founder's widow and then married her. At one time Schlitz was the largest brewery in the world. Frederick Miller bought the Planck Road Brewery in 1855, and the massive operation that is there today still brews.

While Miller Brewing (MillerCoors) still produces millions of barrels each year, Pabst closed the brewery and contract-brews Schlitz, Blatz, and other classic brands. (That will change in 2016 when they open a small brewery again near their old site.) Thanks to the birth of craft breweries in the 1980s, Milwaukee's brewing tradition is alive and well—and growing every year. In addition to the many breweries beyond this page, you will also find beer-related attractions that you should consider on any *pilsgrimage* to the Great Brew City. Museums, restaurants, revived or repurposed old buildings, and more. Have a look; Milwaukee is going to take some time if you really want to explore it well.

Big Bay Brewing Co.

Founded: October 2010
Brewer: Jeff Garwood
Website: www.bigbaybrewing.com
Annual Production: 1,000 bbls and growing

Staple Beers:
> » Boatilla Amber Ale
> » Long Weekend IPA
> » Wavehopper Kölsch-Style Ale

Rotating Beers:
> » Summer Tide Wheat Ale

Uncharted Series:
> » Angry Molly Imperial Stout
> » Fun as Helles Imperial Maibock
> » On Deck Farmhouse Ale

Most Popular Brew: Long Weekend IPA

Brewer's Fave: Angry Molly

Where can you buy it? Distributed throughout Wisconsin.

The Beer Buzz: The idea started over a couple of beers. Sound familiar? Jeff had 23 years in the business with Miller Brewing Co. (MillerCoors) and wanted to stay in Wisconsin. He had "enough background in beer to get in trouble but at least make some darn good beers." While we count this as Milwaukee in the book so you don't miss it on a visit to Brew City, this is technically Shorewood, and Big Bay is the village's first and only brewery.

Initially, the flagship beers were brewed at Milwaukee Brewing Co.'s 2nd Street Brewery, and they operated a Shorewood taproom. Now Big Bay is brewed partly at Stevens Point Brewery under an alternating proprietorship agreement and at House of Brews in Madison as a contract brew (though Jeff spends a lot of time at House of Brews doing the brewing himself).

BRENNER BREWING CO.

Opened: 2014
Brewmaster: Mike Brenner
Address: 706 South 5th Street • Milwaukee, WI 53204
Phone: 414-465-8469
Web Site: www.brennerbrewing.com
Annual Production: 650 barrels
Number of Beers: up to 24 taps (including 4–6 guest taps)

Staple Beers:
>   » BACON BOMB RAUCHBIER
>   » CITY FOX PALE ALE
>   » STAR BABY IPA
>   » TEST BATCH 001 AMBER

Rotating Beers:
>   » ANXIOUS PORTER
>   » BUTTERFLY FART
>   » GLÜCKLICH PILS
>   » MAIDEN OPUS (a sour beer aged in cabernet barrels)
>   » WITCHCRAFT IMPERIAL STOUT

Most Popular Brew: City Fox Pale Ale

Brewmaster's Fave: Maiden Opus

Tours? Yes, scheduled $10 tours (includes a pint glass) on the website where you can make a reservation.

Samples: Yes, flights of four pours for about $8.

Best Time to Go: Open Mon and Thu 4–10PM, Fri 2–11PM, Sat 11AM–11PM, Sun 11AM–6PM.

Where can you buy it? Here on tap and in growlers to go, plus six-pack bottles and some bombers and draft accounts in distribution from Fond du Lac to Kenosha, Madison to Sheboygan, but hopes of going farther soon.

Got food? Only a short snack menu, otherwise food friendly and close to many Mexican places.

Special Offer: Buy your first Brenner beer, get one free when you get your book signed.

Directions: From I-43 heading south take Exit 311 for National Ave and go east (toward the lake) on Mineral St and turn left on 5th St. The brewery is 2.5 blocks north on the right. From downtown, 6th St takes you south to a round-about after the bridge of the river; get out of the circle at 5th St and continue 2 blocks. The brewery is on the left.

The Beer Buzz: Mike Brenner has homebrewed since the 90s, and when he decided he wanted to be part of a beer renaissance here in Milwaukee, to regain the city's former beer glory, he attended the Master Brewer program at Siebel in Chicago, finishing the program in Munich. With money from his

loans for a grad school program, he bought a $5,000 brew system to get started. He then spent a year raising money for his project, a process followed closely by expectant fans on social media.

He found this location in Walker's Point on Milwaukee's south side and now runs a 30-barrel system using city steam to power the boils. The taproom is an industrial space with high ceilings but painted white walls and abundant local art make it a bright room. A long bar and a collection of tables have lots of space, and there are TVs and a projection TV for the wall, typically reserved for games or special events. A garage door opens to the street in season.

Brewing is an art, and here at Brenner Brewing there are also art galleries. Founder/brewmaster Mike Brenner used to run an art gallery, and one of his passions is still promoting art in the community. While a 6,800 sq. ft. area of this building is dedicated to his brewery, about 20,000 sq. ft. more are home to art studios and a contemporary art gallery.

There's a lot of serendipity going on here. Mike's first brew, Maiden Opus, is a sour. A rare choice for one's first brew, no? A mechanical problem led to what could have been a wasted batch, but instead it ended up in some wine barrels and resulted in a fantastic beer. Butterfly Fart happened when wheat beer yeast was mistakenly put into a pilsner batch. When the error was discovered, orange, lemon, and lime zest, plus coriander and nutmeg were added, and the result became a popular summer beer without a style category.

Free WiFi. Facebook.com/BrennerBrewing and Twitter @BrennerBrewing

Stumbling Distance: Call this area Little Mexico: within a 1–3 block radius lie some of the city's best Mexican food: *La Fuente, Café La Paloma, Conejito's Place, Botanas*, and *Cielito Lindo*.

Urban Harvest Brewing is 3 blocks south on 5ᵗʰ and *MobCraft Beer* is 2 blocks north.

MILWAUKEE NIGHTLIFE & DRINK CULTURE INFO

For an always-changing nightlife guide and articles pertinent to the Milwaukee bar scene and drink culture in general, look for a copy of the free magazine *Milwaukee Alcoholmanac* (alcoholmanac. com). About 70 pages of articles, photos and ads about drink and food and drink in Brew City. A new issue comes out every two months. Facebook.com/Alcoholmanac

BAR ON THE RUN

Way back in the day, **Potosi Brewing** (Zone 1) used to have a bar on wheels to take around to special events. Here in Milwaukee they've put a new twist on that idea. Get on board the Pedal Tavern for the most unusual pub crawl. The mobile tavern has room for 16 (10 seats have pedals) and is often booked for groups. Choose from some pre-made routes or put together your own. Individuals can join as well during specified times for about $25 for a 2 or 2.5-hour ride. The tavern does not actually serve alcohol but gets you Happy Hour prices at each of the many pubs and breweries you will hit. The **Historic Third Ward** and **Walker's Point** are popular touring areas and home to several breweries (pedaltavern.com, 414-409-8022).

PHOTOGRAPH COURTESY OF POTOSI BREWING CO.

Company Brewing

Founded: 2015
Brewmaster: George Bregar
Address: 735 E Center Street • Milwaukee, WI 53212
Phone: 414-930-0909
Website: www.companybrewing.com
Annual Production: 250 bbls
Number of Beers: 32 taps (14 for beer, including guests)

Possible Beers:
- » Bounce House (session wheat)
- » HighLow (American pale ale)
- » Hopsided IPA
- » Lunchpauze Saison
- » Night Rye'd (rye porter)
- » Oaky Doke (white oak red ale)
- » Pomp and Pamplemousse (grapefruit IPA)
- » ... plus many others including session pale ales, saisons, belgian styles

Most Popular Brew: Pomp and Pamplemousse

Brewmaster's Fave: Lunchpauze Saison

Tours? Yes, by appointment or by chance.

Samples? Yes, 8-oz pours called "cuppers"

Best Time to Go: Open Tue–Thu 4pm–12am, Fri–Sat 4pm–2am, Sun 4pm–10pm (kitchen 5–10pm, brunch 10am–2pm). Closed Mondays. "Tappy Hour" runs weekdays from 4–6pm.

Where can you buy it? Here on tap in cuppers and pints and in growlers to go.

Got food? The menu, served 5–10 daily (and brunch on Sat–Sun from 10am), is a wee bit eclectic. Appetizers (octopus, fried pig's ear, mushroom rate, etc.), vegetarian, fish and meat dishes, and a mix of Wisconsin, pub, and healthy.

Special Offer: Get Tappy Hour pricing during your book signature visit.

The Beer Buzz: Formerly Stonefly Brewing (and Onopa Brewing Co. before that), this brewpub has new ownership. George Bregar, a home-brewer and former director of coffee for Colectivo is a resident of the neighborhood and has long wanted to open a brewpub here. Conveniently, one was already occupying the space. He did a complete makeover of the place, bringing in maple flooring from ReStore which has become maple wall covering. The bar once resided in the Schlitz Brewery tasting room. Everything they serve is on tap: the beer, wine, soda, even cocktails, thus happy hour here is referred to as Tappy Hour. George operates a 7-barrel system to keep those beer taps busy, and he doesn't want to lock himself into any particular beer or style.

Company Brewing's tagline is "Quality Nourishment," which extends to the food and the beer and their mission to foster good company—as in companionship and community not the corporation sort. This is, first and foremost, a neighborhood brewpub. Parking is on the street.

Free WiFi. Facebook.com/CompanyBrewing

Stumbling Distance: *Fuel Café* (www.fuelcafe.com, 818 E Center St, 414-374-3835) is a popular coffeehouse with sandwiches just down the street in this funky eclectic neighborhood. (They also contribute one of their brews to one of Lakefront Brewery's brews.) *Nessun Dorma* (2778 N Weil St, 414-264-8466) is a personal favorite, serving gourmet sandwiches and wine, with a nice beer selection of Belgians and microbrews. *Centro Café* (centrocaferiverwest.com, 808 E Center St, 414-455-3751) serves some really nice and reasonably priced Italian right across the street. *Milwaukee Beer Bistro* (2730 N Humboldt Blvd, 414-562-5540, milwaukeebeerbistro. com) has 13 taps and 50+ bottled/canned beers, plus a lunch, dinner, and brunch menu that is predominantly beer-infused.

THE MUSEUM OF BEER AND BREWING

Really, how is it that Milwaukee does not have a museum dedicated to beer yet? These things take time, but rest assured some people are on it. The Museum of Beer and Brewing is dedicated to preserving and displaying the proud history of beer and brewing throughout the world and especially North America. At present this museum is mostly virtual, but that does not mean you have no place to go. The museum may one day have a permanent site, but in the meantime this society organizes events (even beer and cheese pairings) and exhibits in the Milwaukee area. Check their website for what's coming up, virtual exhibits, a gift store, and some really interesting articles related to brewing history (brewingmuseum.org).

MILWAUKEE'S BEER GARDENS

Milwaukee is a bit of a German town, isn't it? Summer in Germany means beer gardens, so it's no surprise that Milwaukee follows suit. Milwaukee County Parks host the various bier gartens.

Rules are you can bring your own food and non-alcoholic beverages but there is no outside alcohol and you can't bring a grill. Often there is live music and the event is quite family friendly and typically pet friendly as well. Glassware for your beer requires a refundable deposit; you are not allowed to take them home or purchase them except where indicated.

Estabrook Park Beer Garden

The Landing at Hoyt Park

Scout Lake

Humboldt Park Beer Garden

Milwaukee County Parks Traveling Beer Garden™ as the name suggests, has no permanent home. It sets up in several locations throughout the city during a 16-week summer schedule that includes many different parks. Sprecher Brewing and Sprecher Restaurant & Pub collaborate to provide the beer, sodas, hard sodas, and German food, and seating and polka playing follows with them. (county.milwaukee.gov/Parks/BeerGardens)

EVERY PICTURE TELLS A (BREWERY) STORY

Milwaukee photographer Paul Bialas has a thing for historical breweries. His large, hard-cover books are collections of black and white shots of the Milwaukee area breweries that in some instances have fallen into ruins or been repurposed. The photos are fascinating looks at these old structures as works of art, and his first two—Schlitz, Brewing Art and Pabst, An Excavation of Art—are tributes to the past. His latest work, however, combines shots of old structures with the new ones when he takes on the city's largest brewery in Miller, Inside the High Life. Each book goes beyond the images and includes CDs containing 70 minutes of interviews and anecdotes from former employees. Find out more about Paul and his work, and order his books at lakecountryphoto.com. Contact him at pjbialas@yahoo.com.

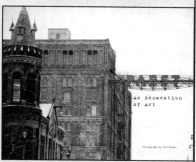

PHOTOS COURTESY OF PAUL BIALAS

District 14 Brewery & Pub (D14 Brewery)

Opened: September 2014
Brewmaster: Matt McCulloch
Address: 2273 S Howell Ave • Milwaukee, WI 53207
Phone: 414-744-0399
Web Site: www.d14beer.com
Annual Production: 400 barrels
Number of Beers: 10 on tap, plus occasional firkins

Staple Beers:
  » Chocomatic Love Machine Stout
  » Dirty Blonde
  » Local Legend Brown Ale
  » Malty McHoppinstein APA

Rotating Beers:
  » Blackr Eye Rye Pale Ale
  » Captain Trips Triple IPA
  » Cobblestone Farmhouse (brown saison)
  » La Ferme Pavée
  » 7-Grain Imperial Stout
  » 20 Franc Gold (Belgian tripel)
  » Workman's Comp Triple Saison
  » … barrel aging in planning

Most Popular Brew: Whatever's new

Brewer's Fave: "The beer I haven't had yet"

Tours? Not really, but bar stool tour/chat if he's available.

Samples: Yes, flights of 4 five-oz pours for $2–3 per glass.

Best Time to Go: Open Tue–Thu 3pm–12am, Fri 3pm–2am, Sat 12pm–2am, Sun 12pm–12am. Closed on Mondays. Happy hour runs 3–7pm. Live music on occasion.

Where can you buy it? Here on tap and in growlers to go. Limited growlers depending on supply.

Got food? Fresh made pizzas and some snacks. Also food spreads on special occasions.

Special Offer: One half-price flight of 4 beers during your signature visit.

Directions: Follow Kinnickinnic Ave (WI 32) south into Bay View and Howell splits in a V to the right. The brewery is there on the right at the split before the corner at Lincoln Ave.

The Beer Buzz: Matt started homebrewing in 2005 and was soon doing it every weekend. His father, a teacher, was a smart investor and left him some good money when he passed away. Matt looked for a way to invest it and that weekend habit gave him an idea. He didn't want to try to compete with the larger distribution breweries. One day he stopped in at Public in Kenosha and it clicked: he could do this in a corner bar space. He chose Bay View as it was up and coming, and the 20s–40s art and music loving demographic here is strong. The 1890s building, once an IGA in the '30s, needed some major renovation including bringing it up to fire code. He did all the woodwork himself, and it includes 9 varieties of hardwood. The bar top and back bar are made of basswood, the tables are of cherry. There are coat/purse hooks and outlets under the bar. The windows looking in on the brewhouse are actually old convenience store cooler doors. The boys and girls bathroom doors came from a 1922 Beloit grade school. The kayak frame you see is the last father-son project they worked on together. Matt credits his father for the financial and physical skills he needed to pull this whole thing off.

Variety is the theme here, and the tap list changes quite often. Matt brews one or two new beers each week. Current beers are posted on a chalkboard behind the bar. Local art adorns the walls and there's a dartboard. There are TVs, but they only come on for special events such as a Packers game. Parking is on the street.

ATM onsite. Facebook.com/d14beer and Twitter @District14MKE

Stumbling Distance: *Goodkind* (2457 S Wentworth Ave, 414-763-4706, goodkindbayview.com) has a nice farm to fork menu with large and small plates, an impressive tap list of 20 carefully chosen beers plus specialty bottles. *Sugar Maple* (441 E Lincoln Ave, 414-481-2393, mysugarmaple.com) has a dive bar environment and 60 craft tap selections. *Café Centraal* (2306 S Kinnickinnic Ave, 414-755-0378, cafecentraal.com) is a Euro café with related food and Belgian beers. *Burnhearts* (2599 S Logan Ave, 414-294-0490, burnhearts.tumblr.com) has 24 choice taps, a cask, great cocktails, and a crap ton of bottles/cans. *Odd Duck* (2352 S Kinnickinnic Ave, 414-763-5881, oddduckrestaurant.com) does superb, creative, shareable small plates and creative cocktails. *Guanajuato Mexican* (2317 S Howell Ave) gets raves.

Horny Goat Hideaway (Horny Goat Brewing Co.)

Founded: 2009
Brewmaster: Brian Sauer
Address: 2011 S. 1st Street • Milwaukee, WI 53207
Phone: 414-482-4628
Website: www.hornygoatbrewco.com
Number of beers: 10 on tap; 13 in distribution

Staple Beers:
» Hopped Up and Horny IPA
» Horny Blonde Lager
» Tango Delta Tangerine IPA

Rotating Beers:
» Archer Apple Brown Ale
» Black Vanilla IPA
» Brownie Porter
» Cereal Killer (Oatmeal Stout)
» Chocolate Peanut Butter Porter
» Cucumber Saison
» Dry Stout
» Hometown Wheat
» HornaCopia Pumpkin Ale
» Laka Laka Pineapple Hefe
» Monica Pale Ale
» Nutty Wishes (Nut Brown Ale)
» Oktoberfest
» One-Eye Double IPA
» Red Vixen – Red Ale
» Slim Billy
» Watermelon Wheat
» Whoa Nelly! Scotch Ale
» Zincognito Zinfandel IPA

Most Popular Brew: Hopped Up and Horny IPA

Brewmaster'sFave: Whoa Nelly! Scotch Ale

Tours? On request.

Samples? Yes, $10 for six 3-ounce beers.

Best Time to Go: Open Mon–Fri 11AM–close, Sat–Sun 10AM–close. Happy Hour is Mon–Thu from 3–6PM with drink, appetizer and other daily specials.

here can you buy it? On tap here and in growlers to go. Horny Goat cans and draft can be found in 25 states (AL, AR, Brazil, CO, GA, IL, IN, KA, KY, LA, MD, MI, MN, MO, NC, ND, NJ, NY, OH, PA, SC, SD, TN, TX, WI, WV) and Brazil.

Got food? Yes, a menu with sandwiches and burgers, Loaded Tater Tots, Hopped Up Buffalo Wings, Epic Burger (bacon added into patty), Carne Asada Tacos, Funky Chicken (Sandwich with jalapeño popper cheese), Bruschetta Pizza, Crab Cake Benedict, and Breakfast Burrito. The Friday Fish Fry was rated one of Milwaukee's best.

Special Offer: Free tap of Horny Goat with book signing.

Directions: Along I-43/94 just south from the center of Milwaukee, take Exit 312 for Becher Street heading east. Go just under a quarter mile east to First Street and go left (north). The pub is just before the river on the left.

The Beer Buzz: This building was once temporary living quarters for firemen and the pumping station which provided all the water pressure to fire hydrants in the Kinnickinnic area in the 1930s. Well, it's still a pumping station of sorts, pumping beer into your glass. Inside the bar you'll find nine big-screen TVs, a private party room, and a view of the brew system. Outdoors is just as fun with four heated sand volleyball courts, seating for up to 500, and a bar with 75 places to hunker down with a pint. By land or by sea: the bar has boat slips for you, Captain, and plenty of parking for the rest of you. Watch for Big Band Brunches on Saturdays and Sundays from 11AM–5PM.

Free WiFi. Facebook.com/hornygoathideaway and Twitter @HGBrewpub

Stumbling Distance: You are close to the heart of Bay View here: See outstanding beer bars *Roman's Pub* (www.romanspub.com, 3475 S Kinnickinnic Ave, Milwaukee, 414-481-3396) and *Sugar Maple* (mysugarmaple.com, 441 E Lincoln Ave, Milwaukee, 414-481-2393). And the quirky and awesome sharable plates eatery, *Odd Duck Restaurant* (oddduckrestaurant.com, 2352 S Kinnickinnic Ave, 414-763-5881). Visit the *Mitchell Park Domes* (524 S. Layton Blvd, 414-649-9830). These three 85-foot-high glass beehive domes showcase a variety of plants from around the world as well as a lightshow in the evenings. See floral gardens, tropical jungle, and even a bit of the desert.

CRUIZIN' FOR SOME BOOZIN'

Check out listings in the back of the book for a way to float your way around to some breweries here in Milwaukee!

LAKEFRONT BREWERY

Founded: 1987
Brewmaster: Marc "Luther" Paul
Address: 1872 N. Commerce St. • Milwaukee, WI 53212
Phone: 414-372-8800
Website: www.lakefrontbrewery.com
Annual Production: 44,000 bbls
Number of Beers: 10 year-round, 11 seasonals, and various limited releases

Staple Beers:
- » BRIDGE BURNER STRONG ALE
- » EAST SIDE DARK
- » EXTENDED PLAY IPA
- » FIXED GEAR
- » FUEL CAFÉ COFFEE STOUT (organic)
- » IPA
- » KILSCH PILSNER
- » NEW GRIST GLUTEN-FREE PILSNER (organic)
- » NEW GRIST GINGER-STYLE GLUTEN-FREE ALE (organic)
- » RIVERWEST STEIN

Rotating Beers:
- » BEER LINE ORGANIC BARLEY WINE
- » BELGIAN WHITE (organic)
- » BIG EASY IMPERIAL MAIBOCK
- » CHERRY LAGER
- » GROWING POWER (farmhouse style organic pale ale)
- » HOLIDAY SPICE LAGER
- » IBA
- » IMPERIAL PUMPKIN
- » LOCAL ACRE Lager (also a fresh-hop version)
- » OKTOBERFEST
- » PUMPKIN LAGER
- » WISCONSINITE SUMMER WEISS
- » *My Turn Series Beers* plus barrel aged versions

Most Popular Brew: Riverwest Stein (in Milwaukee), Fixed Gear (out of state), New Grist (in Canada)

Brewmaster's Fave: Bridge Burner

Tours? Every day in summer (not on Sunday otherwise), but hours vary according to day and season. Check the website! You can (should) buy tickets in advance online. Seriously, this is one of the best tours in the Midwest—Bob Freimuth was awarded best brewery guide in Milwaukee, and *Maxim* and *Tripadvisor* rate the tour as tops. Bob drinks with the guests. OK, they *all* drink with the guests. I'm partial to Brother Jim's tours. $8 includes a souvenir pint glass, four 6-oz pours. ALSO, after your tour receive a dated "Beer On Us" coupon, good for a free Lakefront beer at several places listed on the back before a certain hour that day. If tours sold out on Saturdays, you can still get a mini-tour with samples. **Homebrewers take note:** a 90-minute technical tour with pairings is on Sundays at 11AM for about $30.

Samples? Before, during, and after the tour.

Best Time to Go: Fridays for a Fish Fry, but any old time is nice. There's a dock for boats (kayaks?) in the summer and boat tours that include two other brewery tours on the river (see Booze Cruises in back).

Where can you buy it? Bottles and draft throughout Wisconsin. Nationwide in 37 states, a bit in Canada, and even Japan if you know where to look. (I do!) At Miller Park serves Lakefront in sections 112, 214, 123, 225.

Got food? Yes, serving classic Wisconsin fare daily. On Friday evenings from 4–9PM enjoy a fish fry with live polka band!

Special Offer: A Lakefront Brewery bumper sticker.

Directions: From I-43 take Hwy 145 East at 4th Street. Go east on Juneau Ave to Water St. Turn left on Water St to Pleasant St. Turn left, cross the bridge and go to Commerce St. Turn right. The brewery is on the river just before the Holton Street Bridge.

The Beer Buzz: Russ and Jim Klisch come from a long line of brewery history. Yes, their grandfather drove the street sweeper for Schlitz back in the 30s. This microbrewery, situated just under the Holton Street Viaduct, occupies the former coal-fire power plant that once gave the juice to Milwaukee's first light rail. Now the Klisch's make some juice of their own here in this historic neighborhood at the foot of Brewer's Hill. Lakefront was the first U.S. brewery brewing under its own label to be certified organic. Organic is a catchy title—and important quality—for modern times, but as Russ points out, old school brewing was organic already at a time when industrial farms and widespread chemical use didn't exist. New Grist has gained notoriety as a gluten-free beer (no wheat or barley) using sorghum and rice for grains, and the Fuel Café Stout uses Milwaukee's roasted Alterra coffee from the cool and quirky local coffeehouse from which the beer takes its name. Watch for the My Turn series, a different brew every time. Everyone in the brewery is part of your beer. These are made from start to finish by someone other than Luther. Dan the Tax/Compliance Manager made a Baltic Porter and won bronze in 2012 at the World Beer Cup.

Local Acre is brewed with Wisconsin ingredients from within 100 miles, but Wisconsinite takes it one step further. Not only are the malted barley, wheat, and hops from Wisconsin, but so is the yeast! Jeremy King of Northern Brewer Supply harvested an indigenous wild strain which was then isolated for brewing. It's known as the Lakefront strain.

For the total Wisconsin experience, don't miss the Lakefront Palm Garden's Friday Fish Fry complete with live polka band.

Stumbling Distance: You can see the old breweries—Schlitz, Pabst and Blatz—from atop Brewer's Hill. Nearby *Café Brücke* (2101 N. Prospect Ave, 414-287-2053, Tues–Sat 5–9 PM) is a German-themed mom and pop restaurant with great beer and reasonably priced eats. You can also cross the river on the Holton St Marsupial Bridge—a walkway/bike path hung under the viaduct—and get to Brady Street where you will find a whole slew of great bars including *The Nomad Pub, The Hi Hat, The BBC, Hooligan's, The Palm* and *Roman Coin. Trocadero's* (1758 N Water St, 414-272-0205, open daily) is a Euro café with year-round outdoor seating. Weekend brunch is highly regarded. Check out *The Wicked Hop* (www.thewickedhop.com, 345 N Broadway, 414-223-0345) in the Historic Third Ward—they exclusively serve Lakefront's Poison Arrow IPA. Lakefront also brews Motor Oil for the Motor Bar & Restaurant at the *Harley Davidson Museum* (harley-davidson.com, 400 W Canal St).

PABST MANSION: LIFE AS A BEER BARON

Frederick Pabst brought us a Blue Ribbon beer back in 19th century. Jacob Best opened a brewery in 1844 (four years before Wisconsin became a state) which his son Phillip took over. Pabst, a steamship captain, married Phillip's daughter Maria and invested in the brewery as well. He became president of it in 1872 before changing the brewing company's name to his own in 1889. The blue ribbon was an award from competition but it wasn't until 1899 that the beer itself became known as Pabst Blue Ribbon Beer. Over a million barrels were being brewed before the turn of the century.

A beer baron of Pabst's caliber desired some serious digs, and this Flemish Renaissance Revival mansion is a real beauty. Completed in 1892, the mansion was wired for electricity and had a state-of-the-art heating system. The good captain filled it with great artwork and spared no expense on the interiors. Pabst died in 1904, however, and his wife two years later. From 1908 to 1975 the Archdiocese of Milwaukee occupied the home, but it was sold once again. This time someone had plans for something much more beautiful and magnificent, a true tribute to the times… er, a parking ramp? Seriously?

Fortunately for all of us, Milwaukee entrepreneur John Conlin stepped in and held the house until Wisconsin Heritages, Inc. could round up the dough to keep it from the wrecking ball. It has been no small expense to save this tremendous piece of Milwaukee's history, and restorations

on the mansion continue. Much of it has been completed; however, this has been a painstaking process especially as some of the skills that went into making it are no longer readily available.

A tour of this mansion is a must on any brew visit to Milwaukee, and you can either guide yourself or join a guided tour on the hour. Reservations are required for the latter. Behind the Scenes and Private Tours are also available for about double the normal price. No photos allowed.

Open Mon–Sat 10 AM–4 PM and Sun 12–4 PM. Closed Wednesdays mid-January through February, and Easter. Special hours and prices during the holiday season. Wheelchair accessible and parking. Admission is $12 for adults ($13 from mid-Nov to mid-Jan).

2000 West Wisconsin Avenue • Milwaukee, WI 53233
www.pabstmansion.com | 414-931-0808

HISTORICAL ATTRACTION:
BEST PLACE IN MILWAUKEE!

It's not just bragging. "Best" is a big beer name in Milwaukee. Before Pabst Brewing became Pabst Brewing, it was actually the brewery of Jacob Best Sr. who founded it in 1844 (before Wisconsin became a state). Best's son Phillip and Phillip's son-in-law, the venerable Captain Frederick Pabst, made a huge success of it, and Pabst eventually took it over and gave the brewery his name. The brewery closed in 1996 but you can still find Pabst Blue Ribbon (PBR) in bars as far away as Nepal (seriously). It is the beer of choice of hipsters everywhere. And you can have one at the end of this tour in the brewery's Blue Ribbon Hall. Be sure to get your picture taken with Captain Pabst in the courtyard. The tour takes you through the story of Pabst, starting in Blue Ribbon Hall, moving on to the recently restored Great Hall and the captain's office, and ending in the Sternewirt, the guest hall.

Several Wisconsin beers are on tap in the beer hall and guest hall. Tours cost about $8 (cheaper depending on how old you are) and walk-up tours are on Monday, Wednesday & Thursday at 1 & 3PM, Friday, Saturday & Sunday at 11AM, 12 & 1PM. Private and group tours are available year round and can be scheduled any day. Be aware that weddings here are becoming increasingly popular (over 100 per year!) and can occasionally affect the tour schedule.

Best Place's gift shop doesn't just sell t-shirt, caps, and other Best Place paraphernalia; it also has an assortment of rare and collectible Pabst items from the old brewery itself as well as a number of others. This is super for collectors of breweriana. Best Place at the Historic Pabst Brewery, the former Pabst Corporate Offices and Visitor's Center is a Certified Historic Structure on the National Register of Historic Places. And there is much more going on out here. Brewhouse Inn & Suites is up the block, and a new Pabst brewery is planned for the old church around the corner.

Directions: To get there from I-43 (if heading north) take the exit for WI-145. Keep right at the fork following signs for WI-145/ McKinley Ave and merge onto WI-145. At N 6th Street go right and take the first right onto W Juneau Ave. Turn slightly right onto Winnebago for a half a block. Turn left at N 8th Street. Take the first right onto W Juneau Ave. If you're coming from the north though, take exit 72E for Highland Ave/11th St. Turn left at W Highland Ave. Turn left on N 8th St and take the first left onto W Juneau Ave. Or just type the address into your GPS maybe. Whew.

Best Place at the Historic Pabst Brewery
901 W. Juneau Avenue | Milwaukee, WI 53233
www.bestplacemilwaukee.com | 414-630-1609

Combine a tour here with a visit to the Pabst Mansion for a discounted price! Call 414-779-1663.

MILLER BREWING CO. (MILLERCOORS)

Founded: 1855
Brewmaster: David Ryder
Address: 4251 W State Street • Milwaukee, WI 53208
Phone: 414-931-2337
Website: www.millercoors.com or www.shopmillerbrewing.com
Annual Production: 7.4 million bbls here; 60.5 million worldwide

Staple Beers brewed here:
  » COORS LIGHT
  » MILLER GENUINE DRAFT
  » MILLER HIGH LIFE
  » MILLER LITE
  » LEINENKUGEL'S SUMMER SHANDY and seasonals
  » REDD'S APPLE ALE

Most Popular Brew: Miller Lite

Tours? Free hour-long tours of the historic Miller Caves, Miller Inn, and the plant floor typically Mon–Sat from 10:30–3:30 on the half hour. Open Sundays Memorial Day through Labor Day. Call 800-944-LITE for daily updates or visit them on Facebook.

Samples? 2–3 samples at the end of the tour which vary by MillerCoors brand each day.

Best Time to Go: Monday–Friday. Saturday can be busy and they don't take reservations.

Where can you buy it? Where *can't* you buy it? World famous!

Got food? Pretzels in the Miller Inn.

Special Offer: The girl in the Moon Gift Shop, located at 4251 W. State Street, will offer 10% off any one item of your choice. Offer excludes sale or clearance merchandise. Please mention promo code: Beer Guide.

Directions: From I-94 west take Hwy 41 north to the State Street/Vliet Street exit. Turn right (south) on 46th Street, then left (east) on State Street. Go a half block east on State and the Visitor Center is on your right (south).

The Beer Buzz: Frederick J. Miller settled in Milwaukee in 1855 with a special brewer's yeast and an ambition to brew "confoundedly good beers." The story begins when Miller emigrated from Germany to Milwaukee and bought Plank Road Brewery (built by Charles Best). The beer was immediately popular, and he was soon selling well beyond Milwaukee. You can still see a brewhouse he built on State Street with "F. Miller" and "1886" visible at the top. He passed the brewery to his sons in 1888 and they built the Miller Inn, the Refrigeration building, and the Stables. The oldest part of the Milwaukee Brewery is the storage caves, built in the 1850s by the Best brothers and later expanded by Frederick Miller to keep beer cold through the sometimes-hot Wisconsin summers; they are still on the tour route today. Beer drinkers had their first taste of High Life on December 30, 1903, and soon it picked up the moniker "Champagne of Bottled Beer." (Later shortened to Champagne of Beers after 1967.) The brewery survived Prohibition making

near beer, soda, and malt syrup, and modernized as soon as it was repealed. After World War II, Frederick C. Miller, a grandson of the founder, worked to make it the fifth largest American brewery. Miller died after a plane crash in 1954 (see the Caves photo), and the presidency of the brewery left the Miller family for the first time. Philip Morris bought it in 1970. Miller Lite was introduced in 1975, starting a whole new trend toward light beers which—along with a series of popular "Great taste … less filling" celebrity ads—helped make Miller the second largest brewer in the United States. In 1988 Miller acquired Jacob Leinenkugel Brewing of Chippewa Falls, Wisconsin, but has continued to run it as an independent operation. In 2002, Miller Brewing was bought by South African Breweries and became part of SAB Miller, one of the largest brewers in the world. In 2008, SAB Miller and Molson Coors entered into a joint venture to combine the U.S. and Puerto Rico operations of Miller Brewing Company and Coors Brewing Company and form a high-potential new brewing company with a unique foundation of famous beer brands—including Blue Moon Belgian White, Cripsin ciders, Italy's Peroni Nastro

Azzurro and the Czech Republic's Pilsner Urquell. MillerCoors is one of Wisconsin's largest employers, with more than 1,300 employees and a payroll of nearly $175 million in the state. In 2014, state and local taxes paid totaled $83 million and the company purchased $700 million in goods and services from 1,600 Wisconsin-based companies. To this day, Miller beers are brewed with the same yeast strain Frederick carried with him from Germany.

Legend Has It: The iconic Miller High Life Girl in the Moon—one of the oldest advertising symbols in the U.S.—dates to 1907, when it was trademarked by Miller ad director A.C. Paul. The story is Paul was hunting alone in northern Wisconsin and became lost in the woods, spent the night there, and had a vision of a woman perched on the moon. Despite many stories and myths, the model for the Miller Girl in the Moon is unknown. Stories claim that she was a granddaughter of Miller founder Frederick J. Miller, and different Miller family branches claim that their grandmother or great-grandmother was the model.

Facebook.com/millerbrewerytour

Stumbling Distance: Head over to *Miller Park* to watch the Milwaukee Brewers play some ball. During the holidays, take a drive down to the Plank Road Brewery to see the awesome light show set to music. You may have seen something similar in one of their commercials. For a killer bar burger, you can't miss *Sobelman's Pub & Grill* (milwaukeesbestburgers.com, 1900 W Saint Paul Ave, 414-931-1919).

MILLER PHOTOGRAPHS COURTESY OF PAUL BIALAS.

MILLER CAVES

Built by Charles Best, these caves are all that remains of the original Plank Road Brewery, which Miller founder Frederick J. Miller took over in 1855. The 44-inch thick walls are made of brick and limestone, and the caves made a great cool place for fermentation, aging, and storing beer. Ice blocks cut from frozen lakes and hauled by horses kept them cool in winter and sawdust and hay insulated them in summer. The caves went back 600 feet and could hold as many as 12,000 barrels. Brewery president Frederick C. Miller created a tour program in 1952 and made a caves museum. The gas lighting was replaced by electricity and the displays were added. The museum officially opened in October 1953, and Milwaukee's famous pianist Liberace was part of the dedication ceremony.

The photo, taken on December 17, 1954, is of one of the famous "Cave Dinners" and shows Frederick C. Miller having lunch with other members of the Wisconsin State Brewers Association. Later that same day Miller was fatally injured in a plane crash at Mitchell Field in Milwaukee. Also killed were his son Frederick C. Miller, Jr. and the two pilots, Joseph and Paul Laird. That was the last cave dinner until a fundraiser for the Museum of Beer and Brewing revived the tradition. Today, the Caves are on the official Miller consumer tour route and are still used for special events, including dinners and concerts.

PHOTOGRAPH COURTESY OF MILLER BREWING

Milwaukee Ale House

Founded: 1997
Brewmaster: Robert Morton
Address: 233 N Water Street • Milwaukee 53202
Phone: 414-276-2337
Website: www.ale-house.com
Annual Production: 1,400 bbls
Number of Beers: 12 on tap: 9 regular, at least 3 rotating styles all the time

Staple Beers:

- » Booyah Apricot Saison
- » Hop Freak Double IPA
- » Hop Happy IPA
- » Litta Bitta Session IPA
- » Louie's Demise Amber Ale
- » O-GII Imperial Wit
- » Outboard Cream Ale
- » Polish Moon Milk Stout
- » Pull Chain Pale Ale (APA)
- » Sheepshead Stout
- » Ulao Belgian Wit

Rotating Beers: (see The Beer Buzz)

Most Popular Brew: Louie's Demise Ale

Brewmaster's Fave: Booyah

Tours? No, but it is one of two stops for the Brew City Queen (see Booze Cruises).

Samples? Yes, four 5-oz samples for $7 or six for $9.

Best Time to Go: Open daily at 11AM. Happy hour specials Mon–Fri (and another on Thu night from 9–close!), trivia night on Wednesday, Karaoke on Thursday, live music on Fri–Sat at 9:30PM.

Where can you buy it? Growlers at the bar plus six-packs in cans and bottles throughout Wisconsin, Chicago, the Twin Cities and Fargo. Plus various draft accounts.

Got food? Yes, a hand-crafted, fresh menu with suggested beer pairings. Weekly food specials allow Chef Grant to

experiment with incorporating seasonal brews into the dining experience. A classic Wisconsin Fish Fry is featured on Fridays.

Special Offer: $2 off MKE Brewing beers 4–7PM during your signature visit.

The Beer Buzz: Welcome to the Historic Third Ward of downtown Milwaukee. Once a warehouse and manufacturing district, the Third Ward is now a thriving arts and entertainment neighborhood of renovated brick and timber buildings. This particular structure dates from the late 1880s when it was a saddlery; the old beer wagons used to come here to service horses and repair wagons. Jak Pak Co. bought the building in the 1940s, and it became the first manufacturer to mass-produce hula hoops. By the mid-70s, the building was empty, and so it sat until someone had an idea.

Jim McCabe, an electrical engineer by trade, saw the potential of the old district and felt the city needed a local brew and entertainment venue. The Milwaukee Ale House became one of the first to move into the neighborhood just as the idea of reviving it took off. The City's Riverwalk runs directly behind the brewpub, so there's outside seating and a few boat slips as well. Schooners actually used to dock here to get fitted for sails before sailing back into Lake Michigan. The beer names have good stories—ask your bartender. The beer here has been so successful that the same group of beer nuts running the show at this location opened a second, larger brewery over on 2nd Street: Milwaukee Brewing Co. (see separate listing). Up in Grafton you can find another *Ale House* (1208 13th Ave, Grafton, 262-375-2337) serving the beers brewed here in Milwaukee. Live music is common, and the bar has a couple of pours coming from beer engines.

Not only is this Milwaukee Brewing Co.'s birthplace, but it is also the testing grounds for any new or experimental beers. Test batches, seasonals, and cask-conditioned brews come and go, and a number of guest taps are curated by the brewers as well.

Free Wifi. Facebook.com/milwalehouse and Twitter @alehouse

Stumbling Distance: Six blocks from here on the shore of Lake Michigan Santiago Calatrava's architectural masterpiece, the *Quadracci Pavilion* at the *Milwaukee Art Museum* (www.mam.org, 414-224-3200). The museum has a sizeable collection including many works by Wisconsin-born Georgia O'Keeffe. Even if art doesn't do it for you, do not miss the Quadracci opening and closing its "sails" at 10, 12, and closing time. The world's largest music festival is the 11-day *Summerfest* also on the water's

edge right next to the museum. The event features eleven stages with the best music in a variety of genres—just a 5-block walk from here. The pub sponsors several charitable events throughout the year including *Louie's Last Regatta* for Children's Hospital of Wisconsin and *Mid-Winter Brew Fest* for the MACC Fund usually in February. Check out *The Wicked Hop* (www.thewickedhop.com, 345 N Broadway, 414-223-0345) for some fine beer selections and the *Milwaukee Public Market* (milwaukeepublicmarket. org, 400 N Water St) for an assortment of local vendors selling eats, deli items and cheese, candies, wines, beers, even fresh seafood.

GATEWAY TO WISCONSIN I

From late April/early May through October, the *Lake Express* (www.lake-express.com, 866-914-1010), a comfortable, high-speed passenger and car ferry, makes two (three from July to September) round-trip crossings of Lake Michigan between Muskegon, Michiga,n and Milwaukee. The trip takes 2.5 hours and comes into Milwaukee just south of where the Summerfest grounds are. Take the I-794 overpass heading south and the first exit (Exit 3) takes you down to the port area.

MILWAUKEE BREWING COMPANY 2ND STREET BREWERY

Founded: 2007
Brewmaster: Robert Morton
Address: 613 South 2nd Street • Milwaukee, WI 53204
Phone: 414-226-2337
Website: www.mkebrewing.com
Annual Production: 12,000 bbls and growing
Number of Beers: 14+ beers

Staple Beers:
» BOOYAH APRICOT SAISON
» HOP HAPPY IPA
» LITTA BITTA BELGIAN WIT
» LOUIE'S DEMISE AMBER ALE
» OUTBOARD CREAM ALE
» POLISH MOON MILK STOUT

Rotating Beers:

Seasonal "Timed Release" series:
» "ADMIRAL" STACHE
» BLACK IRON
» HOPTOBERFEST
» INCREASE WHEAT
» SASQUASH
» WEEKEND @ LOUIE'S (with Rishi's Organic Blueberry Rooibus and Hibiscus teas)

Herb-In Legend Series (16-oz cans):
» HOP FREAK DOUBLE IPA
» O-GII

Destination Local (750ml bottles):
» ANTI MATTER
» DARK MATTER
» DOPPELVISION
» LOUIE'S RESSURECTION (4-pack bottles)
» RECOMBOBULATION
» WALK OFF TRIPEL

Most Popular Brew: Louie's Demise Ale

Brewmaster's Fave: Booyah

Tours? Yes, $10 gets you the tour, a pint glass, a free beer token for elsewhere and beer samples. Tours are scheduled (see website) on Fridays and Saturdays plus there's a 5–7PM Open House on Saturdays with casual samplings. Check the website for schedule and make reservations, however, walk-ins are also welcome.

Samples? Yes, can't have a tour without samples.

Best Time to Go: Other than stopping by to buy beer to go, the public visits are limited to the tour times.

Where can you buy it? There's beer to go here Mon–Thu 4–6PM, Fri 3–8PM and Sat noon–7PM. Distributed throughout Wisconsin, the Chicagoland area, the Twin Cities and Fargo.

Got food? Nope.

Special Offer: A highly prized trinket when you get your book signed.

The Beer Buzz: Just a few blocks south of sister brewhouse Milwaukee Ale House, this brewing facility opened in 2007 to meet a higher demand for the three staple beers heading to market in cans and bottles. Equipment includes an in-house lab from Pabst, grain handling equipment from a caffeine plant in Milwaukee, and water tanks from Texas. Ain't it funny how beer just brings things together? Housed in what used to be a produce company, the facility offers the brewers an opportunity to bottle a boatload of beer and go far beyond Metro Milwaukee.

The beer names typically have some kind of story. For Booyah, you'd need to head to the Green Bay area where Walloon immigrant culture brought this throw-everything-in sort of soup. Polish Moon, however, is right down the block at the former Allen-Bradley building: a lighted, four-face clocktower that's bigger than Big Ben. Overlooking what was once the Polish neighborhood, the clock shone down on workers on their way to their jobs in the wee hours.

The brewers are concerned about being environmentally friendly. The cans are actually more efficient and less wasteful than glass bottles. They have a grant for some solar panels for water-heating purposes, and they make their own biodiesel from used fryer oil which sometimes runs the boilers. In 2013, the brewery was accepted into the Wisconsin DNR's Green Tier Program because of their sustainable practices. By the way, the MKE you see on the packaging is the airport code for Milwaukee's airport, General Mitchell International Airport.

Facebook.com/milwaukeebrewing and Twitter @MKEbrewco

Stumbling Distance: Go here first, get the tour, and then stumble back to *Milwaukee Ale House* to lean over a pint and further contemplate what you've learned today. *Hinterland Erie Street Gastropub* (222 East Erie Street, 414-727-9300) offers some very nice dining of the gourmet type and gets its beer from its own brewery up in Green Bay. For an incredible locally-sourced dinner, make reservations for *Braise* (braiselocalfood.com, 1101 S. 2nd St, 414-212-8843) which practices Restaurant Supported Agriculture, and serves gourmet dishes from a menu that constantly changes based on what's available. Arguably the best eco-foodie experience in Milwaukee. Get fresh cheese curds across the street at *Clock Shadow Creamery* (clockshadowcreamery.com, 138 W Bruce, 414-273-9711) and fresh ice cream at *Purple Door* (purpledooricecream.com, 138 W Bruce, 414-231-3979) in the same room!

PABST REPURPOSED: BREWHOUSE INN & SUITES

What could be a better beer experience than to go to Milwaukee for all the brewery visits and then spend the night in an historic brewery?? For years the massive brick buildings of the old Pabst Brewery have stood vacant, a sad reminder of the decline of Milwaukee's brewing in the late 20th century. But forget that—we are in the new Golden Age of Beer here in the Brew City with so many fine brewers and more breweries in planning. Development projects amid the old Pabst site have brought us the very cool Best Place in the former hospitality center and offices. Up the block from there, where the big Pabst sign still crosses high over the street, you can stay the night in the former brew house.

The $19 million redevelopment of the late 1800s buildings has brought Milwaukee a uniquely beerstoric hotel property. Called the **Brewhouse Inn & Suites**, the 90-room hotel offers studios as well as one- and two-bedroom accommodations for extended stays. You can still see the original copper brew kettles all polished up like they were still in operation. A large, stained-glass window featuring a picture of the legendary beer icon King Gambrinus has also been preserved. Winding staircases, a mezzanine-area skylight, and some beer themes in six of the suites create an atmosphere one wouldn't have imagined. Three of the suites have balcony views of downtown. An outdoor patio offers gas grills and terrace seating. In the old mill house is a pub-style restaurant which will soon also have its own outdoor beer garden.

Also within the complex is a **Jackson's Blue Ribbon Pub** (1203 N 10th St, 414-276-7271, jacksonsbrp.com) which serves American bistro fare and keeps a long tap list of great beers.

The **Pabst Brewery** has been given a second life. Book a stay here for your next pils-grimage to Milwaukee!

1215 N. 10th Street, Milwaukee | 414-810-3350
brewhousesuites.com | Facebook.com/BrewhouseInnSuites

PABST IS BACK?

In July of 2015 it was announced that Pabst, the legendary Milwaukee Brewery that closed in 1996, was coming back to Milwaukee. While the brewery shut its doors, Pabst had continued as a corporation, buying up labels of beers—many of them old favorites such as Schlitz, etc.—and keeping them on the shelves in your local liquor store. All of this was done through contract brewing with other companies. As the corporate offices moved around a bit—Texas, Chicago, California—impassioned fans in Milwaukee wanted that beer back in Brew Town. (Oddly enough, the Miller Brewery here in Milwaukee was, in fact, brewing Pabst here and still is.)

Then the news broke. Pabst had purchased the 1871 First German Methodist Church that still stands within the former brewery complex. In fact, this is the second time Pabst has bought this property. In 1898 they acquired and repurposed it to serve as an employee restaurant and lounge (the Forst Keller), which became best known for its Friday fish fry. Naturally.

The abandoned brewhouse has already been repurposed as a hotel, Brewhouse Inn & Suites, and the hospitality center and corporate offices are now open to the public as Best Place, a gift shop, event hall, bar, and fascinating tour.

The new Pabst brewhouse will have a 10,000-barrel capacity, with a likely production of perhaps 2,000 barrels per year to start. While they won't be brewing the iconic Pabst Blue Ribbon, the production here will include tinkering with pre-Prohibition beer recipes and old-time favorites such as Old Tankards Ale, Kloster, and Andecker, to name a few. New brands are also possible.

The first floor will function as a brewery and tasting room. Right through the center of the church beneath the high ceilings will run an open bar and the stained glass windows will spill their light on either side. The second floor will be a restaurant/bar developed by Mike Eitel (notable restaurateur of Café Hollander and The Nomad World Pub fame).

International award-winning D.I.R.T. Studios, which developed nearby Zilber Park (next to Brewhouse Inn), are designing a preservation park west of Best Place incorporating historic memorabilia. A beer garden behind the church will feature a wall with signatures of former brewery workers. Over 10 years ago, as the entire Brewery Complex stood vacant and decaying, no one could have imagined the impressive rebirth here plus the return of Pabst.

MobCraft Beer

Founded: 2013 (Taproom open Jan/Feb 2016)
Brewmaster: Andrew Gierczak
Address: 505 South 5th Street • Milwaukee, WI 53204
Phone: _____
beer@mobcraftbeer.com
Web Site: www.mobcraftbeer.com
Annual Production: 3,600 barrels
Number of Beers: 12–15 on tap (some guest taps); 20+ beers per year

Staple Beers:
   » Batshit Crazy (coffee brown ale)
   » Hop Gose the Grapefruit (grapefruit gose/IPA hybrid)
   » Yard Beer (American adjunct lager)

Past Winner Beers:
   » Aloha Danke Shön (cocoa, coconut and coffee witbier)
   » Vanilla Wafer Porter
   » Wheat Men Can't Jump (wheat IPA)
Monthly crowd-sourced batches, and a new sour beer every other month

Most Popular Brew: The monthly crowd-sourced brew.

Samples: Yes, sample flights available.

Best Time to Go: Open Tue–Sun 11am–12am, subject to change.

Where can you buy it? Growlers, cans, bombers, kegs to go. Distribution throughout Wisconsin and northern Illinois at select places, plus they can ship to 42 states.

Got food? Yes, a pizzeria inside the brewery.

Tours? Yes, by chance or by appointment. Watch the website for a future schedule.

Special Offer: A free pint of MobCraft beer during your signature visit.

Directions: From I-43 heading south take Exit 311 for National Ave and go east (toward the lake) on Mineral St and turn left on 5th St. The brewery is on the left just before the big roundabout. From downtown, 6th St takes you south to this roundabout; get out of the circle at 5th St and the brewery is right there at the corner.

The Beer Buzz: What if you could suggest some crazy beer ideas and someone would make it? This is how MobCraft first got everyone's attention: Crowd-sourcing brews. Brewer Andrew studied fermentation science at University of Wisconsin-Madison, and has brewed for Leinie's and made ethanol at an ethanol plant. His twin brother Tony went to college with co-founders Henry Schwartz and Giotto Troia and taught them how to homebrew. Andrew came over to help often, and they decided to look at the possibilities of opening a brewpub. For a bunch of young guys, that idea looked awful expensive, so they went back to the drawing board. How could they get something going without a lot of investment, and how could they do something different? Crowd sourcing. Followers on the web and in social media would propose some often wacky beer ideas, the public would vote, and MobCraft would come up with a recipe for the winning suggestion. This caught on fast. They brewed under an alternating proprietorship arrangement with Madison's House of Brews and started filling draft accounts and selling bombers. They added cans in the summer of 2015, but their space at HOB was getting cramped. They settled on this Milwaukee location (leaving Madisonians heartbroken) and brought in a 30-barrel brewhouse from Quality Tank Solutions (manufactured in Marshfield, WI). A separate 2,000 sq ft room houses oak barrels and foeders for their sour beer production.

This old brick and cinder block building originally housed a metal manufacturing outfit but had functioned as an indoor parking lot for the last several years. The 2,000 sq ft taproom has a bar of reclaimed wood, a stage for live music, windows into the brewhouse and the sour room, and three garage doors that open to outside seating in seasonable weather. Parking is on the street.

Don't go thinking all their beers are suited to adventurous palates. Even the crazy concoctions may be more subtle than you expect, and that Yard Beer is as approachable as anything. To the amusement of Packers fans, MobCraft collaborated with Green Bay's Badger State Brewing to produce Dubbel Czech, a double blonde that plays on Quarterback Aaron Rodgers' discount double-check State Farm insurance commercials.

Free WiFi. Facebook.com/MobCraftBeer and Twitter @MobCraftBeer

Stumbling Distance: *Conejito's Place* (539 W Virginia St, 414-278-9106, conejitos-place.com) is right behind them, serving cheap and popular Mexican fare on paper plates. *The Iron Horse Hotel* (500 W Florida St, 888-543-4766, theironhorsehotel.com) is an awesome biker-themed boutique hotel with a great patio bar. *Great Lakes Distillery* (616 W Virginia St, 414-431-8683, greatlakesdistillery.com) makes small-batch gin, whiskey, rum, vodka, absinthe and more, and does tours, tastings and events. Open daily.

Brenner Brewing is 2 blocks south on 5th and *Urban Harvest Brewing* is 5.

Rock Bottom Restaurant & Brewery

Founded: March 1997
Brewmaster: David Bass
Address: 740 N Plankinton Avenue • Milwaukee, WI 53203
Phone: 414-276-3030
Website: www.rockbottom.com/milwaukee
Annual Production: 1,100 bbls
Number of Beers: 11 on tap, 40 per year

Staple Beers:
- » Heartland Wheat (a rotating wheat line)
- » Hop Bomb IPA
- » Liquid sun light lager
- » Naughty Scot Scotch Ale
- » Specialty Dark (rotation, anything brown or darker)

Rotating Beers:
- » Alt
- » Baltic Porter
- » Belgian Dubbel and Tripel
- » Bock
- » Dark Lager
- » Dunkelweizen
- » Imperial Stout
- » Kölsch
- » MaiBock
- » Octoberfest
- » Pale Ales
- » Pilsner
- » Porter
- » Red Ale
- » Cask-conditioned ales and many more

Most Popular Brew: Liquid Sun

Brewmaster's Fave: Pilsner

Tours? Yes, ask your server. Groups should make appointments. Saturdays are best, especially in summer.

Samples? Yes, six 4-oz beers for about $6.

Best Time to Go: Open from 11 AM. Summer opens the great patio on the river with an outdoor bar. Happy hour runs Mon–Fri 3–6.

Where can you buy it? Here on tap and to go in growlers.

Got food? Yes, and some menu items are paired with particular beers. The BBQ ribs have stout in the sauce, the chili has beer in it, and the ballpark pretzel is brushed with ale.

Special Offer: Free sampler when you get your book signed.

The Beer Buzz: Rock Bottom originated in Denver, Colorado, and in twenty years has come to open 34 other locations including this one in an old bank building on the river in downtown Milwaukee. Despite being part of a larger chain, the brewpub does brew on premises and mills its own grain. The main floor offers a full menu restaurant and a bar that backs up against the brewhouse under glass. You can still see the old vault downstairs where there is another bar with a more casual bar atmosphere. The best place to hang—at least in nice weather—is outside on the terrace. An outside bar serves you as you watch the river go by.

Listen for the hostess answering the phone: "Hello, you've hit Rock Bottom." The name comes from the original brewpub which was on the ground floor of the Prudential building in Denver. Remember the insurance ads? "Get a piece of the rock." Am I dating myself here?

David started like many as a homebrewer. It's one thing to brew in your basement, but quite another to nail a gold medal at the Great American Beer Festival as he did with 106 Pilsner in 2009. Rock Bottom is one block from the Milwaukee Trolley route and reachable by boat/kayak on the Milwaukee River. Become a Rock Rewards member (membership is free) and receive great deals, email news, and invitations to special events.

Stumbling Distance: This is close to the *Bradley Center* (where the Bucks play). You are also a block or two from *Riverside* and *Pabst* theaters. This is a good place to head after a concert or performance. Actually, you're really not far from anything here. *Water Street Brewery* is close, as is *Milwaukee Ale House*. Or *Grand Avenue Mall*. Or the *Milwaukee Public Museum* or *Milwaukee Performing Arts Center* or… well, you get the picture. In summer, check out the live music of *River Rhythms* on Wednesdays in Pierre Marquette Park three blocks north. *Cathedral Square Jazz in the Park* is every Thursday and three blocks east. Right across the river is a commemorative *statue of the Fonz* from the classic TV show Happy Days (set in Milwaukee). The famous *Safe House* (779 N Front St, 414-2712-007, safe-house.com), a spy-themed bar, is also near the Fonz. Be sure to find out the password.

Sprecher Brewing Co.

Founded: 1985
Brewmaster: Randy Sprecher
Address: 701 West Glendale Avenue • Glendale, WI 53209
Phone: 414-964-2739
Website: www.sprecherbrewery.com
Annual Production: 22,000 bbls
Number of Beers: 20 beers/10 sodas on tap; 20+ beers (plus 4 Chameleon beers, 3 hard products)

Staple Beers:

- » Abbey Triple (Premium Reserve)
- » Black Bavarian
- » Hefe Weiss
- » IPA^2 (Premium Reserve)
- » Pipers Scotch Ale (Premium Reserve)
- » Pub Ale (non-bitter, English-style, deep brown)
- » Russian Imperial Stout (Premium Reserve)
- » Special Amber (lager)
- » Stout

Chameleon Beers:

- » Firelight
- » Hop on Top
- » Ryediculous
- » Witty
- » Also: Hard Root Beer, Hard Ginger Beer, Hard Apple Pie

Rotating Beers:

- » Dopple Bock (Premium Reserve)
- » Generation Porter (with Dutch cocoa and raspberry)
- » Mai Bock (dry hopped)
- » Oktoberfest
- » Summer Pils
- » Winter Brew (Munich bock)

Series Beers: All American Pale Ale, Hooligan, Hopfuzion, Redhead Ale, Wisconsin Pale Lager

Watch for bourbon-barrel-aged brews and Limited Releases

Most Popular Brew: Special Amber, Black Bavarian

Brewmaster's Fave: Mai Bock

Tours? Yes, but reservations are highly recommended (414-964-2739) as some tours fill up fast. The tour is kid friendly (they make sodas too) and prices are adults $5, seniors $4, minors $3, and military free. Tours start weekdays at 3; Sat and Sun from noon to 4:20. Friday, Saturdays and Sundays have *Reserve Tastings* for $20 which bring out the premier and limited edition brews and pair them with artisanal cheeses. Check the website for tour additions and updates.

Samples? Yes, four 7-oz beers, unlimited soda, and a commemorative tasting glass.

Best Time to Go: Anytime is good. Watch for special events.

Where can you buy it? Here on tap and bottled, of course, and in area taverns, stores, and restaurants. Distribution is heaviest regionally. The beer sells as far east as Massachusetts, as far west as California and south to Florida. Much of the Midwest especially around Wisconsin has it too.

Got food? Yes, pizza, large soft pretzels, Nueske's landjaeger sausage (locally made since 1933!), and cheese curds.

Special Offer: A Sprecher trinket of some sort.

Directions: Just off of I-43 heading north from Milwaukee, one street south of the 77A exit.

The Beer Buzz: After returning from military service in Germany, Randy Sprecher could not find (or afford) the kind of flavorful beer he enjoyed in Augsburg. Frustrated, he decided to build his own brewery and worked toward that goal. After completing a special studies program in fermentation science at UC-Davis, Sprecher became a brewing supervisor at Pabst Brewing Company in Milwaukee in the early 1980s. When Pabst downsized, he established Sprecher brewery—the first craft brewery in Milwaukee since Prohibition—in 1985, with $40,000 in capital, a gas-fired brew kettle and repurposed used equipment. Randy Sprecher first brewed Black Bavarian in 1969, and as a signature beer, it has earned accolades from beer critics in *Men's Journal*, *Beer Advocate Magazine* and the *Washington Times*. Most recently it won the 2014 World Beer Cup Gold Medal (Scharzbier), and I must say it's my favorite Sprecher brew. Among other notable awards, Sprecher Brewery won the 2004 GABF Small Brewery of the Year and Small Brewery Brewmaster of the Year. In the last few years, Sprecher introduced some low-alcohol "hard" products, starting with a hard version of their famous root beer, followed by Hard Ginger Beer and Hard Apple Pie.

As a company Sprecher believes it is important to have a positive effect on the local economy and has been dedicated to using locally produced ingredients as much as possible—cherries from Door County, cranberries from the area, ginseng from around Wausau, honey from Germantown.

The tour reveals some Bavarian murals in the bottling room and the tasting room is designed to look like a bier garten. Up to 20 beers and 9 sodas are on tap to sample. Stop in the gift shop on your way out. Sprecher is active on social media—follow them and you'll know about upcoming events and beer releases. Don't forget about their whole other line up with **Chameleon** beers (which are also on tap in the tasting room).

Stumbling Distance: Just a block away is the best butter burger you will ever have at *Solly's* (414-332-8808, 4629 N Port Washington Rd), a family-run joint since 1936. Homemade pie and a fish fry. (Say, that rhymes.) Celebs know about it too, and there is a plate for regular customer and long-time voice of Milwaukee Brewers baseball, Bob Uecker. Sprecher sodas are on tap. Less than 10 minutes east is *Draft and Vessel* (4417 N Oakland Ave, 414-533-5599, draftandvessel.com), offering 16 rotating taps for sampling, drinking, or growler filling. Various snacks and large bottles also for sale.

CHAMELEON BREWING

If you're searching for this new Wisconsin brewery, the trail will lead you right to the front doors of Sprecher. Brewed by the same folks who do your Black Bavarian, Chameleon is sort of set apart from the other Sprecher products, intended to appeal to another market, a younger one and drinkers who prefer lighter session beers. These are less traditionally European than the Sprecher line and aiming to stand out as simply Wisconsin craft ales. Chameleon beers are created and brewed by Sprecher's brewmaster, and they're high-quality, winning awards at Los Angeles International Commercial Beer Competition—Gold for Hop on Top, Bronze for Ryediculous IPA—and a Gold for Witty from the Beverage Tasting Institute. (chameleonbrewing.com)

SPRECHER AND BEER GARDENS

Each summer the Milwaukee County Park System operates Sprecher's two Traveling Beer Gardens™. Throughout the summer the Traveling Beer Gardens™ stop in different parks for 12 days where they serve Sprecher beers, sodas and hard products from renovated fire trucks. Light snacks and pizzas are available from a concessions trailer; Sprecher's Restaurant & Pub serves Usinger's brats as well. Opening day at each stop, beer and soda are free while they last. Schedules for times and locations are at sprecherbrewery.com or the park system's website (county.milwaukee.gov/Parks/BeerGardens).

PHOTOGRAPH COURTESY OF ANNE SPRECHER

10TH STREET BREWERY

Founded: 1996
Brewmaster: Dan Pierson
Address: 1515 North 10th Street • Milwaukee, WI 53205
Website: www.leinie.com
Annual Production: 45,000+ barrels (estimate)
Number of Beers: varies

Beers:
- » BIG EDDY'S CHERRY DOPPELSCHWARZ
- » BIG EDDY'S RUSSIAN IMPERIAL STOUT
- » BIG EDDY'S ROYAL NEKTAR
- » BIG EDDY'S UBER-OKTOBERFEST
- » LEINENKUGEL'S IPL

Tours? Not open to the public!

Special Offer: Not participating.

The Beer Buzz: Not everyone knows this brewery is even here. Passing by on Interstate 43 one could easily mistake the big Leinie's banner as a mere billboard. But this is the 10th Street Brewery, or the "Tiny Leinie" if you prefer. It's not actually so tiny when you consider the 45,000 barrels it produces each year. Built in 1986, G. Heileman's Brewing used it to produce Blatz beer, one of the old brands it had purchased. Leinenkugel's Chippewa Falls brewery needed help keeping up with demand, so in 1996 they purchased this place and started brewing here as well. While supplementing production of Leinenkugel's year-round and seasonal beers, 10th Street is also home to Big Eddy. No, that's not the hefty security guard at the gate, it's Leinie's own line of craft brews, named for the spring next to which the original Chippewa Falls brewery was built. Each year you can expect to see new Big Eddy beers. Veteran brewer Dan Pierson is 10th Street's brewmaster.

Urban Harvest Brewing Co.

Opening: November, 2015
Brewmaster: Steve Pribek
Address: 1024 South 5th Street • Milwaukee, WI 53204
Phone: _____
Web Site: www.urbanharvestbrewing.com
Annual Production: 100–150 barrels
Number of Beers: up to 12 taps

Staple Beers:
  » 414 Golden Ale
  » Ach Ya Der Hey-fe Weizen
  » Black Puppy Pale Ale
  » Corkscrew IPA
  » Espresso Amber
  » Falls Pilsner
  » H.C. IPA
  » Nookie Nookie (pale ale)
  » Oktoberfest
  » Old Towne Amber
  » PriBock
  » Who the Helles Alice?

Image Courtesy of Urban Harvest

Rotating Beers:
  » Big Ring Bourbon Red
  » Blood Orange Wheat
  » Bourbon Barrel Brown
  » Cascade IPA
  » Chocolate Whiskey Stout
  » Corkscrew Double IPA
  » Festive Gourds
  » Imperial Blood Orange Wheat
  » Pumpkin Ale
  » Maple Brown
  » Weizenbock
  » Wicket Summer Wheat

Most Popular Brew: Too soon to tell.

Brewmaster's Fave: Espresso Amber or Corkscrew IPA

Tours? Yes.

Samples: Yes, sample flights available.

Best Time to Go: Open Wed–Thu 4–10PM, Fri–Sat 2–11PM, for starters. Check the website to be sure.

Where can you buy it? Here on tap and to go in growlers.

Got food? No, but food friendly and area menus available.

Special Offer: Your first pint of their house beer free when you get your book signed.

Directions: From I-43 heading south take Exit 311 for National Ave and go east (toward the lake) on Mineral St and turn right on 5th St. The brewery is on the left. From downtown, 6th St takes you south to this roundabout; get out of the circle at 5th St and continue 5 blocks south and the brewery is on the left.

The Beer Buzz: You may have seen Brewer Steve around at some Milwaukee area beer festivals serving his beer. In 2013 he brewed under the name Mill Street Bierhaus, and it looked like at any moment they were going to open a brick and mortar place for us to visit. The plans were frustrated by a series of sites and leases falling through, sometimes even at the last minute, and to further complicate things, Mill Street Brewery in Toronto wasn't too keen on their name. That's all water under the Water Street Bridge. Steve is back with a new brewery name and sweet location near a couple other breweries. "Things happen for a reason," he says. He found a nondescript place in Walker's Point on Craigslist, got in touch

---

RIDE THE TROLLEY!

Milwaukee has a $1 trolley that takes about 40 minutes to make a full loop of some of the best places in downtown. Milwaukee Ale House and Water Street Brewery are on the route, while Rock Bottom and some great beer bars—The Wicked Hop, for example—are just a block off. Other stops include the Milwaukee Art Museum, the Historic Third Ward, Old World Third Street, Discovery World and the Amtrak station. The trolley passes every 20 minutes and runs from late May or early June to early September, Wed–Sat 11AM–9PM. A downloadable map is online. Check the Milwaukee Downtown web site at milwaukeedowntown.com or call 414-562-RIDE.

with the landlord, signed a lease, and was suddenly moving forward again, no hassles.

This is a three-story Cream City brick building with wood floors, previously occupied by a theater company. It came with a 54-seat theater. The 4,000 sq ft on the first floor is divided between brewing space and a taproom with a bar and tables. Rather than a typical tap system, they use 2 chest freezers (keezers) with a wood collar for the taps. Windows along the front let in a lot of light. His 2-barrel system is visible on the first floor, and the fermentation vessels and a walk-in cooler are in the basement.

Steve has been brewing since 1999. He always had the brewery idea in mind (no restaurant), but knowing the brewpub was the thing to do at the time, he didn't pursue it. Then Greg York of *Rustic Road Brewing* did a presentation for the Milwaukee Beer Barons and put the nano-brewery idea in his head. Greg told him if one doesn't do it now, it's not going to happen. The nano concept is to go in with lower costs and do unique batches in smaller amounts to get yourself up and running before taking on big ideas. Expect numerous creative and unique seasonals and limited releases.

Free WiFi. Mug Club. Facebook/Urban-Harvest-Brewing-Company

Stumbling Distance: *Crazy Water* (839 S 2nd St, 414-645-2606, crazy-waterrestaurant.com) is an upscale fusion sort of bistro set in an old tavern. *Botanas* (816 S 5th St, 414-672-3755, botanasrestaurant.com) serves casual Mexican fare. *Brenner Brewing* is 3 blocks north and *MobCraft Beer* is 5.

CREAM PUFFS AND CRAFT BEER

The Wisconsin State Fair is perhaps best known for its Original Cream Puff, which has been served there since 1924. The number eaten each year is creeping up on a half million. This being Wisconsin, of course, we have to bring beer into this mix. The Micro is an open-air pavilion serving beer from Wisconsin breweries (16 in 2015). Beer education events, pairings, some cheese and sausage plates, and even a keg killer t-shirt giveaway for those who finish a barrel are part of the fun. Flight School is a separate bar within, serving beer flights of select beers/styles. The Micro even has its own app and FB page (Facebook.com/themicrofair). The state fair runs 11 days in early August. (640 S 84th St, West Allis, 800-884-FAIR, wistatefair.com)

Water Street Brewery

Founded: 1987
Brewmaster: George Bluvas III
Address: 1101 N Water Street • Milwaukee, WI 53202
Phone: 414-272-1195
Website: www.waterstreetbrewery.com
Annual Production: 600 bbls
Number of Beers: 8–9 on tap

Staple Beers:

- » Bavarian Weiss
- » Honey Lager Light
- » Old World Oktoberfest
- » Punch You in the Eye PA
- » Raspberry Weiss
- » Victory Amber

Rotating Beers:

- » Belgian Wit
- » Black IPA
- » Black Lager (Schwarzbier)
- » Doppelbock
- » Imperial Stout
- » Irish Stout
- » Saison
- » … and many more!

Most Popular Brew: Honey Lager Light/Oktoberfest

Brewmaster's Fave: Pale Ale

Tours? Yes, but by appointment.

Samples? Yes, $8 gets you seven to nine 4-oz beers.

Best Time to Go: This place hops a bit more at night and is popular with the twenty-something and university crowd. It gets busy around lunch and dinner.

Where can you buy it? Growlers and tap accounts at sister restaurants: Louise's, Trinity, Harp, Black Rose, Solo Pizza—all in Milwaukee, plus the Water Street locations in Delafield, Oak Creek and Grafton.

Got food? A full menu. Scotch eggs, beer-marinated Usinger bratwurst are total Wisconsin, the rest ranges from sandwiches to pasta, steak and seafood. A little upscale.

Special Offer: Not participating.

The Beer Buzz: Owner R.C. Schmidt wanted to start something that paid a little homage to his German heritage. That'd be beer, of course, and when he opened Water Street there weren't any brewpubs in the state and less than 100 in the whole country. The building itself dates to 1890 and is one of the first commercial structures in the city to have electricity. It had served various purposes over the years—grocery store, floral warehouse, apartments. When it was renovated, efforts were made to keep the stamped tin ceiling and Cream City brick. The project was one of the first in a renaissance of a rundown neighborhood that is now quite trendy. The dining is great and the ambience classy but social—don't expect pool tables or live music. The breweriana collection here is amazing and the Schlitz reverse-glass corner sign is a true rarity. The collection includes 6,000 cans on display, tap handles, coasters, serving trays and neon signs and can be seen at all three brewpub locations.

George started brewing when he was 17 years old because "the government wouldn't let me buy it, but I could get ingredients." A friend first showed him how to make wine out of apple juice. Later he worked under great brewmasters at Lakefront and Water Street (where he started working in 1999). Now he does quadruple duty here and at Water Street Lake Country out in Delafield as well as Water Street in Grafton and Oak Creek.

Stumbling Distance: *Uber Tap Room and Cheese Bar* (1048 N 3rd St, 414-272-3544, ubertaproom.com)—the name says it all—36 on tap and paired with that other thing Wisconsin is famous for. *Milwaukee Public Museum* (www.mpm.edu, 800 W Wells St, 414-278-2728) is in walking distance from here and home to an IMAX theatre. *The Pabst Theater* (www.pabsttheater.org, 144 E Wells St, 800-511-1552) is just a great place to see a concert and also just down the street. After a show, the crowd often comes to Water Street. The 1883 *Historic Turner Restaurant* (1034 N. 4th St, 414-276-4844) offers more great dining in a historical setting. This is one of the best Friday fish fries in town and Water Street beer is on tap. Looking for other brewpubs nearby? Check out the Milwaukee Trolley.

WATER STREET OAK CREEK BREWERY

Opened: 2015
Brewmaster: George Bluvas III
Address: 140 West Town Square Way • Oak Creek, WI 53154
Phone: 414-301-5290
Website: www.waterstreetbrewery.com
Annual Production: 800 bbls
Number of Beers: 8–9 on tap

Staple Beers:
- » BAVARIAN WEISS
- » HONEY LAGER LIGHT
- » OLD WORLD OKTOBERFEST
- » PUNCH YOU IN THE EYE PA
- » RASPBERRY WEISS
- » VICTORY AMBER

Rotating Beers:
- » BELGIAN WIT
- » BLACK IPA
- » BLACK LAGER (Schwarzbier)
- » DOPPELBOCK
- » IMPERIAL STOUT
- » IRISH STOUT
- » SAISON
- » … and many more!

Most Popular Brew: Honey Lager Light/Oktoberfest

Brewmaster's Fave: Pale Ale

Tours? Yes, but by appointment.

Samples? Yes, $8 gets you seven to nine 4-oz beers.

Best Time to Go: Open daily at 11AM and popular for weekend brunches 10AM to 3PM.

Where can you buy it? Growlers on site and tap accounts at sister restaurants: Louise's, Trinity, Harp, Black Rose, Solo Pizza—all in Milwaukee, and Water Street Lake Country in Delafield and Water Street's Grafton location.

Got food? A full menu. Scotch eggs, beer-marinated Usinger bratwurst are total Wisconsin, the rest ranges from sandwiches to pasta, steak and seafood.

Special Offer: Not participating.

Directions: From I-94 take Exit 322 and go east on WI 100/Ryan Rd for 1.6 miles. Turn left on Shepard Ave, go 0.6 mile, and turn left on Centennial Dr. After 0.2 mile, turn right on Village Green Ct and left on Town Square Ct.

The Beer Buzz: Water Street, one of the oldest brewpubs in Milwaukee expanded first to Delafield, then to Grafton with a third location, and now here in Oak Creek. The beers remain the same as Brewmaster George does quadruple duty here and in the other locations.

The restaurant, like the other Water Street locations, has breweriana on the walls, but a huge collection in this case. The main dining area offers booth and table seating. Like in Delafield and Grafton, there is a small brew system tucked inside. There is additional seating in another room.

SWEET MULLETS BREWING CO.

Founded: March 2012
Brewmaster: Josh Kueffer
Address: N58W39800 Industrial Road, Ste D, Oconomowoc, WI 53066
Phone: 262-456-2843
Website: www.sweetmulletsbrewing.com
Annual Production: 600 bbls
Number of Beers: 14 on tap, 30 throughout the year

Staple Beers:
- » 505 EXPORT STOUT
- » RYE BOB

Rotating Beers:
- » THE CAPTAIN PILSNER
- » DARK MATTER
- » 501 RED ALE
- » JORGE JALAPEÑO ALE
- » MECO HEFEWEIZEN (with ginger)
- » OISHI (sour beer aged in oak barrels with Japanese spices)
- » WILD-HOPPED BUCKWHEAT
- » Several sour stouts: DARKNESS, TOIL AND TROUBLE

Most Popular Brew: Jorge Jalapeño Ale or Dark Matter

Brewmaster's Fave: Wild-hopped Buckwheat

Tours? Yes, by appointment.

Samples: Yes, a flight of six 5-oz beers for about $14

Best Time to Go: Open Mon, Wed–Thu 4–10ish, Fri 4–11ish, Sat 12–11ish, Sun 12–10ish. Double check hours on the website.

Where can you buy it? Here on tap and in growlers to go, and a few draft accounts.

Got food? Yes, a menu designed around the beers and revamped in summer 2015.

Special Offer: A free pint of house beer when you get your book signed.

Directions: Coming into Oconomowoc from the west side on Highway 16, take a right (south) on Division Street into an industrial park. Go left on Industrial Road and the brewery is on your left.

The Beer Buzz: Like many famous brewers, original founder Mark Duchow got his start in Milwaukee. He was washing kegs in 1992 at Water Street Brewery and worked his way up to head brewer. George, who's brewmaster there now, was his assistant. He put some time in at Gray's in Janesville, then opened a brewery called Flatlanders in Illinois. Then Oconomowoc Brewery. Then on to Mount Horeb Brewery. When that became The Grumpy Troll, he went to Iowa City, then quit for a while before he got the itch again and did some work in Texas and North Carolina. In 2006, Mark went back to The Grumpy Troll until he decided it was time to move back to Oconomowoc, where Mark grew up and opened this brewpub. New partners joined him in ownership in 2015, and Mark's assistant Josh took over as head brewer while Mark set off on another project.

The beers have won awards over the years, including a bronze at the World Beer Cup in 2010 for the stout, and a silver for Rye Bob that same year. Sour beers are big here.

Stumbling Distance: Many people talk up what a great community theater Oconomowoc has. Check out *Theatre on Main's* website for a schedule of events and get some tickets for before/after a brewpub visit. (www.theatreonmain.org, 25 S Main St, 262-560-0564). *The Crafty Cow* (153 E Wisconsin Ave, 262-354-8070, craftycowwi.com) is a local craft beer bar with a pub menu. For a great selection of craft beers, stop in at *Sonoma Cellars* (1290 Summit Ave, 262-567-7500, www.sonoma-cellars. com). Their original location is in Delavan (1807 East Geneva St, Delavan, 262-740-2200), not far from *Geneva Lake Brewing*. The website offers a blog with reviews and new arrivals.

St. Francis Brewery & Restaurant

Founded: 2009

Brewmaster: Scott Hettig

Address: 3825 South Kinnickinnic Avenue • St Francis, WI 53235

Phone: 414-744-4448

Website: www.stfrancisbrewery.com

Annual Production: 450 bbls

Number of Beers: 7–10 on tap

Staple Beers:
- » Envy – IPA
- » Greed – Session IPA
- » Lust – Weissbier
- » Sloth – Brown Ale
- » Wrath – Amber Ale
- » Kitzinger Kölsch
- » (also hand-crafted sodas including 49 Maples Root Beer, Cherry, Orange Cream, Vanilla Caramel and Cherry Cola)

Rotating Beers:
- » Gluttony – Rotating Seasonal
- » Pride – Rotating Seasonal
- » Monthly cask-conditioned ales

Tours? By appointment, $5 includes two samples.

Samples? Yes, a sample platter goes for $8.

Best Time to Go: Open Mon–Thu 11AM–10PM, Fri–Sat 11AM–11PM, Sun 10AM–9PM.

Where can you buy it? On tap here and in growlers to go. Distributed in 6-pack bottles throughout Wisconsin. Watch for their summer beer garden at Humboldt Park.

Got food? Yes, a full pub menu with sandwiches, soups, and salads. Fridays host fish fries. Beer is worked into a couple of dishes including the ale-braised beef, stout BBQ sauce on some ribs, a Kölsch-marinated bratwurst and the classic beer cheese soup.

Special Offer: A free can koozie or key chain bottle opener while supplies last.

Directions: Take I-794 to Howard Ave and go east toward the lake just a short distance to Kinnickinnic Ave and you can see the pub on your left.

The Beer Buzz: You can't miss this place at the corner of a busy intersection: a grain silo stands in the middle of its outdoor seating area. The newly built 7200 sq-foot-building has a long bar, plenty of dining (and banquet) space and that breezy terrace in the sun. Parking is off street and easy. Regulars can join a mug club for discounts and special offers. St. Francis is a nice little community just south of Milwaukee and this is its first brewery.

Scott is a native Wisconsinite—born in Milwaukee, raised in Slinger— who started by homebrewing for 10 years or so, before he grew unhappy with his day job. The classic turn-a-hobby-into-a-career. He interned at Rock Bottom Restaurant and Brewery in Milwaukee and then was a full-time assistant brewer for nine months at two of Rock Bottom's locations out in Cleveland. When this position opened, he headed back to Wisconsin. In December 2011 he had the opportunity to take a sabbatical and spent about 7 months helping out a brewer in southwestern Germany. The brewery began bottling in 2013 and updated their beer menu to the Seven Deadly Sins theme. In conjunction with Milwaukee County Parks, the brewery operates a cash-only summer beer garden in Humboldt Park (ATM onsite).

Facebook.com/SaintFrancisBrewery

Stumbling Distance: Just north of here on Kinnickinnic (or K K as locals call it) are two of the best beer bars in the Milwaukee area: *Roman's Pub* (www.romanspub.com, 3475 S Kinnickinnic Ave, Milwaukee, 414-481-3396) and *Sugar Maple* (mysugarmaple.com, 441 E Lincoln Ave, Milwaukee, 414-481-2393).

Fixture Brewing Co.

Founded: December 21, 2012
Brewmaster: Steve Fix
Address: 716 Clinton Street • Waukesha, WI 53186
Phone: 262-446-0770
Web Site: www.fixturebrewing.com

Staple Beers:
  » Fox River Red
  » 1906 Forward Pass
  » The Sha-Shank Stout
  » Totem Bourbon Ale
  » Walk a Shame Apple Ale
  » Wizard Weissbier

Rotating Beers:
  » Belgian Saison
  » Black IPA

Tours? Yes, by chance or by appointment.

Samples: Yes.

Best Time to Go: Open 5pm–close Tue–Sat. Live music on weekends, and trivia night on Tuesdays.

Where can you buy it? Here on tap and in growlers to go.

Got food? No, but food friendly.

Special Offer: Not participating.

Directions: From I-94, take Exit 295 and turn left on Redford Blvd. Drive 1.9 miles and follow the slight right as the road becomes North St. Go 1.1 miles, turn left on Madison St, and 800 feet later, turn right on Clinton St. The brewery is on the right.

The Beer Buzz: Originally, Steve had been looking to open a live music venue and brewery in Milwaukee's Bay View neighborhood, and even had a property picked out. The amount of renovation and repairs the space required didn't make for a winning situation,

so he took over what was Totem Bowl out in Waukesha. (You can still see a bowling ball on the building façade.) He had previously managed Main Stage bar in Waukesha, so running a music venue is right up his, um, alley, and this place immediately became known for live performance. This is also Waukesha's first brewpub. (Fox Head and Weber Waukesha Breweries were the last of the city's breweries and closed in 1962.)

Expect live music on Friday and Saturday nights, some sports on the TVs from time to time, trivia on Tuesdays, and a laidback vibe.

Facebook/fixturebrewingcompany and Twitter @fixturebrewing

Stumbling Distance: *Jimmy's Grotto* (314 E Main St, 262-542-1500, jimmysgrotto.com) serves pizza and more but is known for their "deep-fried pizza," what they call Ponza Rotta. Waukesha was also the hometown of guitar legend **Les Paul**, and the *Waukesha County Museum* (101 W Main St, 262-521-2859, waukeshacountymuseum.org) will reopen sometime in 2016 with their exhibit dedicated to him. Phone first!

Big Head Brewing Co.

Opened: September 2013
Head Brewer: Rich Gross
Address: 6204 West State Street • Wauwatosa, WI 53213
Phone: 414-257-9782
Web Site: www.bigheadbrewingco.com
Annual Production: 300 barrels
Number of Beers: 7 on tap

Staple Beers:
» Big Head Blonde
» Big Head IPA
» SMaSH (single malt, single hop ale)

Rotating Beers:
» Various specialty, experimental and seasonal brews

Most Popular Brew: Big Head IPA

Tours? Yes, by chance or by appointment.

Samples: Yes, flights of seven 4-oz pours for about $10.

Best Time to Go: Open Wed–Fri 4–10PM, Sat 1–11PM. Happy hour runs 4–6PM Wed–Fri. Closed on Sun–Tue.

Where can you buy it? Here on tap and in growlers to go.

Got food? Free popcorn. Snacks and jerky, frozen pizzas. Food friendly, so carry in what you want.

Special Offer: $1 off your first Big Head beer when you get your book signed.

Directions: From I-94, take Exit 307A toward 68th/70th St. Turn north on 68th St and go 1.1 miles. Turn right on State St and go 0.4 mile. Turn left on 62nd St and the brewery is in the brick building on your left, despite what the street address might suggest about State St.

The Beer Buzz: Andrew Dillard, whose self-proclaimed oversized noggin this brewery was named for, founded this place with homebrewing partners Pat Modl and Pat Fisher in 2013 in hopes of making diabetic-friendly beer. However, Andrew's day job transferred him, and that never happened. Brewer Rich took over as head brewer.

Wauwatosa's first (and still only) brewery, Big Head is located in a 5,000 sq ft cinder block construction warehouse. Inside the front door is a taproom with a small bar—actually a small counter hanging from chains. A chalkboard on the wall lists the brews on tap. A couple coolers bear pictures of The Fonz and Richie from *Happy Days* on the doors: Real Cool and Cool. Mismatched tables and chairs are arranged about the room, and the tap room spreads through a garage door into the next room where you can find the brewhouse and the restrooms. For your drinking entertainment, they have shuffleboard, darts, pinball, cornhole, and even beer pong. There's an old piano, and they host live music most Wednesdays and Fridays.

Free WiFi. Growler Club. Find them on Facebook and Twitter @bigheadbrewery

Stumbling Distance: Go west on State Street into the heart of Wauwatosa ('Tosa, as the locals say) and you'll pass *Leff's Lucky Town*, (7208 W State St, 414-258-9886) for burgers, beer and sports TV; *Café Hollander* (7677 W State St, 414-475-6771) for Euro gastropub fare, a big beer list heavy on Belgian imports; *Café Bavaria* (7700 Harwood Ave, 414-271-7700) for German cuisine and beer, and several other eateries in between. *Meritage* (5921 W Vliet St, Milwaukee, 414-479-0620, meritage. us) serves creative American bistro fare with local, seasonal ingredients and a good wine list and nice craft beers. Best liquor store in town is *The Malt Shoppe* (813 N. Mayfair Rd, 414-585-0321, maltshoppetosa.com) with Certified Cicerone Beer Servers, a huge selection of beers, and 30 taps for growler fills.

A GALLERY OF GROWLERS

Ray's Growler Gallery & Wine Bar (8930 W North Ave, Milwaukee, 414-258-9521, raysgrowlergallery.com) is part of Ray's Liquor, an excellent place to find your favorite craft beers and more. The store is open all week, but the tasting room upstairs opens Wed–Sun and offers tap takeovers, educational events, and, of course, growler fills during its more limited hours. "Every single beer that we tap into at Ray's Growler Gallery will either be a beer made exclusively for the Gallery, a rare brewery-only release, or a special selection that will not be available anywhere in bottle." Convinced yet? They also serve by the glass.

RIVERSIDE BREWERY & RESTAURANT

Founded: October 2005
Brewmaster: Chris George
Address: 255 S Main Street • West Bend, WI 53095
Phone: 262-334-2739
Website: www.riversidebreweryandrestaurant.com
Annual Production: 240 bbls
Number of Beers: 8 on tap, 27 or so per year

Staple Beers:
>> BENT RIVER BERRY WEISS
>> DIZZY BLONDE WEISS
>> MAIN STREET AMBER ALE

Rotating Beers: *(2 or 3 Brewer's Choices)*
>> BEE HOME SOON HONEY ALE
>> BROKEN OAK ABBEY DUBBEL ALE
>> CLEV'S AGED OLD WORLD OKTOBERFEST
>> FEELIN' LUCKY IRISH STOUT
>> IMPERIAL PALE ALE
>> IRON TRAIL PALE ALE
>> LUNA NEGRA ESPRESSO STOUT
>> MUGGLES' FUGGLES ESB
>> RASPBERRY FRUIT WEISS
>> SCATHING WIT

Most Popular Brew: Main Street Amber Ale

Brewmaster's Fave: "I will not pick a favorite from among my children."

Tours? Yes, available some Fridays, best by appointment. Call the brewery!

Samples? Yes, seven 4-oz mugs for about $8.95.

Best Time to Go: Happy hour is 3–5 ($1 off hours beers), Friday night fish fry. In warm weather, go for the outside seating. Live music in the bar on Saturday nights. Be sure to join the Mug Club for some good deals.

Where can you buy it? Only here on tap or in growlers to go.

Got food? Yes, a wide selection in fact. Beer-battered cheese curds and mushrooms, beer cheese soup, excellent ribs, steaks, seafood, top-notch sandwiches, and the fish fry offers cod, walleye, lake perch, and shrimp.

Special Offer: A free pint.

Directions: Follow Hwy 33 through town to the west side of the river and take Main St south through a traffic circle. Riverside will be down the street on your left past the Walnut St intersection.

The Beer Buzz: The brewpub is just south of the quaint downtown and its collection of historic buildings and shops in a Cream City brick building on the river. This used to be a vacuum cleaner store but has since been totally remodeled in a sort of 1920s décor with breweriana and photos of pre-Prohibition scenes on the walls. (The place received a local award for interior design.) Outdoor dining has two options: the sidewalk along the street and the terrace along the river. Owner Wayne Kainz was the manager of another restaurant, and when he and his wife, Dana, decided to open their own place, the downtown association brought him the brewpub idea. Riverside Brewery and Restaurant has that hometown restaurant appeal, and quality food served with great beer is never a bad thing. It's a good place to meet up with friends or family and has a touch of class.

Stumbling Distance: The downtown is a nice collection of little shops in historic buildings and walking distance from the pub. If walking's your thing, the path along the river is nice enough and features a series of sculptures. *Dublin's* (110 Wisconsin Ave, 262-338-1195, dublinswi.com) occupies an old Victorian house, serves fine food and has 40 fine beers on tap. The *Museum of Wisconsin Art* (wisconsinart.org, 205 Veterans Ave, 262-334-9638) showcases Wisconsin artists only with permanent and temporary exhibitions. Are you ready for a Wisconsin-style safari? *Shalom Wildlife Sanctuary* (shalomwildlife.com, 1901 Shalom Drive, 262-338-1310, $8/person) gives a two-hour guided wagon ride through 100 acres full of bison, elk and deer. Shalom Dr is five miles north of town off Hwy 144. Be sure to call for a reservation.

841 BREWHOUSE

Founded: 2015
Head Brewer: Mark Strelow
Address: 841 East Milwaukee Street • Whitewater, WI 53190
Phone: 262-473-8000
Website: www.841brewhouse.net
Annual Production: 200 bbls
Number of Beers: 12 taps; 4 house beers, plus guest taps

Staple Beers:
  » AMBER LAGER
  » WHEAT ALE

Rotating Beers:
  » RYE ALE

Most Popular Brew: Wheat

Brewer's Fave: Wheat

Tours? No, but you might meet the brewer by chance.

Samples? Yes, four 3-oz glasses for about $5.

Best Time to Go: When you're thirsty. Funhunters gets a good lunch crowd. Dining room closes at 9PM. Closed Mondays!

Where can you buy it? Here on tap and in growlers to go.

Got food? Yes, a full bar and full menu, including a Friday fish fry (cod, walleye) and prime rib on Fri/Sat. Here's something unusual: hand-dipped, battered *Colby* cheese curds (not cheddar).

Special Offer: Your first pint of 841 Beer for $2 during your signature visit.

Directions: Business Hwy 12 is Milwaukee St. If you come in on Hwy 59 from the north or south, it passes the pub on Milwaukee as well.

The Beer Buzz: On the east side of town, this supper club draws 'em in for the food as well as the microbrews. Since 1972, there has been a restaurant on this site. Randy Cruse got a brew kit for Christmas and ended up bringing craft beer to Whitewater at his restaurant Randy's Funhunters, and in 2015, he passed the torch. Randy sold the business to Jim Burns who has long had success with Ray's Family Restaurant over in Edgerton. His son Lucas Burns manages here. They remodeled the interior but have kept the beer on. Randy guided Mark in the beginning before passing the reins to him as head brewer.

The restaurant is a bit brighter and more modern than before. A long wood bar meets you as you walk in. Booths and tables are off in the dining room, and there's outside seating as well. The brewhouse is visible through windows in the back corner. Nine TVs spread throughout make this a good place to catch a game.

Free WiFi. ATM onsite. Facebook.com/841Brewhouse

Stumbling Distance: Nightlife in Whitewater is downtown where the college-aged patrons hang out. *Casual Joe's* (319 W James St, 262-458-4751, casualjoes.com) has great local BBQ from the chef behind the fine dining restaurant *The Black Sheep*. The town is also the southern end of the Kettle Moraine Scenic Drive. Starting at Cty H/Hwy 12, a 115-mile stretch meanders north through the natural beauty left behind by the glaciers of the last Ice Age. Whitewater Lake is popular with boaters. *Frosty's Frozen Custard* (535 E Milwaukee St, 262-473-2320) is just down the road and offers some great frozen delights.

SECOND SALEM BREWING CO.

Opened: 2014
Head Brewer: Christ Christon
Address: 111 West Whitewater Street • Whitewater, WI 53190
Phone: 262-473-2920
Web Site: www.secondsalem.com
Annual Production: 175 barrels
Number of Beers: 12 on tap; up to 11 house beers plus a guest tap

Staple Beers:
» THE BEAST OF BRAY ROAD AMBER ALE
» BONE ORCHARD IPA
» OLD MAIN GOLDEN ALE (OMG)
» THE REAPER (AMERICAN PALE WHEAT)
» SECOND SALEM PORTER
» WITCHTOWER PALE ALE

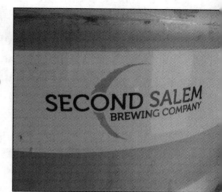

Rotating Beers:
» CHRISTMAS SPICED ALE
» FULL SLEEVE IBA
» WILD MAN OF LA GRANGE HEFEWEIZEN

Area 53 (190) Series: (limited small batches)
» COFFEE PORTER, SAISON, ETC.

Most Popular Brew: Old Main Golden Ale

Brewer's Fave: He's a seasonal drinker, but likes his IPAs

Tours? By chance or by appointment. It's a small system.

Samples: Yes, flights of four for about $5.

Best Time to Go: Open Mon–Fri 11AM–close, Sat–Sun 10AM–close. Happy hour Mon–Fri 3–6PM.

Where can you buy it? Here on tap and to go in growlers, and some 22-oz bombers to come in the immediate area and perhaps select stores in Madison or Milwaukee.

Got food? Yes, a full menu with appetizers, soup/salad, sandwiches/burgers, and a few entrees. Watch for daily specials and a Friday fish fry that includes walleye.

Special Offer: Buy your first house beer, get the second one free during your signature visit.

Directions: From US 12 crossing south of Whitewater, go north on Janesville St 0.8 mile, and turn right on Whitewater St. Go 0.5 mile and it is on the right.

The Beer Buzz: Second Salem is an old nickname for Whitewater. As you look at all the beer names and imagery you get the impression this might be a Halloween theme, but the truth is Whitewater earned that nickname for a rich local folklore that involves everything from ghosts and witches to werewolves. Bone Orchard IPA is named for the three cemeteries in town.

Speaking of history, this building dates back to the nineteenth century, its past lives including time as a blacksmith's, leather shoe factory, Model T assembly line, and a furniture store. Brewer Christ's father ran a restaurant up front, but in 2010, Christ took over and converted the back section to a craft beer bar called Lakefront Pub. His goal was to add brewing one day. He and Thayer Coburn talked about the idea but were missing something critical: a brewer. A year later, Karl Brown, a history professor with some brewing experience, took a teaching job at University of Wisconsin-Whitewater and became the last piece of the puzzle. They put a one-barrel system up front and soon started serving house beers. Brewer Karl got the ball rolling and left it to Christ who in turn brought in a couple of assistant brewers to help him keep up with demand. A bit of

contract brewing at House of Brews in Madison soon became necessary, and now they are in the hopes of expanding their system.

The taproom moved up front where there are tall and regular tables and a long bar, plus a couple of TVs. You can also shoot pool or play darts. Midway back in the building is a lounge space with couches. That former backroom bar opens for overflow, and there's a patio behind the building overlooking the lake beyond the railroad tracks. A painting of Nicholas Klinger's Brewery, an 1864 brewing company that would become Whitewater Brewery in the early 1900s, hangs on the wall in back. That brewery closed in 1942.

Posters on the walls and their corresponding beer labels offer some very cool artwork designed by graphic artist Sarah Hedlund. The Area 53 beers (a play on Area 51 and the 53190 zip code) are small test batches that go on tap to see how patrons like them. The popular ones may become regular beers.

Free WiFi. ATM onsite. Facebook/SecondSalemBrewing and Twitter @secondsalem

Stumbling Distance: *The Sweet Spot* (226 W Whitewater St, 262-473-5080, sweetspotwhitewater.com) serves baked goods, breakfast and lunch items and has two locations: this coffee shop and the bakehouse (1185 W Main Street). *The Black Sheep* (210 W Whitewater St, 262-458-4751, EatAtBlackSheep.com) offers farm-to-table fine dining.

ZONE 3

Black River Falls: Sand Creek Brewing Co.
Bloomer: Bloomer Brewing Co.
Chippewa Falls: Brewster Bros. Brewing Co.
Chippewa Falls: Jacob Leinenkugel Brewing Co.
Dallas: Valkyrie Brewery
Eau Claire: The Brewing Projekt
Eau Claire: K Point Brewing
Eau Claire: Lazy Monk Brewery
Eau Claire: Norsky Northwoods Brewpub
Ellsworth: Common Man Brewing
Hudson: Pitchfork Brewing
La Crosse: City Brewery
La Crosse: Pearl Street Brewery
La Crosse: Turtle Stack Brewery
Menomonie: Lucette Brewing Co.
Menomonie: Real Deal Brewing
New Richmond: Barley John's Brewing
New Richmond: Brady's Brewhouse
River Falls: Rush River Brewing Co.
Somerset: Oliphant Brewing Co.
Spring Valley: Mines Creek Brewing
Wilson: Dave's BrewFarm

Sand Creek Brewing Co.

Founded: 1999
Brewmaster: Todd Krueger
Address: 320 Pierce Street • Black River Falls, WI 54615
Phone: 715-284-7553
Website: www.sandcreekbrewing.com
Annual Production: 9,000+ bbls
Number of Beers: 14–16 each year

Staple Beers:
- » APA (hand-drawn tattoo on label by local tattoo artist Jimmy Fingers)
- » Badger Porter
- » English-style Special Ale
- » Oscar's Chocolate Oatmeal Stout
- » Sand Creek Hard Lemonade
- » Wild Ride IPA
- » Woody's Easy Ale (low hop, low abv session ale)

Rotating Beers:
- » Black Currant Ale
- » Cranberry Special Ale (fall)
- » Double Oscar's Oatmeal Stout (also on nitro)
- » Frank's Double IPA
- » Groovy Brew (Kölsch, summer)
- » Imperial Porter
- » Oderbolz Bock
- » Oktoberfest (a.k.a. Black River Red)
- » Rye Doppelbock
- » Three Stooges hard lemonades

Most Popular Brew: Oscar's Chocolate Oatmeal Stout

Brewmaster's Fave: Depends on season/mood/hangover (or Oscar's).

Tours? Yes, Fridays 3–5PM year round. From May–Sept also Saturdays noon–4PM.

Samples? Yes, freebies and sample trays for about $8 with eight 5-ounce beers and a special reserve beer.

Best Time to Go: Taproom open Mon–Fri 8AM–5PM for growler fills or bottle sales only. *Karner Blue Butterfly Festival* in July, when 500 people tour the brewery that day or *Sand Creek Brewery Oktoberfest*, the first Saturday in October right in a huge tent with crafts and music all day and night. Watch for live music events.

Where can you buy it? Pints here plus growlers, bottles, cases, pub kegs, ¼ and ½ barrels. Throughout Wisconsin, parts of Minnesota, Iowa and Illinois (mostly Chicago area).

Got food? No, but on Friday nights you can bring in something to pass— they always seem to find something. Food trucks come in once a month (whenever there's live music).

Special Offer: A free pint and a hearty handshake and/or pat on the back.

The Beer Buzz: The brewing force is strong in this one! Beer has been happening here since 1856 when Ulrich Oderbolz opened his brewery on this very same site. It was sold and renamed Badgerland Brewery but went beer belly up in 1920. (Yep, Prohibition!) Then all hell broke loose here: turkeys, land mines, Coca Cola, and finally just storage, until 1996 when Jim and Dave Hellman remodeled the brick building and started Pioneer Brewing Co. In 1998, they acquired Wisconsin Brewing Co. from Wauwatosa and moved those brews to Black River Falls. Meanwhile, out on a farm near Downing, WI, Cory Schroeder and Jim Wiesender turned a farm shed into a brewery (talk about retro) and a semi-trailer into a beer cooler. Pudding tanks for mash kettles? If the tank fits... Thus was born Sand Creek Brewing Co., and in 2004 they bought Pioneer and left the farm. Original Pioneer Brewmaster Todd stayed on with the new owners and the lagers and ales kept flowing. They also contract brew another

30+ beers and have been responsible for a variety of great beers such as Fulton in Minneapolis, Half Acre in Chicago, and Door County Brewing to name a few. In 2000, Sand Creek took two golds at the World Beer Cup (Oscar's and Black River Red)—the first microbrewery to do it and followed up with another gold in 2002 for Oderbolz Bock. The tasting room feels like you are hanging with the neighbor guy at a bar he put in his basement—except this neighbor also happens to have a half dozen or so great homemade beers on tap. A bigger taproom is in planning and might happen in 2016.

Infinity Beverages in Eau Claire (infinitybeverages.com) takes Double Oscar's and Rye Doppelbock and distills them and ages them in whiskey barrels to make two varieties of Beerskey.

Stumbling Distance: *Rozario's* (42 N 1st St, 715-284-0006) near Main St is the best pizza in town and has beer on tap. Get your fresh cheese curds at *Mocha Mouse* (themochamouse.com, 715-284-2541, 500 Oasis Rd, Hwy 54 exit 116 by the orange moose) and sample any of the cheeses or have breakfast, lunch or a cup of Joe or some ice cream. Visit the *Black River Chamber of Commerce* (blackrivercountry.net, 800-404-4008) for current ATV- and snowmobile-trail conditions along with scuba diving (no, seriously), paddling (see my book *Paddling Wisconsin*) and biking info. *Laura's Brickhouse Grill & Saloon* (44 Main St, 715-284-2888) will get you a Friday fish fry, a Saturday prime rib, and several Sand Creek taps.

BLOOMER BREWING CO.

Founded: 2012
Head Brewer: Dan Stolt
Address: 1526 Martin Road • Bloomer, WI 54724
Phone: 715-271-3967
Web Site: www.bloomerbrewingco.com
Annual Production: 120 barrels
Number of Beers: 6 on tap

Staple Beers:
» BLOOMER BEER
» BLOOMTOWN BROWN
» BUCKINGHAM ALE
» DUNCAN SPRING IPA
» STOLTY'S A-HORIZON STOUT
» WEATHERED BRICK

Most Popular Brew: Buckingham Ale

Brewer's Fave: Duncan Spring IPA

Tours? Yes, by chance or appointment.

Samples: Yes, four 5-oz pours for about $5

Best Time to Go: Open Wed 5–10PM, Sat 1–8PM, but he may add Fridays. Call or see website.

Where can you buy it? Here on tap and to go in growlers, and maybe a couple local draft accounts.

Got food? Only free popcorn, but food friendly. *Firewoods Traveling Pizzeria* (firewoodspizzeria.com) parks outside the 2nd and 4th Wednesday of the month.

Special Offer: Your first 12-oz house beer is free during your signature visit.

Directions: From US 53, take the exit for WI 40 and head east into Bloomer for 0.8 mile. Turn right on Main St, then left on 17th Ave and continue 0.3 mile. Turn left on Martin Rd and the brewery is on the right in the back of an industrial building set back far from the street. Follow the signs on either side of the building to get to the brewery. (ADA-entry to the left.)

The Beer Buzz: Bloomer Brewing is located in the former Bloomer Brewing building from 1874. Down in the basement is an old lagering cave built into the hillside. Brewer/founder Dan went to Fort Lauderdale to visit his eldest son who took him to a Brew on Premise with 120 recipes to make a batch together. That started him on the brewery idea and his wife Cindy thought he was nuts. She's reassessed his sanity since he opened this place and gets a steady stream of locals and travelers. Dan's actually been renting this space since 1985 when he set up his own septic and excavation business here, and he's been fixing up the space. (The stout's name, A-Horizon, is a digging term referring to the dark top soil layer.)

Dan has the local polka station on while he's brewing. Gets him in the mood. He started with 40–80 gallon batches but may be going bigger soon. All his brews have 5% corn in them for lighter flavor and drink-ability. His spent grain goes to a local farmer.

The taproom shows some breweriana and eclectic curios, and a couple of other rooms have more collectibles. A room with a pool table has a few dozen hunting trophies mounted on all the walls. A small stage occupies a corner of the taproom for occasional live music.

Mug Club with smart copper cups. ATM onsite.
Facebook/bloomer-Brewing-Co

Stumbling Distance: Next door right on the street is *The Next Place Bar & Grill* (1602 Martin Rd, 715-568-2566, thenextplacebar.com), which serves 75 different burgers. *Bob's Processing* (2430 S Main St, 715-568-2887) has very popular beef sticks and hot dogs to take home. *Fat Boys Family Restaurant* (1312 Main St, 715-568-4464) is the place to get pizza.

BREWSTER BROS BREWING CO. & CHIPPEWA RIVER DISTILLERY

Opened: October 2015
Brewmaster: Jim Stirn
Address: 402 West River Street • Chippewa Falls, WI
Phone: _____
Web Site: www.brewsterbrosbrewing.com | www.chippewariverdistillery.com
Annual Production: 1,500 barrels
Number of Beers: 6–8 on tap

Beers:
- » IPA
- » PORTER
- » STOUT
- » Some lighter beers and seasonals planned as well

Brewmaster's Fave: Stout

Tours? Yes, by chance or by appointment.

Samples: Yes, sample flights available.

Best Time to Go: Open Thu–Fri late afternoon, Sat midday into evening, Sun midday to early evening. Check website for current hours.

Where can you buy it? Here on tap and in growlers to go, and distributed in bottles and on draft in the greater Chippewa Valley area.

Got food? There's no kitchen so maybe something simple such as meat and cheese plates.

Special Offer: $1 off your first pint during your signature visit.

Directions: From US 53, take Exit 96 and head east into Chippewa Falls on Business WI 29/River Street for 1.7 miles. The brewery is on the left at the corner of River and Taylor Streets.

The Beer Buzz: Chippewa Falls has long been famous for an historic brewery, but now they're sharing the place with a new kid in town. Founded by a couple of mechanical engineers, Jim Stirn and Kurt Schneider, the brewery is also a distillery.

Jim and Kurt worked together years ago here in Chippewa Falls, and remained friends and hunting buddies ever since. Jim took up homebrewing in about 2000, finding pleasure in the process as much as the beer itself.

Kurt once started a small business then sold it and had the itch to get back into working for himself. They started with the craft distillery idea, noting the recent growth in that industry, and added the brewery knowing it had similarities but also could generate revenue sooner.

They needed equipment and wanted to stay close to the design aspect so rather than just buying something, they created MSP Engineering with a third partner to design and build equipment for brewing and distilling. They then coordinated various suppliers and tradesmen to manufacture their own system. They first built a 3-vessel system and control set as a test system for homebrewing and developed the larger brew system for the brewery based on that design. They did the same with the distillery.

Both still have day jobs.

They looked around in the Twin Cities and parts of Wisconsin before finding this building right on the Chippewa River at the edge of downtown. Kurt grew up and still lives here, while Jim lived here and grew up south in Alma. He lives in Minnesota and commutes on weekends to the brewery/distillery. The building was a beer distributor in the '50s, and through the years, an auto parts store, a video rental and tanning salon (yes, at the same time), and now returns to its beer roots. The building was two buildings joined as one, and Kurt and Jim added a room with glass on three sides to show off the still. An outdoor beer garden and deck above the building for a river view are planned. The brewing system occupies one half of the building visible through more windows. The cocktail room/tasting room has a bar, tables and tall tables, but is not a typical tavern or sports bar full of TVs. It aims to be more of a conversational sort of location. Remodeling exposed the old tongue-and-groove ceiling with big steel beams, and the cement block walls have a lot of windows. They will run through various beer styles as they work out what lineup is popular for their patrons, and the distillates include vodka and gin to start, while the whiskey is aging. Off-street parking.

Free WiFi. Find them on Facebook.

Stumbling Distance: The *Fill-Inn Station* (104 W Columbia St, 715-723-8282) is run by Kurt's cousin and has deep-fried cheese curds, 10 different burgers, pizza, and a Friday fish fry, prime rib Saturday. *Bresina's Carryout* (10 Jefferson Ave, 715-723-7869) is rated the best chicken and fish fry, but as the name suggests you need a place to eat it, so maybe grab some Brewster Bros beer and cross the street here to *Irvine Park* along the river for a picnic. *Mahli Thai Restaurant* (212 N Bridge St, 715-861-5333, mahlithaicuisine.com) gets high marks for their curry.

Jacob Leinenkugel Brewing

Founded: 1867
Brewmaster: John Buhrow
Address: 124 East Elm Street • Chippewa Falls, WI 54729
Phone: 888-534-6437
Website: www.leinies.com
Annual Production: 350,000+ bbls (estimated)
Number of Beers: 10 (8 year round, 9 seasonal)

Staple Beers:
» Berry Weiss Bier
» Creamy Dark
» Helles Yeah
» Honey Weiss Bier
» India Pale Lager
» Leinie's Original Lager
» Red Lager
» Sunset Wheat

Seasonal Beers:
» Big Eddy Beers (Leinie's special higher abv. craft brand)
» Big Butt Doppelbock
» Canoe Paddler (Kölsch)
» Oktoberfest
» Snowdrift Vanilla Porter

The Shandies:
» Cranberry Ginger Shandy
» Grapefruit Shandy
» Harvest Patch Shandy
» Summer Shandy (lemon)

Most Popular Brew: Summer Shandy

Brewmaster's Fave: Year round: Original Lager, Seasonal: Oktoberfest

Tours? Yes, $5 tours including 5 samples and a branded sample glass are scheduled every half hour. Go to the Leinie Lodge, not the brewery.

Samples? Yes, $5 gets you five 5-oz samples (and the tour if you want it).

Best Time to Go: The Leinie Lodge is open daily, Mon–Thu & Sat 9AM–5PM, Fri 9AM–8PM, Sun 11AM–4PM. Oktoberfest is a nice time to be here.

Where can you buy it? In all 50 states, but most widely distributed in the upper Midwest.

Got food? Maybe some pretzels. Root beer is available if you don't want to sample beer.

Special Offer: A free pint glass with any $10 purchase.

Directions: Follow Hwy 124 to the Elm St intersection. Turn onto East Elm Street and you'll see the Leinie Lodge on your left.

The Beer Buzz: This is a bit of a shrine for those of you who grew up knowing Leinie's as a local brewery. It's the seventh-oldest working brewery in the US and a *pils*-grimage here is indeed a must. In the 1840s, Matthias Leinenkugel brought his family from Prussia (now part of Germany) to settle in Sauk City where he started brewing. Is brewing genetic? Could be. His sons opened two more: one in Eau Claire (where an uncle already had one) and another in Baraboo. Another son Jacob wasn't about to be left out and moved north eventually finding the lumber center of Chippewa Falls. Apparently lumber workers like beer. Lots of it, in fact.

And so it was that he and John Miller founded Spring Brewing Co. The oldest building here is a former malt house built in 1877. Why would that be built before a brewhouse, you may ask? In the beginning they brewed in the homes built in a line right out front. (A couple of those home were moved elsewhere in town years ago.) At that time they brewed as many as 400 barrels in a year. John Miller left in 1884, and when they built a proper brewhouse in 1890, they were able to produce half of that... in a single day. (Today they brew upwards of 1200 barrels daily.) Jacob's name was added to the brewery's name, and not long after "Spring" was dropped. They continued to grow, survived Prohibition with Leino near beer and soda water, and until 1945, still delivered beer by horse and wagon. The name became household in Wisconsin.

Fast forward to 1988: Miller Brewing Co. (now MillerCoors), second largest brewer in the world, buys Leinie's. Purists clutch their chests, breaths are held, there is much gnashing of teeth. Somewhere in the distance a dog barks. But the brewery was not dismantled or swallowed up, and the old classic Leinie's has emerged bigger and better than before, producing some rather exceptional large market beers in a microbrew style. At the 2006 World Beer Cup, Sunset Wheat got bronze and Honey Weiss silver while Red Lager took gold in 2002. To keep up with sales, Leinie's operates 10th Street Brewery in Milwaukee which is also where they brew Big Eddy, their own line of craft beers named for that original spring that still exists behind the brewery. Honey Weiss is made with Wisconsin honey from Hauke Honey in Marshfield.

The Leinie Lodge, separated from the brewery itself by Duncan Creek, is where you go for the tours and tastings, and it contains a huge amount of merchandise as well as some exhibits of Leinie breweriana and history.

Stumbling Distance: One of the best rated eateries in town is *Chippewa Family Restaurant* (1701 Kennedy Rd, 715-723-4751, chippewarestaurant. com). *Bresina's Carryout* (10 Jefferson Ave, 715-723-7869) is rated the best chicken and fish fry, but as the name suggests you need a place to eat it. (Picnic in the park?) Leinie's hosts or gets involved with a lot of little fests and such, but one of the most unusual is the *Family Reunion*. On the Saturday of Father's Day weekend head out to meet Leinenkugel brothers Jake, Dick, and John as they host a free get together featuring some live music, tours, and plenty of brats, beer, chips, beer, pickles, cookies, and of course beer. All free to 3000 participants. The event lasts from noon to sunset and the first 100 guests get a little extra gift.

ALTERNATIVE USES FOR BEER CANS

So craft beer is starting to embrace the beer can. Besides recycling them, there are plenty of other ways to repurpose them. Consider these:

Party wear. Not sure what to wear to the next beer fest? How about a hat made out of cans and yarn? This will surely be hitting the runways in Paris (Paris, Wisconsin, population 1,473).

Davis Thuecks is sporting his grandpa's hat and shirt here. His friend, Robin Reese, apparently left his at home.

My great uncle John Lajcak had a knack for making furniture out of beer cans. A bit on the smallish size, but stylish.

If beer could fly…

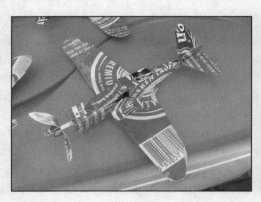

Remember Body on Tap shampoo? Me neither, but it was back in the 70s when it was believed beer would give your hair body. Back when the big curl was all the rage for the ladies, the steel cans made great rollers and the beer helped set the hair. A big thanks to Pat Breister and Sara Napiwocki down at Madison College for the re-enactment and Kristin Abraham, the brave volunteer. There was no permanent damage—other than possible emotional scarring.

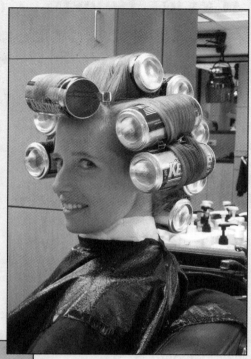

VALKYRIE BREWING CO. (FORMERLY VIKING BREWING CO.)

Founded: 1994
Brewmaster: Randy and Ann Lee
Address: 234 Dallas St. West, Dallas, WI 54733
Phone: 715-837-1824
Website: www.valkyriebrewery.com
Annual Production: 300 barrels
Number of Beers: 22+ annually, up to 16 on tap

Staple Beers:
  » BIG SWEDE (Swedish-style Imperial Stout)
  » DRAGON BLADE (American retro lager)
  » RUBEE RED (a Marzen style lager)
  » WAR HAMMER (coffee, oatmeal, milk porter)

Rotating Beers: (Most are seasonal batches and new ones come up once or twice a month.)
  » ABBY NORMAL (Belgian tripel – Aug)
  » BLAZE ORANGE EXOTICALLY SPICED BEER
  » CRIMSON WONDER (Scotch Ale – Dec)
  » 4 BITTEN FRUIT
  » GOLDEN HORN (Weizenbock)
  » HOT CHOCOLATE (Fair Trade organic cocoa & cayenne pepper)
  » INVADER DOPPELBOCK
  » LIME TWIST (wheat beer)
  » NIGHT WOLF (German-style Schwarzbier)
  » RAVEN QUEEN (Black Wheat IPA with Star Anise)
  » SUPERNOVA (Royal Australian India Pale Ale)
  » VELVET GREEN (Dry Irish stout)
  » WHISPERING EMBERS (Oktoberfest with beechwood-smoked malt – Sept)

Most Popular Brew: War Hammer

Brewmaster's Fave: Randy: Invader Doppelbock, Ann: Big Swede

Tours? Yes, free "deep" tours most Saturdays at 1PM (check website for when they are gone for Beer Shows) or by appointment.

Samples: Yes.

Best Time to Go: The tap room is open Fridays 4–8 and Saturdays noon–8, but Thu–Sun in summer months. Don't miss Oktoberfest. Taproom usually closed in Jan/Feb, but tours continue.

Where can you buy it? In six-pack bottles (and occasional 22-oz bombers), mostly in Western, Northwestern, and Central WI, plus Madison and Milwaukee. Here in the Beer Cave you can build your own 6-, 9-packs or cases, plus growler fills in the taproom.

Got food? No, but there's free popcorn, the taproom is food friendly, and on Thursdays in summer, brats are served custom-made with their beer by Louie's Finer Meats in Cumberland.

Special Offer: A bottle of beer, sure, why not?

The Beer Buzz: Tiny Dallas makes a not-so-tiny mark on the beer map with this husband-and-wife operation. Housed in the basement of an old brick building on the main street, this was originally a Ford dealership selling Models T and A. (Was Ford a perv?) In the 30s it became a creamery and a handful of other things thereafter. Why did Randy open a brewery? "We were out of work at the time." Unemployment is the mother of invention. Or is it Randy's wife and co-brewer Ann? She comes up with a lot of the brew ideas and Randy makes the recipes. A stout with cocoa and cayenne? You better believe it. Dallas was dry until the early 60s, so heads turned when the brewery opened under its original name Viking Brewing and became one of the pioneers of microbrewing in the 90s in western Wisconsin. Randy sold the Viking name to an Icelandic brewery that wanted it worse than he did, and began brewing again as Valkyrie, a mythical Norse female who determines who lives and dies in battle. The

tour lasts an hour and a half and is comprehensive, not just a show of what he's doing but also explanations of the different kinds of beers.

The sign on the building may still say Viking Brewing. The brewery is in the basement but the taproom is upstairs in front. Inside is a bar in the corner next to the walk-in cooler Beer Cave for bottle sales. The walls are painted like castle stones and along with the cool mural were all painted by Ann. Weapons and chain mail, most made by a local metalworker, hang on the wall, and you can see a giant pair of knockers on the double doors to the back room. The booths are re-claimed from an old Pizza Hut, and a homemade fire & water fountain symbolizes the Nordic Tree of Life, Yggdrasil. Games, such as cribbage and chess, are onsite if you come to linger. Be aware that Valkyrie brews unpasteurized beer. If you pick some up, take good care to keep it cool and out of the sun until you're ready to drink it!

Trivia note: Randy ran for state governor in 2002 as the BEER Party candidate. Hard to believe, but he didn't win. And now we are facing beer taxes. See where not voting gets you??

Stumbling Distance: This isn't far from lake country and nearby Chetek, and the surrounding area draws a lot of fishermen and outdoors types. Since Prohibition, Chicago travelers have come here for cabins. *Clicker's Restaurant and Bar* (210 W Dallas St, 715-837-1416) has the best eats in town and a Friday night fish fry. If you're into antiques, hit up *Old Farmer's Mercantile* (115 W Dallas St, 715-837-1919). Eyeball some local pottery at *Losse Clay Studio* (201 W Dallas St, 715-837-1109). 17 miles south is a good bed & breakfast: *Hay River House* (E4517 CR FF, Boyceville, 715-702-1809, hayriverhouse.com).

THE BREWING PROJEKT

Founded: 2015
Brewmaster: Eric Rykal
Address: 2000 Oxford Ave, Building #3 • Eau Claire, WI 54703
Phone: 715-214-3728
Web Site: www.thebrewingprojekt.com
Annual Production: 1,000 barrels
Number of Beers: 12 on tap

Staple Beers:
> » GUNPOWDER IPA
> » IPZ (India Pale Zwickel)
> » WISCOAST (hoppy wheat ale)

Rotating Beers:
> » BELGIAN QUAD
> » BLACK IPA
> » BLUEBERRY WIT
> » CHAMOMILE WIT
> » FARMHOUSE LAGER
> » FIRST BORN (raspberry chocolate chipotle stout)
> » GINGER TRIPEL
> » MILK STOUT (with molasses and bourbon-soaked vanilla beans)

Most Popular Brew: Gunpowder IPA

Brewmaster's Fave: IPZ

Tours? Yes, by appointment or by chance.

Samples: Yes, order a Pick 3—three 5-oz samples for about $4.

Best Time to Go: Open Wed–Fri 4–10PM, Sat 12–10PM.

Where can you buy it? Here on tap and to go in growlers, distributing 16-oz cans and some draft accounts as far east as Wausau, maybe some in Madison.

Got food? No, but food friendly, and possible food trucks.

Special Offer: Half off your first pint during your signature visit.

Directions: Business Highway 12 runs right through Eau Claire, crossing Chippewa River downtown on Madison Street Bridge. On the west side of the bridge, go north on Oxford Ave/US 12 and stay straight through the curve where Platt St/US 12 goes left. This will take you to the parking lot and the brewery is Building #3 beyond it to the left.

The Beer Buzz: The Brewing Projekt may be the finest example for how complicated and absurd old post-Prohibition laws still are. When founder (but not owner!) Will Glass, a Chippewa Falls native, got out of the Marine Corps, he went home again and worked a bit for Leinenkugel's before he and his wife decided to open Eau Claire's excellent craft beer bar, The Fire House back in 2009. By this time, Will had taken up homebrewing, so as the Firehouse became successful, he and his wife Rebecca figured the next step was to start brewing their own. This turned out to be way more difficult than they had imagined.

After Prohibition, laws went into effect that a person could not own a bar *and* a brewery. This became a long story of back and forth with the government, and for a time they had even considered getting a legal divorce so each of them could own one business. Even then they were told that Will would also have to give up legal claims on his children who were indirect joint interests and thus still a no-no. Literally asking for your first born (and second and third). The solution is that his wife took over the bar 100% as a sole proprietor. His father owns the brewery. And Will? He works as an unpaid volunteer at his father's brewery because he can't legally take a paycheck here while his wife owns the bar. Oh, it gets better. Brewer Eric's wife worked at a bar downtown. She had to quit so that Eric could work here. Time to change the laws, wouldn't you say?

Brewing runs the gamut here through lagers and ales, and all sort of creative brews come and go. The taproom has no TVs or WiFi, just some background tunes and an LCD screen with the beer menu. Seating is either at the bar or some heavy wood tables. A garage door opens to an outdoor patio with picnic tables in the front of the building. The 20-barrel brewhouse is right there at the edge of the space. Cribbage and cards are on hand.

Facebook/thebrewingprojekt and Twitter @brewingprojekt
Instagram @thebrewingprojekt

Stumbling Distance: Be sure to check out *The Fire House* (202 Gibson St, 715-514-0406, eauclairefirehouse.com), the best beer bar in town, with 40 rotating taps and 2 casks—and they even fill growlers.

K POINT BREWING

Opened: 2015
Head Brewer: Lon Blaser
Address: 4212 Southtowne Drive • Eau Claire, WI 54701
Phone: 715-834-1733
Web Site: www.facebook.com/kpointbeers
Annual Production: 24–150 barrels
Number of Beers: 8 on tap (some may be guest beers)

Staple Styles:
  » PALE ALE (same grains but alternating hops combinations)
  » A porter/stout
  » An Irish red/amber/brown ale
  » Seasonals

Most Popular Brew: Too early to tell.

Brewer's Fave: Lon: Pale Ale | Tom: Brown Porter

Tours? By chance or by appointment.

Samples: Yes, sips to taste but no flights yet.

Best Time to Go: Open Mon–Fri 7AM–8PM, Sat 7:30AM–8PM, Sun 8AM–5PM.

Where can you buy it? Only here on tap and to go in growlers. They have 32- and 64-oz Hydroflasks as well as glass growlers.

Got food? Yes, a changing menu featuring breakfast sandwiches, baked goods, tapas, and excellent house-roasted coffee. A wood-fired pizza food truck, Tutto Bene, parks outside occasionally.

Special Offer: One half-priced pint of K Point Beer during your signature visit.

Directions: From I-94 take Exit 68 and head north on WI 93 for 0.6 mile. Turn left on Damon St and an immediate left on Southtowne Dr and The Coffee Grounds is on your right.

The Beer Buzz: Looks like a coffee shop, no? Eric and Julie Nelson started The Coffee Gourds, roasting beans in a mall back in 1990. It would become successful and grow, expand into a new location, and become a notable specialty shop that not only roasted and served great coffee, but also sold food, gourmet products, wines, and the finest selection of bottled craft

beers in town. Eventually they outgrew the other location and opened up here. Brewer Lon, now a retired physician, has homebrewed since 1982 when he was "too poor to buy beer." Eric had long had the idea to bring him in to do a little onsite brewing, and finally in 2015 he convinced him. Lon is joined by another longtime homebrewer, Tom Breneman who got his first brew kit for Christmas in 1992. They started on a Sabco ½ barrel system but already have aims to get a larger system and move into 2,100 square feet of space in the next room to increase production to about 150 barrels per year and set up a taproom. Lon and Tom make sessionable beers, aiming to be true to style and with the intent of providing an educational element which fits in nicely with the various tasting and pairing events of The Coffee Grounds.

At printing, the taproom is a stand alone counter in the center of The Coffee Grounds, with taps and a fine assortment of spirits. Tables are nearby and it all blends together with the coffee, deli (with gourmet cheeses!), and liquor store.

Free WiFi. Facebook/K Point Brewing

Stumbling Distance: *Manny's Cocina* (4207 Oakwood Hills Pkwy, 715-514-0818, mannyscocina.com) serves fine Mexican fare with an emphasis on the seafood of the Pacific coastal region.

Lazy Monk Brewery

Founded: May 2011
Brewmaster: Leos Frank
Address: 97 West Madison Street • Eau Claire, WI 54703
Phone: 715-271-5887
Website: www.lazymonkbrewing.com
Annual Production: 460 barrels
Number of Beers: 12 on tap, including a few WI guest beers

Staple Beers:
» Bohemian Pilsner
» Bohemian Dark Lager

Rotating Beers:

» Baltic Porter
» Bock
» Mai Bock
» Marzen

» Oktoberfest
» Summer Lager
» Vienna-Style Lager
» Winter Lager

Most Popular Brew: Bohemian Pilsner.

Brewmaster's Fave: It depends, which child do you like more?

Tours? Yes.

Samples: Yes, a paddle of 4 beers for about $4

Best Time to Go: Initial plans for taproom hours are Tue–Fri 4–10PM, Sat 2–10PM, but those are likely to increase. Call or check the website.

Where can you buy it? Here on tap and in growlers to go. Distributed in Wisconsin in cans as far away as La Crosse, Madison, Milwaukee, and Appleton.

Got food? Not right away, but watch for it in the future probably.

Special Offer: Not participating.

Directions: Business US 12 runs through downtown Eau Claire and crosses the Chippewa River on the Madison Street Bridge. The brewery is on the west side of the bridge, south side of Madison St near the corner of Madison St and Oxford Ave.

The address is 320 Putnam Street until fall 2015.

The Beer Buzz: Brewer/owner Leos Frank was born and raised in what was then Czechoslovakia (now central Slovakia). We didn't have enough room or consonants to spell his hometown. When he moved here, he couldn't find a beer he enjoyed and missed the brews of his culture. "It is a beer culture, it is part of life. Not too many people think they could make it, but they expect to have it." There were just a few microbreweries at that time just starting up. "I stopped drinking beer at one point. Until someone told me, 'Do you know you can make it at home?'" It all started as a hobby and became an obsession.

"I started with a 40 gallon kettle, the biggest I could find. Then 55. Not enough." Then he had a guy from Menomonie make him a 5.5 barrel kettle. That's how it all got started. "Then I got a stainless steel fermenter and really started feeling like a pro." The name makes reference to the tradition of the monks while adding a kick-back-and-relax attitude to it. In deciding how to package, he realized the bottled six-pack is rather pricey. So he decided to go with returnable packaging, namely the growler. This worked well for a while, but then he added 16-oz cans. The taproom, known as the Monk Cellar, was always popular so Leos decided he'd expand. In 2015, Lazy Monk moved to the former Charlson Building & Design building, a 17,000-square-foot facility which includes a 5,000-square-foot German/Czech-style Bier Hall taproom with communal seating and a fireplace, as well as an outdoor beer garden/deck overlooking the Chippewa River.

Stumbling Distance: *Eau Claire Downtown Farmers Market* (300 Riverfront Terrace, 715-563-2644, ecdowntownfarmersmarket.com) is just across the bridge, as is the *Chippewa River State Trail* popular with cyclists. Definitely check out *The Coffee Grounds* (thecoffeegrounds.com, 4212 Southtowne Dr, 715-834-1733) which is much more than a cool coffee shop with a nice menu of food—it is also a stellar beer cellar with over 450 brews, and now their own nanobrewery: *K Point Brewing. Infinity Beverages Winery & Distillery* (930 Galloway St, Ste 4, 402-374-6542, infinitybeverages.com) has a tasting lounge.

Northwoods Brewpub and Grill

Founded: 1997
Brewmaster: Tim Kelly
Address: 3560 Oakwood Mall Drive • Eau Claire, WI 54701
Phone: 715-552-0510
Website: www.northwoodsbrewpub.com
Annual Production: 1,200 bbls
Number of Beers: 16 on tap; 28 beers per year

Staple Beers:
- » Birchwood Pale Ale
- » Bumbl'n Bubba's Buzz'n Brew (honey golden ale)
- » Floppin' Crappie (light caramel-colored ale with honey)
- » Half Moon Gold
- » Kelly's Stout
- » Lil' Bandit Brown Ale
- » Mouthy Muskie Light Ale
- » Poplar Porter
- » Prickly Pike's Pilsner
- » Red Cedar Red Ale
- » Rowdy Rye
- » Walter's Premium Pilsener
- » White Weasel Light Ale
- » Whitetail Wheat

Rotating Beers:
- » Buckshot Bock
- » Bumbl'n Bubba's Lingonberry Light (an actual berry)
- » Dunkelweizen
- » Irish Stoat Ale
- » Oktoberfest Lager
- » Ripplin' Red Raspberry Wheat
- » Wall IPA

Most Popular Brew: Floppin' Crappie

Brewmaster's Fave: Lil' Bandit Brown

Tours? Yes, anytime.

Samples? Yes, a sampler with eight 4-oz beers for $5 and a free 8-oz beer with a brew tour.

Best Time to Go: Open Mon–Sat 7AM–close, Sun 8AM–close. Happy hour is 11–6 Mon–Fri. Popular with the college crowd on Friday and Saturday nights.

Where can you buy it? Here on tap and in growlers to go, and distributed in the area and north of Eau Claire in six-packs. Grocery stores in Eau Claire, Hayward, Chetek and some regional taverns.

Got food? Yes, they have a full menu, are big on burgers, open for breakfast and the typical Friday fish fry, deep-fry cheese curds.

Special Offer: A free house beer or soda when you get your book signed.

Directions: The brewpub is on the frontage road on 53 just north of the I-94 interchange. Exit US-53 at Golf Rd and go west a short block to Oakwood Hills Parkway. Turn right (north) here and Oakwood Mall Drive is on your left.

The Beer Buzz: Where once were 800 acres of farmland is now a major shopping area. In the middle of all this is a pond saved from the surrounding development, and next to that is a brewpub. Founder/owner Jerry Bechard, a Wisconsin native, actually started homebrewing when he lived in Colorado. His co-workers (fans and test subjects of his beers) named Bumbl'n Bubba's Buzz'n Brew upon the arrival of Jerry's newborn son. When Jerry bought the Norske Nook in 1990, he was making the move into some of the best pies around and bread (which isn't too far off from beer (liquid bread), or so the monks of Europe would have said). But the call of beer is strong, and in 1995 he decided he needed to make beer commercially and began Northwoods Brewing Co. Brewmaster Tim grew up with Jerry, and Jerry wanted him to brew. So Tim went off to Siebel Institute to study, already knowing where he'd be working when he was done. Long ago the famous local brew was Walter's Premium, and when the brewery found that this brand was dead, they revived it. They consulted with some lifelong Walter's drinkers until Tim dialed in the best guess of the original pilsner recipe.

The interior aims at rustic for the Northwoods theme, and the pond-side beer garden and patio are great in the summer. Their Lil' Bandit Brown Ale won silver at the Great American Beer Festival in 2000 while Floppin' Crappie wowed the crowd and took a best beer title at Sturgis in 2004. The restaurant menu shows some Norwegian items as well as about 25 specialty pies from the on-site bakery.

Facebook.com/northwoodsbrewpub

Stumbling Distance: If you are ready to shop till you drop, the surrounding area is chock full of places to do so. If you are not so inclined but with someone who is, the brewpub can be your refuge! Gyros anyone? *Olympic Flame* (2920 London Rd, 715-835-7771) gets raves. Unassuming place in a strip mall. Great food, friendly people. *Carson Park* has the Paul Bunyan Camp (a recreation of a 19th century logging camp), a working quarter-scale railroad, and the baseball stadium where former Milwaukee Brave and Brewer Hank Aaron first played as a pro. The *Chippewa Valley Museum* (www.cvmuseum.com, 715-834-7871, free on Tues, closed Monday during school year, $4 adult) is also with exhibits about local history and the native Ojibwe (Chippewa), as well as some historic buildings. And the turn of the century ice cream parlor is serving ice cream sodas. Check in at *The Coffee Grounds* (www.thecoffeegrounds.com, 3460 Mall Dr Hwy 93, 715-834-1733) for beer of the month, tastings, and now the in-house *K Point Brewing*.

Common Man Brewing, Inc.

Founded: May 2015
Head Brewer: Sam Korpela
Address: 193 East Main Street • Ellsworth, WI 54011
Phone: 715-941-4060
Web Site: www.commonmanbrewing.com
Annual Production: 400 barrels
Number of Beers: 20 taps (4–6 of their own beers), 2 nitro taps

Staple Beers:
» Common Man POB (Plain old beer) (blonde)
» IPA
» Nut Brown

Rotating Beers:
» Imperial brews

Brewer's Fave: Imperial IPAs

Samples: Yes, $2 5-oz pours.

Tours? Yes, by chance or appointment. Watch Facebook for Beer 101 and tasting events.

Best Time to Go: Closed Mondays. Open Tue, Wed, Thu, Sun 12–10PM, Fri–Sat 12–12. Two daily happy hours from Tue–Thu.

Where can you buy it? Here on tap and in growlers and howlers to go. Possible local draft accounts in the future.

Got food? Yes, appetizers, salads, sandwiches/burgers, and flatbreads, plus cheese & sausage boards. A full bar.

Special Offer: Buy your first beer, get one free during your signature visit.

Directions: US 10 and US 63 pass right through town as Main Street. The brewery is on the south side of the road set back in a short strip of shops behind a parking lot near the center of town.

The Beer Buzz: When you walk in and see all the lunch pails decorating the taproom, you understand Common Man is a tip of the hardhat to the working man. Owner/founder Russ Korpela hales from Ashland, WI where he grew up in a family with blue collar roots. When he and his brewing son Sam were brainstorming for a brewery name, Common Man appealed for that reason. Russ had had the idea for some time and kept looking for a good place to open up. Somewhere with passing traffic, a good economy, and perhaps under-served in terms of craft beer or good eats. When he found a place in Ellsworth, one with wide open space and a garage door out the side, he knew this was it. Being located 6 blocks from his home didn't hurt either.

Brewer Sam was a Food Science major at the University of Wisconsin, brewing even before he could legally drink. Other than the science knowledge of his degree, he had no formal brewing training. This is a nano-brewery operation, and they took their inspiration from Peter Gentry at One Barrel Brewing in Madison. They aim to brew sessionable beers and occasional firkins. The flagship beers will be lighter in style but the brewer also brews bigger and varied beers. POB aims to be a crossover brew, bringing converts to craft beer.

Russ knows bars and marketing, but not cooking, so he hired a good chef to develop a pub-style comfort food menu that walks that fine line between dive bar and supper club. Food is locally sourced whenever possible.

The brewpub is at the end of a short strip of stores on Main Street. Tin siding fronts the L-shaped bar and serves as wainscoting, and of course there are many lunch pails scattered throughout the room. Straight Edge Metal Art in Manitowoc did their cool sign on the wall. The garage door in back opens to a small patio area. There are a couple TVs, some board games, and music is playing.

Free WiFi. Facebook/commonmanbrewing and Twitter @cmbrewinggcfb

Stumbling Distance: Ellsworth is the Cheese Curd Capital of Wisconsin, so be sure to visit *Ellsworth Cooperative Creamery* (232 N Wallace St, 715-273-4311, ellsworthcheese.com) for some fresh curds, various cheeses and a ton of other area products. *Sailer's Meats* (600 W Winter Ave, Elmwood, 715-639-2191, sailersmeats.com) has 5 generations and a slew of awards behind it. (18 miles east of here). *Vino in the Valley* (W3826 450th Ave, Maiden Rock, 715-639-6677, vinointhevalley.com) offers some very cool seasonal outdoor dining. (10 miles SE of here)

Pitchfork Brewing

Founded: August 2013
Brewmaster: Mike Fredricksen
Address: 709 Rodeo Circle, Suite 104 • Hudson, WI 54016
Phone: 715-245-3675
Web Site: www.pitchforkbrewing.com
Annual Production: 600 barrels
Number of Beers: 7 on tap plus a firkin; 29+ beers per year

Staple Beers:
  » Barn Door Brown
  » German Pilsener
  » Pitchfork Pale Ale
  » Plus housemade root beer

Rotating Beers:
  » Sugar Shack Maple Lager
  » Vanilla Rose Imperial Porter
  » And loads of styles including local IPAs, English Porter, etc.

Most Popular Brew: Pitchfork Pale

Brewmaster's Fave: Munich Dunkel

Tours? Yes, detailed free tours on Sunday afternoons (not during Packers games) and includes a couple of samples.

Samples: Yes, flights of five 5-oz pours for about $6.

Best Time to Go: Open Wed–Thu 3–8PM, Fri 3–10PM, Sat 12–10PM, Sun 11:30AM–7:30PM. Closed Mon–Tue. Packer game days are popular. Watch for two festivals on site: Spring Fest in May and Harvest Fest in October. Check the website.

Where can you buy it? Here on tap and in growlers and 22-oz bombers to go. Some growlers and bombers in local liquor stores and a few draft accounts in Hudson.

Got food? Free popcorn, but also food friendly. *Paddy Ryan's* has an appetizer menu just for the brewery.

Special Offer: Buy your first Pitchfork beer, get 1 free when you get your book signed.

Directions: From I-94, take Exit 4 for US 12 going north about 0.3 mile. Turn left on Rodeo Dr, go 0.2 mile, and take a left on Rodeo Dr again. The brewery is in the line of shops on the right.

The Beer Buzz: Brewer Mike homebrewed with a buddy for 20 years and worked for 6 at Northern Brewer. He's a beer judge and started the local homebrew club. He's also a bit of a beer activist: in 2011 the Wisconsin Department of Revenue determined homebrewers couldn't take their beer out of the house, to friends, competitions, etc. Working with the Wisconsin Homebrewers Alliance, Mike rallied local officials and went to testify in Madison, and in April 2012, Senate Bill 395 passed and homebrew could be shared again and taken to competitions and exhibitions.

Sarah and Jason Edwards contacted Mike and wanted to start something, and his wife Jessie had been pushing him for years. They spent a year planning it and found a vacant space just off the interstate. They refurbished the place in an environmentally and agriculturally conscious fashion. The bar top is repurposed flooring, the tables were once doors, and the sconces are Kerr jars with chicken water bowls. Spent grain goes to a farmer and the brewing uses recirculated water. Two fermenters are dedicated to lagers. He uses whole-leaf hops, not pellets, and his alpha-acid hops are all local. He's not a fan of Yakima hops. Mike doesn't chill with glycol, but actually has different refrigerated spaces for specific temperatures. He has over 300 recipes so you can expect a lot of variation in the tap list.

The taproom has a couple of TVs (Packers games) and a few booths and tables in the storefront windows. He does an Irish Coffee Stout infused with Irish whiskey for Paddy Ryan's next door. That Vanilla Rose Imperial Porter (barrel-aged with vanilla beans) sells out in under an hour.

Free WiFi. Growler's Club Card. Facebook/PitchforkBrewing and Twitter @PitchforkBeer

Stumbling Distance: *Stone Tap Gastropub* (517 2nd St, 715-808-8343, stonetaphudson.com) has some great food and the best tap list in town. *Casanova's Liquor Store* (236 Coulee Rd, 715-386-2545, casanovaliquor. com) has an excellent selection of craft beers including 20 taps for growler fills. *Paddy Ryan's* next door has pub grub.

CITY BREWERY

Founded: November 1999 (1858)
Brewmaster: Randy Hughes
Address: 925 S. Third Street • La Crosse, WI 54601
Phone: 608-785-4200
Website: www.citybrewery.com
Annual Production: 2,000,000 bbls (100% contract brewing)
Number of Beers: 40+

Brewmaster's Fave: "The one in my hand, but La Crosse Lager is my table beer."

Tours? No public access, though there are some historical markers outside.

Samples? No.

Best Time to Go: La Crosse Oktoberfest (see Festivals in back of book).

Got food? No.

Special Offer: Not participating.

Directions: Highways 14/61 go right through the city and the brewery is on it where it meets 3rd Street.

The Beer Buzz: This isn't any longer a place to tour or drink at, but it is a bit of history and a photo op: Look for the world's largest six-pack and you've come to the right place. On Third and Mississippi St, this is the former G. Heileman Brewery, founded as a partnership in 1858 and officially G. Heileman's in 1890. Remember Old Style and Special Export? "Pure brewed from God's country; you can travel the world over and never find a better beer." In the late 19th century, after the death of her husband, Johanna Heileman was one of the first women presidents of a US corporation. In 1959, G. Heileman began buying up other breweries and became a bit of a giant producing 17 million barrels altogether. Bond Corporation of Australia bought G. Heileman in 1987 and then the brewery was passed about until it was sold to Pabst in 1999. All the breweries shut down and found different purposes except this facility which became City Brewery, owned partly by employees of the former company. The 1870 home of Gottlieb and Johanna Heileman is right across the street and holds the offices. The brewery sits on an artesian well from which it takes its water for brewing.

Brewmaster Randy was here 22 years with G. Heileman and all of City Brewery's years since. He studied biology at UW-La Crosse and went straight to the brewery to do lab work, ie. beer analysis. He's been brewmaster since 1995. Several beers have taken home awards including 2000 World Beer Cup Silver for City Lager/Light, La Crosse Lager/Light, silver for City Lager, La Crosse Lager, and Festbier at the 2004 World Beer Championships, and more silver for Winter Porter and Pale Ale at 2005 World Beer Championships. For a while City Brewery maintained ownership of the La Crosse brands, but since the sale of those, the brewery is doing contracted brews exclusively, and now has brewing facilities also in Latrobe, PA and Memphis, TN. Besides the big sixer, you can see some historical plaques here on the way to the other La Crosse breweries.

Stumbling Distance: *Kramers Bar & Grill* (1123 3rd St, 608-784-8541) next door is a good place to get a bite. Menu is mostly burgers and the like, plus deep-fried white cheddar cheese curds and beer-battered shrimp. If you are already road-tripping here, don't miss the *Great River Road* from Prescott to Prairie du Chien (by way of La Crosse). Signage is clear (a green pilot's wheel) and Hwy 133 goes all the way to Potosi (100 miles/2 hrs), home of *Potosi Brewery* and the *ABA National Brewery Museum*. The bluffs are beautiful and the drive is recommended by several national publications. Granddad Bluff is most popular for a view of the river valley and the city.

PEARL STREET BREWERY

Founded: 1999
Brewmaster: Joe Katchever
Address: 1401 S Andrew Street • La Crosse, WI 54603
Phone: 608-784-4832
Website: www.pearlstreetbrewery.com
Annual Production: 3,000+ bbls
Number of Beers: 8 on tap here; 10 in distribution

Staple Beers:
- » D.T.B. (Brown Ale)
- » DANKENSTEIN I IPA
- » EL HEFE (Bavarian-style Hefeweizen)
- » ME, MYSELF AND IPA
- » PEARL STREET PALE ALE (APA)
- » RUBBER MILLS PILS
- » THAT'S WHAT I'M TALKIN' 'BOUT ORGANIC ROLLED OAT STOUT!

Rotating Beers:
- » APPLEWEIZEN (August in bottles)
- » BEDWETTER BARLEYWINE
- » EVIL DOPPLEGANGER DOPPLEBOCK
- » HARVEST ALE
- » LIEDERHOSEN LAGER OKTOBERFEST (Sept in bottles)
- » RASPBERRY TAMBOIS (Belgian-style sour)
- » SMOKIN' HEMP PORTER (April 20)

Most Popular Brew: D.T.B. but Pale Ale and IPA are close behind

Brewmaster's Fave: "I tend to drink the hoppier beers, but a good bock is a great thing!"

Tours? Yes, Friday one tour at 5PM, Saturdays from 1PM–4PM on the hour, or call with your group or for a special event. Tours are about $6 and include a pint glass, a pint of beer and a coupon. Check the website to be sure.

Samples? Yes, a flight of 2-oz pours of all 8 beers for about $7.

Best Time to Go: Tasting room open Tue–Thu 4–8PM, Fri 3–10PM, Sat noon–7PM. La Crosse is in the Guinness Book for having the most bars per capita. It's an exciting town with festivals and ongoing events year round. The city is particularly jovial during Oktoberfest or Great River Jazz Fest in August. Watch for their Anniversary Party, the Annual Winter Ball in February, a Fri–Sat event with food and beer pairings with area chefs and restaurants, special beers only made for this weekend, plus live music, and beer releases every 1.5 hours.

Where can you buy it? Here on tap and to go in Pearl Street growlers only and four- and six-packs. Distributed throughout Wisconsin and parts of SE Minnesota on draft, in four- and six-pack bottles, and some 22-oz bombers.

Got food? Just free pretzels at the bar, but La Crosse has lots of great restaurants that deliver right to the brewery.

Special Offer: A free pint when you get your book signed!

Directions: From I-90 take the Hwy 35/53 exit south to the first traffic light and go left on to George Street. After you've gone over the bridge over the train tracks, take a left at the 2nd set of traffic lights (Saint Andrew St) and go half a block down on the left to the four-story La Crosse Footwear building.

The Beer Buzz: Brewmaster Joe lived in Colorado and worked at several breweries there before journeying to La Crosse to found Pearl Street, which takes its name from its original location on Pearl Street downtown. Things were going well and he was putting out 12 different beers annually, but growth was inevitable. The new facility was up and running before renovations were even complete. They have much more space in this renovated boot factory from the early 1900s. It was once home to

TOUR DE PEARL

If you like cycling for your beer, this awesome Pearl Street summer promotion is for you. Every summer the brewery puts on its Tour de Pearl. Your registration fee (about $20–25) gets you a tour badge/lanyard, t-shirt, bonus tour card, keychain, and promotional coupons and freebies from sponsors. Both La Crosse and Madison have their own Tour de Pearl from June–August. On your own time, pedal to each of the stages (Madison has 20+, La Crosse 40+!) and order a pint of Pearl Street beer at each of them to get your tour card stamped. Completing a certain number of stages gets you an entry for a chance to win the grand prize (a sweet new bicycle). The end-of-tour party is held at the Lac Crosse Area Bicycle Festival (explorelacrosse.com) in La Crosse on the Saturday of Labor Day Weekend. Register online at pearlstreetbrewery.com/tour-de-pearl and follow Facebook.com/TourDePearl for organized rides.

La Crosse Footwear which moved its operations to China in 2001 and left the factory empty. And as with most emptiness, beer just seems like the best solution for filling it. In 2015, they added several new fermenters to keep up with demand. The taproom has a long curving concrete bar and a scattering of mismatched tables. A small stage hosts free live music most Fridays and a cooler holds forth to-go beer. They have a nice little gift shop here as well. Foosball, ping pong and board games are provided for your entertainment.

Free WiFi. ATM onsite. Facebook.com/pearlstreetbrewery

Stumbling Distance: The Mississippi is king here, and to take in a view of it and have some great eats, head down to *La Crosse Pettibone Boat Club* (2615 Schubert Pl, 608-784-7743, under the big blue bridge to Minnesota). Boaters can use the marina, and outside seating features a tiki bar. Famous for hand-dipped cheese curds, Pettibone serves anything from nice dinners to casual burgers. Open from May–Oct. And of course the biggest beer event in town is also one of the biggest in the state: *La Crosse Oktoberfest.*

TURTLE STACK BREWERY

Opened: June 2015
Brewmaster: Brent Martinson
Address: 125 South 2nd Street • La Crosse, WI 54601
Phone: 608-519-2284
Web Site: www.turtlestackbrewery.com
Annual Production: 300 barrels
Number of Beers: 6–8 on tap; 50 different beers each year

Beers:
- » Beers vary greatly and seasonally
- » German, English, Belgian, American styles

Most Popular Brew: Too soon to tell

Brewmaster's Fave: "I have a hard time picking a beer"

Tours? Yes, by chance or by appointment. It can be done from a bar stool.

Samples: Yes, sips to decide, or 4-oz pours for about $1.25 each.

Best Time to Go: Open Wed–Sat for starters. (Call or check website/Facebook.)

Where can you buy it? Here on tap and eventually growlers to go, plus area draft accounts when they are ready.

Got food? Just snacks, but food friendly and local menus are on hand. Occasional food trucks park outside.

Special Offer: Not participating at this time.

Directions: US 53 passes north–south through La Crosse and 2nd St runs parallel to the west. Take Main St or Pearl St toward the river from US 53 and the brewery is just north of the corner of Pearl and 2nd St.

The Beer Buzz: You know the way turtles climb on top of each other on logs and rocks while sunning themselves? That's a turtle stack. With the proximity of the Mississippi River and its own legion of stackable turtles, the name seemed appropriate for this most recent brewery to open in La Crosse. Then again it might be inspired by a certain children's story turtle who rhymes with Mertle.

Located in a 1880s building, in the city's historic architecture district, Turtle Stack is the creation of founder/brewer Brent Martinson. Hooked on homebrewing by a friend years ago, his hobby turned into a basement full of equipment. He already had a science background and started to believe beer was his future. Brent is originally from Fargo, ND but moved to La Crosse years ago. He left for Delafield to brew at Water Street Brewery for about 5 years but returned to La Crosse in 2013 to finally move forward on his own place. He eventually found this old building which had housed a printer for 60 years, a saloon, a mattress spring factory, and most recently, a clock shop. When they tore out the insides of the building, they found a 100-year-old wood floor underneath. Brent's small system allows him to keep switching things up on the taps, and that's exactly what he aims to do. Styles will range widely, though public response may determine some brews that end up on more often than others.

Free WiFi. No TVs. Music in the background, eventually some live acoustic music down the road. It's really about the beer and conversation.

Facebook/turtlestackbrewery

Stumbling Distance: While not a brewery, *Bodega Brew Pub* (122 4th St S, 608-782-0677, bodegabrewpublax.com) nevertheless is an impressive craft beer bar, with hundreds from around the world plus good food. *Buzzard Billy's* (222 Pearl St, 608-796-2277, buzzardbillys.com) is around the corner for casual Cajun/Creole and beer. Right across the street from there is *The Cheddarhead Store (608-784-8899),* the original home of those foam cheesehead hats and a bunch of other Wisconsin products/apparel/souvenirs. *The Charmant Hotel* (101 State St, 866-697-7300, thecharmanthotel.com) is a new boutique hotel in a repurposed 1898 candy factory. Great place to crash and has a rooftop bar.

LUCETTE BREWING CO.

Founded: 2011
Head Brewer: Jon Christiansen
Address: 901 Hudson Road • Menomonie, WI 54751
Phone: 715-233-2055
Website: www.lucettebrewing.com
Annual Production: 2,200 barrels
Number of Beers: 16 on tap (10–12 Lucette beers, small-batch exclusives, plus guest WI beers)

Staple Beers:
- » THE FARMER'S DAUGHTER SPICED BLONDE ALE (coriander and grains of paradise)
- » HIPS DON'T LIE BAVARIAN-STYLE WEISSBIER
- » RIDE AGAIN AMERICAN PALE ALE
- » SLOW HAND AMERICAN STOUT

Belgian Series:
- » DOUBLE DAWN BELGIAN STYLE IMPERIAL GOLDEN ALE
- » SHINING DAWN BELGIAN-STYLE GOLDEN ALE

Rotating Beers: (15 BBL Batch Series)
- » RYE'D ON MAN – Rye Brown Session Ale

Most Popular Brew: Farmer's Daughter

Brewer's Fave: Shining Dawn

Tours? Maybe, check the website.

Samples: Yes, sample flights.

Best Time to Go: The eatery should be open Wed–Sun but check the website for current hours.

Where can you buy it? Here on tap and to go in growlers. Distributed mostly in western Wisconsin and the Twin Cities metro area on draft or in six-packs of 16-oz cans or 750 ml cork & cage bottles. They self-distribute to Madison as well.

Got food? Yes, wood-fired Neapolitan-style pizza.

Special Offer: 10% off the purchase of Lucette Brewing merchandise during visit.

Directions: From I-94 take Exit 41 for Hwy 25 and head south through downtown on Hwy 25. Go west on Hwy 29, across from the university, and follow it ¾ mile and you'll see Lucette in a white building on your left (south side).

Cyclists: This is right off the Red Cedar State Trail.

The Beer Buzz: Lucette is the name of Paul Bunyan's girlfriend (or so it was decided in a statue-naming contest in Minnesota) and big Paul is a legendary lumberjack popular around these parts where the lumber industry once boomed. From the road, this place could be mistaken for a farmhouse, painted white, a porch out front. Don't expect a big industrial brewery. They wanted to fit in with their surroundings. Co-founder Michael Wilson is very serious about the local aspect of beer and part of his business philosophy is making a difference not just for himself, but for the businesses that support him—thus the use of local ingredients as much as possible.

Mike is originally from Minnesota, and while studying at University of North Dakota he determined that he wanted to be involved with the craft brewing industry. He dabbled in homebrewing and learned he wasn't good at it, but that wouldn't deter him. He moved to Menomonie and got experience in distribution. He met his business partner Tim Schletty who had a retail background. The two had experience in two of the three aspects of a brewery; now they only needed the all-important brewer. They hired Jon Christiansen who has been brewing with them since day one. Jon got his start at Water Street Lake Country in Delafield and spent some time at Joseph James Brewery in Vegas before being hired by Lucette Brewing.

In 2015, the brewery tripled the size of the building to accommodate Lucette Wood-fired Eatery. The 120-seat restaurant features a hand-cut stone oven from Naples for Neapolitan-style pizzas made with locally sourced ingredients. Patrons sit right in the middle of the brewery, not far from the canning line, for an open and visual beer and food experience.

Free WiFi. Facebook.com/LucetteBrewingCompany and Twitter @lucettebrewing

Stumbling Distance: *Red Cedar State Trail* runs right past the brewery. If you're a biker, this is a nice ride. See Biking for Beer in the back of the book.

REAL DEAL BREWING (THE RAW DEAL)

Founded: 2006 (brewing since 2014)
Brewmaster: Ryan Verdon
Address: 603 South Broadway • Menomonie, WI 54751
Phone: 715-231-3255
Web Site: www.rawdeal-wi.com
Annual Production: 40 barrels
Number of Beers: 8 taps, 4 year round beers, some guest taps, 1 nitro tap

Staple Beers:
- » DRIFTLESS ORGANIC PALE ALE
- » MILK STOUT
- » RAW RYE (a.k.a. GEOFF)
- » SCOTCH ALE

Rotating Beers:
- » BARLEYWINE
- » BEGLIAN QUADRUPEL
- » ENGLISH MILD
- » FARMHOUSE SAISON
- » IMPERIAL BELGIAN RYE SAISON
- » … various big beers and session beers, all unfiltered and unpasteurized

Most Popular Brew: Driftless Organic Pale Ale

Brewer's Fave: Changes all the time. (Rye Beer #5 at the time)

Tours? Yes, scheduled on website or Facebook.

Samples: Yes, four 4-oz pours for about $4.

Best Time to Go: Open Mon–Sat 6:30AM–8PM, Sun 9AM–6PM. Watch for seasonal hour changes and live music twice a month.

Where can you buy it? Here on tap or to go in your own growlers or Raw Deal's howlers.

Got food? The Raw Deal is first and foremost a coffee shop, with bagels, fresh juices/smoothies, cold press coffee on nitro, and bottled beer and wine.

Special Offer: Get a free hop patch with the purchase of your first beer during your signature visit.

Directions: Highways 12, 25 and 29 come together as Broadway St. heading south through town. Look for The Raw Deal on the corner at the intersection of Broadway and 6th Ave.

The Beer Buzz: Owners of previous editions of this book may recognize The Raw Deal as a former Stumbling Distance listing in the book. They roast their own coffee and serve a changing menu of organic and local dishes and desserts in a cozy, community-centric space. Now they are serving their own beer as well with the same devotion to quality: "No Crap on Tap. Period."

Brewer Ryan is a graduate of the beer-propriately named UW-Stout right here in town, and during his student life he hung out here at The Raw Deal doing his chemistry homework for a Food Science major. He'd come for coffee in the morning, beer in the evening. He started homebrewing with a kit from Northern Brewer, and when he took some time off from school, he worked at Rush River Brewing on the bottling line and doing odd jobs. When the owners here learned he brewed beer, they asked him to make a beer with their coffee in it. Soon they were tossing the idea around for a brewpub, and in June 2014 he started brewing here.

Ryan does many half-batches of experimental brews but also likes to keep down-to-earth session beers on tap. He loves farmhouse ales and English styles, and wants to keep beer as beer, "not something expensive and

snobby." He does occasional collaboration brews with Lucette Brewing in town. The local homebrewers have a good relationship with him and they meet here every week.

The building dates to 1905 and spent some time as an auto parts store. When the Fedderly family renovated the place to create The Raw Deal, they uncovered the pressed-tin ceiling, wood floors and brick walls. The large storefront windows and other windows high on the side wall let in a lot of light, and the assortment of used tables and comfortable couches makes this a very homey place. A 10-seat bar on the left toward back is where the beer is served, and the back bar is made from a fireplace mantel salvaged from a nineteenth-century mansion in Winona, MN. The Raw Deal roasts its own coffee beans, and you can see the roaster in the front window. This is a modern take on a public house, a community gathering space that brews coffee *and* beer. Check out the tap handle with Ryan's face on it, a gift from his assistant who studied graphic arts.

Free WiFi. On Facebook.

Stumbling Distance: *Zanzibar Restaurant & Pub* (228 Main St E, 715-231-9269, zanzibarmenomonie.com) has good food and is great for cocktails. *The Waterfront Bar & Grill* (512 Crescent St, 715-235-6541) has a reputable fish fry and a good tap list. If you enjoy disc golf, there are 4 courses in Menomonie.

BARLEY JOHN'S BREWING CO.

Opened: August 2015
Brewmaster: Bob McKenzie
Address: 1280 Madison Avenue • New Richmond, WI 54017
Phone: 715-246-4677
Web Site: www.barleyjohnsbrewery.com
Annual Production: capable of 10,000 barrels
Number of Beers: 16 taps; some guest taps

Staple Beers:
  » LITTLE BARLEY SESSION ALE
  » OLD 8 PORTER
  » 6 KNOT IPA (STOCKYARD IPA at the brewpub in MN)
  » WILD BRUNETTE WILD RICE BROWN ALE

Rotating Beers:
  » Maibock, Oktoberfest, Belgian styles, Doppelbock, Scotch Ale,
     and many more

Most Popular Brew: Too soon to tell.

Brewmaster's Fave: Old 8 Porter

Tours? Yes, check the website for the schedule.

Samples: Yes, four 5-oz pours.

Best Time to Go: For starters, open Thu–Fri 4PM–10PM, Sat 12PM–12AM,
Sun 12–8PM. But check the website to be certain!

Where can you buy it? Here on tap and in growlers to go, as well as kegs
and cans. Four-packs of 16-oz cans and kegs distributed in Western WI
and in MN, primarily in Twin Cities Metro initially.

Got food? Yes, eclectic café style with small plates and appetizer sorts of

things, snacks, bacon popcorn, pretzel, pickles, olive sampler, chips and dips, small sandwiches, meat and cheese plates, relish trays, and salads. No deep fryer.

Special Offer: A free 4-beer sampler flight with your book signature.

Directions: Coming into New Richmond from the south on WI 65, turn left on Richmond Way and go 0.6 mile. Turn right on Madison Ave, and of 0.4 mile to find the brewery on the right.

The Beer Buzz: John Moore and his wife Laura Subak have been running a highly successful brewpub in the Twin Cities area called Barley John's Brew Pub. Success compelled them to expand, but he'd have to buy a whole new brewhouse to increase capacity. Minnesota law prevents brewpubs (as opposed to production breweries) from distributing, and you can't own both. Someone told him he ought to go to beer-friendly Wisconsin, and New Richmond came up as a really nice community to work with. The City recommended a new build, but John was hesitant.

The law in MN says no owner of a brewpub in MN can have any owner-ship of a brewery *anywhere*. They consulted a lawyer, and it turns out the State of Minnesota considers a married couple as two separate entities. So Laura owns the brewpub now, and John owns the brewery. In Wisconsin this would be a problem (see The Brewing Projekt's story), but as they are married in Minnesota, they are in the clear. In the end they found they may have been able to do that separate ownership plan in Minnesota, but oh well, Wisconsin is happy to have them. The 30-barrel brewhouse occupies the great space in back. Brewer Bob attended the Heriot-Watt University's Brewing School in Scotland and worked with Bill Burdock at the now defunct Sherlock's Home in the Cities and spent 3-plus years at Third Street Brewhouse in Cold Spring, MN.

The building, at the corner of Madison and Wisconsin, is almost 14,000 square feet. The taproom has a long bar of birch wood, seats 75, and has a fireplace in the corner. Hops grow on a trellis outside, and some apple and cherry trees in the yard will eventually contribute their fruits to brews. There's a TV, some background music, and you might find a cribbage board lying around.

Free WiFi. Facebook/Barleyjohns and Twitter @barleyjohns

Stumbling Distance: Nearby *45th Parallel Distillery* (1570 Madison Ave, 715-246-0565, 45thparalleldistillery.com) does tours and tastings.

Brady's Brewhouse

Founded: October 10, 2010
Brewmaster: Luke Nirmaier
Address: 230 South Knowles Avenue • New Richmond, WI 54017
Phone: 715-246-9960
Website: www.bradysbrewhouse.com
Annual Production: 250 barrels
Number of Beers: 8–9 on tap, plus random firkins

Staple Beers:
- » Derailed Pale Ale
- » Harvester Oatmeal Stout
- » Hop Tornado IPA
- » Sunny Golden Wheat
- » Vagadond Irish Red

Rotating Beers:
- » Drag Buster Brown Ale
- » Hefweizen
- » Oktoberfest
- » Smoked Rye Porter

(Basically, a strong ale, a weekly special, and two seasonals are always on tap)

Most Popular Brew: Hop Tornado IPA

Brewmaster's Fave: Oktoberfest

Tours? Yes, by chance from 9–5; see if Luke is around.

Samples: Yes, a flight is $12 for eight 5-oz pours.

Best Time to Go: Open for lunch and dinner, from 11AM. Happy Hour all day Mon, Tue–Fri 3–6PM and Tue/Thu 10PM–close. Discount growler refills on Mondays.

Where can you buy it? Only at the bar or take-away in growlers.

Got food? Full menu with good burgers and pizza, including deep-fried cheese curds, beer cheese soup, and so much more. Good whiskey selection here.

Special Offer: $1 off your first house beer when you get your book signed.

Directions: Highway 65 comes right into New Richmond and becomes

Knowles Avenue. If you are coming from the south, watch for Brady's on the right between 2nd and 3rd Streets.

The Beer Buzz: There's a lot going on here. Great food, house-brewed beer, TVs, and plenty of space to kick back and relax with friends or family. The kitchen has a wood-fired oven, and the bar also offers a wide assortment of wines and cocktails. Itinerant Brewer Rick Sauer started the ball rolling and was then joined by Luke Nirmaier who took over when Rick left. Luke started in college and jumped in at Brady's via the kitchen. When he applied for a job, he recalls, "I brought in a six-pack—here's my portfolio." It got him in the door and after doing most of the brewing with Rick supervising, it wasn't a big deal when he found himself taking the reins alone.

A 10-gallon batch of R&D beer is typically on tap, so there's always something new to try. Brady's is family friendly and one of the finest places to eat in town. A room upstairs in back overlooks the brewhouse.

Free WiFi. ATM on site. Facebook.com/bradysbrewhouse

Stumbling Distance: Get a tour and tasting over at *45th Parallel Distillery* (45thparallelspirits.com, 1570 Madison Ave, 715-246-0565)—be sure to call for an appointment. *Star Prairie Trout Farm* (starprairietrout.com, 400 Hill Ave, Star Prairie, 715-248-3633) just north of town lets you catch 'em or just take home already caught and cleaned.

RUSH RIVER BREWING CO.

Founded: May 2004
Brewmasters: Dan Chang and Nick Anderson
Address: 990 Antler Court • River Falls, WI 54022
Phone: 715-426-2054
Website: www.rushriverbeer.com
Annual Production: undetermined
Number of Beers: 10

Staple Beers:
» BUBBLEJACK IPA
» DOUBLE BUBBLE IMPERIAL IPA
» LOST ARROW PORTER
» MINION IPA
» SMALL AXE GOLDEN ALE (Wisconsin-style Hefeweizen with local wheat)
» THE UNFORGIVEN AMBER ALE (dry-hopped)

Rotating Beers:
» LYNDALE BROWN ALE (Aug–Nov)
» NEVERMORE CHOCOLATE OATMEAL STOUT (winter)
» ÜBER ALT (April–July)
» WINTER WARMER (Oct–Jan; based on Scotch Ale with a malty emphasis)

Most Popular Brew: The Unforgiven Amber Ale

Brewmaster's Fave: Bubblejack IPA

Tours? Free tours with samples the second Saturday of each month at 1PM. Numbers are limited, and you must reserve a spot (use the website).

Samples? Yes.

Best Time to Go: Taproom open Thu–Sat 4–10PM.

Where can you buy it? Here on tap and distributed in six-pack and twelve-pack bottles. Their website shows their distribution in western Wisconsin, the Madison area, and eastern Minnesota (especially the Twin Cities).

Got food? Nope.

Special Offer: Not Participating.

The Beer Buzz: Dan and Nick were co-workers at a brewery in Seattle when they met. Nick's from Minneapolis and Dan hails from Milwaukee, so the logical place to set up shop was right in the middle, just inside the border of Wisconsin, as it turns out, in Maiden Rock. Dan put in some time at Summit Brewing Co. in St. Paul to perfect his art while Nick worked in retail to gain experience in that all-important aspect of the microbrewing world. Robbie Stair, a third partner, brought a site to the table—his farm on Lake Pepin. The twenty-barrel brewhouse, designed and built by the three owners, was a showcase of ingenuity. Then in March 2007, they packed up the farm, as it were, and moved into a new facility in River Falls. This change means more beer is a-flowing and bottles became available, but also we, the public, can now stop in for a tour.

Stumbling Distance: Fill your belly with some highly regarded local home-style cooking at *River Falls Family Restaurant* (702 North Main Street, 715-425-9440). Paddle or trout-fish the Kinnickinnic River (see my book *Paddling Wisconsin*).

ARE YOU A WISCONSIN BEER LOVER?

I mean, like *officially*? The Wisconsin Brewer's Guild brings together many of the state's great craft brewers and the businesses that support them to promote the art and educate the public about good beer. You may not be a brewer, but you can still join the club as a Wisconsin Beer Lover. Annual fees are about $30 and benefits include quarterly newsletters, VIP benefits at events sponsored by the guild, and discounts at some of the member breweries… and, of course, a lovely t-shirt. Go to their website to get an application or to find more information: wibrewersguild.com. Like them at Facebook.com/wibrewersguild

Oliphant Brewing

Founded: Spring 2013
Brewmaster: Matt Wallace and Trevor Wirtanen
Address: 350 Main Street, Suite 2 • Somerset, WI 54025
Website: www.oliphantbrewing.com
Annual Production: 360 bbls
Number of Beers: 10 on tap, plus 2 nitro taps

Beers: Nothing permanent—always rotating! But common returns:
  » Brown Sugar Brown Brown
  » EnnuIPA (different hops every time)
  » Milkman Manbaby (milky weizen dunkel stout)
  » Party on Wayne (black ale)
  » Party on Garth (blonde ale)

Tours? By appointment.

Samples: Yes, flights of 3.5-oz pours, 6 for $10, 12 for $17.

Best Time to Go: Open Thu–Fri 4–9PM, Sat 12–9PM, Sun 12–7PM; later hours in summer.

Where can you buy it? Here in pints and howlers, growlers and 32-oz "Crowlers" (on demand cans) to go. Some area draft accounts and at Liquor Depot next door.

Got food? Fresh cheese curds, beef & cheese. Bring your own if you want.

Special Offer: Bring this book in and receive a pretty good high-five (maybe even a great one?). Also, if you get a permanent face tattoo of their logo, they'll give you free beer for life!

Directions: Take Hwy 64 west from New Richmond and take the Business 64 exit into Somerset. This becomes Main Street. You'll see Liquor Depot and the brewery is around back past a mural of a chameleon on the wall of the building.

The Beer Buzz: Some of their story is a bit suspect, but trouble is I can't figure out which parts. Best to quote them: Trevor and Matt "met in Nepal at the secret caves underneath Mt. Everest fighting the Secret Ninja of the would-be American Communists group 'El Luchadores.' Trevor was mortally wounded until he saw a toucan, smelled Fruit Loops, and was reborn. At that very instant, Matt fell asleep and dreamed of the Oliphant. The Oliphant approached Matt with his hot pink sucker-fins and commanded him to open a brewery and distillery in Somerset, Wisconsin, to spread the liquid consciousness of the Oliphant to the people."

Fortunately, Trevor and Matt had been brewing for a while prior to their mind-numbing experience with the Oliphant. Trevor started homebrewing on a whim with the help of a friend's equipment and instantly became a fervent supporter of fermentation in all aspects. Next thing Matt knew, Trevor was forcing him to participate in weekly brewing sessions at times in the morning when no one should be brewing. Although not the career path they originally planned on, (Trevor has a Master's Degree in Music Composition and Matt double majored in English and Anthropology) they felt like it was in everyone's best interest not to get on the wrong side of the Oliphant and to do what it told them to do. You know… for the children.

The brewery is in the back space of a shared building that once packaged 7-Up, and at another time, some guy was in here building armored vehicles, but something happened and he fled the country. Don't ask too many questions. Now a garage door opens to a patio at the edge of the parking lot behind the building. The started the taproom here and much later opened up space in the adjoining room. You are drinking literally where they are brewing. No, seriously: they move portable brewing equipment in here when the taproom is closed. This may change as they expand a bit into that other room. They feature an ever-rotating tap list of beers. "We believe in having constant variety, and we feel that having only a few beers that we brew over and over is more akin to manufacturing than crafting. We are brewers, not manufacturers, and we strive to create something that will keep our patrons excited and surprised." Jeremy Hughes does their chalkboard art for the beer menu. Taylor Berman is the creator of the giant chameleon. They've got cornhole and Giant Jenga, board games and comic books, or Free Wifi if you'd just prefer not to talk to anyone.

Stumbling Distance: *Liquor Depot* (350 Main St, 715-247-5336) has a good assortment of Wisconsin products. *Pizza Planet* (253 Main St, 715-247-3399, pizzaplanetsomerset.com) serves carry out as well (hint, hint, taproom). 18 holes await at *Somerset Disc Golf Course* (390 Tower Rd, facebook.com/somersetdiscgolf). Your local cheese is made at *Bass Lake Cheese Factory* (598 Valley View Trail, 715- 247-5586, blcheese. com) and they also serve sandwiches, burgers and such. Go tubing down the Apple River with *Float Rite* (floatrite.com, 715-247-3453) but be sure not to take glass out on the water. Find an alternative growler for Oliphant beer (Crowler?).

MINES CREEK BREWERY

Founded: July 2014
Brewmaster: Dave Boisen
Address: S345 Hidden Fox Court • Spring Valley, WI 54767
Phone: 715-778-5513
Web Site: www.minescreekbrewing.jimdo.com
Annual Production: 10 barrels
Number of Beers: 3 taps

Staple Beers:
  » CANADIAN PALE ALE
  » DIRTY BLONDE ALE
  » NUT BROWN ALE

Rotating Beers:
  » COLUMBUS NIGHT DARK IPA
  » KÖLSCH
  » NORWEGIAN FARMHOUSE ALE
  » OKTOBERFEST

Most Popular Brew: Nut Brown Ale

Brewmaster's Fave: He likes German styles best.

Tours? No, but if you catch him brewing, he'll show off his little Sabco Brew-Magic.

Samples: Yes, a taste to choose, but no flights yet.

Best Time to Go: This is a seasonal brewery at a golf course, so it is open daily during golf season. Around May 1 the first batch appears, and beer should be available through September and into October perhaps. Phone first!

Where can you buy it? Here on tap in 4-, 8-, 12- and 16-oz pours, but no growlers at the moment (maybe soon).

Got food? Just a bit of bar food, burgers, cheese curds, pizza, but there's no wait staff.

Special Offer: Not participating.

Directions: WI 29 passes through Spring Valley. Watch for Van Buren Road on the west side of town and take that north 0.4 mile. Turn right on Silver Fox Dr and it runs right into the golf course. The brews are served at the bar.

The Beer Buzz: This may be the smallest nanobrewery in Wisconsin and it's not even open year round. Golf course owner Guy Leach and Brewer Dave live near each other and their kids are about the same age. Dave was sharing his homebrew with Guy and they thought it would be nice to have some fresh beer out at the golf course. So Guy applied for a brewpub license and here you are. The first brews were Nut Brown Ale, Dirty Blonde Ale, and Canadian Pale Ale, and they became crowd favorites. They might not always be on tap as Dave makes 10-gallon batches, and brews come and go.

Several years ago he was looking for career change. In exasperation, he said to his wife, "When I retire I am gonna brew beer by day, drink beer by night." She and his two kids got him a Mr. Beer Kit as a gift. Over $15,000 later, Mines Creek is on tap overlooking the links. Dave grows 10 different varieties of hops at home.

Dave works at UW-Stout (a beery sounding university if there ever was one) and brews on weekends generally. His undergrad degree was in history, and he admits that part of his brewing fascination is the story behind each beer style. He learned the Norwegians couldn't grow hops too far north and so they added juniper to their beers. And so he brews a Norwegian Farmhouse Ale. Generally he sticks to German Reinheitsgebot rules and keeps beers simple: water, malt, yeast and hops. This is the only tap beer at the golf course, and it's "Plain Jane brewing," as he calls it. "It's not a lot of money, but I'm having a lot of fun."

The two-story main building once held the clubhouse downstairs and a proper restaurant upstairs. Now it's a bar with a limited bar menu. The scenic 18-hole course is rather popular with golfers from the Twin Cities. The view out over the golf course from the windows in the small, 70s decor bar is rather nice. A couple big screens often show golf, but of course Packers or Badgers football or Brewers baseball will be on—though this is not really a sports bar.

WiFi. Facebook/Mines-Creek-Brewing

Stumbling Distance: Obviously, you can golf a round here at *Spring Valley Golf Course* (345 Hidden Fox Ct, 715-778-5513, playspringvalleygolf. com). *Cady Cheese Store* (126 WI Highway 128, Wilson, 715-772-4218, cadycheese.com) is on the way to *Dave's BrewFarm* in Wilson if you're heading that way. Go 70 feet underground into a geological wonder at *Crystal Cave* (W965 WI-29, 715-778-4414, acoolcave.org) south of town. Tours and gem panning, good family fun.

Dave's BrewFarm—A Farmhouse Brewery

Founded: March 2008
Chief Yeast Wrangler: Dave Anderson
Address: 2470 Wilson Street • Wilson, WI 54027
Phone: 612-432-8130 (*see note below)
Website: www.davesbrewfarm.blogspot.com
Annual Production: 100 bbls
Number of Beers: 8 taps at the farm, too many styles to list!

Rotating Beers:
  » AuBEXXX
  » BrewFarm Select
  » Matacabras
  » Mocha Diablo
  » SOB OMG (sour orange basil)
  » Anything goes here! You never know what to expect!

Most Popular Brew: Mocha Diablo

Brewmaster's Fave: "You want me to pick my favorite child?!? Depends on the mood. I usually say the beer in my right hand."

Tours? Yes, they do free tours and have open taproom hours in the LaBrewatory, but they vary. Make an appointment or watch the blog or Facebook page.

Samples? "Oh yes, the best way to sell my beers!"

Best Time to Go: Taproom is open every other weekend more or less. Check the blog or the Facebook page to be certain.

Where can you buy it? For now, only in the taproom.

Got food? No, but peanuts in the shell are usually on hand.

Special Offer: A 15% discount on a BrewFarm T-shirt.

Directions: Take Exit 28 off I-94, head north about 2.5 miles to 80th Ave. Take a right onto 80th to the "T" intersection. You can't miss the red barn board building with the wind generator on the 120-ft tower making power!

The Beer Buzz: Like many, Dave's brewing problem started with home-brewing in 1992, and progressed with him going to the Siebel Institute in

1996. By then he was too far gone and wanted to open his own brewery. He conceived of the "BrewFarm" in 1995. Dave wanted to brew beer and be out in the country in a farmhouse setting. He brewed for the short-lived Ambleside Brewery in Minneapolis and Paper City Brewery in Holyoke, MA, worked for a variety of beer distributors, worked both importing and exporting craft beer, and consulted with start-up breweries in places around the world, including Vietnam, Italy, and Israel. In the end he landed in Wilson, WI, to finally make the BrewFarm a reality. Dave started brewing here and an immediate demand compelled him to do some contract brewing offsite, producing cans and bottles. After a short while he decided that didn't feel right for him, so he cut the contract and now just brews at the farm. He's a one-man show, and this is quality not quantity.

Dave's beer is looking pretty green. You can see Jake, the 120-foot-tall 20kW wind generator that provides nearly all the power for Dave's brewery and home. (One blog entry shows his electric bill was 81-cents one month!) The beer name Matacabras comes from a Spanish term for a wind that "kills goats." But Wisconsin wind is a bit nicer; here on the wind-powered farm, it brews beer! Throw in some recycled dairy equipment repurposed for beer plus a solar thermal system in the works, and this is about as eco-friendly as a brewery can get. Drink some beer to protect the environment.

*At the time of writing, Dave was in a sort of transitional period. The brewery has been for sale, on and off the market a couple times as he decided what he's going to do next in this life. Someone may come in and buy the whole package and continue brewing here, or maybe not. Be sure to check the blog above or Facebook before trying to visit.

Stumbling Distance: There's not much out here, but if you are looking for a good place to eat, try *Peg's Pleasant View Inn* (3015 US Highway 12, Wilson, 715-772-4610). *Lucette Brewing* and *Real Deal Brewing* are in Menomonie another 20 minutes east on I-94.

ZONE 4

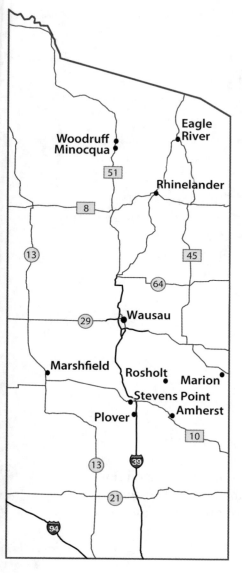

Amherst: Central Waters Brewery
Eagle River: Tribute Brewing Co.
Marion: Pigeon River Brewing Co.
Marshfield: Blue Heron BrewPub
Minocqua: Minocqua Brewing Co.
Plover: O'so Brewing Co.
Rhinelander: Rhinelander Brewing Co.
Rosholt: Kozy Yak Brewery
Stevens Point: Stevens Point Brewery
Wausau: Bull Falls Brewery
Wausau: Great Dane Pub and Brewery
Wausau: Red Eye Brewery
Woodruff: Rocky Reef Brewing Co.

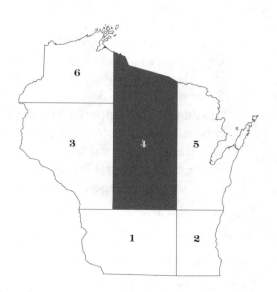

CENTRAL WATERS BREWING CO.

Founded: January 1998
Brewmaster: Paul Graham
Address: 351 Allen Street • Amherst, WI 54406
Phone: 715-824-2739
Website: www.centralwaters.com
Annual Production: 11,000 bbls
Number of Beers: 15 on tap; 20+ beers each year

Staple Beers:
- » GLACIAL TRAIL IPA
- » HONEY BLONDE
- » HORICON SESSION IPA
- » MUD PUPPY PORTER
- » OUISCONSING RED ALE
- » SATIN SOLITUDE IMPERIAL STOUT
- » SHINE ON ALE

Rotating Beers:
- » BREWHOUSE COFFEE STOUT
- » HEADLESS HERON
- » ILLUMINATION DOUBLE IPA
- » LA PETIT MORT
- » LAC DU BAY (English IPA)
- » OCTOBERFEST LAGER
- » RYE BARREL CHOCOLATE PORTER
- » SLÁINTE SCOTCH ALE
- » SPACE GHOST (Imperial Stout with ghost peppers)
- » SUMMARILLO INDIA-STYLE PALE LAGER
- » and BREWER RESERVE SERIES: bourbon barrel-aged brews (Barleywine, Stout, Cherry Stout, and Scotch Ale) and CELLAR SESSIONS, barrel-aged brewery anniversary brews and more.

Most Popular Brew: Glacial Trail IPA

Brewmaster's Fave: The one in his hand.

Tours? Yes, Fri at 5PM, Sat at 3PM, but check the website to be sure.

Samples? Yes. Sample platters of 5 pours for about $8.

Best Time to Go: The Tap Room is open Fri 3–10PM, Sat 12PM–10PM, Sun 12PM–5PM. Open for retail sales Mon–Thu 8AM–4PM, Fri 8AM–10PM, Sat 12PM–10PM, Sun 12PM–5PM.

Where can you buy it? Here on tap and in growlers, bottles and kegs to go. Bottles and kegs around Wisconsin, Minnesota, Illinois.

Got food? No.

Special Offer: A free Central Waters sticker when you get your book signed.

Directions: From US Hwy 10 take the Cty Rd A exit and go north 0.7 mile. Turn left on Washington St, go 0.2 mile and turn left on Allen St. Go 0.3 mile and the brewery is on the right.

The Beer Buzz: Paul calls it a "hobby gone out of control." He was brewing in his dorm room when he was 18. Perfectly legal to buy the ingredients, but he wasn't allowed to drink his results. And I'm sure he didn't. Actually, at first, he really didn't—it was so bad, he said, he couldn't. He was just playing around but soon got the hang of it (as one can tell from the great beer here). Mike McElwain and Jerome Ebel opened the brewery first in a 1920s former Ford Dealership in Junction City in a small brick building with a flapping screen door that opened right out onto the highway through town. Paul called it a "glorified homebrew system," and he did the boils in a 300-gallon cheese starter tank with a commercial hot water heater element attached to the bottom. Converted dairy tanks functioned as fermenters, and the whole operation was built by hand. After 3 years Paul and Clint Schultz bought the brewery, and soon after Anello Mollica took Clint's place. Success led to expansion and Central Waters started a brewpub in Marshfield (now the independent Blue Heron) and moved the brewery into new digs in Amherst in 2006. The current brewing facility was the first green-powered brewery in the state (though no longer the only). Besides energy efficient lights and equipment and radiant-heat flooring, they have a bank of twenty-four solar collectors. In October 2011, they added 20,000-watt solar photovoltaic panels which provide 20% of their annual power needs. As they like to say at the brewery: "Making the world a better place, one beer at a time." Their Barleywine has gotten a couple of awards, and Bourbon-Barrel Barleywine and Bourbon Barrel Cherry Stout have both taken gold at Great American Beer Festival. Special releases are anxiously anticipated.

Facebook.com/CWBrewing

Stumbling Distance: *Tomorrow River Supper Club & Motel* (9971 Cty Rd KK, 715-824-3113), a block off the end of Main St, is a notable local restaurant with a Friday fish fry. Stay the night in Amherst at *Amherst Inn B&B* (303 S Main St, 888-211-3555, amherstinn.com). *Go paddling* on either the Waupaca River or the tubing-easy (but fun) Crystal River in nearby Waupaca (See my book *Paddling Wisconsin*).

CENTRAL WISCONSIN CRAFT COLLECTIVE

What started out as the Grain Circle Tour, has since evolved into this collective of craft fermentation and distillation. This cluster of breweries plus a winery and distillery make for a nice little roadtrip in Central Wisconsin—and yes, you can bike it, if you prefer.

Leave the driving to someone else and book a private ride for your group:
Lamers (715-421-2400)
Xecutive Limousine (715-344-1153)
Courtesy Cab (715-342-8863)
Hop Head Tours based in Madison does on-demand tours (608-467-5707, hopheadtours.com)

The rails-to trails *Tomorrow River Trail* connects Plover to Amherst on a flat 14.8 mile ride. Biking the entire circle is about 55 miles.

For more information contact Stevens Point Area Convention & Visitor Bureau: 715-344-2556 | www.stevenspointarea.com.

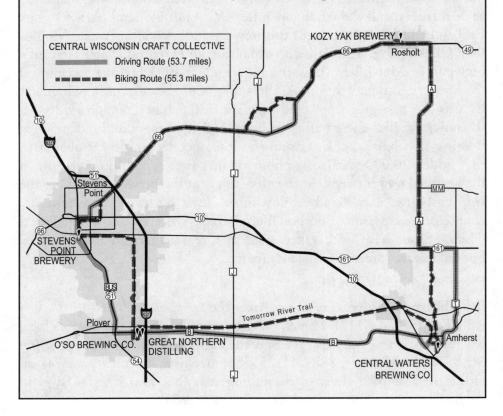

TRIBUTE BREWING CO.

Founded: February 2012
Brewmaster: Marc O'Brien
Address: 1106 Bluebird Road • Eagle River, Wisconsin 54521
Phone: 715-480-2337
Website: www.tributebrewing.com
Annual Production: 400+ bbl
Number of Beers: 4–8 of their own on tap, plus 10–12 guest Wisconsin beers

Staple Beers: (subject to change)
  » BAREFOOT CHARLIE IPA
  » BLUEBERRY TRAIN WHEAT ALE
  » GHOST LIGHTS AMBER LAGER (Vienna style)
  » OLD EAGLE CHOCOLATE PORTER
  » 28 LAKES LAGER (Dortmunder style)

Rotating Beers:
  » BUCK SNORT COFFEE STOUT
  » BUCKSKINNER BOCK
  » FINN'S IRISH RED ALE
  » FROSTWATCH CRANBERRY WHEAT ALE
  » MELE KALIKIMAKA COCONUT PORTER
  » SUMMER KAMP BELGIAN STYLE WITBIER
  » WHITE LEGS JALAPEÑO WHEAT ALE
  » … and more planned!

Most Popular Brew: Blueberry Train Wheat

Brewmaster's Fave: Barefoot Charlie IPA.

Tours? No.

Samples: Yes, a sampler tray of 6 of their beers.

Best Time to Go: The taproom is open Tue–Fri 3–9PM and Sat 1–9PM. Closed Sun–Mon.

Where can you buy it? Here on tap and in pre-filled growlers—pre-filled to ensure proper carbonation and sanitation. Growlers available at *Trig's Cellar 70's* in Eagle River, Minocqua & Rhinelander, *Stein's Lincoln Street Liquor* in Rhinelander and at *Paul's Pump & Pantry* in Eagle River.

Got food? Free peanuts and popcorn, or have pizza delivered.

Special Offer: $1 off your first pint of Tribute beer during your signature visit.

Directions: From downtown Eagle River head north on Highway 45 to Airport Road. Go left here and the next street is Bluebird Road. Go left again (south) and the brewery is on the right side.

The Beer Buzz: This isn't founder Bill Summers' first involvement with the craft beer scene. He and a few others originally started Eagle River's Great Northern Beer Festival (greatnorthernbeerfestival.com). Now he and his wife VaLynda run the fest with the help of volunteers. After the short-lived Loaf & Stein brewpub came and went in the late 90s, there was really no craft beers for locals to enjoy. Bill did some research and visited a lot of places to see what sort of place might work for a brewpub. In the 1990s the trend was to buy an old brick building downtown somewhere (as South Shore in Ashland or Angry Minnow in Hayward) and refashion it into a pub. Then he saw brewers moving into industrial parks and airport hangars. In the end, Bill felt this model made a more casual atmosphere, made clients comfortable, and gave everyone more space. They were more talkative and laid back.

Bill found this building out near the highway and the airport and decided it was perfect. The former home to a log home design company and their woodcrafting shop, it had a good vibe. "Like going into a garage party, a

keg in the corner." In fact, the brewery opens a garage door in nice weather for some good air. The style is all industrial: Barrels under the bar, cement floor, warehouse lighting, and galvanized metal utility panels along the walls. A couple of antennae towers frame the bar. You can also see Bill's collection of over 150 growlers. No pool tables or jukebox. What you'll get here is just a great place to hang out and talk craft beer or play cribbage, Battleship or other games.

Brewer Marc is president of the L.U.S.H. Inc. homebrew club in the Northwoods and has won some awards for his homebrews. He and Bill were at a club meeting at Minocqua Brewing Co. a several years ago and tossed around the idea of going pro. And in 2012 that happened. Their beer is on tap at a lot of Northwoods bars and restaurants with a waiting list until they are able to increase production. Tribute names their beers as a "tribute" to local historical people, places or events.

Stumbling Distance: Eagle River is on the Chain of Lakes, the largest inland fresh water chain of lakes in the world with 28 connected bodies of water. So boaters, fishermen, and paddlers will find Nirvana here. Right across the street from the brewery is the *World Championship Snowmobile Derby Track* (derbytrack.com). *Leif's Café* (800 N Railroad St, 715-479-2766) is walking distance and is famous for breakfast and brunch. *Riverstone Restaurant & Tavern* (riverstonerestaurant.com, 219 Railroad St, 715-479-8467) has an eclectic dinner menu, a Friday fish fry, and very good wine and beer list.

Pigeon River Brewing Co.

Founded: July 18, 2012
Head Brewers: Nate Knaack and Brett "Bub" Hintz
Address: W12710 U.S. Highway 45 • Marion, WI 54950 **
Phone: 715-256-7721
Website: www.pigeonriverbrewing.com
Annual Production: 600–700 barrels
Number of Beers: 18 on tap (some guest taps)

Staple Beers:
- Buxom Lass Scottish Ale
- German Hefeweizen
- Townie (cream ale)
- Wet Willy Oatmeal Stout

Rotating Beers:
- Belgian White
- Chipotle Porter
- On Your Knees Midnight Wheat
- Red IPA
- Spring Fugue Bock
- Vanilla Jimmy Java Porter (aka The VJJ)
- Seasonals

Most Popular Brew: Townie

Brewer's Fave: Nate: German Hefe | Bub: He drinks anything.

Tours? Yes, if the brewers are there, you can ask.

Samples: Yes, a flight of all their beers 4.5-oz pours for about $6.

Best Time to Go: Hours are Wed–Fri 4pm–close, Sat 11am–11pm, Sun 11am–8pm. Closed Mon–Tues. Double check the website. The Iola Old Car Show, the largest in the Midwest, takes place on a long weekend in July in nearby Iola.

Where can you buy it? Here on tap and in growlers to go. Draft accounts from Shawano to Fond du Lac and the Fox Cities. Bottling is on the horizon.

Got food? Yes, a full kitchen with handcrafted pizza, hand-pattied burgers, wings, and appetizers (cheese curds). Friday fish fry.

Special Offer: One free pint when you get your book signed.

Directions: The brewery is at the west edge of town on the north side of Highway 45 set back a bit from the road.

The Beer Buzz: Nate and Matt grew up in the same town of 1200 or so, yet didn't meet until they both ended up at the University of Wisconsin-Platteville. For a short while the university even had its own microbrewery in the student union. Nate had already started brewing in high school, and both he and Matt joined the UWP Homebrewing Club. (Nate was president.) They decided early on that brewing was something they wanted to do professionally and set up a five-year plan to make it happen back in Marion.

Nate then married his high school sweetheart Kayla, a UW business graduate who has been instrumental in getting the administrative details of the whole project in order. "Without her we wouldn't be where we're at," says Nate. When the right place opened up for a brewpub in the fall of 2011, Nate and Kayla picked it up, planning to wait until they were ready for the next step. Two weeks later, O'so Brewing called; they were in the midst of a big move and upgrade and were looking to sell their old brew system. Things just kept falling into place. Kinda like an avalanche, all at once, until Pigeon River Brewing opened for business on July 18, 2012 in honor of the feast day of St. Arnold of Metz, patron saint of brewers.

The 5000 square foot facility was previously a restaurant and bar with a banquet hall. So one side was ready to handle a brewpub, while the banquet hall required more remodeling to become a brewhouse. You can see right into it through windows from the bar side. The brewpub has a warm atmosphere about it, with old breweriana on the walls for decoration.

According to Nate, their mission is to "keep people excited about local beers they may not have heard of." So along with their own brews you can get a few more rotating guest beers from Wisconsin. Dupont Cheese makes a beer cheese with their Scottish Ale and they sell it on site.

**Double check the address, they may be crossing the street in 2016, at which time they will start bottling.

Stumbling Distance: As Nate puts it, Marion is "sitting at the gateway to the Northwoods" on Highway 45. A snowmobile trail crosses the property. An area special event that draws a big crowd is *Caroline Lions Colorama* (carolinelionscolorama.com), the first weekend of October. Of other local interest is *Dupont Cheese Inc.* (dupontcheeseinc.com, N10140 Hwy 110, 800-895-2873) five miles south on 110 which makes some stellar cheeses.

Blue Heron BrewPub (West 14th Restaurant)

Founded: 2005
Head Brewer: Ron Hulka
Address: 108 W 9th Street • Marshfield, WI 54449
Phone: 715-389-1868
Website: www.blueheronbrewpub.com
          www.west14threstaurant.com
Annual Production: 300 bbls
Number of Beers: 10–12 on tap

Staple Beers:
» Honey Blonde (made with local Hauke Honey)
» Hop Heart IPA
» Loch Ness Strong Scotch Ale
» Tiger's Eye (English mild with pale ale malt and English Fuggles hops)

Rotating Beers: (a few possibilities)
» Angry Leprechaun Irish Red
» Bock Your World
» Dubilee Dubbel
» Grapefruit IPA
» Hub City Lager
» Oktoberfest
» Pack-Man Porter
» Parkin's Pilz (German-style pilsner)
» pREDator
» Rauchbier
» Red, White & Wheat American Hefeweizen
» Rye-man Simon (red rye saison)
» Shadowfax White Wit
» Tapper's Tripel
» Wisco Yeti Robust Brown

Most Popular Brew: Honey Blonde

Brewmaster's Fave: Shadowfax

Tours? Yes, by appointment, usually Saturdays.

Samples? Yes, five 5-oz samples for $6.

Best Time to Go: Open Mon–Sat at 11AM. Closed Sundays. Watch for pint of the day discount.

Where can you buy it? On tap here and the restaurant upstairs and in growlers to go (plus sixth- and half-barrels. Occasionally on tap at O'so

Brewery in Plover and a couple others beer bars. Growler options run the gamut, from glass to steel, 2 liter German-style, a stainless steel gallon mini-keg with CO2 tap on it.

Got food? Great food, in fact! Full pub menu with pizza. Pasta alla Phil is a big hit (bowtie pasta with 3 cheeses, chicken, bacon in a creamy sauce). Fried pickle slices are excellent. Upstairs is fine dining (but no tie required). From grilled ribeye to alligator stir-fry, this is great stuff. Beer cheese soup with andouille sausage. Friday night Fish Fry!

Special Offer: A free pint of house beer during your signature visit.

Directions: Coming into town on Business Hwy 13 (Central Ave), look for 9th St on the south side and the brewpub is on the corner on the west side across 9th from Holiday Inn.

The Beer Buzz: I was thrilled to death to know that my birth home was to have a brewpub. In 2005, Central Waters Brewery got together with Marshfield's finest restaurant and set up a brewpub/restaurant in this renovated brick creamery. The Parkin family built this dairy processing plant in 1941 and operated it until 1966. The ice cream here was tops and the family figured prominently in the so-called milk wars when grocers and dairy farmers formed the first cooperatives. The "Got milk?" people are part of that organization that John Parkin helped put together. Now you can still see some ice cream molds and some painted bricks on the wall which were used to match label colors on the ice creams. Check out the We Want Beer photo near the restrooms—anti-Prohibition marchers all decked out in suits and fedoras. Who said beer drinkers didn't have class?

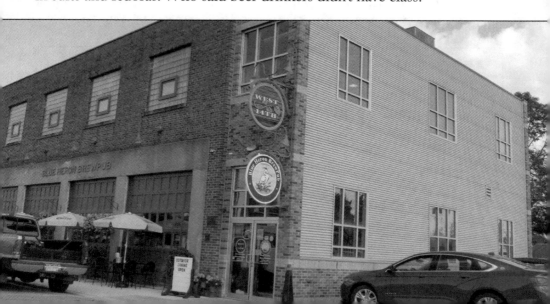

Marshfield hadn't had its own beer since local mail-order cheese pioneer John Figi made an attempt to keep the Marshfield Brewery alive after its long run from 1889 to 1965. Figi Brewing Co. lasted less than two years. In 2008, the brewpub became independent of Central Waters Brewery and was renamed Blue Heron. Sister establishment West 14th Street Restaurant is upstairs, and if you are wondering why such a name for a place on West 9th, it's because the restaurant moved here from that previous address well after establishing a good reputation with the moniker. A couple of TVs show sports, and a small gift shop by the door sells the pub's paraphernalia. One tap is always reserved for a M.A.S.H. (Marshfield Area Society of Homebrewers) brew, and a Hop Harvest beer is made each year from fresh hops picked by the club. When the previous brewer left for Eugene, Oregon, Ron came from Rusty Truck Brewing in Oregon to replace him.

Free WiFi. Facebook.com/blue.brewpub and Twitter @BluHeronBrewPub

Stumbling Distance: At the Central Wisconsin Fairgrounds east on 14th Street you will find the *World's Largest Round Barn*. Come on, it's at least a photo op! *Lumberyard Bar & Grill* (1651 N Central Ave, 715-387-1920) has a good craft beer list. Just north of town off Cty Hwy E, *JuRustic Park* (www.jurustic.com, M222 Sugar Bush Ln, 715-387-1653) is a collection of large critters fashioned out of scrap metal. For fresh cheese curds and a great variety of other cheeses (including aged varieties), don't miss *Nasonville Dairy* (nasonvilledairy.com, 10898 Hwy 10 West, 715-676-2177) The world's largest block of cheese? Well, at least the container for it. Head west on Hwy 10 to Neillsville and you can't miss this roadside attraction with a talking cow and the Wisconsin Pavilion from the 1964 World's Fair.

WHY CREAMERIES?

And gas stations?!? You may notice that some of the breweries occupy buildings with similar stories. More than a couple are renovated creameries from the early part of the twentieth century. Why such a common brewing site? Sloped tiled floors with drains in the middle—lots of filling and draining and mopping goes into the brewing process. Plus some of the old stainless steel dairy tanks are perfectly suited for brewing beer. Who knew? Basically any building that already has adequate drains for brewing is a bonus as refitting such a system into an old building can be quite an undertaking.

Minocqua Brewing Company

Founded: 1997 / January 2006
Brewmaster: Ryan White
Address: 238 Lake Shore Drive • Minocqua, WI 54548
Phone: 715-356-2600
Website: www.minocquabrewingcompany.com
Annual Production: 600 bbls and growing each year
Number of Beers: 7–8 at all times

Staple Beers:

» Bare Naked Brown Ale
» Minocqua Pale Ale
» Pudgy Possum Porter
» Roadkill Red Ale (8.5% abv)
» Whitey's Wheat Ale
» Wild Bill's Wild Rice Lager
  (made with native Wisconsin rice)

Rotating Beers:

» Dark Dwarf (Black IPA)
» Hefeweizen
» Honey Cranberry Ale (for Beef-A-Rama using local cranberries)
» Oatmeal Stout
» Scottish Ale
» Vanilla Cream Ale

Most Popular Brew: Red Ale or Wheat Ale or Pale Ale

Brewmaster's Fave: Either the Pale Ale or the Wild Rice Lager.

Tours? No.

Samples? Yes, $12 for seven 5-oz beers.

Best Time to Go: Closed on Mondays, otherwise open 11 AM–close. Visit in summer when the town goes from Unincorporated to almost 200,000 people. Winter brings in snowmobilers. Beef-A-Rama shouldn't be missed! Watch for live entertainment on the weekends in the upstairs Divano Lounge.

Where can you buy it? On tap here and in growlers and howlers to go. Minocqua Winter Park has their beer on tap in winter months.

Got food? Yes! Expect a pub menu but with a gourmet twist. Beef and brie open-face sandwiches, sharp cheddar nuggets and calamari are popular. Try the wheat ale and smoked gouda soup or the wild rice veggie burger. They use Vern's Cheese out of Chilton, WI. Also there's a fish fry serving perch and cod and Alaskan whitefish for fish and chips.

Special Offer: A free pint when you get your book signed!

Directions: Hwy 51 splits into two one-way streets, northbound and southbound, in the middle of town at Torpy Park. Take the southbound branch and the brewery is next to Torpy Park to the west.

The Beer Buzz: Like the mythological Phoenix rising literally from its own ashes, the MBC, under new ownership, came back in 2006 and started brewing again after fire destroyed much of the guts of the building. The brewpub/restaurant is located in a 1927 brick Masonic Temple—I asked if there were any secret rooms; they *claim* they didn't find any. Brothers Ryan and Dustin White, along with their parents, salvaged the place and re-opened it even as they were restoring the second floor. In 2009 they added the upstairs Divano Lounge which has become a nice source of good live music in the community bringing in big names from around the Midwest. Music tends toward folk, bluegrass, and originals. The lounge also functions as an event space or just a nice option for drinks while you're waiting for a table in the restaurant downstairs. There's always something going on in the summer around Minocqua and the MBC has a nice downtown location right on the water and next to a small shady park.

Stumbling Distance: *The Cheese Board* (www.thecheeseboard.com, 8524 Hwy 51, 877-230-1338) has a variety of Wisconsin cheeses and does gift boxes. *Otto's Beer & Brat Garden* (509 Oneida St, 715-356-6134) serves Sheboygan brats and over 80 different beers. The outdoor beer garden makes this a great summer hangout. Perhaps the quirkiest time to come here is for *Beef-A-Rama* (www.minocqua.org, 800-446-6784). First celebrated in 1964, the annual festival is the last Saturday in September. Friday night is a kickoff with polka music, then the next day 1500 lbs. of beef is roasted for the 10,000 or so that come out for the event. An arts and crafts fair is part of it, but the central moment is the Parade of Beef and sandwiches from the roasters along the sidewalks downtown. Heading north a bit to Boulder Junction, check out *Aqualand Ale House* (10450 Main St, Boulder Junction, 715-385-0380, aqualandalehouse.com) with 20 taps, including 3 of their own brand brewed at *Corner Pub* in Reedsburg.

O'so Brewing Company

Founded: 2007
Brewers: Marc Buttera and Team O'so
Address: 3028 Village Park • Plover 54467
Phone: 715-254-2163
Website: www.osobrewing.com
Annual Production: 6,350 bbls
Number of Beers: 40 taps (¾ O'so and ¼ Wisconsin guest taps)
7 year round plus many seasonals and specialty beers in distribution

Staple Beers:
 » The Big O (sort of a farmhouse ale)
 » Convenient Distraction (750 ml, Imperial Porter w/vanilla, coffee)
 » Hopdinger (Pale Ale)
 » Hop Whoopin' (IPA)
 » Memory Lane (German-style pilsner)
 » Night Train (Oatmeal Porter)
 » Rusty Red

Rotating Beers:
 » Dank (Imperial Red)
 » Doe in Heat (American-style pilsner)
 » The Dominator Dopplebock
 » Lupulin Maximus (IPA with a hop cone in the bottle!)
 » O-toberfest
 » Picnic Ants (saison with Brettanomyces)
 » Sweet Lady Stout
 » O'so Extreme Beers: a variety of wood cask aged beers, especially well regarded sours ales
 » Plus a new one-off monthly: e.g. Black my Eye-PA, Black is the New Orange, Dr's Bock…

Most Popular Brew: Hopdinger

Brewmaster's Fave: He likes the stuff he's been putting in barrels.

Tours? Yes, Saturdays at 2, 3 and 4 PM, with a $2 donation to a different local charity each month.

Samples? A flight of as many samples as you want from the 40 taps at $2 each.

Best Time to Go: The Tap House is open Mon–Fri 3–9PM, Sat noon–9PM, but often longer hours in summer, so check the website. Watch for their anniversary party in November which is also a Toys for Tots event.

Where can you buy it? Here on tap and in growlers, six-packs, 750 ml bottles, and kegs to go. Distributed in bottles and kegs all over Wisconsin and Chicagoland, and a wee bit in England (the UK, not a cheekily named Wisconsin town). Watch for the O'so Boombox, a case of 12 with at least 4 different brews. Some exclusive 750 ml bottles are only sold in the Tap House.

Got food? Bring your own or order in; it's all cool. Restaurants all around them.

Special Offer: 10% off of O'so merchandise when you get the book signed.

Directions: From I-39/US-51, take Exit 153 at Cty Rd B/Plover Road heading west. Take the first left on Village Park Drive and you will go 1.5 blocks and see O'so across the big parking lot on your right.

The Beer Buzz: Co-owner/brewer Marc Buttera started homebrewing in 1994. His first brew? Barleywine. Not a bad start, but he soon found there was no place to get supplies. So he and his wife Katina opened one: Point Brew Supply. "It was so tiny," says Katina, "customers had to wait in the hall for the previous customer to check out." After the second location, the couple moved into a new location, opening a brewery adjoining the supply shop.

They started on repurposed dairy equipment and used equipment from Central Waters and the now defunct Falls Brewery and Denmark Brewing. The growth was stupendous, and this wasn't going to be enough to keep up. In November 2011, O'so opened some much bigger digs. The brew supply is still next door, but now there is room to move (and grow) in a big brewing area which lies behind the windows from an also sizeable Tap House. There are 40 beers on tap here, not just the O'so line up and rotating special O'so brews, but also an assortment of other Wisconsin craft beers.

The brewing philosophy is "freestyle," thinking outside the box. A bit of whimsy goes a long way in helping a good brewer stand out in the crowd. They mostly brew ales, with a few lagers from time to time—Dopplebock, Oktoberfest, and the like. The name of the brewery comes from an old picture in a local restaurant with a delivery truck from O'so Beverage Co. and its claim: "O'so Good!" An appropriate name for a super good beer. An "O" is worked into all the labels.

O'so is very into their local community, thus the donation of their tour fees to different charities each month and various other charitable events. Part of the proceeds from one of their beers, Memory Lane, goes to the Alzheimer's Association of Wisconsin. It's nice to be able to drink for a good cause! Marc and the O'so Team have really been into sours lately and now have a stockpile of over 400 casks. You will see various sours on tap or in 750ml bottles at the liquor stores. Also, in support of funky beer, they produce some wort for Funk Factory Geuzeria in Madison.

Stumbling Distance: Next door is *Mikey's* (mikeysbarandgrill.com, 3018 Village Park Dr, 715-544-0157) serving good food and 40 beers on tap (anyone kicked out of O'so at 9 generally goes here). *Bamboo House* (ploverbamboohouse.com, 715-342-0988), also next door, is an Asian bistro, serving Chinese, Japanese and Southeast Asian fare. The brewery's location is right behind a big home center, so ladies, if your husband says, "I gotta run to Menard's and pick something up," he might not be back as quickly as you expected. *Christian's Bistro* (3066 Village Park Dr, 715-344-3100, christiansbistro.com) finer dining with some deliciously creative menu items.

RHINELANDER BREWING CO.

Founded: 1882
Brewer: Minhas Craft Brewery
Address: 59 South Brown St., Rhinelander, WI 54501
Phone: 715-550-2337
Website: www.rhinelanderbrewery.com
Number of Beers: 7

Beers:
- » RHINELANDER ORIGINAL
- » RHINELANDER EXPORT LAGER
- » RHINELANDER LIGHT
- » CHOCOLATE BUNNY STOUT
- » MYSTICAL JACK TRADITIONAL ALE
- » IMPERIAL JACK DOUBLE IPA
- » THUMPER AMERICAN PALE ALE

Most Popular Brew: Rhinelander Original

Tours? Nothing to tour yet, however, some people stop in to say hello or maybe have a sip.

Best Time to Go: Weekday, office hours.

Where can you buy it? Statewide in bottles. On tap here in Rhinelander.

Special Offer: Not participating.

The Beer Buzz: I think we need to call this a resurrection in progress. That founding date is the real deal. Rhinelander has been around a long, long time. Founded by Otto Hilgermann and Henry Danner, it was once one of Wisconsin's dominant breweries. Prohibition stopped the beer flow but it picked right up again until 1967 when the brewery closed. But there were too many fans about, and Joseph Huber Brewery in Monroe (now Minhas Craft Brewery) soon bought up the label and recipe and brought it back to the market. Have you ever heard of a "Shorty"? Rhinelander was the first to put out the squat little 7-ounce bottles of beer. Sort of a little pick-me-up I guess.

But the story doesn't end in Monroe. In 2009, Jyoti Auluck bought up the brands and assets and has intentions of building a brewery again back in Rhinelander. Minhas, in the meantime, does all the brewing, and they added a few craft brews to the lineup in late 2011. For now, Rhinelander is a two-room office downtown. Brenda, the marketing coordinator, holds down the fort and says she gets walk-in traffic all summer. There's no tour; just some posters on the wall, some old cases, but she might be able to offer you a taste. I think most people just want to chat about old Rhinelander beer memories. And what's wrong with that?

Stumbling Distance: *The Brick Restaurant & Spirits* (16 N Brown St, 715-369-2100, thebrickrhinelander.com) has good food and a nice tap list. *Rhinelander Logging Museum Complex* (www.rhinelanderchamber. com, Business Hwy 8, 715-369-5004) is free but only open Memorial Day to Labor Day. A logging camp replica and an old Soo Line depot are part of a fascinating look into the hodag-fearing, beer-drinking life of the loggers. *Hodag Country Festival* (www.hodag.com, 715-369-1300) is a long weekend event in mid-July that draws over 40,000 and features some big names in country music and plenty of space to camp. Tickets go on sale the November before! Fishing is big here including the *Saldo Hodag Muskie Challenge* with a $20K prize and the *Ice Fishing Jamboree* the second weekend in February. Contact the Chamber of Commerce for lots more information (www.rhinelanderchamber.com, 800-236-4346).

THE MYTHICAL HODAG, THE FEARSOME BEAST OF THE LUMBERJACKS

Kozy Yak Brewery

Founded: August 2012
Brewmaster: Rich Kosiec
Address: 197 North Main Street • Rosholt, WI 54473
Phone: 715-677-3082
Web Site: www.kozyyak.com
Annual Production: 60 barrels
Number of Beers: 4–6 on tap (4 flagships, 1 seasonal, 1 specialty)

Staple Beers:
- » Chicken Coop Cream Ale
- » Rosholt Red Beer

Rotating Beers:
- » Chocolate Milk Stout
- » Doubleday Northern Brown Ale
- » Ike "Steel Beach Picnic" IPA
- » Indy IPA
- » Minnow Ginger Ale
- » Night Ops (Top Gun with dark grains)
- » R^{34} Porter Beauregard Southern Brown Ale
- » The Shot Revolutionary Porter
- » State of Confusion Strong Ale
- » Top Gun American Amber
- » Try Rye Again American Rye Ale
- » Yak "Lighter Than Normal Beer" Ale
- » Znoozen Saison

Most Popular Brew: Chicken Coop Cream Ale

Brewmaster's Fave: Bock

Tours? Well, it's kinda small to tour. But he'll show you if he's not busy.

Samples: Yes, flights of beer or wine.

Best Time to Go: Open Thu 5–8PM, Fri and Sat 3–10PM. Open later in March, and latest after Memorial Day. Best to call or check Facebook.

Where can you buy it? Here on tap and to go in Grunters (growlers). Wine for sale by glass or bottle.

Got food? Yes, German-style malt beer pretzels, gourmet pizzas with Rich's housemade dough, plus their own wine for the non-beer people.

Special Offer: A free Kozy Yak coaster while supplies last.

Directions: WI 66 passes right through Rosholt just northeast of Stevens Point. At Main St, turn north and the brewery is on the left at the end of that first block.

The Beer Buzz: Population 466. Breweries 1. Not a bad per capita ratio, really. Owners Rich Kosiec and Rose Richmond started with grapes, not grains, planting a few vines and adding more until by 2007 they had a 6.5-acre vineyard. They decided to open Fresar Winery (fresarwinery.com) downtown where they might get some traffic. While shopping for yeast online, Rich saw a beer kit on clearance (with a bock recipe) and picked it up. He loved it and went to Point Brew Supply (O'so Brewing's shop in Plover) for more ingredients, and quickly moved from extracts to grains.

A son of Norwegian immigrants, J.G. Rosholt built a sawmill in these parts, and when he sold some land to the railroad in 1902, the line passed through here and the little town enjoyed a boom from the sale of timber and potatoes. By the 70s, however, those days were gone and people were leaving for work elsewhere. Rich and Rose are doing their best to keep a pulse going here, and wine seemed a place to a start. Fearing the wine would not be enough, Rich figured he should add beer as well. Easier said than done: A brewery needed no liquor license, but the winery did and it can't self-distribute. So they couldn't sell their wine in the taproom. They needed to change to a brewpub, but this meant they had to serve food. So, Rich converted a closet to a kitchen and got a pizza oven. What may have been a formality is now quite popular, and from time to time he sells so much pizza he goes through the day's dough. At least, finally, he could serve his wines *and* beers... except in bottles. To sell bottles, the Fed says this must be a brewery! So in the end, this is a winery (selling from another part of the house), and to the State of Wisconsin they are a brewpub. To the Federal government, this is a brewery. Everyone happy? Super.

The brewery and winery occupy an old house in bustling downtown Rosholt. A large deck out front overlooks Main Street. The taproom has a bar and seating area as well as a fireplace. PVC pipe functions as the bar rail and the tap handles are upside down carved wooden bottles. His 2-barrel system occupies one of the back rooms, and he still does a lot of homebrew-sized 5 gallon batches so he is constantly be trying different things. Despite having 1–2 new beers each week, for a while he was creating unofficial label designs for each. You can see many of them around the place. The winery is a separate room of the building. Most of the wines are sweet, and there are several fruit varieties.

A teacher once mispronounced the family surname "Kosiak" and thus the brewery's name of Kozy Yak. Rich served on the U.S.S. Eisenhower and during the Iranian hostage crisis in 1980, they went 152 days without a port call, setting a record that would stand 15 years. The captain can authorize 2 drinks per sailor every 45 days without a port call, and during that time Rich says the beers flown in were ridiculously expensive. What's a guy to do? Ike IPA is also "Steel Beach Picnic," which is how they referred to a party on the flight deck.

Yaks grunt when they are happy, thus not growlers, but refillable "grunters" for sale.

Facebook.com/KozyYakBrewery

Stumbling Distance: Great barbecue in Rosholt? Yep. *The Brick Pit House* (107 N Main St, 715-677-4740) is impressive.

Stevens Point Brewery

Founded: 1857
Brewmaster: Gabe Hopkins
Address: 2617 Water St, Stevens Point 54481
Phone: 715-344-9310 / 800-369-4911
Website: www.pointbeer.com
Annual Production: 120,000 bbls
Number of Beers: 16 (also 5 gourmet soft drinks)

Staple Beers:
> » Point Amber
> » Point Belgian White
> » Point Beyond the Pale IPA
> » Point Cascade Pale Ale
> » Point Drop Dead Blonde Ale
> » Point Onyx Black Ale
> » Point Smiley Blue Pilsner
> » Point Special Lager

Rotating Beers:
> » Point Coast Radler Beer
> » Point Nude Beach Summer Wheat
> » Point Oktoberfest
> » Point St. Benedict's Winter Ale
> » Point Apricadabra Apricot Wheat Ale

Whole Hog Limited Edition Brewmaster's Series: 6-Hop IPA, Espresso Stout, Peach Hefeweizen, Pumpkin Ale, Russian Imperial Stout

Ciderboys Hard Ciders: Cranberry Road, First Press, Grand Mimosa, Mad Bark, Magic Apple, Peach County, Pineapple Hula, Raspberry Smash, Strawberry Magic

James Page Beers: A Capella Gluten Free Pale Ale, Bastian Black Forest Cake, Casper White Stout, Healani Pineapple Hefeweizen, Yhabba Dhaba Chai Porter

Most Popular Brew: Point Amber

Brewmaster's Fave: James Page's Casper White Stout

Tours? Yes, call ahead for tour times and reservations (800-369-4911)! Free gift at the end of the tour!

Samples? Yes, two 10-oz samples with the tour.

Best Time to Go: Any season! *Pointoberfest* in late September is an annual fundraiser promising plenty of Point beer, live music, and local food vendors. Admission is limited to 1000 tickets, $20 in advance/$25 at the door.

Where can you buy it? Besides Wisconsin, look throughout the Midwest and beyond. Over 30 states!

Got food? Nope.

Special Offer: Buy one get one free brewery tour.

Directions: Look for Francis St off Business Hwy 51 just north of Forest Cemetery. Go west on Francis to Water St.

The Beer Buzz: This is the fifth oldest continuously running brewery in the US, and it was the site of my first *pils*-grimage back in 1988 when a retired brewery employee Bill ("Bilko") still did the tours. I clearly recall him jabbing me in the shoulder and saying, "And you know what *kreusening* is, dontcha?" I didn't. Partners Frank Wahle and George Ruder started making Point Special Lager back in the mid-1800s. They supplied the troops during the Civil War. Prohibition, of course, meant near-beer and soft drinks, but the brewery survived those dry years and the Great Depression (notice the one started before the other) and came back with Point Bock. Mike Royko, a syndicated columnist from Chicago, declared

Point Special the best beer in America in 1973, but for the longest time it remained a very local brew, and even in the 80s I still remember saying, "When you're out of Point, you're out of town." Finally, in the 90s Point crossed state lines and became available in Minnesota and Chicagoland. They do some contract brewing now too, and they brought back Augsburger. And like Leinie's, though a large regional brewery, they have moved beyond the standard American pilsners and offer various alternatives. Back in 2003 Point Special took the Gold at Great American Beer Festival beating Bud and Miller. In 2009 the brewery introduced a line of extreme beers with bold flavors and higher alcohol content called Whole Hog Limited Edition Brewmaster's Series. The brewery

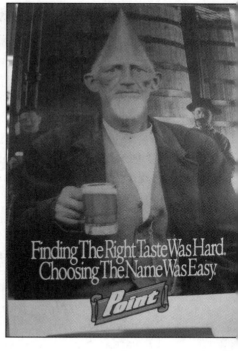

also purchased James Page brand beer in 2005 and began producing it for sale in the Minnesota market. The brewery has had six expansions in the last six years, investing nearly $7 million in upgrades and new equipment, bringing their capacity to 150,000 barrels!

Stumbling Distance: Hanging around town you should head to The Square—the historic downtown hosts a number of taverns (more than 10!) all serving the hometown brew. *Guu's on Main* (1140 Main St, 715-344-3200, guusonmaintavern.com) has an excellent beer menu plus good burgers and fish fry. The *Bottle Stop* (35 Park Ridge Dr, 715-341-7400) is an awesome liquor store with deep knowledge of Wisconsin craft beer! *Rusty's Backwater Saloon* (www.rustys.net, 1715 West River Dr, 715-341-2490), five miles southwest of Point off Cty P, is known for amazing Bloody Marys and also serves Cajun smelt, cheese curds, a variety of sandwiches and a fish fry. *SentryWorld* (www.sentryworld.com, 601 Michigan Ave North, 866-479-6753) is a Robert Trent Jones Jr.-designed par 72 golf course, a must for golfers. Colors are phenomenal here in fall. A twenty-minute drive away in Rudolph is *Wisconsin Dairy State Dairy Co.* (6860 State Rd 34, 715-435-3144) which offers free tours and fresh cheese curds and ice cream.

Bull Falls Brewery

Founded: September 2007
Brewmaster: Mike Zamzow
Address: 901 E Thomas Street
Wausau, WI 54403
Phone: 715-842-2337
Website: www.bullfallsbrewery.com
Annual Production: 3,000 bbls
Number of Beers: 7 plus seasonals

Staple Beers:
» BAVARIAN-STYLE HEFEWEIZEN
» BULL FALLS MARATHON (a revived regional Marathon City Brewery recipe)
» FIVE STAR ALE (English Amber Ale)
» HOLZHACKER LAGER (Munich-Style Lager)
» MIDNIGHT STAR (Schwarzbier)
» NUT BROWN ALE
» OATMEAL STOUT

Rotating Beers:
» BOURBON-BARREL OATMEAL STOUT
» EDEL BOCK (Maibock)
» OKTOBERFEST
» OPTI-LAGER (Munich-style Lager, brewed for Wisconsin Valley Fair)
» RAUCHBIER (Bamberg-style Smoked Lager)
» TRADITIONAL BOCK
» WEIZENBOCK
» WHITE WATER ALE

Most Popular Brew: Five Star Ale

Brewmaster's Fave: Midnight Star

Tours? Yes, groups of 10 or more and by appointment. $5 includes the tour, a souvenir mini-stein and a 14-oz Bull Falls beer.

Samples? Five 5-oz pours for $8

Best Time to Go: Open Mon–Thu 4–11PM, Fri 4PM–12AM, Sat 1PM–12AM. Closed on Sundays!

Where can you buy it? Here on tap and in growlers to go and four-pack 16-oz cans. Distribution is strong in the greater Wausau area but now statewide distribution has extended into major markets such as Green Bay, Oshkosh, Appleton, Milwaukee, Madison, La Crosse, Eau Claire and spaces in between. Also find them in the Twin Cities area in Minnesota.

Got food? Free shell-on peanuts and menus from some local places that deliver pizza and sandwiches. Food friendly.

Special Offer: Buy 1 beer, get 1 free.

Directions: From Hwy 51 take N Mountain Road (Cty Rd NN) east to River Dr at Lake Wausau. Then go north until Thomas St and go right to the end.

The Beer Buzz: Big Bull Falls, was the original name of Wausau during the lumber era when giant White Pine were prevalent in northern Wisconsin. The Bull Falls waterfalls are located right in the city on the Wisconsin River which runs through town. That stretch of the river provides an Olympic-caliber course for whitewater kayaking and canoeing during the summer in Wausau. Bull Falls Brewery was named after the original city name: Big Bull Falls.

Let this be a warning to wives everywhere: "My wife got me a beer kit ten years ago," says Mike. Prior to this he was and still is a co-owner of a software company that develops and markets software to county Social and Human Service Departments in Wisconsin. Someone informed him of some brewing equipment up in Eagle River that had been sitting on the market for a while. He got a good deal on it and then stored it locally for five years. Mike and Don Zamzow bought the current brewery building in 2007 as well as a used 10-barrel system that was located in Stevens Point, Wisconsin. They sold the smaller 3-barrel Eagle River system to a place out in Peekskill, New York without ever having brewed a batch in it. In 2013, Bull Falls completed a 8,000-square-foot addition to the building bringing in a 30-barrel brewhouse, six 60-bbl fermenters and two 90-bbl fermenters, and canning and kegging lines. The grand total with construction and equipment was nearly $2.6 million and has allowed them to greatly increase production and market reach.

When Mike and partners submitted a Bull Falls Brewery trademark, they received a challenge. "Yours is too close to ours and it will cause confusion in the market place." The offended company? Red Bull. An attorney from California argued that someone might confuse Red Bull with the local microbrewery. One option was to go to Federal court to tell them they were ridiculous. Unfortunately, ridiculous people with money versus reasonable people without it... well, you know how THAT ends. After four years a three-page agreement was developed. Bull Falls can't use any bovine animals in their advertising. The words Bull and Falls cannot be separated. The colors blue and silver are not to be used in the fashion they do. And they are not allowed to brew root beer and call it Bull Falls Root Beer.

An interesting beer note: Mike's great uncle Walter A. Zamzow was treasurer of the now defunct Marathon City Brewing Company which closed in 1966. The brewery had been brewing beer for over 100 years. Mike had been searching for the recipe for Marathon Superfine Lager. The son of a worker who was involved with tearing down the old Marathon City Brewing Co. building had the log book from 1954 which his father had found during the demolition. Inside was a July 30, 1954 recipe for Marathon's beer. In 2009, Mike brought it back and reintroduced the beer to the community as Bull Falls Marathon. The resurrected brew is available every year in Marathon, Wisconsin, on Labor Weekend at the Marathon Fund Days celebration, as well as at the Bull Falls brewery taproom. Like traveling back in time.

Also of note, the Wausau-area distributor is an independent Pepsi distributor. Local deliveries of Bull Falls beer are sharing the ride with Pepsi and coffee. Not only that, but the family that owns this distribution company is part of the Wolf family that owned and operated the old Wausau Brewing Co. (1917–1961). So they are back in the beer business, you can say.

Facebook.com/bullfallsbrewery

Stumbling Distance: *Angelo's Pizza* (www.angelospizzawausau.com, 1206 N 6th St, 715-845-6225) is good for ordering in at the brewery tasting room. *City Grill* in the *Jefferson Street Inn* (www.jeffersonstreetinn.com, 203 Jefferson St, 715-848-2900) is also a good spot for eats. *Red Eye Brewing* isn't far away and also serves great food.

THE GREAT DANE PUB AND RESTAURANT

Founded: 2009
Head Brewer: Dan Weber
Address: 2305 Sherman Street • Wausau, WI 54401
Phone: 715-845-3000
Website: www.greatdanepub.com
Annual Production: 1,200 bbls
Number of Beers: 12

Staple Beers:
  » CROP CIRCLE WHEAT ALE
  » EMERALD ISLE STOUT
  » GEORGE RUDER'S GERMAN PILS
  » JOHN STONER'S OATMEAL STOUT
  » LANDMARK LITE ALE (pilsner)
  » OLD GLORY APA
  » SPEEDWAY IPA
  » STONE OF SCONE SCOTCH ALE
  » WOODEN SHIPS ESB
  » WOOLY MAMMOTH PORTER

Rotating Beers:
  » DUNKBRAU
  » IMPERIAL RED ALE
  » SAISON
  » SPRUCE TIP PORTER
  » ÜBER BOCK
  » ...and a rotating beer engine choice

Most Popular Brew: Stone of Scone Scotch Ale

Tours? By chance or appointment but always welcomed.

Samples? Yes, a sip to decide, or sampler platters of four beers for about $6.50 (add 2 more for $2.50).

Best Time to Go: Open Sun–Thu 11AM–12AM, Fri–Sat 11AM–2:30AM. Happy hour 4–6PM with free popcorn. Each day there's a Brewer's Choice pint on discount.

Where can you buy it? Here on tap and in growlers, pub kegs, half barrels (with 24-hour notice) to go. Some distribution in cans now as well. See their Madison/Fitchburg locations in Zone 1.

Got food? Yes, a full menu of soups, salads, burgers, and entrees. The bratburger (created on a dare) is an original with bacon on a pretzel bun. Beer, brat and cheese soup is Wisconsin in a bowl. Beer bread is standard, fish and chips available, and a load of other great dishes. Friday night pilsner-battered fish fry!

Special Offer: A free 10-oz beer

Directions: From Interstate 39/Highway 51 take Exit 191 heading east on Sherman Street. The Dane is right there on the right (south) side of the road just a stone's throw from the exit.

The Beer Buzz: Located just off the highway, and thus convenient to anyone heading past Wausau for the Northwoods, this place originally opened in 2000 as Hereford and Hops, a grill-your-own steakhouse with a rather nice brewpub. A few good brewers passed through and on to other gigs, and when the steakhouse didn't make it, the venerable Great Dane from Madison stepped in. The pub has plenty of parking, and inside you'll find the brewhouse behind glass and open to daylight from the other side. Circular booths in the main bar make a stylish lounge atmosphere while billiards, darts and the usual Dane shuffleboard give you something to do with your hands when you're not holding a beer. A beer garden with an outdoor bar was added in 2011 with room for 100. A fireplace takes the bite out of winter. Six TVs pipe in important games. If you have a wedding or work party, the Dane has private space for up to 300!

Stumbling Distance: *Milwaukee Burger Company* (2200 Stewart Ave, 715-298-9371, milwaukeeburgercompany.com) has 40 on tap. *Rib Mountain* is more of a hill, but we take what we can get here in the Midwest. At one billion years old, it is one of the oldest geological formations on the planet. And what do we do with it? Ski on it. *Granite Peak Ski Area* (www.skigranitepeak.com, 3605 N Mountain Rd, 715-845-2846) offers 72 runs as well as lodging and lessons. From Hwy 51 take Cty Hwy NN and the entrance is just over half a mile down. The state park here at the top charges a fee and offers camping, trails, and picnic areas. Exit 51 Cty Hwy N West. Turn right (west) at the first intersection (Park Dr) and go about 2.5 miles to the top. Get a close-up look at some whitewater with *Wausau Kayak Canoe Corporation* (www.wausauwhitewater.org, 1202 Elm St, 715-845-5664). They offer training courses for all levels, and if you prefer to stay dry come see one of three national and international competitions.

RED EYE BREWING COMPANY

Founded: 2008
Brewmaster: Kevin Eichelberger
Address: 612 Washington Street • Wausau, WI 54403
Phone: 715-843-7334
Website: www.redeyebrewing.com
Annual Production: 532 bbls
Number of Beers: 10 on tap

Typical Beers:
  » BLOOM (Belgian wheat)
  » SCARLET 7 (Belgian-style dubbel with caramelized black mission figs)
  » THRUST! (American-style IPA)

A Rotating Dark Beer:
  » CHARLATAN IMPERIAL STOUT   » VERUCA STOUT
  » MIND'S EYE RYE PORTER

Rotating Beers:
  » BELGIAN BLONDE WITH   » OKTOBERFEST
    RASPBERRY   » PUMPKIN ALE
  » A CART RIDE TO MEXICO   » SCHWARZBIER
    MAIBOCK   » SERENDIPITY DOUBLE IPA
  » GERMAN PILS   » VIENNA LAGER
  » LEMONGRASS RYE   » TARTAN TODDY SCOTCH ALE
  » MAN PANTS KÖLSCH   » WISKANSAN TORNADO INDIA
  » NITRO ENGLISH NUT BROWN   BROWN ALE

Most Popular Brew: Thrust

Brewmaster's Fave: He's partial to his lagers

Tours? Yes, for large groups only and by appointment.

Samples? Yes, 4 samples for $5.50, plus $1.50 each additional.

Best Time to Go: Open Mon–Sat 11AM–close. Happy hour is 4–6PM, Mon–Fri. Closed on Sundays.

Where can you buy it? Here on tap and in growlers and howlers to go, plus some draft accounts.

Got food? Yes, great artisan food. Try the wood-fired oven pizzas. The menu offers paninis, grass-fed beef burgers, wraps, soups, and salads as well as few signature entrees. For a gourmet take on Wisconsin's beer cheese soup, check out Red Eye Beer & Brie Bisque. An in-house smoker makes great ribs, chicken and more.

Special Offer: A free pint of beer during your signature visit.

Directions: From Hwy 51 take the Hwy 52 exit east which becomes Stewart Ave. Follow it across the Wisconsin River. It splits, and as you go right it becomes one-way. Follow it and it becomes First St, then Forest St. before it joins Grand Ave. Do not follow this to the right; rather stay left and turn onto 6th St and continue two blocks to Washington St and turn right.

The Beer Buzz: Kevin used to brew over at the now defunct Hereford and Hops (which reopened as The Great Dane here in Wausau). He is a creative brewer making some remarkable stuff and really likes Belgians (you may notice that two of the house beers are Belgian). He bought a brew system that had been sitting for four or five years for a good price and opened Red Eye. His promise: "Red Eye Brewing Company will never serve a beer that is not worthy of the most articulate beer drinker's palate."

He's also serious about his pizza. The oven came all the way from Italy. They ferment the dough overnight and hand toss it as it should be for an Italian pie. Most of the food is locally sourced and there is no deep fryer here. Plus, every item on the menu is paired with one of the beers. Watch for the Black Eye Series which features super premium beers in limited batches. This is Kevin showing off. Good stuff and worth marking the calendar for. A lot of people stop in frequently to fill their growlers, and Red Eye has become a social center for cyclists, especially after a day's ride. In 2015 they expanded their parking lot (it was getting crowded).

Free WiFi. Facebook.com/RedEyeBrewing

Stumbling Distance: Next door is *Patina Coffeehouse* (610 Washington St, 715-298-0497, patinacoffeehouse.com) serving smoothies, café food

and Milwaukee-roasted Colectivo coffee. You are just minutes from *Bull Falls Brewery*.

Rocky Reef Brewing Co.

Founded: 2015
Brewmaster: Tyler Smith
Address: 1101 1st Avenue • Woodruff, WI 54568
Phone: 262-339-1230
Web Site: www.rockyreefbrewing.com
Annual Production: 360 barrels
Number of Beers: 8 on tap plus 4 guest taps; 14 beers in a year

Staple Beers:
> » A Big Red Hen
> » HoWITzer
> » Just Wheat It
> » Musky Bite IPA
> » Never Fail Pale Ale
> » Soft Landing (dark ale)
> » Staycation (blonde ale)
> » Up Nort Lakehouse Saison

Rotating Beers:
> » Imperial Black IPA
> » Imperial IPA
> » ...plus seasonals and random one-offs

Most Popular Brew: Soft Landing

Brewmaster's Fave: Up Nort Lakehouse Saison

Tours? Yes, if they're free they'll show you around.

Samples: Yes, flights of four or eight 5-oz beers for $6 and $12.

Best Time to Go: Open Mon, Wed–Thu 4–9PM, Fri 4–10PM, Sat 12–10PM, Sun 12–6PM. Closed Tuesdays. Watch for possible seasonal changes.

Where can you buy it? Here on tap and to go in growlers, and some local draft accounts planned for the future.

Got food? No, just some free popcorn and other snacks, but food friendly.

Special Offer: A free sample glass (5 oz) of Rocky Reef beer during your signature visit.

Directions: Where US 51 and WI 47 cross in the center of Woodruff, go east (south) on WI 47 one block and it's on your right.

The Beer Buzz: Co-owners and co-brewers Tyler Smith and Christie Forrer had been homebrewing for a couple years when they decided to go part-time at their jobs as they laid the plans for a brewery in Milwaukee. When the time came to pull the trigger, they ended up here in the Northwoods. Christie's grandparents have a cottage in Boulder Junction, so she had been up here a lot throughout her life. In the summer of 2014, she and Tyler saw this place for sale. They liked the idea of a small town and so plans changed and they moved up here. The family cottage is on Rocky Reef Lane, so the name raises a glass to some great memories.

Tyler brews daily while Christie works as assistant brewer when she's not handling the rest of the operation. They are planning an unlimited rotation of styles and recipes, and they like to try new things, but a few favorites will end up being regular beers. They started on a one-barrel system, but as soon as they opened, they were already realizing they'd need to bump up their capacity, hopefully by sometime in 2016. Expect a little outdoor beer garden that summer as well.

The big metal-sided building houses their small brewing space and a taproom. They built the bar and 20 stools themselves. Two picnic tables and a ping pong table take up some space as well. Decoration is simple and a chalkboard lists the beers on tap, and the tap handles and flight paddles are designed to look like Northwoods street signs. The 2 TVs come on for sports, plus there are board games and Giant Jenga.

Free WiFi. Find them on Facebook and Instagram @RockyReefBrewing

Stumbling Distance: *Monical's Pizza* (360 US-51, 715-358-9959, monicals.com) in Arbor Vitae does thin- and thick-crust pies for sit-down or takeout. Heading north a bit to Boulder Junction, check out *Aqualand Ale House* (10450 Main St, Boulder Junction, 715-385-0380, aqualandalehouse.com) with 20 taps, including 3 of their own brand brewed at *Corner Pub* in Reedsburg.

ZONE 5

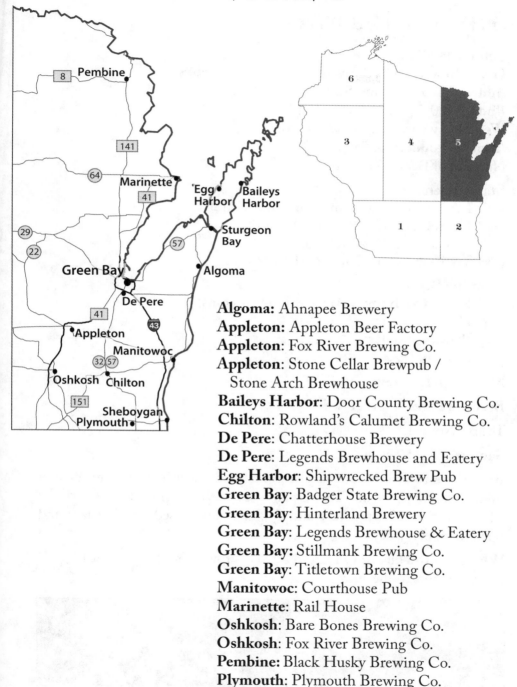

Algoma: Ahnapee Brewery
Appleton: Appleton Beer Factory
Appleton: Fox River Brewing Co.
Appleton: Stone Cellar Brewpub /
 Stone Arch Brewhouse
Baileys Harbor: Door County Brewing Co.
Chilton: Rowland's Calumet Brewing Co.
De Pere: Chatterhouse Brewery
De Pere: Legends Brewhouse and Eatery
Egg Harbor: Shipwrecked Brew Pub
Green Bay: Badger State Brewing Co.
Green Bay: Hinterland Brewery
Green Bay: Legends Brewhouse & Eatery
Green Bay: Stillmank Brewing Co.
Green Bay: Titletown Brewing Co.
Manitowoc: Courthouse Pub
Marinette: Rail House
Oshkosh: Bare Bones Brewing Co.
Oshkosh: Fox River Brewing Co.
Pembine: Black Husky Brewing Co.
Plymouth: Plymouth Brewing Co.
Sheboygan: 3 Sheeps Brewing Co.
Sturgeon Bay: Starboard Brewing Co.

Ahnapee Brewery

Founded: 2013
Head Brewer: Nick Calaway
Address: 105 Navarino St. • Algoma, WI 54201
Phone: 920-785-0822
Web Site: www.ahnapeebrewery.com
Annual Production: 550 barrels
Number of Beers: 8 on tap

Staple Beers:
- » Little Soldier (American Amber Ale)
- » Long Goodbye (Bavarian Helles)
- » Noble IPA (English Style)
- » Two Stall Chocolate Milk Stout

Rotating Beers:
- » Fun Guy- Brown Ale (with mushrooms)
- » Helles in Red
- » Pain in the Rye
- » Session IPA

Most Popular Brew: Two Stall

Brewer's Fave: Noble IPA

Tours? Not yet.

Samples: Yes, $2 each.

Best Time to Go: Hours vary seasonally, so check the website. Winter hours: closed Mon and Tue. Open Wed 4–9pm, Thu 12–9pm, Fri–Sat 12–10pm, Sun 12–5pm. July and August, only closed on Tuesdays and open noon every day.

Where can you buy it? On tap ad to go in growlers and 25-oz bottles, plus draft accounts in the surrounding counties.

Got food? Yes, flatbread pizzas, snack boards, and hot pretzels.

Special Offer: Not participating.

Directions: WI 42 passes north–south through Algoma. Near the center of town just south of the Ahnapee River, go east 0.2 mile toward the lake on Navarino St and the brewery is on the left.

The Beer Buzz: The name Ahnapee Brewing dates back to 1868, and while you might think someone just resurrected an old name for this little craft brewery, the connection is much stronger than that. The original brewer, a Civil War veteran by the name of Henry Schmiling, is the great-great-great-great uncle of owners Aric and Brad Schmiling, and their modern winery occupies the old brewery building which ceased beer production in 1886. Lagering tunnels underneath now hold wine instead of beer. Brewer Nick has homebrewed since he was 18. He worked at Titletown Brewing for a few years, but not as a brewer. Nevertheless, he was able to get feedback on homebrews and learn a bit on the side as he worked his way up from busser to general manager. He took the general manager position here at the winery, and when the brewing idea moved forward, he took that on as well. He brews the beers offsite in a repurposed creamery nearby.

The taproom is housed in a converted two-stall garage down the block from the winery. Inside is a low L-shaped bar under a peaked corrugated-metal ceiling. A few tables sit along the wall, and a back room offers windows overlooking the Ahnapee River. In season, an outside deck lies beyond this with tall chairs and sort of bar-rail.

Be sure to also check out *von Stiehl Winery* (920-487-5208, vonstiehl. com) which makes 30 different varieties of grape and fruit wines and gets cherries from Door County and some of their grapes from their own Stony Creek Vineyard just outside of town. The winery is open year round, offering scheduled tours—daily from May through October, Saturdays from November through April.

Free WiFi. Facebook/ahnapeebrewery

Stumbling Distance: *Caffè Tlazo* (607 4th St, 920-487-7240, caffetlazo. com) is a marvelous little café in town with loads of teas, coffee, and a fresh, often organic menu for breakfast, lunch and dinner. *Skaliwags* (312 Clark St, 920-487-8092, skaliwags.com) offers finer dining with great seafood. Algoma is also a prime port for recreational fishing. Go angling for trout, salmon or steelhead on Lake Michigan. *Kinn's Sport Fishing* (60 Steele St, 800-446-8605, kinnskatch.com) next door is a good charter fishing service.

Appleton Beer Factory

Founded: December 2012
Brewers: Ben Fogle and Carl Pierce
Address: 603 West College Avenue • Appleton, WI 54911
Phone: 920-364-9931
Website: www.appletonbeerfactory.com
Annual Production: 500 bbls
Number of Beers: up to 9 on tap

Staple Beers:
- » Amber Ale
- » American Pale Ale
- » Black Ale
- » Blonde Ale
- » Brown Ale
- » Hefeweizen
- » Oatmeal Stout

Rotating Beers:
- » Belgian Tripel
- » Belgian Wit
- » Light Lager
- » Oktoberfest
- » …and various experimental one-offs and a bit of barrel-aging.

Most Popular Brew: Blonde Ale or Hefeweizen

Brewmaster's Fave: "Mostly ales. Amber, Brown, Black, IPA, Hefe…"

Tours? Yes, by chance or by appointment for groups. A self-guided tour is in the works.

Samples: Yes, customizable flights of 4-oz beers, $1 per regular beer and $1.25 for specialties.

Best Time to Go: Open Mon–Tue 11AM–close (4PM–close in summer), Wed–Sun 11AM–close. Kitchen closes 8PM Sun, 9PM Mon–Wed, 10PM Thu–Sat. Happy hour is 4–6PM Sun–Thu. Call in advance for reservations for large tables on weekends. Double check the hours online.

Where can you buy it? Here on tap and to go in growlers, plus draft accounts around town.

Got food? Yes. Jeff's wife Leah, the executive chef, developed a beer-centric menu, and there are some very notably delicious items here that are a bit uncommon.

Special Offer: Half off your first pint of house beer when you get your book signed!

Directions: Easy peasy: From US 41 just take College Avenue east into town. The "factory" will be on your right just after you cross the railroad tracks.

The Beer Buzz: I've had a few brewers say they are putting their own system together, meaning recycling some dairy equipment or other clever re-engineering, but when Jeff Fogle showed me his operation I was dumbfounded. He was literally building it. He was a pipe welder for Anheuser Busch and ended up in design management for them, working on multi-million dollar projects. So welding together some tanks from sheets of metal was just a tiny version of what he used to do.

The "factory" looks the part, set in a 1940s brick auto-parts building. The front bar/tasting room has polished concrete floors and warm wood ceilings, and the bar along the back brick wall. Beyond that is a larger high-ceiling space where you can see the brew system around you and a stage for occasional live music. Another room up front provides more dining space. Recycled wood was used for the tables.

Jeff's son Ben, a mechanical engineer is in charge of the brewing. Jeff learned from his own father in 1983 and then passed the pleasure on to his son Ben in 2005. Rounding off Team Fogle is Ben's wife Mairi who handles marketing.

Stumbling Distance: If you need your Wisconsin cheese fix, head over to *Arthur Bay Cheese Company* (237 E Calumet St, 920-733-1556) for the best selection in town. On Saturday mornings in summer, part of College Ave nearby closes for the *Appleton Farm Market* (appletondowntown.org). In winter the market moves indoors. Don't miss the awesome *Mile of Music* (mileofmusic.com), a four-day mostly free music festival in August hosted by 65+ venues, including *Appleton Beer Factory*. More free music happens every summer Thursday at Houdini Plaza on College Ave. Houdini fans should visit the *The History Museum at the Castle* (330 E College Ave, 920-735-9370, myhistorymuseum.org) with its exhibit dedicated to the escape artist/illusionist who called Appleton home.

Fox River Brewing Co.

Founded: 1998
Brewmaster: Kevin Bowen
Address: 4301 W. Wisconsin Avenue • Appleton, WI 5491
(inside Fox River Mall)
Phone: 920-991-0000
Website: www.foxriverbrewing.com
Annual Production: 1,400 bbls
Number of Beers: 9 on tap
Staple Beers:

> » 2 Dams Blonde Ale
> » Blü Bobber Blueberry Ale
> » Crooked Dock American Pale Ale
> » Marble Eye Scottish Ale

Rotating Beers:

> » Abbey Normal
> » Badger Bitter ESB
> » Belgian Black
> » Black Fox IBA
> » The Chief
> » Defibrillator Doppelbock
> » 1853
> » Fox Tail Pale Ale
> » Foxtoberfest
> » German Pils
> » Hoppyface IPA
> » Maibock
> » Optic IPA

> » Oshkosh Best Bitter
> » Paine's Pilsner
> » Raspberry Wheat
> » Red Baron Alt
> » Shakedown IPA
> » Slam Dunkel
> » Titan Porter
> » Trolleycar Stout
> » 2x4 Imperial Pilsner
> » Upside Brown Ale
> » Vader's Imperial Stout
> » Vanilla Cream Ale
> » WI Coffee Stout

Most Popular Brew: Crooked Dock APA

Brewer's Fave: He's a hop head, so Crooked Dock APA

Tours? On request, call ahead.

Samples? Yes.

Best Time to Go: Open Mon–Sat 11–10PM, Sun 11–8PM. Happy Hour runs Mon–Fri 3–6PM & 9–close, Sat 9–close, Sun 7–close.

Where can you buy it? Here (and at their Oshkosh location) on tap plus growlers, quarter- and half-barrels and some local taverns serve it. Bottles are distributed in NE Wisconsin from Sheboygan to Green Lake on up to Ashland (but just shy of I-39 to the west, so not Stevens Point or Wausau… yet).

Got food? Of course. The menu features a variety of steaks, seafood, pastas, sandwiches, and pizzas and much more on their full menu.

Special Offer: $2 pint on your first Fox River beer, additional pints regular price.

Directions: From Hwy 41 take the College Ave exit and go east to S Appleton St. Go right (south) and take a right on Water St before crossing the Fox River. It's inside the mall.

The Beer Buzz: Fox River Brewing Co. could be the highlight to a giant shopping mall trip for any true-brew connoisseur. This food court couldn't get any better—it boasts a brewery with a restaurant inside it! Kevin is working double duty, with this location and Oshkosh's Fox River Brew Co. (but each is brewed on site). This Fox River Mall location incorporates the waterfront theme of its sister brewery with an interior highlighting deep-water blues and a freshwater feel. There is an open kitchen, pizza oven, and an outdoor patio for the summer season. Serving lunch and dinner daily, their full menu offers steaks, pasta, seafood, pizzas, and sandwiches to accompany the handcraft beers. Kevin Bowen started at the restaurant in Oshkosh years ago and he began helping out in the brewery: cleaning kegs, filling bottles and such. After studying at Siebel Institute he worked for a few other brewhouses before returning to Fox River Brewing Co.

Stumbling Distance: *World of Beer* (149 Mall Dr, 920-903-8337, worldofbeer.com) does "beer school" events and has 52 taps and 500 bottles of beer on the wall. The former *White Clover Dairy* (489 Holland Ct, Kaukauna, 920-766-5765 ext.2), now part of Arla Foods, is a cheese store in nearby Kaukauna. You can see havarti being made at the factory and then buy some great cheddars, gouda, edam and more in the little white house next door. Take Hwy 441 around the east side of Appleton and take Cty CE (Holland Rd) east to Holland Ct. Look for *Fox River Brewing* in Oshkosh: 1501 Arboretum Drive, Oshkosh, 920-232-2337.

STONE CELLAR BREWPUB (STONE ARCH BEER)

Founded: 2004
Brewmaster: Steve Lonsway
Address: 1004 S Olde Oneida Street • Appleton, WI 54915
Phone: 920-731-3322
Website: www.stonecellarbrewpub.com
Annual Production: 3,200 bbls
Number of Beers: 11 on tap

Staple Beers:
» ENGLISH SIX-GRAIN ALE (corn, barley, oats, rice, wheat, rye)
» HOUDINI HONEY WHEAT
» MARQUETTE PILSNER
» PIE-EYED IPA
» STONE ARCH STOUT
» SCOTTISH ALE
» VANISHING VANILLA STOUT

Rotating Beers:
» ADLER BRAU
» AMERICANA PALE ALE
» BLINDSIDED BARLEYWINE GOLD MEDAL
» BLUEBERRY WHEAT
» CAFFEINATOR
» DARK ALE
» DOPPLEBOCK
» ESB
» FIRST SNOW ALE
» GRAND CRU
» I.R.B.B.A.I.O.R.S.
» LEMONGRASS RYE
» PUMPKIN SPICE
» RASPBERRY PORTER
» STONETOBERFEST
» ...and fruit beers in summer

Most Popular Brew: Scottish Ale

Brewmaster's Fave: IPA

Tours? Yes, by appointment.

Samples? Yes, six or ten 4-oz samples for $10.

Best Time to Go: 11AM–close daily, except for a few holidays. The beer garden is awesome in the summer and often features live music on Tuesdays and Saturdays.

Where can you buy it? Here on tap and in growlers, bottles, and kegs to go. On tap at numerous Fox River Valley pubs and distributed in six-packs in 20 counties in WI.

Got food? Yes, lunch and dinner. Bangers and mash, shepherd's pie, goulash, fish and chips, Scotch egg, deep-fried Wisconsin cheese curds, ale-steamed shrimp, cheese, sausage and beer for two, burgers, pizzas, and a Friday fish fry.

Special Offer: $1 off your first pint Stone Arch beer during your signature visit.

Directions: From Hwy 41 take the College Ave exit and go east 3 miles and turn right (south) on South Appleton St and it becomes Oneida. Go right, cross the bridge and take the second left (east) on S Olde Oneida. The brewery is on the right.

The Beer Buzz: Situated between the locks in a building called Between the Locks, this brewery carries on a long tradition on this site. In 1858 Anton Fischer, a German immigrant, founded the first brewery in Outagamie County and helped build the Fox River canal system. His Fischer Brewery was sold just a couple years later to Carl Meunch, a foreman from the Schlitz Brewery in Milwaukee. In 1884 the building lost a battle with fire and needed to be rebuilt. George Walter Brewing Co., the producer of Adler Brau, lasted until 1972. When the old building was converted into a little collection of stores and offices, Adler Brau Brewery and Restaurant tried to make a go if it as a micro-brewery. In 2004, father and son partners Tom and Steve Lonsway took over the tradition. And one more thing: the building is haunted by "Charlie."

While studying science in college, Steve went to England for a semester and fell in love with beer history and beer itself and decided it had to be his career. "Beer is such a part of the culture there." And so it is here as well. He started *Homebrew Market* in 1993 (which sold ingredients and equipment for making beer, wine, and soda for 20 years). He attended the Siebel Institute in Chicago and then for six years did the brewing for both Fox River Brewing Co. locations until breaking out on his own. His brews have gotten some awards: Marquette Pilsner (Gold), Between the Locks (Silver) 2005, and others for Barleywine (Gold), Six-Grain, Stout, and Scottish Ale. He brews those 3,000+ barrels each year seven barrels at a time.

You may notice the beers are under the trade name Stone Arch Brewhouse. This is all still Stone Cellar, but in order to get approval to sell his beer offsite, Steve had to change the name. Still the same beer, still the same location. The only thing different is a taproom expanded in 2015 where they often host beer releases. They also brew a special beer each year for the awesome August festival **Mile of Music**—Americana Pale Ale.

Stumbling Distance: *Skyline Comedy Café* is in the same building. Stop in at the *Outagamie Museum* (330 E College Ave, 920-733-8445, $5, open Tues–Sat 10–4, Sun 12–4, add Mon during summer) and see A.K.A. Houdini, an exhibit dedicated to the famous escape artist, an Appleton native (or so he claimed). *Simon's Specialty Cheese* (www.simonscheese.com, 2735 Freedom Rd, Little Chute, 920-788-6311, north on Hwy 41 exit Freedom Rd) has the fresh cheese curds as well as over 100 types of cheese (free samples), various fudge flavors (more samples), and a cheese mini-museum with a video about the cheese making process. *Octoberfest* (www.octoberfestonline.org) as well as *License to Cruise* (a classic car show) and *Applefest* are held downtown on College Ave in late September. "A mile of fun," as they call it. Do not miss *Mile of Music* (mileofmusic.com), an amazing event featuring over 200 artists, 65+ venues, and 800+ live performances every August.

Door County Brewing Co.

Founded: January 2013
Brewmaster: Danny McMahon
Address: 2434 County Road F • Baileys Harbor, WI 54202
Phone: 920-839-1515
Web Site: www.doorcountybrewingco.com
Annual Production: 3,500 barrels
Number of Beers: 10 on tap; 6 bottled for distribution

Staple Beers:

>   » Bare Bottom Madness (oatmeal pale ale)
>   » Little Sister Witbier
>   » Pastoral Farmhouse Ale
>   » Polka King Porter

Rotating Beers:
>   » Biere De Seigle
>   » Big Sister Belgian Wit (with hibiscus)
>   » Silurian Stout
>   » Four seasonal farmhouse ales

Most Popular Brew: Little Sister.

Samples: Yes, flight of five 3-oz pours for about $10

Brewmaster's Fave: Biere de Seigle or Bare Bottom Madness

Best Time to Go: Closed in January. *Winter hours:* Fri 1–10PM, Sat 11AM–10PM, Sun 1–5PM. *Summer hours:* daily 11AM–10PM. Music on the weekends.

Where can you buy it? Here on tap and to go in growlers, howlers, and 25-oz containers, and distributed in 6-pack bottles and draft accounts throughout Wisconsin, as well as the Twin Cities, St. Cloud, and Duluth areas.

Got food? Only some cheese plates and curds, and food trucks on occasion in summer. Otherwise, food friendly, so bring your own.

Tours? Yes, scheduled on the website, one on Friday, two on Saturday. They are free, include samples, and are limited to 25 people. The brewery is a stop on a Door County Trolley tour that includes a visit to Shipwrecked Brewpub as well.

Special Offer: A free pint of Door County beer during your signature visit.

Directions: Take WI 57 into Baileys Harbor and go west 0.2 mile on County Rd F and it's on the right. From the bay side in Egg Harbor, take WI 42 to County Rd EE and go east 6.5 miles to County Rd F, go right and another 0.7 mile the brewery is on the left.

The Beer Buzz: It may seem an obvious brewery name for its location within Wisconsin's most recognized county outside the state, but the fact is every fiber of this brewery is connected to Door County—from their ingredients to the styles and the beer names. Their goal is to get all the barley for their malt locally as well as the hops. President John McMahon co-founded the brewery with his son Danny, the head brewer. John's wife Angie is general manager, and their other son Ben manages the taproom and music bookings. John and Angie raised the boys here in Door County.

"Don't trust a brewer without a beard," Danny told me, with a knowing nod. Danny went to school in Minneapolis and took up homebrewing as a hobby, but to step it up to pro, he attended the Siebel Institute. Door County has a rich history of Belgian immigrants—this was the largest population of Wallonians outside Wallonia (southern Belgium)—and Danny appropriately is into Belgian styles, especially farmhouse ales and sours. These are yeast-forward beers, and he is working on harvesting local yeasts.

The brewery was originally a bar, then a feed store, then a grocery store, and now comes back to beer. The owners have brought back the feed mill design, with touches such as barn doors fashioned into tables and the original columns and wood beams exposed with pieces of bark still on them. Rather than staining the wood back in those days, they burned them with a torch creating an unusual look. A '49 Chevy truck appears on the brewery logo, so Vintage truck doors with targets and bullet holes on them adorn the taproom. There's also a gift shop. All production on the

7-barrel system in the basement is for the taproom, while they have an alternating proprietorship arrangement at Sand Creek Brewing in Black River Falls for the bottles and distribution. By 2017 they may be looking into a larger space elsewhere in Door County for a production facility.

What's in a name? Local color and regional history. The four seasonal farmhouse ales are named after historical Door County Belgian farms, while Little Sister and Big Sister are two islands on the Green Bay side of the peninsula. There actually was a Polka King: Freddie Kodanko, a local character who loved the oompah music, used to play 45s and LPs of it at area events while wearing a crown and cape. He liked his drink a bit much and lost his driver license, so he ended up driving around on his red tractor, which didn't require one. Silurian Stout is not a geeky reference to Dr. Who, but rather a nod to a geological period between the Ordovician and Devonian Periods, 443.7 to 416.0 million years ago, when warm seas covered the area and laid down the materials that would become limestone and eventually the dolomite that underlies the peninsula. Thus, the fish fossil on the label. (A professor from the Field Museum in Chicago informed them their fish was from the wrong period, but who's gonna know that? A professor from the Field Museum, apparently.)

Mug Club. Facebook/DoorCountyBrewingCo and
Twitter @DoCoBrewingCo and Instagram @doorcobrewing

Stumbling Distance: *Blacksmith Inn on the Shore* (8152 WI-57, 800-769-8619, theblacksmithinn.com) is an outstanding bed & breakfast here in town. *AC Tap* (9322 WI 57, 920-839-2426) is a cash-only bar serving lunch and dinner and a reputable fish fry. Burgers, pizza and fish fry at *Cornerstone Pub* (8123 WI-57, 920-839-9001) are also nice. *Door County Trolley* (8030 Hwy 42, Egg Harbor, doorcountytrolley.com) runs a variety of tours in the area, from cherry themes to ghost tours in the fall. But don't miss their Classic Beer Tour, which includes tasting stops at both Door County Brewing and Shipwrecked Brewpub. Bookings are handled by Zerve at 866-604-5573. Pay a visit to the *Cana Island Lighthouse* (8800 E Cana Island Rd, dcmm.org) and see the light stations on a lovely walk through *The Ridges Sanctuary* (8270 WI 57, 920-839-2802, ridgessanctuary. org). Ten miles up the highway in Sister Bay, try *Bier Zot* (10677 Bayshore Dr, Sister Bay, 920-854-5070, Facebook.com/BierZot) a Belgian beer café with a long list of brews and Euro café fare.

Don't miss the *Door County Beer Festival* in mid-June here in Baileys Harbor! (doorcountybeer.com)

ROWLAND'S CALUMET BREWING (ROLL INN BREW PUB)

Founded: September 1990, first beer on tap
Brewmaster: Patrick Rowland
Address: 25 N. Madison Street • Chilton, WI 53014
Phone: 920-849-2534
Website: www.rowlandsbrewery.com
Annual Production: 400 bbls
Number of Beers: 30 per year, 11 on tap

Staple Beers:
» CALUMET AMBER
» CALUMET DARK
» CALUMET OKTOBERFEST
» CALUMET RYE
» FAT MAN'S NUT BROWN ALE

Rotating Beers:
» BITTER BITCH BELGIUM ALE
» BUCHOLZ ALT (formulated with Luther from Lakefront Brewery)
» CALUMET BOCK
» CALUMET ICE
» CALUMET KOLSCH
» CALUMET PILSNER (brewer's grandfather's recipe, a 1950 Coal miner from West Virginia)
» CALUMET WHEAT
» CONNOR JOHN'S SCOTCH ALE
» DETENTION ALE
» GUIDO'S GRAND IMPERIAL STOUT
» HONEY LAGER
» HUNTER'S CHOICE
» KELLY'S IRISH RED LAGER
» MADISON STREET LAGER (a pre-Prohibition pilsner)
» MITTNACHT PILSNER (Schwarzbier)
» MORTIMER'S ALE (English-style ale formulated with Kirby Nelson of Wisconsin Brewing)
» TOTAL ECLIPSE

Most Popular Brew: A dead heat: Nut Brown or Oktoberfest

Brewmaster's Fave: "Whatever we have the most of—we make it exactly the way we like it."

Tours? Yes, by appointment.

Samples? Yes, $9 for eleven 3-oz beers and a root beer.

Best Time to Go: Open Tue–Thu 2PM–2AM, Fri–Sun 12PM–2:30AM. Closed Mondays, except holidays. Watch for the local street party in August, Crafty Applefest, or the brewery's famous Wisconsin Micro Brewers Beer Fest in May.

Where can you buy it? Growlers on site or 45+ area bars with draft accounts.

Got food? Pickled eggs and turkey gizzards? You make the call. "Eight or nine beers and it'll be the best food you ever had in your life." Also popcorn and pizzas made in Fond du Lac.

Special Offer: A free 7-oz glass of the reason they're in business so long.

The Beer Buzz: Built around 1870, the building was Chilton's first firehouse and later city hall. At one time church services were held upstairs. John Diedrich made a tavern out of it in 1937, officially (though the back bar's mirror indicates 1926, so it may have been a speakeasy during Prohibition). Bob and Bonita Rowland opened the bar in '83. As the drinking age went from 18 to 19 and then to 21, Bob dealt with a lagging customer base and decided to take his homebrewing public. The Old Calumet Brewing Co. closed in 1942 when the Feds made an example of them for not paying beer taxes, and Bob saw it fit to adopt the name for what in 1990 was the 3rd smallest brewery in the US in the smallest city to have one. Madison Street Lager, a pre-Prohibition American-style lager, was formulated by Bob and Carl Strauss, the former head at Pabst for 40 years. Calumet Ice was the result of an equipment malfunction and the engineer sent out by the company to find the problem was Dan Carey, now the brewmaster at New Glarus Brewery. There's a handwritten note behind the bar from Kirby at Capital Brewery. As Bob once put it, "Brewers in Wisconsin are like cohorts in the same crime." Bob's son Patrick carries on this awesome

family tradition. This is a true tavern, not to be missed, and laden with breweriana and some great stories. Small town prices are a bonus!

Stumbling Distance: *Vern's Cheese* (www.vernscheese.com, 312 W. Main St, 920-849-7717) has fresh curds on Tue and Thu evenings (or the following mornings) and various string cheeses besides a huge selection of other cheeses. *Ledge View Nature Center* (W2348 Short Rd, 920-849-7094, ledgeviewnaturecenter.org) is a 105-acre wooded park with a 60-ft observation tower and a couple miles of hiking trails. $6–7 scheduled tours are available for three natural caves here. Expect to get dirty and you might want to do this *before* you hit the brewpub. The park is free and open from dawn till dusk, but only till 4:30 at the office. Pick strawberries, buy honey or maple syrup, go on hay rides and explore a corn maze in fall at *Meuer Farm* (meuerfarm.com, N2564 Hwy 151, Chilton, 920-418-2676).

LOCAL INGREDIENTS—BRIESS MALT

Beer can only be as good as its ingredients. Garbage in, skunk beer out. So we are fortunate to have the Briess Malt and Ingredients Co. (briess.com), North America's leading producer of specialty malts, right here in Chilton, Wisconsin. Briess produces over 50 styles of malt—more than any other malting company in the world! Ignatius Briess started malting barley back in the 19th century in Moravia in what is now the Czech Republic. World Wars do little for business, and so grandson Eric brought the operation to the US in the 1930s. Great-grandson Roger saw that craft brewers could not buy in quantities as big as a box car and, sensing the coming trend toward hand-crafted microbrews, had the brilliant notion to start producing and bagging specialty malts in the 1970s. Specialized roasters were necessary to get the darker malts. Today they have 3 malt houses in Wisconsin, including this original one, plus one in Waterloo and the largest, a reactivated malthouse, in Manitowoc which doubled their capacity. (And there are two more there that could be brought back online when needed!) You'll find bags of Briess Malt in the back rooms of nearly all of the microbreweries in Wisconsin. Now *that's* some local beer.

Trivia note: Briess President Gordon Lane brews with his daughter at his own little brewery in Brookfield: Biloba Brewing.

CHATTERHOUSE BREWERY (GEORGE STREET CONNECTION)

Founded: 2015
Head Brewer: Terry Taylor
Tap Room: 614 George Street • De Pere, WI 54115
Phone: George St Connection: 920-336-8750
Web Site: www.chatterhousebrewey.com
Annual Production: 500 barrels
Number of Beers: 3 on tap (16 on tap at bar)

Beers:

- » CHATTERHOUSE ALE
- » COFFEE PORTER
- » DE PERE DRAFT
- » 1893 DARK ALE
- » NO SACRIFICE GLUTEN FREE ALE
- » Hard Cider

Most Popular Brew: Chatterhouse Ale

Brewer's Fave: No Sacrifice (by default, see below)

Tours? By appointment.

Samples: Yes.

Best Time to Go: The bar is open 2PM–close. The restaurant is open for lunch 11AM–2PM, and dinner 4–11PM. Happy hour runs Mon–Fri 3–7PM.

Where can you buy it? Only here on tap and in growlers and howlers and bottles to go.

Got food? Yes, a full bar and full menu with burgers/dogs/sandwiches, soup/salad, curds, wings, and Brewpub pizzas.

Special Offer: A vaguely defined trinket… maybe, if something is on hand.

Directions: Coming across the Fox River on WI 32 from the west, enter the traffic circle and take the second exit onto Wisconsin St. At the next corner turn right on George St and go 1.5 blocks east and George Street Connection is on the right.

The Beer Buzz: The Chatterhouse Supper Club operated here from 1893, the second oldest building in De Pere, and now a brewery of the same name finds a space here within George Street Connection, a restaurant and bar. The dining room is to the left when you walk in, while a bar, with a continually growing amount of craft beer, is on the right. A small tasting area for the brewery is in the back of the dining area.

Brewer Terry's dad homebrewed, and when Terry was five, he showed how to cap a beer bottle for show and tell. Part of Terry's service was a 3-year stint in Belgium as a protective service agent for NATO (read "bullet catcher"), and while stationed there he developed a taste for great beer. Since he can no longer consume gluten, his favorite of his brews is that gluten-free one.

Brewer Terry started homebrewing in 2003, sharing with friends, and got licensed in February 2015. He took a buyout from a telecommunications job, settled in on a horse ranch in Denmark, WI (5675 Maribel Rd), and picked up some used equipment from Von Stiehl winery (Ahnappe Brewing). Then he started having seizures from PTSD-triggered epilepsy and couldn't drive and deliver brew. (He can now, however.) Now he is hoping for a zoning variance in Denmark so that he can open a tasting room there. Until then, this will do nicely.

He is the landlord of this double building, and when father and son Dale and Ken Oldenburg wanted to open a music venue sort of craft brewpub, they all agreed his tasting room would fit right in. The bar has a couple TVs, a jukebox, pool, darts, and pinball in back. A projection screen comes out during Packers games.

Free WiFi. Facebook/Chatterhouse-Brewery and
Twitter @chatterhouswBre

Facebook.com/
GeorgeStreetConnection

Stumbling Distance: Other good beer lineups in De Pere include *Graystone Ale House* (3711 Monroe St, 920-347-2727, graystonealehouse.com) and *Brickhouse Craft Burgers & Brews* (500 Grant St, 920-338-2337, brickhouseburgersandbrews).

LEGENDS BREWHOUSE & EATERY

Founded: 2001
Brewmaster: Ken Novak
Address: 875 Heritage Road • De Pere, WI 54115
Phone: 920-336-8036
Website: www.legendseatery.com.
Annual Production: 50 bbls
Number of Beers: 6 on tap

Staple Beers:
- » ACME AMBER
- » DUCK CREEK DUNKEL
- » FOUNDERS HONEY WEISS
- » LONGTAIL LIGHT

Rotating Beers:
- » CLAUDE ALLOUEZ IPA
- » CROCODILE LAGER
- » HALF MOON BRICK BELGIAN TRIPEL
- » HARVEST MOON OKTOBERFEST
- » IXTAPA BLONDE ALE
- » JACK RABBIT RED ALE
- » RUDOLPH'S RED-NOSE ALE (Christmas)

Most Popular Brew: Acme Amber

Brewmaster's Fave: IPA

Tours? If Ken's out there, otherwise try to make an appointment.

Samples? Yes, $5 for six 2-oz beers.

Best Time to Go: Friday and Saturday nights, Packer game days, or after an event at St. Norbert College. Fridays the beers are on special. Sunday brunch is popular. Happy Hour is 2–6 PM Mon–Fri.

Where can you buy it? On-site growlers with super cheap refills.

Got food? Yes, Friday fish fry (perch), beer cheese soup, wings, and ribs are notable.

Special Offer: Not participating.

Directions: Cross the Fox River heading east in De Pere and then go right (south) on S. Broadway. Where the road curves and Hwy 32 continues, go straight on Cty PP until you reach Heritage Road. Then go right (west).

The Beer Buzz: This used to be Splinters Sport Bar. The new owners remodeled a bit, and moved the bar to the side. Like the other locations, this has a sports bar theme. Read a bit about Ken at the Green Bay location listing.

Sit outside on the deck during the summer. During football season, come see the Monday Night Kickoff Show. Green Bay Packer players host a live TV show talking to guests, fans, and friends. You will need a reservation for the TV show. Free WiFi on site.

STUMBLING AROUND DE PERE

Less than a quarter of the population of Green Bay, De Pere nevertheless shouldn't be overlooked. A *Packers Heritage Trail* trolley tour might actually take you here because *St. Norbert College* (www.snc. edu), right on the Fox River, is where the Packers stay for training camp. Autograph seekers often hunt there in summer. The campus also has the usual sporting, arts, and cultural events associated with a fine liberal arts college. Go Green Knights! Near the college is *Luna Café* (330 Main Ave, 920-336-1557, lunacafe.com), not just a great coffee shop but a roaster as well. That's the Luna in Hinterland's excellent Luna Coffee Stout (and Lunatic Imperial Stout). *Brickhouse Craft Burgers & Brews* (500 Grant St, 920-338-2337, brickhouse-burgersandbrews) is also nearby with rotating taps and 1 of 2 places that serves the brews of tiny RockPere Brewing.

On the east side of the river is Chatterhouse Brewing served inside George Street Connection. A short walk from there is *Seroogy's Homemade Chocolates* (144 N Wisconsin St, 800-776-0377, seroogys. com), satisfying your sweet tooth since 1899. They roast coffee too (and it ends up in one of Badger State Brewing's beers). Don't miss breakfast and baked goods at *Alpha Delights* (143 N Wisconsin St, 920-339-9144, alphadelights.com) right across the lot from there. *Chateau De Pere* (201 James St, 920-347-0007, chateaudepere.com) is a perfect place to spend the night right here. The *Fox River Trail* runs through here, connecting you all the way to Downtown Green Bay about 5 miles north.

And of course, De Pere has local cheese and fresh curds: just south of town is *Scray Cheese* (2082 Old Martin Rd, 920-347-0303, scray-cheese.com). Family run since 1924, they make award-winning Edam, Gouda, Fontina and Cheddar, among others. Plus there's ice cream and a drive up window.

RockPere Brewing Co. (De Pere)

Founded: 2014
Brewmaster: Mark Riggle
Address: Town of Rockland, WI (De Pere)
Web Site: www.rockpere.beer
Annual Production: 12 barrels
Number of Beers: 5 beers

Staple Beers:
» Ay Yi Yi P, Eh?
» Easy Peasy Light Amber Ale
» Peachy Wheat
» Ski Trail Winter Ale
» Uncle Fritz Francisco Oatmeal Stout

Most Popular Brew: Easy Peasy

Brewmaster's Fave: Ski Trail

Best Time to Go: Check the two establishments for opening hours but make sure they have some left! Watch for Green Bay's Craft Beer Week in May if you want to meet the brewer.

Where can you buy it? Only two places to find this stuff:

Red Restaurant (106 S Broadway, Green Bay, 920-544-4156, redrestaurantgb.com) in bottles.

Brickhouse, (500 Grant St, De Pere, 920-338-2337, BrickhouseBurgersAndBrews.com) on tap.

Special Offer: Not participating.

The Beer Buzz: With production of a barrel per month, this is officially Wisconsin's tiniest brewery. Nevertheless, Mark Riggle, a homebrewer for 30 years, has gone through all the official hoops of Federal and local authorities to brew commercially. While others might groan at the thought of it, Mark reports the process was quick and smooth, even his label approval. To satisfy Federal requirements for an acceptable brewing space he merely needed to wall off the third stall of his garage. If he had done this 10 years ago, he'd be all in, but at this stage ("damn, if I was a younger man") he doesn't want outside investment and he doesn't have the time, so he brews on a one barrel system.

So far it's been good. He needs more time, and he'd be brewing every other day. "I went from little tiny buckets to bigger buckets." The Green Bay area brewing community has been supportive. He got a lot of help from the guys at Badger State and Joe Karls at Hinterland is a good friend. Joe let him learn a bit how to use "the big buckets" at Hinterland. Mark's wife Jill Larson is a master chemist (a professor) who also has his back when necessary.

From 'R' Farm to Your Face, One Barrel at a Time! is the brewer's motto, and while Mark sells only to two establishments, he is often sold out before he finishes brewing the next batch. The oatmeal stout is named after a miniature donkey on his farm. Ski Trail has 10 different spices and flavor ingredients added, including maple syrup from his

brother. He has grown his own barley and tried to malt it… and will probably never try that again. He does grow three kinds of hops, uses his own well water, and may roast small quantities of dark malts. He built himself a walk-in cooler but used a Pepsi glass-door cooler for his fermenter in the beginning. He's got no bigger plans at this point so for now he keeps a low profile and is just having some fun. For now, the only place to try this beer is at the two restaurant/bars. There's no special offer, but you can still get your book signed there to record your successful beer hunting excursion.

Shipwrecked Brew Pub

Founded: 1997
Brewmaster: Rich Zielke **Head Brewer**: Sam Koelling
Address: 7791 Egg Harbor Rd, Egg Harbor 54209
Phone: 920-868-2767, 888-868-2767
Website: www.shipwreckedmicrobrew.com
Annual Production: 800 bbls
Number of Beers: 7 on tap

Staple Beers:
» Bayside Blonde Ale
» Captain's Copper Ale
» Door County Cherry Wheat
» India Pale Ale
» Lighthouse Light
» Peninsula Porter

Rotating Beers:
» Maibock
» Pumpkin Patch Pumpkin Ale
» Spruce Tip Ale
» Summer Wheat

Most Popular Brew: Lighthouse Light

Brewmaster's Fave: IPA

Tours? No.

Samples? Yes, seven 3-oz samplers for $7.

Best Time to Go: In summer Door County is swarming with tourists, and you may have to wait to be seated. Late spring or early fall might be better times to go if you want to avoid the crowds. From about Nov–Apr they are only open Fri–Sun with special hours around the holidays. Watch for Door County Beer Fest in June in Baileys Harbor.

Where can you buy it? Growlers on site and kegs on order and throughout Wisconsin. Six-pack bottles all over Wisconsin and in the Chicago and Twin Cities areas.

Got food? Yes, a pub menu including beer-boiled brats, pulled pork sandwiches, fried cheese curds, salads, and a chicken dish made with Door County cherry wine sauce.

Special Offer: $1 taps during signature visit (for bookholder only).

Directions: Highway 42 passes right through town, and the pub is right on it at the bend in the road where Horseshoe Bay Dr connects from the west.

The Beer Buzz: Owned by the Pollmans of the Door Peninsula Winery (and Door County Distillery), this was the first brewpub in the ever popular Door County. The brewpub was merely an idea for a good place to hang out and get a beer, and the food developed after that. The building dates back to the late 1800s when it attracted lumberjacks and sailors looking for a drink. Al Capone frequented the bar, and tunnels beneath it functioned as potential escape routes to other parts of the town. Shipwrecked also is known for its spirits—not whiskey and the like, but the ghostly kind. One of several frequently spotted apparitions is Jason, Capone's illegitimate son who hanged himself (perhaps with help) in the attic. Ask about the other haunts.

Brewer Rich brewed in Colorado for 12 years at Estes Park Brewery. He had been tending bar and moved over to the brewery side and just "kinda lucked into it." He moved to Door County in 2008 inheriting the recipes at Shipwrecked and adding some of his own such as the IPA. While he misses the mountains sometimes, he was landlocked in Colorado and loves the water and endless shoreline of Door County.

The bar is topped with metal like a truck's running boards, and the room is decorated with a sailing theme. Besides the bar there is a separate dining room, and there are windows into the brewhouse. The patio out front is great for sunsets.

Facebook.com/ShipwreckedBrewPub

Stumbling Distance: *Door Peninsula Winery* (www.dcwine.com, 800-551-5049, 5806 Hwy 42) is ten minutes south in Carlsville. Tours are $3 and 45 wines are on hand for free tasting. Also, attached to the winery is *Door County Distillery* (doorcountydistillery.com, 920-746-8463) which produces vodka, fruit-infused vodkas, brandies, gin, and whiskey. The distillery offers tastings, but you can taste the at the winery as well. Door County is famous for its cherries, and the season starts around mid-July. There are places to pick them or just stop at one of many roadside stands. Fish fries are less common than the fish boil, a tradition unique to Door County. *Pelletier's* (920-868-3313, Fish Creek, open May–Oct) is recommended for theirs. Whenever traveling up here during early spring, late fall and winter, it is advisable to call ahead to see what is open. Many places in Door County shut down during the off season. Too tired to stumble? There are eight guest rooms above the bar *(Upper Deck Inn at Shipwrecked)!*

TAKE AWAY: DOOR COUNTY DELICIOUS

Door County is synonymous with cherries. Various producers and shops sell cherries and cherry products throughout the peninsula (wisconsin-cherries.org). One good recommendation is *Schartner's Farm Market* (6476 WI Hwy 42, Egg Harbor, 920-743-8617); another is *Hyline Orchard Farm Market* (8240 WI Hwy 42, Fish Creek, 888-433-2087). But honestly, there are loads of them.

Schoolhouse Artisan Cheese (schoolhouseartisancheese.com) carries cheese from 30+ Wisconsin cheesemakers plus some specialty meats with locations in both Egg Harbor (7813 Highway 42, 920-868-2400) and at Ellison Bay (12042 Hwy 42, 920-854-6600) inside Savory Spoon Cooking School (Recommended! Savoryspoon.com)

Renard's Cheese & Deli (2189 County Rd DK, Sturgeon Bay, 920-825-7272, renardscheese.com) is right off WI Highways 42/57 as you head north to Sturgeon Bay, and along with their fresh curds, they offer a load of other cheeses made inhouse or elsewhere. Tons of other products as well, including…

Salmon's Meat Products (107 4th St, Luxemburg, 920-845-2721, salmonsmeatproducts.com) Some of the best wieners you'll ever find plus brats, bacon, various sausages and more. Vince Lombardi went to these people for meats, and I pack a cooler for every trip to Green Bay/Door County to stock up. You don't have to get to Luxemburg though, because several select stores carry them—only in this NE corner of the state. (Pronounce the L; it's not like the fish.)

BADGER STATE BREWING CO.

Founded: February 1, 2013
Brewmaster: Sam Yanda
Address: 990 Tony Canadeo Run • Green Bay, WI 54304
Phone: 920-634-5687
Web Site: www.badgerstatebrewing.com
Annual Production: 1,300 barrels
Number of Beers: 24 taps (8 guests)

Staple Beers:
- » BUNYAN BADGER BROWN ALE
- » GREEN CHOP SESSION IPA
- » WALLOON WITBIER

Rotating Beers:
- » DUBIOUS RUFFIAN CHOCOLATE STOUT
- » HONEY KÖLSCH
- » JALAPEÑO PORTER
- » MEAN GREEN NEW ZEALAND HOP IPA
- » ON WISCONSIN RED ALE
- » PORTE DES MORTS MAPLE PORTER
- » SAISON
- » VIVE LA BELGE! BELGO-PALE ALE
- » various IPAs and Stouts
- » …plus frequent assorted pilot batches and barrel-aging.

Most Popular Brew: Green Chop IPA, On Wisconsin, but Walloon in summer.

Brewmaster's Fave: If forced to choose, one of the IPAs.

Tours? Public tours are typically scheduled on Saturdays, cost about $10, and can be signed up for via a link on their website.

Samples: Yes, 4-oz pours for $2 each or more for bigger beers.

Best Time to Go: Open Wed 3–9PM, Thu–Sat 2–10PM, Sundays during Packers games only.

Where can you buy it? Here in 4-, 10-, and 16-oz pours, plus growlers or cans to go. Distributed throughout Door County and Northeast WI down to Sheboygan/Oshkosh for now, in four-packs of 16-oz cans.

Got food? No, but food friendly. Occasional food trucks, especially on game days and catered events. Menus onsite for delivery, even from nearby restaurants that only deliver here.

Special Offer: A free 4-oz sample when you get your book signed.

Directions: From I-94 or from Ashland Ave/WI 32, turn onto Lombardi Ave and head toward Lambeau Field. Just east of the stadium, turn south on Holmgren Way. Turn left on Brett Favre Pass, follow it as it turns right, and then the next left is Tony Canadeo Run. The brewery is 300 feet along on the left beyond a big parking lot.

The Beer Buzz: Close enough to Lambeau to tailgate, Badger State Brewing was founded by Andrew Fabry whose family has a bit of Belgian blood in them. Andrew had a merry Christmas in 2011 when his brother bought him a brew kit. His friend Mike and Mike's cousin Sam had him over to learn a bit, and they brewed a batch in Sam's garage in 90+ degree July heat. The discomfort didn't dampen any enthusiasm.

When Andrew finished university in Madison, he headed back to Green Bay to stand at a crossroads: law school or beer. Tough choice, right? Disappointment in the local craft beer scene as compared to Madison's at the time, he sat down and wrote up a business plan. Andrew had worked for a distributor in high school and in bars in college, so he had experience in 2 of the 3 tiers of the beer industry but not the manufacturing side of it. Mike passed on the idea, and Sam remained silent on the matter until about a year later when frustration with his own job and Andrew's relentless efforts to convince him finally got him on board as head brewer.

They took over a vacant storage space in a much larger industrial building. Saranac and Hudson-Sharp occupy the other two spaces. They sold their first kegs in December 2013, and when they started selling growlers out the back door six months later, they knew they needed a taproom.

They had a lot of room to work with (and still do for brewery expansion), so the taproom is spacious with a large three-sided bar built of reclaimed pallet wood at center and abundant tables throughout the room. Two big TVs show sports (especially such games being played at the nearby stadium), music plays, and board games are on hand. There's even a gift shop. A glass utility door looks in on the brewhouse and opens for tours or larger crowds. Out a side door is a grassy area with a few picnic tables functioning as a beer garden. You can see the lights of Lambeau to the west of here. A factory sized parking lot serves the building.

The brewery logo includes a badger—the state's nickname that derives from the mining heritage, not the testy creature itself—and a pick and shovel, and barley on the sides.

Free WiFi. Facebook/BadgerStateBrewingCompany and Twitter @badgerstbrewco

Stumbling Distance: *Green Bay Distillery* (835 Mike McCarthy Way, Ashwaubenon, 920-393-4403, greenbaydistillery.com) has a full menu, WI beers, house-made vodkas, and TVs for the game. Filled with memorabilia from the all-star former quarterback, *Brett Favre's Steakhouse* (1004 Brett Favre Pass, 920-499-6874, brettfavressteakhouse.com) is next door and can deliver the goods to the taproom. Tour *Lambeau Field* or visit the *Packer's Hall of Fame* (packers.com). The stadium is the stuff of legends. Named after the year Curly Lambeau and George Whitney Calhoun organized the Green Bay Packers, *1919 Kitchen & Tap* is a gastropub with 40 beers on tap in the atrium at Lambeau Field.

HINTERLAND BREWERY (GREEN BAY BREWING CO.)

Founded: 1995
Brewmaster: Joe Karls
Address: 313 Dousman Street • Green Bay 54303 (*In late 2016/early 2017 Hinterland will relocate to the new Titletown District west of Lambeau Field.*)
Phone: 920-438-8050
Website: www.hinterlandbeer.com
Annual Production: 6,000 bbls
Number of Beers: 14 on tap

Staple Beers:
- » INDIA PALE ALE
- » LUNA STOUT
- » LUNATIC IMPERIAL STOUT
- » PACKERLAND PILSNER
- » PALE ALE
- » PUB DRAUGHT (pale ale-style, under nitro)
- » WHITE CAP WHITE IPA

Rotating Beers:
- » BOURBON-BARREL DOPPELBOCK
- » BOURBON-BARREL IMPERIAL STOUT
- » BOURBON-BARREL GRAND CRU
- » CHERRY WHEAT
- » GRAND CRU
- » MAPLE BOCK
- » OKTOBERFEST
- » SAISON
- » THIS AIN'T NO PILSNER! IMPERIAL STOUT
- » WHITEOUT BOURBON-BARREL IMPERIAL IPA
- » WHITEOUT IMPERIAL INDIA PALE ALE
- » WINTERLAND

Most Popular Brew: Luna Stout

Brewmaster's Fave: "Depends on my mood and time of the year."

Tours? Yes, Saturdays at 3 and 4PM. Cost is $10 and includes a pint glass and two beers. Check website and sign up there.

Samples? Yes, eight beers for $14.

Best Time to Go: In late summer and early fall there are lots of area events. Packers game days. Summer is the slowest time of year, but the courtyard patio is a great place to hang outside. Happy hour is 4–7PM Mon–Sat.

Where can you buy it? Bottles and drafts of most brews are available in Green Bay, Milwaukee, Madison, Door County, and throughout the state of Wisconsin. Florida, Illinois, Iowa, Indiana, Minnesota, Nebraska, North Carolina, U.P. Michigan and Ohio now also have it!

Got food? Yes, but don't expect greasy pub fare—this is a high-class menu. Seafood is flown in daily from Maine, Seattle, and Hawaii. Wood-fired oven pizzas, noodle bowls, grass-fed beef burgers.

Special Offer: A glass of their beer when you get your book signed.

The Beer Buzz: Broadway Street, once famous for seedy bars, now has a collection of fine restaurants and shops. Beer meets class in this upscale and classy restaurant/pub on the corner of Dousman and Broadway, just west of the Fox River. This is Packerland, after all—the building was formerly a meat-packing plant, and the hook receptacles can still be seen in the ceiling. Sound like a dismal place? Not on your life! The atmosphere is relaxed, the décor elegant. The upstairs lounge has an eclectic music library and is a popular post-work-day gathering place. The menu includes a lot of local game, and a wood-fired oven is on hand for some fine pizzas. Founder Bill Tressler studied journalism in college and started editing brewing magazines in the 90s. So the logical next step, of course, was to open a brewery. Rahr Green Bay Brewing Co. was the longest running brewery in the city, operating from 1858 to 1966 and the corporation name here is a nod to them. Hinterland was the first brewpub to bring hometown brew back to Green Bay. The beers have won many medals including silver medals for the Pale Ale and IPA and a World Champion

medal for Maple Bock. Hinterland ships its beers to its second fine-dining gastropub down in Milwaukee (222 East Erie Street, 414-727-9300). The building is not exactly massive, yet a rather large brew system has been magically packed into every available space with occasional structural alterations to accommodate large tanks. Very impressive. Joe has a pound of coffee in each barrel of their most popular beer, Luna Stout, and I took some on The Today Show at Lambeau Field back in 2011 for Al Roker to try.

Stumbling Distance: *Titletown Brewing Co.* is just across the street. Look both ways—you've been drinkin'. See Stumbling Around Downtown Green Bay.

STUMBLING AROUND DOWNTOWN GREEN BAY

Hinterland and *Titletown* Breweries are right next to each other, and *Stillmank* is not far east. This puts a beer focal point right in the heart of downtown Green Bay, thus providing you some other cool things to do just stumbling distance away. Downtown is divided by the Fox River. Hinterland and Titletown are on the **west side** at Dousman/Main St bridge. Both touch on Broadway. Once a sort of sketchy area, revitalization has transformed it into a collection of great eateries, bars and shops, and on Wednesday evenings from Jun-Oct, On Broadway (onbroadway.org), a farmers market, closes off Broadway.

Highlights here include *Red Restaurant* (106 S Broadway, 920-544-4156, redrestaurantgb.com) with a fantastic fusion menu showing touches of Asian influences and changing regularly. Good cocktails and a nice selection of craft beer in bottles (including RockPere, a nano-nano-brewery that only serves here and at *Brickhouse* in De Pere.) Inside Titletown's brewery complex is *The Cannery Public Market* (320 N Broadway, 920-388-3333, thecannerymarket.com) with field-to-fork foods, fresh cheese curds being made before your eyes, a deli, beer and wine retail and many specialty products, primarily local in origin. Shop for home or sit and eat here with a selection of draft beers.

Before you cross the bridge, there is the *Neville Public Museum* (210 Museum Pl, 920-448-4460, nevillepublicmuseum.org) covering some Wisconsin history from the Ice Age to the 1940s, plus frequent traveling exhibits.

Just over the bridge on the **east side,** Washington Street runs parallel to the Fox River. Another farmers market closes this street as well Saturday mornings from May-Oct. One of Green Bay's best craft beer bars, *Ned Kelly's* (223 N Washington St, 920-433-9306, nedkellyspub.com) is here, as is craft-beer-friendly *Hagemeister Park* (325 N Washington St, 920-884-9909, hagemeister-park.com). *Adams Street Pub* (121 N Adams St, 920-593-2383, adamsstreetpub.com) has great bar food (curds! Fish fry!) and a huge beer list. *The Libertine* (209 N Washington St, 920-544-6952, thelibertine209.com) is a cool, relaxed craft cocktail bar, extremely serious about mixology (enough to get the notice of *The New York Times* and other national outlets). No TVs or blaring music, just expertly mixed drinks and about 11 craft beers on tap.

Great burgers at a cheap price await at old-school *Al's Hamburger* (131 S Washington St, 920-437-5114). *Polito's* (201 N Washington St, 920-544-5086, politospizza.com) does pizza by the slice. For grapes rather than grains, visit *Captain's Walk Winery* (345 S Adams St, 920-431-9255, captainswalkwinery.com) The 1930 *Meyer Theatre* (117 S Washington St, 920-433-3343, meyertheatre.org) is the local concert/performance venue.

The City Walk portion of the *Packers Heritage Trail* (packersheritagetrail.com) is a self-guided walking tour chronicling the local legends of football with 17 commemorative plaques and some statues. The centerpiece is located at Washington and Cherry Streets. There are also Packing Plant and Lambeau-Lombardi sites outside downtown, and a *trolley tour* for the entire heritage trail (downtowngreenbay.com/tours) which covers the whole city. The tours line up with some Packers training camp dates, too (800-895-0071, candmpresents.com).

The Fox River Trail (dnr.wi.gov) runs right along the east bank in downtown and goes all the way south to Wrightstown.

Quality Inn & Suites Downtown (321 S Washington St, 920-437-8771) is walking distance to all of these places. *St. Brendan's Inn* (234 S Washington St, 920-884-8484, saintbrendansinn.com) also has rooms plus an Irish pub.

You cannot come to Green Bay and not at least see *Lambeau Field*, the legendary home of the Green Bay Packers. Tours are available (packers.com, 920-569-7512 (press 1)). *The Packer Hall of Fame* (remodeled 2015) is another pilgrimage site for football fans right inside the stadium, and *1919 Kitchen & Tap* which serves excellent food and keeps 40 on tap. To get here from downtown, go west 3 blocks on Dousman to take a left (south) on Ashland. This will take you to Lombardi Avenue and you will turn right (west) and you're almost there. They live and die by football in this town. Bars will be hopping on game day; streets may be empty... until the game lets out anyway.

Don't miss **Green Bay Craft Beer Week** in May (gbcraftbeerweek.com) and Restaurant Week in July (gbrestaurantweek.com), a good time to explore the scene here.

For more downtown Green Bay goings-on, check downtowngreenbay.com

LEGENDS BREWHOUSE & EATERY

Founded: 1998
Brewmaster: Ken Novak
Address: 2840 Shawano Drive • Green Bay, WI 54313
Phone: 920-662-1111
Website: www.legendseatery.com
Annual Production: 60 bbls
Number of Beers: 6 on tap

Staple Beers:
- » ACME AMBER
- » DUCK CREEK DUNKEL
- » FOUNDERS HONEY WEISS
- » LONGTAIL LIGHT

Rotating Beers:
- » CLAUDE ALLOUEZ IPA
- » CROCODILE LAGER
- » HALF MOON BRICK BELGIAN TRIPEL
- » HARVEST MOON OKTOBERFEST
- » IXTAPA BLONDE ALE
- » JACK RABBIT RED ALE
- » RUDOLPH'S RED-NOSE ALE
  (Christmas)

Most Popular Brew: Duck Creek Dunkel

Brewmaster's Fave: Belgian Tripel "The best beer I've ever made!"

Tours? If Ken's out there, otherwise try to make an appointment.

Samples? Yes, $5 for six 2-oz beers.

Best Time to Go: Friday and Saturday nights, Packer game days. Fridays the beers are on special. Sunday brunch is popular. Happy Hour is 2–6 PM Mon–Fri.

Where can you buy it? Here on tap and in growlers on site.

Got food? Yes, Friday fish fry (perch), beer cheese soup, wings, and ribs are notable.

Special Offer: Not participating.

Directions: Head west on Shawano Ave (Hwy 29 West) off of 41 North, take Hwy 2 west to Riverdale Drive and turn right (north) and Legends is on the right, just past the *Village Green Golf Course*.

The Beer Buzz: Prior to this Legends, there was an old bar of the same name with an adjoining baseball field on this site. Thus, the name. The new building was completed in 1998, and the owners wanted a brewpub. Ken heard through a friend and got the job (nice friend!). Ken got his start homebrewing in 1993 with a kit he received as a gift, and he did his first beer on Christmas Day. He likes the hours and that no one tells him when he has to work or how to do it. The drawback, he says, "I work alone a lot. Not a lot of people to talk to."

Two large projection screen TVs are the flagships for a whole fleet of TVs piping in the day's sporting events. Sunday brunch is popular with folks staying around for noon kick-offs. Free WiFi is available and parking is off-street. They do their own root beer as well.

Stumbling Distance: Here it is, the local color you may have been scouring the pages for: *BOOYAH!* This is the regional hearty chicken-vegetable soup often made in mass quantities. *Rite View Family Dining* (2130 Velp Ave, 920-434-8981) makes 42-gallon batches. They also serve broasted chicken, Friday fish fry, cheese curds, and offer views of an old stone quarry and a yard full of peacocks. *Townline Pub & Grill* (2544 Lineville Rd, Suamico, 920-434-7943, town-line.com) has a lot of craft beer north of here.

Stillmank Beer Co.

Founded: May 2012
Brewmaster: Brad Stillmank
Address: 215 North Henry Street Road • Green Bay, WI 54302
Phone: 920-785-2337
Website: www.stillmankbrewing.com
Annual Production: 1,400 barrels
Number of Beers: 8 taps

Staple Beers:
  » BEE'S KNEES (honey rye ale)
  » SUPERKIND (Green Bay IPA)
  » WISCO DISCO (unfiltered amber ale)

Rotating Beers:
  » BOCK OF THE FUTURE
  » DOUBLE DISCO
  » PERKY PORTER

Most Popular Brew: Wisco Disco

Brewmaster's Fave: Wisco Disco

Tours? Yes, by appointment or by chance.

Samples: Yes, flights of three 5-oz pours for about $5.

Where can you buy it? Here on tap in 12- and 16-oz pours, and in growlers or cans to go. Distributed in 4-pack 16-oz cans and draft accounts in various places throughout Wisconsin: Eau Claire, Madison, Door County, Central Wisconsin, the Fox River Valley, and growing.

Got food? No, only snacks, but food friendly.

Special Offer: $3 off one growler during your signature visit.

Directions: Going east from the Fox River on Main Street, turn left on Deckner, and left again on Henry St and the brewery is on your left.

Cyclists: Right off the Baird Creek Trail which connects to the East River Trail and via streets to the Fox River Trail

The Beer Buzz: Milwaukee-native Brad Stillmank got his start as a homebrewer in the late 90s, throwing parties with his creations in college out in Colorado. The first batch was "good enough to keep me going. We were really surprised, actually, and emptied all the bottles over the weekend." In

2002 he started with keg washing and worked his way up to the brewhouse at Ska Brewery in Colorado but left in 2007 and moved to Green Bay with

his wife to start a family. He brewed for a while for the now defunct Black Forest Dining and Spirits, but decided there is no greater joy than brewing it for yourself. He worked as a craft beer specialist for a distributor in De Pere for 8 years, brewing on the side. When Wisco Disco was ready, he took it to Milwaukee Brewing Co. to be contract brewed, giving him some income to prepare for his own brewery. In 2014 he bought a building in April and brewed the first batch in August. The taproom opened two months later. The brewhouse was the indoor lumberyard of an old building supply store. The taproom was office cubicles and a showroom was torn down to open up a parking lot. The taproom has exposed ceiling beams, a bar at one end and a few picnic tables and tall tables.

Brad has certifications from the UC-Davis Institute of Brewing and Distilling and is a beer judge and a Certified Cicerone™ (sis-uh-ROHN), what you might call a beer sommelier. Brad tries to use local ingredients. All his hops are from Wisconsin, his malt is from Briess (Chilton), his honey comes from Bellevue, and the coffee is roasted locally. He calls Superkind his "gateway IPA."

Stumbling Distance: *Anduzzi's Sports Club* (900 Kepler Dr, 920-544-0874, anduzzis.com) toward the east side near I-43 has good food, 18 beers on tap, 28 TVs and great weekday happy hours. *Titletown Brewing* and *Hinterland Brewery* are 10 minutes from here. See Stumbling Around Downtown Green Bay.

TITLETOWN BREWING CO.

Founded: 1996
Brewmaster: David Oldenburg
Address: 200 Dousman Street • Green Bay, WI 54303
Phone: 920-437-2337
Website: www.titletownbrewing.com
Annual Production: 10,000 bbls
Number of Beers: 6 year-round beer, about 25 new recipes/year plus one-offs
Tasting Room: 16 on tap, *Brewpub:* 14 on tap plus 2 casks

Staple Beers:
  » "400" HONEY ALE (blonde ale with local wildflower honey)
  » CANADEO GOLD (Kölsch)
  » DARK HELMET SCHWARTZBIER
  » GREEN 19 IPA
  » JOHNNY "BLOOD" RED (Irish-style red ale)
  » CTRL "ALT" DELETE

Rotating Beers: (the list is endless, but here are a few)
  » BRIDGE OUT STOUT
  » DOUSMAN STREET WHEAT
  » OKTOBERFEST
  » BELGIANS
  » AMBERS
  » PORTERS
  » BROWNS
  » DOUBLE IPAs
  » …plus some barrel-aging, smoked beers, and occasional sours such as NED FLANDERS SOUR BROWN

Most Popular Brew: Green 19 IPA

Brewmaster's Fave: The beer in his glass.

Tours? Yes, scheduled on the website and for a nominal fee that includes some sampling.

Samples? Yes, sips to help you choose and flights for sale.

Best Time to Go: **Brewpub:** Open daily at 11AM. Hoppy hour 2–6PM. Join the Hoppy Campers Club. *Brewery Tap Room:* Wed–Fri 3–11PM, Sat 11AM–11PM. *Warning:* Tap room may close for private events, so double check the website.

Where can you buy it? On tap here in proper pints (20 oz) and in growlers and bottles to go, and some draft accounts around the state, plus 6-pack bottles of some of their core beers.

Got food? Brewpub: Yes, a great pub menu. Fish and chips, pizzas, artichoke dip, perch on Friday, deep-fried cheese curds, spicy beer cheese soup, the on-site baker makes beer breads. In fact, many of the entrees use beer in some way. The dinner entrees are excellent as well. **Tap room:** snacks and pizza.

Special Offer: A free pint o' beer when you get your book signed.

Directions: From US Highway 41 take Shawano Ave exit and go east to Ashland Ave. Go left (north) two blocks and take a right on Dousman St. The brewpub is on the left just before the bridge over the Fox River. The brewery and taproom is across the street from the brewpub; you can't miss the giant smokestack with Titletown on it.

The Beer Buzz: Overlooking the Fox River, Titletown occupies a former train station that is listed in the National Register of Historic Places. Built in 1898, it was a stop for the Chicago & Northwestern railway. Prior to that, it was the Fort Howard Military Reservation. This was a center of the community when the "Peninsula 400" passenger service still ran.

Three presidents rolled through on whistle-stops: Taft, Franklin Roosevelt and Eisenhower. The "400" ended service in 1971 and in '87 C&NW sold the tracks to Milwaukee to Fox River Valley Railroad. By 1994, after a couple more sales, it was just an empty building. That's when founder Brent Weycker, a fellow student union employee in college with yours truly, decided he would open a brewpub so that I would have something to write about 10 years later, and so we could all drink beer again just like we never, never did on the job. No, never. Well, hardly ever.

Brewmaster David started homebrewing in 2002 and then apprenticed here for many years. When the lead position opened up, he was a brew-in. Nearly everything produced here is sold over the counter (except for just a few tap accounts). It's an impressive amount of beer, but then this is Green Bay. Railyard Alt got silver at 2008's Great American Beer Festival, Dark Helmet took bronze a year later, followed by a gold for Boathouse Pilsner in 2010. (For those of you visiting from another planet, Titletown is the nickname of Green Bay, in recognition of the many championships won by the beloved Packers.) In 2011, I personally shared a growler of David's Expect the Wurst (bratwurst ale) with Al Roker when they did the *Today Show* right on the turf at Lambeau Field. My 1:40 of fame.

In 2014, Titletown opened a much expanded brewery with a state-of-the-art brewhouse, a bottling line, a tap room, event spaces, and rooftop drinking areas (indoor and outdoor). A former vegetable cannery, the

160-year old building had been vacant since 2003, and its massive smokestack rises above with the name Titletown emblazoned on it. The brewery stands across the street and parking lot from the train station brewpub. The brewery tap room was once the boiling room for the vegetables, with kettles cut into the floor and the skylights above to let out the steam. It's a huge space with high ceilings, and during Packers games and other notable events, a

screen is unrolled for projection TV. The long bar, with a foot rail from the old train at Bay Beach Amusement Park, runs along one wall with Art Deco design and blue lighting at night. One of the old kettle holes holds tempered glass so you can see through the floor (no skirts or kilts allowed). Two large garage doors open to Broadway St in season, and there is a front door and street parking here—though many park in back and enter through a hall from the side facing the former train station. Watch for the Beerbler, a true Wisconsin bubbler (drinking fountain) that will shoot beer instead of water. (In development at time of writing.)

Titletown provided beers to Cher-Make which created flavored summer sausages with them, available for sale at the bar.

That football player statue in front of the train station used to be at the Packers Hall of Fame. Titletown acquired it years ago and repainted it to be All-Star wide receiver and community hero Donald Driver. The city renamed the side street Donald Driver Way at that time.

Free WiFi. Facebook.com/titletownbrewing and Twitter @titletownbeer

Stumbling Distance: *The Cannery Public Market* (320 N Broadway, 920-388-3333, thecannerymarket.com) also occupies this building, with field-to-fork foods, cheese curds being made, a deli and lots of local products. *Hinterland Brewpub* is right across the street! Like the railroad theme going on here? Check out the *National Railroad Museum* (www.nationalrrmuseum.org, 2285 S. Broadway St, 920-437-7623) which has over 70 locomotives and cars, including Eisenhower's command train from WWII and the world's largest steam locomotive.

COURTHOUSE PUB

Founded: 2001
Head Brewers: Brian Sobel and Brock Weyer
Address: 1001 S 8th Street • Manitowoc, WI 54220
Phone: 920-686-1166
Website: www.courthousepub.com
Annual Production: 300 bbls
Number of Beers: 6 on tap. Sometimes includes a guest nitro brew.

Beers: (Beers change often)

- AMERICAN AMBER ALE
- CANADIAN-STYLE LIGHT
- CHIEF WAWATAM STEAM LAGER (with Tasmanian hops, it's the official beer of the Maritime Museum and 25¢ per glass goes there)
- CZECH PILSNER
- DOUBLE BOCK
- EXECUTIONER IMPERIAL STOUT
- IMPERIAL RED ALE
- MÄRZEN
- MEXICAN LIGHT
- MUNICH HELLES (malty, mild hops, golden)
- THE PRECEDENCE IMPERIAL PALE ALE
- PUB PORTER
- SCOTTISH ALE
- SING-THAI
- TRIPPEL JON
- UNFILTERED WEISS
- WILLINGER WHEAT

Most Popular Brew: Imperial Red Ale (during the holidays)

Brewmaster's Fave: Munich Helles (really, anything with malt, hops, and alcohol)

Tours? Yes, by appointment or by chance.

Samples? Yes, five beer samplers and a root beer for about $6.

Best Time to Go: Open Mon–Fri 11AM–9PM, Sat 9AM–9:30PM, Sun 9AM–2PM. Happy hour runs Mon–Fri 3–5PM. Friday and Saturday nights offer good dinner specials. This is primarily a restaurant, so don't expect to stay out late here unless you can chat up the bartender. Watch for live music dates on the website.

Where can you buy it? Only here on tap and in growlers to go.

Got food? Yes, serious food for both lunch and dinner. Items range from the more casual sandwiches, burgers, and wraps to steaks, seafood and other dinner entrées such as pecan-encrusted duck with Wisconsin maple syrup glazing or fresh scallops.

Special Offer: A free pint of microbrew when you bring in this book to be signed!

Directions: Take Exit 149 east off of I-43. Then travel east on 151/10/ Calumet Avenue (turns into Washington St) until 8th. Street. The pub is on the southeast corner of 8th and Washington Street in Downtown Manitowoc.

The Beer Buzz: This site was originally home to F. Willinger's Beer Hall, and an old black and white photo behind the bar shows the former beer joint. The pub was rebuilt to the hall's likeness. Once there were five breweries in Manitowoc, but by the mid-70s, there was not a one. Owner John Jagemann wanted to bring back a little of that tradition and so the pub was born. Beer is not the only libation here. Since 2002, the restaurant has maintained a Wine Spectator Award of Excellence. Follow the website's blog to find out about upcoming live music. The beers are brewed in 4-barrel batches, and when they run out, it's on to the next brew. This means a lot of variety in a short period of time. Recently they have been having great success with some imperial brews. They serve those in full pints, by the way!

Stumbling Distance: Look for the big cow and you'll find *Cedar Crest Ice Cream Parlor* (www.cedarcresticecream.com, 2000 S 10th, 800-877-8341). Award winning stuff. Stop in at the *Wisconsin Maritime Museum* (www.wisconsinmaritime.org, 866-724-2356) and tour the submarine U.S.S. Cobia. Twenty-eight subs were built here in Manitowoc during WWII. *Tippy's Bar, Grill and Miniature Bowling* (1713 East St, 920-553-8479) in Two Rivers (pronounced "T'rivers" by locals) serves smelt six days a week! (A small fish which is netted and then fried—and eaten—whole. It's a Wisconsin thing.) The Manitowoc VFW or Eagle's Hall are rumored to have the best fish fries, but there are tons of them here. Get your cheese fix at *Pine River Dairy* (www.pineriverdairy.com, 10115 English Lake Rd, 920-758-2233) south of 151 on Range Line Rd (since 1877). Over 250 varieties!

GATEWAY TO WISCONSIN II

From mid-May to mid-October, the S.S. Badger (ssbadger.com, 800-841-4243), a coal-powered car ferry, makes the four-hour crossing of the big lake to Manitowoc from Ludington, Michigan.

Rail House Restaurant & Brewpub

Founded: 1995
Brewmaster: Kris Konyn
Address: 2029 Old Peshtigo Court • Marinette, WI 54143
Phone: 715-732-4646
Website: www.railhousebrewpub.com
Annual Production: 300 bbls
Number of Beers: 20–24, 16 on tap

Staple Beers:
» Belgian Dubbel
» Big Mac IPA
» Blueberry Draft
» Bock
» Bourbon Oak Cask Ale
» Brewer's Best Pilsner
» Dumb Blonde
» Honey Weiss (Honey from Crivitz, WI)
» Imperial Pilsner
» Irish Red Ale
» Nutty Brown Ale
» Oatmeal Stout
» Oconto Premium Lager
» Scottish Ale
» Silver Cream Pilsner

Rotating Beers:
» Oktoberfest
» Zummer Fest

Most Popular Brew: Silver Cream

Brewmaster's Fave: Nutty Brown

Tours? Not really.

Samples? Yes, large sample car of 4-oz samples for $10, four for $3.50.

Best Time to Go: Open daily 11AM–10PM, 2–for–1 happy hour Mon–Thurs 3–6 PM, Fri 1–5 PM, Sat 1–4 PM. Menominee Water Front Festival is the first long weekend in August.

Where can you buy it? Here on tap and to go in growlers.

Got food? Yes, the menu offers a big variety including Italian (the muffuletta sandwich is highly recommended) and Mexican. Pizzas, beer-battered shrimp, Wisconsin beer and cheese soup, and a big Friday night fish fry. House root beer.

Special Offer: A free house beer during your signature visit.

Directions: The pub is on the right side of US41 as you come into Marinette from the south. Turn right (east) at Cleveland Ave and take the next 2 rights. There are large signs to direct you with the Rail House and Country Inn hotel on them.

The Beer Buzz: The pub was originally in a smaller building on the same lot, and in 1997 it reopened in the new facility. The Silver Cream Pilsner is a bit of nostalgia. It is a reproduction of the turn-of-the-century beer once produced by Menominee-Marinette Brewing Co. (just over the border in the Michigan sister city). The back bar here is a fantastic wood-carved affair all the way from Bavaria. Its original Wisconsin residence was a saloon in Blackwell. Two projection screen TVs are on hand for the big games, and an outdoor covered patio is the place to be in summer.

Kris began homebrewing in college using a couple of plastic pails and a big stainless kettle borrowed from his fraternity house kitchen. At first he used malt extracts and experimented with mini mashes and colder fermenting lagers. (He went to school in the cold U.P. climate of Houghton, MI after all.) One year after graduation he was having a beer with a friend in a brewpub and found himself in a brewing conversation with the owner. The conversation was in fact a cleverly disguised job interview. The next day Kris was offered the brewer position. His first batch of Scottish-style Ale was kegged a month later confirming they had the right guy for the job. Kris loves to try new beers and keeps up on the latest news and ideas

in brewing in technical and scientific publications, beer reviews, magazines and homebrewing blogs and books.

Stumbling Distance: South of town is *Seguin's Cheese* (W1968 US 41, 800-338-7919, seguin-scheese.com) offering a vast assortment of Wisconsin's other finest product and a variety of other local yummies (mustards, jams, sauces). They even ship it. Cheese curds and aged cheddar—can you ask for much else? For you outdoorsy types, grab a

growler from the brewpub and check out one of the 14 cascades that make *Marinette County* the "Waterfalls Capital of Wisconsin" (marinettecounty. com, 800-236-6681). More info on Marinette is found in a chapter from my book *Backroads & Byways of Wisconsin*.

CASK-CONDITIONED ALES

Cask comes from the Spanish word for "bark" like tree bark (cáscara). The little wooden barrel holds the beer in the same way bark surrounds a tree trunk I suppose. This is Old School beer storage (think of the original IPAs on their way to India to be drunk right out of the container) and the beer is unfiltered and unpasteurized.

Cask-conditioned ale goes through its secondary fermentation right in the cask or firkin from which it is poured. The yeast is still active and so still conditioning the brew. In many cases, the cask is right behind the bar, tilted on a shelf so the beer is delivered by gravity, without added carbon dioxide. Cask ale will only last a few days if air is going in to replace that draining beer. Some casks have CO_2 breathers that allow a bit of gas in but not enough to cause more carbonation. By definition, the cask-conditioning can be going on in any tank downstairs as long as it is a secondary fermentation, but the little wooden firkins behind the bar are a rare treat of authenticity.

Bare Bones Brewing Co.

Opened: 2015
Brewmaster: Lyle Hari, Jr.
Address: 4362 County Road S • Oshkosh, WI 54904
Phone: 920-744-8045
Web Site: www.barebonesbrewery.us
Annual Production: 600 barrels
Number of Beers: 12 taps (6 Wisconsin guests)

Beers:
 » Old Bones American Brown Ale
 » IPA
 » Oatmeal Stout
 » Pale Ale
 » American, German, and English styles and some mixes among them plus some sour beers and cask ales

Most Popular Brew: Too soon to tell.

Brewmaster's Fave: Sours and Belgians if he had to pick.

Tours? Yes, watch for schedules online or take your chances.

Samples: Yes, sample flights of 6 for about $9

Best Time to Go: Open Wed Fri 3–9, Sat 11–9 Sun 11–7. Closed Mon–Tue, but that may change. Check the website for current hours.

Where can you buy it? Here on tap and in growlers and howlers to go, plus a few draft accounts in the Lake Winnebago/Fond Du Lac area.

Got food? Yes, local frozen pizzas and some pasties, and food trucks in the future. For now also food friendly and there are menus from local places.

Special Offer: A free pint of Bare Bones beer when you get your book signed.

Directions: From US 45 take the exit for County Road T west toward CR S/Ryf Rd. Turn right on CR S heading north 0.4 mile and the brewery is on the right.

Cyclists: This is just off the Wiouwash State Trail.

The Beer Buzz: Located in a sort of red pole shed just outside of Oshkosh, this brewery shares the space with Puro Clean next door. Both are owned by the husband and wife team of Dan and Patti Dringoli. Dan's a homebrewer, and

when he went to the S.O.B. (Society of Oshkosh Brewers) about his idea to start a brewery, he met Lyle who was planning a one-barrel operation himself. Dan had a 15-barrel system and they agreed it'd be a good idea to collaborate.

Until recently, Lyle had been working in the food industry with cheese and yogurt. He hombrewed over 10 years before this, but his first memory of DIY beer is when he was a kid and his dad came home all excited with a pamphlet about homebrewing. Mom shut him down on that idea right quick. Many years later, Dan picked up a 2-gallon kit, then a bigger one, and so forth, brewing without knowing any other homebrewers for five years. Ten years from the stovetop to the brewhouse.

Dan's other business needed a bigger space, and when he went looking, he found this empty lot at the edge of the bike trail. He built this building for both businesses. He's still operating both. The taproom is in front on the right, with a bar and some pub tables, and a dart board. No TVs, just a flat-screen menu for the beers.

Free WiFi. Mug Club. Find them on Facebook.

Stumbling Distance: For a Wisconsin supper club experience, head over to *Jimmie's Whitehouse Inn* (5776 Main St, Butte Des Morts, 920-582-7211, jimmieswhitehouseinn.com).

Fox River Brewing Co.

Founded: December 15, 1995
Brewmaster: Kevin Bowen
Address: 1501 Arboretum Drive • Oshkosh, WI 54901
Phone: 920-232-2337
Website: www.foxriverbrewing.com
Annual Production: 1,400 bbls
Number of Beers: 13 on tap (9 on the patio)
Staple Beers:
  » 2 Dams Blonde Ale
  » Blü Bobber Blueberry Ale
  » Crooked Dock American Pale Ale
  » Marble Eye Scottish Ale

Rotating Beers:
  » Abbey Normal
  » Badger Bitter ESB
  » Belgian Black
  » Black Fox IBA
  » The Chief
  » Defilbrillator Doppelbock
  » 1853
  » Fox Tail Pale Ale
  » Foxtoberfest
  » German Pils
  » Hoppyface IPA
  » Maibock
  » Optic IPA
  » Oshkosh Best Bitter
  » Paine's Pilsner
  » Raspberry Wheat
  » Red Baron Alt
  » Shakedown IPA
  » Slam Dunkel
  » Titan Porter
  » Trolleycar Stout
  » 2x4 Imperial Pilsner
  » Upside Brown Ale
  » Vader's Imperial Stout
  » Vanilla Cream Ale
  » WI Coffee Stout

Most Popular Brew: Crooked Dock APA

Brewer's Fave: He's a hop head, so Crooked Dock APA

Tours? On request, call ahead.

Samples? Yes.

Best Time to Go: Open Mon–Sat 11–10pm, Sun 11–8pm. Happy Hour runs Mon–Fri 3–6pm & 9–close, Sat 9–close, Sun 7–close.

Where can you buy it? Here (and at their Appleton location) on tap plus growlers, quarter- and half-barrels and some local taverns serve it. Bottles are distributed in NE Wisconsin from Sheboygan to Green Lake on up to Ashland (but just shy of I-39 to the west, so not Stevens Point or Wausau... yet.)

Got food? Yes! The menu features a variety of steaks, seafood, pastas, sandwiches and pizzas and much more on their full menu.

Special Offer: $2 pint on your first Fox River beer, additional pints regular price.

Directions: In Oshkosh, cross the Fox River heading east on Congress (Hwy 21) and it's the first street on the left. You'll see it from the bridge.

The Beer Buzz: Fox River Brewing has always been the beer portion of Fratello's Restaurants but has dropped that name and now both locations are Fox River Brewing. On the banks of the Fox River, this trendy restaurant is one of the most happening spots in town. This restaurant has a view like no other and offers a family-friendly atmosphere with a separate taproom. There are forty slips for boaters, and the patio outside has a large tiki bar with 9 taps. It's a great time in the summer (rumor has it my cousin once danced on a table here—she denies it to the last). Cross the river heading east on Congress (Hwy 21), and it's the first street on the left. You'll see it from the bridge. Kevin Bowen worked at the restaurant years ago and started at Fox River Brewing Co. in an undeclared apprenticeship working from the bottom up: cleaning kegs, filling bottles, and such. After attending Siebel Institute to study the art and science of brewing, he worked for a few other brewhouses before returning to FRB. He's nabbed silver for his Kölsch in 2010 at the World Beer Cup as well as for his Abbey Normal Belgian Dubbel aged in a brandy barrel. In fact, he

has started doing more barrel-aged beers and bringing new brews into the lineup. Foxtoberfest comes on mid-Sept–Oct while Red Baron Altbier comes on tap during the EAA Fly In.

Stumbling Distance: *EAA* (Experimental Aircraft Association) (www. eaa.org) has a museum (just off Hwy 41 adjacent to Wittman Airport, 920-426-4818, open Mon–Sat 8:30–5, Sun 10–5, $12.50) with over 250 historic planes, five theatres, and a flight motion simulator. Don't miss the largest aviation event in the world. The *AirVenture*, when hundreds of experimental and homemade aircraft come to the week-long "Fly In" in late July, is like nothing you've ever seen. *Hughes Homemade Chocolate Shop* (1823 Doty St, 920-231-7232)—look for the open sign on the porch, walk up the driveway and to the side door, and head directly downstairs. If there is a line (which there always is) you'll have to wait on the steps. No displays or candy counters or fancy colors—just clean white boxes of chocolates that get unbelievable raves by choco-junkies. Call first—they are often closed and keep erratic hours. Best around holiday seasons. See the *Brews N Blues Festival* in the Festival section at the back of the book.

Look for *Fox River Brewing* in Fox River Mall in Appleton (4301 Wisconsin, Appleton, 920-991-0000)

OSHKOSH BREWING HISTORY

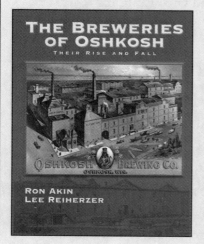

Oshkosh's brewing history goes back a lot further than Fox River Brewing Co. Since the 1840s, the city has been home to more than a dozen breweries and a robust beer culture that continues to thrive. You history and breweriana buffs out there should check out a new book about that old profession (I mean brewing). Co-written by Ron Akin, a retired University professor and breweriana collector, and Lee Reiherzer, a beer columnist and blogger, this is a lively account of beer and breweries in "Sawdust City," with over 400 illustrations. Check out the Oshkosh Beer website and order yourself a copy. oshkoshbeer@gmail.com, oshkoshbeer.blogspot.com

Black Husky Brewing Co.

Founded: March 2010
Brewmaster: Tim Eichinger
Address: W5951 Steffen Lane • Pembine, WI 54156
Phone: 715-324-5152
Website: www.blackhuskybrewing.com
Annual Production: 300 barrels
Number of Beers: 18 or so each year

Staple Beers:
- » Pale Ale
- » Sproose Joose Double IPA (with spruce)

Rotating Beers:
- » Big Buck Brown
- » Deck Dog Summer Ale
- » Harvel the Marvel
- » Jodlerkönig
- » Milk Stout
- » Schutzengel American White
- » Beware of the Dog Series (big beers):
- » Harold Imperial Red
- » Headbutter Barleywine
- » Howler Imperial IPA (dry-hopped with Equinox)
- » Smoke Monster
- » Sparkly Eyes (with spruce)
- » Three Scrutineers Tripel
- » Twelve Dog Imperial Stout

Most Popular Brew: Pale Ale or Sproose Joose.

Brewmaster's Fave: Hard to say. Depends on the time of year. Sproose Joose, I suppose.

Tours? None, not open to the public. Watch the website for changes.

Best Time to Go: Not open to the public at this time. Watch the website for changes.

Where can you buy it? Pembine, for sure. A lot of draft accounts plus 22-oz bombers and ⅙ kegs spread throughout eastern Wisconsin from Marinette to Kenosha. They are heavy in Madison and Milwaukee, and several cities have just one or two places carrying them: Marinette, Green Bay, Oshkosh, Kenosha. They self-distribute, so check the website.

Got food? Nope.

Special Offer: A Laurel and Hardy handshake

The Beer Buzz: This is typically what a serious homebrewer ends up doing when he thinks "career change." He and his wife Toni figured they'd never retire anyway so may as well find something they could do indefinitely. "Find something you love doing, something you really believe in so that it doesn't feel like work." He thought about volunteering at another brewery, but then thought, "Why? So I can learn to clean?" There is a lot to learn, and starting on your own, they felt it was better to just dive right in, as a nanobrewery. "Risks are smaller, and we're poor. We can't afford to borrow $500,000!" The learning curve is steep, but they went from 28 barrels to 200 in a year. They bottled over 20,000 bottles by hand one year. That has gone down as they focus on kegs (65% of their business), but they are still bottling a bit.

The aim is to keep on growing slowly and organically. Half the new accounts they get contact them directly. They don't market a bunch as they are so busy. Tim is on his third generation of brewing equipment. The first kettles were made out of half barrels with the tops cut off. He then moved on to a 1.5-barrel system. Now they have a 3-barrel system, all of it made from recycled dairy equipment. "I'm a hack when I do stuff, but it doesn't stop me from trying. My motto is How hard can it be?" His other motto is "Rarely balanced, Never boring," so expect beers that grab your attention. Some barrel-aging is likely. After three years keeping his day job, Tim phased himself out that job to do this full time. Toni did the same soon after. While they are **not open to the public** at this time, expansion is on the horizon and that could change. Watch their website.

Stumbling Distance: *Newingham's Supper Club* (722 Main St, Wausaukee, 715-856-5966) serves local beef and buffalo, steaks and seafood, and a Friday fish fry (lake perch, cod, walleye). *Four Seasons Resort* (thefourseasonswi.com, N16800 Shoreline Dr, 715-324-5244) is a nice hotel deep in the woods along the Menomonie River, rumored to be an old hangout for Capone types from Chicago back in the day. Stop in at *Pembine Food Depot* (N18678 Hwy 141, 715-324-6499)—they have Black Husky beer.

Plymouth Brewing Co.

Opened: April 20, 2011
Brewmaster: Joe Fillion
Address: 222 East Main Street • Plymouth, WI 53073
Phone: 920-400-1722
Web Site: www.plymouthbrewingcompany.com
Annual Production: 110 barrels
Number of Beers: 14 taps (5 plus guest taps); 43 beers per year

Beers:
- » HubCity Hefe
- » Long Day American IPA
- » Nutt Hill Nut Brown
- » Silber Black Phantom Bike
- » Stafford Oatmeal Stout (with French Vanilla Almond Coffee)
- » … plus many more and some barrel aging

Most Popular Brew: Stafford Oatmeal Stout

Brewmaster's Fave: Silver Black Phantom Bike

Tours? Not really. Casually by chance.

Samples: Yes, sample flights available.

Best Time to Go: Thu 5–10pm, Fri– Sat 5–11pm.

Where can you buy it? Here in pints and half-pints, and in growlers and howlers to go.

Got food? Free pretzel sticks and food friendly. Delivery menus are on hand.

Special Offer: $1 off your first pint of Plymouth brew during your signature visit.

Directions: From WI 23 across Plymouth's north side, take WI 67 south about 1.3 miles and stay straight on Milwaukee St. Turn left on Mill St and go 0.2 mile and the brewery is on the left.

The Beer Buzz: Plymouth Brewing Co. actually used to exist, from 1887-1937, managing to survive Prohibition but then failing shortly after it ended. Joe named his own operation the same and has a collection of breweriana, some of it from that original brewery. The building here dates back to 1923 when it opened as a women's dress shop. Joe built the bar himself, had all the plumbing and electric redone, and kept the old wood floor. Tall tables with beer labels under the glass tops stand along the wall of this narrow and deep shop.

Back in the 90s, Brewer Joe got a homebrew kit, and a year later he was brewing four times a week. It took him a while, like over a decade, but in 2009 he started thinking… why not a brewery? He operates a one-barrel system here and brews a wide variety throughout the year.

Free WiFi. Facebook/Plymouth-Brewing-Company and
Twitter @Plymouthbrewing

Stumbling Distance: Racing fans (or racing curious) should not miss *Road America* (N7390 WI 67, 920-892-4576, roadamerica.com), a popular racetrack with a long history, 10 minutes north. *52 Stafford* (52 S Stafford St, 920-893-0552, 52stafford.com) is an Irish-style inn (think B&B) and pub in town.

3 SHEEPS BREWING

Founded: February 2012
Brewmaster: Grant Pauly
Address: 1327 Huron Avenue • Sheboygan, WI 53081
Phone: 920-395-3583
Website: www.3sheepsbrewing.com
Annual Production: 4,000 bbls
Number of Beers: 5 year round, plus various seasonals and small batches

Staple Beers:
» BAAAD BOY BLACK WHEAT
» CASHMERE HAMMER NITRO RYE STOUT
» REALLY COOL WATERSLIDES IPA
» REBEL KENT THE FIRST AMBER
» SEVEN LEGGED CARTWHEEL WILD IPA

Rotating Beers:
» Nimble Lips, Noble Tongue Series (22-oz bombers)

Most Popular Brew: Really Cool Waterslides IPA

Brewmaster's Fave: "I'm a hop head: the IPA"

Tours? Yes, Fridays at 5PM.

Samples: No, but get a sample flight at Hops Haven upstairs.

Best Time to Go: At the brewery, only during tour times on Fridays. Upstairs, *Hops Haven* (which serves 3 Sheeps) is open Tue–Fri 2PM–close, Sat 11AM–close. Happy hour Tue–Sat 3–6PM (all day Tue).

Where can you buy it? On tap at Hops Haven Bar upstairs from the brewery (1327 N 14th St, 920-458-6572) and in growlers there. Distribution in 6-pack bottles and 22-oz bombers is throughout Wisconsin and in the Twin Cities and Chicagoland areas. There's a tapfinder on the website.

Got food? No, but *The Wicked Grille* (920-917-8269, thewickedgrille.com) connected to *Hops Haven* bar upstairs serves apps, soups/salads, sandwiches/burger, and even a Friday fish fry and fish tacos.

Special Offer: 15% off any apparel purchase during your signature visit at the brewery.

The Beer Buzz: "So many great breweries in Sheboygan have been forgotten," says Brewer Grant. True the brewing history goes way back to 1847 with Gutsch Brewing Co., a year before Wisconsin's statehood. After Prohibition knocked Gutsch out, the still-familiar Kingsbury took over in 1933 brewing until 1974. Heileman had already bought them in 1963, so one could still go "swinging with the King" even after that brewery closed its doors. In fact, 3 Sheeps takes over where another great brewery left off: Hops Haven. 3 Sheeps is set up in the basement of the same building, but you will still find Hops Haven on the sign because a bar remains on site and kept the name while sharing the space with The Wicked Grille, which does the food.

In 2005, Grant started homebrewing when his wife bought him a brew kit. Once he started counting yeast cells, he figured this was getting serious. He took some coursework at the Siebel Institute, and when Hops Haven's former location and equipment became available, he made the leap. Rather than trying to develop a menu and tavern, he decided to just brew the beer and let other entities operate the other two aspects of this unusual all-in-one arrangement.

Grant's amber was first named Enkel Biter. However, many drinkers kept thinking it was Enkel Bitter (seeing double, as can be expected) and so the name was changed to Rebel Kent the First to avoid the suggestion that this was a bitter beer. Funny story about his IPA's name. It comes from a t-shirt that shows a little boy at a crossroads forced to choose: Fame, Fortune, Success? or REALLY COOL WATERSLIDES! Perfectly expresses Grant's choice to leave the financial security of a job he was not passionate about to take the risk on something he really enjoyed. The Nimble Lips, Noble Tongue Series is a collection of limited-release specialty beers in 22-oz bombers and not to be missed.

Stumbling Distance: *Schulz's Restaurant* (1644 Calumet Dr, 920-452-1880) a few blocks up the street is a good place for a burger or a brat. *Legend Larry's* (www.legendlarrys.com, 1632 Michigan Ave, 920-458-9464) is the place for wings. A history of awards backs that statement up. *Charcoal Inn* (1313 S 8th St, 920-458-6988) has a charcoal grill (big surprise, given the name) for brats and burgers. The Sheboygan area is home to a Wisconsin classic: Johnsonville Brats (bratwurst, not rotten children). Check out *Brat Days* (www.sheboyganjaycees.com) in August—1000s of brat eaters, live music and a brat eating contest with serious competitors from around the world.

By the way, brats are "fried" in Sheboygan. A "grill out" or "cook out" is referred to as a "fry out."

Starboard Brewing Co.

Founded: October 2014
Brewmaster: Patrick Surfus
Address: 151 North 3rd Ave. • Sturgeon Bay, WI 54235
Phone: 920-818-1062
Web Site: www.starboardbrewing.com
Annual Production: 120 barrels
Number of Beers: 8 on tap; nearly 100 beers per year

Previous Beers:

- » Abbie Gale's Singel
- » Admiral Bully's IPA
- » American Amber Ale
- » Blarney Stone Irish Red
- » Bowsprit Wit
- » Citra Smash
- » The Demer's Charm Belgian Dark Strong Ale
- » Downtown Brown
- » Edinburgh Ale
- » Erwood ESB
- » Five Minute Fix IPA
- » Fugglestout
- » Imp IPA
- » No Apollogies Double IPA
- » Ryetous Ale
- » Weizen Dunkel

Most Popular Brew: The Demer's Charm

Brewmaster's Fave: The Demer's Charm

Tours? Nothing official, but by chance if someone is free.

Samples: Yes, flights of four 5-oz pours for about $8 or the "1000-Footer" flight, with 8 pours for $16.

Best Time to Go: In season: Open Wed–Thu 2–9PM, Fri–Sat 12–9PM, Sun 12PM–6PM. Watch for winter hours to be shortened.

Where can you buy it? Only here on tap in 10- and 16-oz pours or in growlers to go.

Got food? Small plates such as cheeses, smoked salmon, or chips and dips.

Special Offer: A free serving of kettle chips when you get your book signed.

Directions: From the south on WI 42/57, take the exit for Business 42/57 and follow it through town, crossing the Sturgeon Bay Bridge. Turn left on 3rd Ave and the brewery is on the left. From the north on WI 42/57, turn right on County Rd B/Michigan St. Go 1.4 miles and turn right on 3rd Ave.

The Beer Buzz: Patrick's mother bought him a Mr. Beer Kit for Christmas in 2005. He brewed a batch and it was awful. That didn't deter him, and he brewed a few more extract batches before jumping into all grain brewing. Two years before Starboard opened, Patrick was toying with a business plan, still not taking the idea too seriously. When Ahnapee Brewing opened in Algoma, he and his wife found themselves driving there every weekend. They realized there must be a call for it in Sturgeon Bay too. Ahnapee had a 2-barrel system at that time, and so Patrick was confident he could make it work with a one-barrel. This nano-brewery model affects the tap list. Rather than developing a few mainstays and keeping them on tap, he figured he could experiment a lot more, keep developing new recipes, and give his patrons reasons to come back soon and often for something different. He even has a request board from which he picks one idea a month and brews it. There is some predictability to the tap list: he has six tap targets, so there will nearly always be at least one of each—amber/brown, IPA, pale ale, stout/porter, wheat, and something truly unique, often outside of any single category. Patrick named his Belgian dark strong ale after the Demer, a river in Belgium. Thus far this is the only beer that has been brewed twice, and this repeat occurred when he asked his drinkers to vote on a beer they'd like to see back on tap. It's not just one of the favorites of the brewer.

Sturgeon Bay is famous for shipbuilding and also straddles a ship canal that connects the namesake bay on the Green Bay side of the peninsula to Lake Michigan. Thus, the nautical term for the brewery name. Brace yourself for boat puns and sailing themes.

The tapoom is a light and airy space without any frills. The bar top is repurposed bowling lane wood. There's no TV, no WiFi, but maybe a bit of background music, so it's a great place for a social gathering. Door County Folk Alliance comes in and plays some Irish music once a month. Parking is on the street. Find them on Facebook.

Stumbling Distance: *Bluefront Café* (86 W Maple St, 920-743-9218, thebluefrontcafe.com) has delicious, reasonably priced food, great sandwiches and craft beers. *Nightingale Supper Club* (1541 Egg Harbor Rd, 920-743-5593) has the old school décor and menu, with a Friday night fish fry and prime rib on Thursdays. *Sonny's Pizzeria* (129 N Madison Ave, 920-743-2300, sonnyspizzeria. com) offers Chicago-style pies and more pub food with a view over the water. Watch for Steel Bridge Songfest (steelbridgesongfest.org) in June when 16 venues open up for visiting musicians with a ticketed event at the main stage at the quirky *Holiday Music Motel* (30 N 1st Ave, 920-743-5571, holidaymusichotel.com). Jackson Browne has played here before, a friend of motel owner and musician Pat MacDonald (of "The Future's So Bright, I Gotta Wear Shades" fame).

ZONE 6

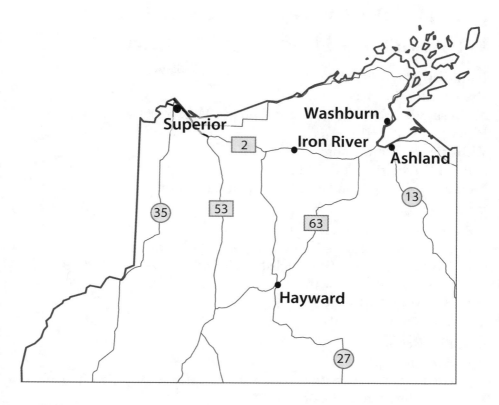

Ashland: South Shore Brewery
Hayward: Angry Minnow Restaurant and Brewery
Iron River: White Winter Winery
Superior: The Thirsty Pagan
Washburn: South Shore Brewery

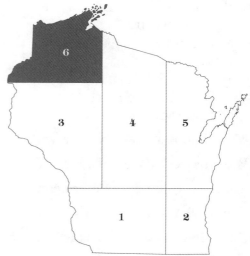

South Shore Brewery (in L.C. Wilmarth's Deep Water Grille)

Founded: May 1995
Brewmaster: Bo Bélanger
Address: 808 West Main Street • Ashland, WI 54806
Phone: 715-682-9199
Website: www.southshorebrewery.com
Annual Production: 1,800 bbls
Number of Beers: 8 on tap, 20+ beers throughout the year

Staple Beers:
- » Inland Sea Pilsner
- » Northern Lights Cream Ale
- » Nut Brown Ale (it's English-style and they've got the darts and crusty bread to go with it)
- » Rhoades' Scholar Stout
- » Wisconsin Pale Ale

Rotating Beers:
- » American Pale Ale
- » Applefest Ale (with local cider direct from the orchard)
- » Belgian-styles Saison and Tripel
- » Bitter Blonde
- » Bourbon-barrel Coffee-Mint Stout
- » Bracket
- » ESB
- » Honey Double Maibock
- » Irish Milk Stout
- » Maibock
- » Porter
- » Pumpkin Beer (with maple syrup)
- » Red Lager
- » Schwarzbier
- » Street Corner 40 Malt Liquor
- » Sumac Wit
- » Weizen Eisbock (rare and amazing)
- » Wheat Doppelbock
- » …Special beers for special events

Most Popular Brew: Nut Brown Ale

Brewmaster's Fave: Inland Sea Pilsner

Tours? Yes, best by appointment.

Samples? Yes, a rack of what's on for about $6.50.

Best Time to Go: Open daily 11AM–close (food served until 10PM). Watch for local festivals: Whistlestop Marathon, Blues and Brews (second weekend in Oct), Applefest in Bayfield (first weekend in Oct), Bay Days in Ashland (mid-July), Red Clay Classic (WISSOTA-sanctioned stock-car race), Firehouse 40 Bike Race, Fat Tire Bike Race, Birkebeiner cross-country-ski race in Hayward, etc.

Where can you buy it? On tap and in growlers to go on site, and bottles distributed throughout much of Wisconsin, western Upper Peninsula Michigan, North Shore of Minnesota, and Duluth Metro area.

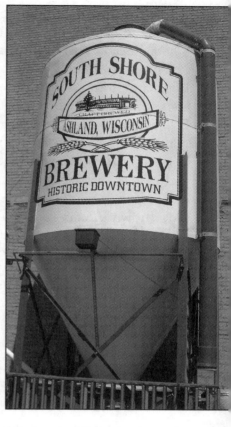

Got food? Yes, salads, sandwiches, and entrees. Walleye fish fry on Fridays and fresh Lake Superior whitefish. Beer cheese soup, ham, mushroom and wild rice soup, pale ale onion soup, and a stout BBQ sauce put the brews in the kitchen. They use malt flour or wort reduction on desserts. The adjoining dining room The Alley serves pizza.

Special Offer: 10% off South Shore Brewery merchandise during your signature visit.

The Beer Buzz: Ashland Brewery made a run from 1886 to 1892, and Ashland Brewing Co. served the city from 1901 to 1937, and it wasn't until South Shore opened up in a renovated railway station that local brew returned to Chequamegon Bay. Originally, the brewery operated with the Railyard Pub in the historic Soo Line Depot downtown. But fire and buildings don't mix, and when they did anyway, the brewery relocated to join Deep Water Grille in one of three Main Street buildings built by Lewis Cass Wilmarth (1833–1907), Ashland's fourth mayor. The brownstone accents and footings are all locally mined, and the cornerstone dates the structure at 1895. The restaurant is the best in town, and it doesn't hurt to have fresh beer on tap. The bar shows some antique stained glass and serves free popcorn. Brewmaster Bo likes to push the envelope a bit on some things. (See the peppermint in that coffee stout!) All of the base malt used in South Shore's beers is grown right there in the Chequamegon Bay / Bayfield Peninsula area and 65% of their hops are from Wisconsin—that's some impressively local beer. Bo collaborates with Iron River mead maker Jon Hamilton at White Winter Winery to make bracket, a sort of cross between mead and ale and precursor to modern beers. Bo's Nut Brown Ale is so popular he says he could get by on that brew alone. With all the continued success, South Shore's growth shouldn't come as a surprise: in 2015 they opened a production facility with limited tasting room hours across the bay in Washburn.

Attached to Deep Water Grille is The Alley, a pizza joint with a lot of TVs for sports. Come for the pizza buffet Thu 4–9PM.

Stumbling Distance: *Frankie's Pizza* (1315 Lake Shore Dr E, 715-682-9980) is the great greasy variety you can't get enough of (does carry out). *Ashland Baking Company* (ashlandbakingco.com, 212 Chapple Ave, 715-682-6010) is an artisan bakery bringing a bit of Europe to the Northwoods. Don't miss *Whistlestop Marathon and Festival* (www.whistlestopmarathon. com, 800-284-9484). Great blues concerts, a Lake Superior fish boil, pasta feed, beer, and running events the second full weekend in October. *Applefest* (www.bayfield.org) is the weekend before up in Bayfield and South Shore hauls out the specialty Applefest Ale for it. 60,000 people turn out for this massive celebration of Wisconsin apples. A rare roadside attraction might be the so-called *"Plywood Palace"* out in nearby Moquah, an odd little tavern that looks like it was nailed together by some fellas that already had a few. *Big Top Chautauqua* (www.bigtop.org, 888-244-8368) is an outdoor music/theatre venue that runs all summer up in Bayfield. *Stage North* (www.stagenorth.com, 123 W Omaha St, 715-373-1194) in Washburn runs music and theater events year round.

ANGRY MINNOW RESTAURANT & BREWERY

Founded: September 2004
Brewmaster: Jason Rasmussen
Address: 10440 Florida Avenue • Hayward, WI 54843
Phone: 715-934-3055
Website: www.angryminnow.com
Annual Production: 670 bbls
Number of Beers: 6–7 on tap, 12–14 per year

Staple Beers:
 » HONEY WHEAT
 » MINNOW LITE
 » OAKY'S OATMEAL STOUT (under nitro)
 » RIVER PIG AMERICAN PALE ALE

Rotating Beers:
 » BELGIAN BLONDE
 » CHARLIE'S RYE IPA
 » DOPPELBOCK
 » HEFEWEIZEN
 » IMPERIAL IPA
 » LAST NOTCH WHEAT
 » McSTUKIE'S SCOTCH ALE
 » MINNOW PILS
 » OKTOBERFEST
 » SAISON OLIVIA
 » VIENNA LAGER
 » … and a couple Belgians around winter

Most Popular Brew: River Pig Pale Ale

Brewmaster's Fave: Rye IPA, River Pig Pale Ale, Stouts in winter

Tours? Yes, by appointment or by chance.

Samples? Yes, $10 for six 6-oz samples.

Best Time to Go: Closed Sundays. Taproom is open Mon–Sat 11AM–close. Call for seasonal hours! Muskiefest is the third week in June each year and the Birkebeiner is in late February.

Where can you buy it? They self-distribute, so growlers at the bar and kegs and cans only in the Hayward area. River Pig Pale Ale and Oaky's Oatmeal Stout are the only brews available in cans either at stores or the brewpub.

Got food? Yes. The menu featuring everything from sandwiches to full meals changes regularly. The emphasis is on locally sourced ingredients. Burgers are popular. Fresh whitefish and perch come from Lake Superior, and crayfish are on the menu. Deep-fried cheese curds are still here, and Friday features the traditional fish fry (walleye, perch, and whitefish). Look for the Lake Superior whitefish sandwich.

Special Offer: A free pint and half off an appetizer!

Directions: Look for Florida Ave to intersect with Hwy 63 just four blocks south of the junction with Hwy 27.

The Beer Buzz: Lumber put Hayward on the map back in the nineteenth century, and the Angry Minnow has inherited a bit of its legacy. The restaurant and brewery occupy a restored 1889 brick building that once served as the offices for Northwest Lumber Co. Exposed brick, hardwood floors, tasteful lighting, and a good menu are notable enough. Like anything, add some great beer and it's all a little bit better. Brewmaster Jason got his start at the Great Dane in Madison as an apprentice and then returned to his hometown to show the results. The name was a twist on the local icon, the massive and elusive muskellunge (that's muskie to you and me). Hayward has the record for the largest one caught. So the pub went with the little guy on the hook who does all the work of catching the big fish. Appropriate for the brewpubs that are the little guys in the beer industry and yet really doing the most impressive work. The bar offers free Wi-Fi.

Stumbling Distance: OK, no one goes to Hayward—angler pro or not—without stopping in to see the giant muskie (over 4 stories tall!) at the *National Fresh Water Fishing Hall of Fame* (www.freshwater-fishing.org, 10360 Hall of Fame Dr, 715-634-4440). Go, and at *least* take a photo. The museum itself lives up to its icon in the fiberglass giant fish menagerie outside—400 fish mounts, classic motors, lures and equipment. *West's Dairy* (www.westshaywarddairy.com, corner of 2nd and Dakota, 715-634-2244) has been around since the 1920s and serves excellent homemade ice cream, malts, sundaes, and some sandwiches. Grab a coffee and some Wi-Fi here too.

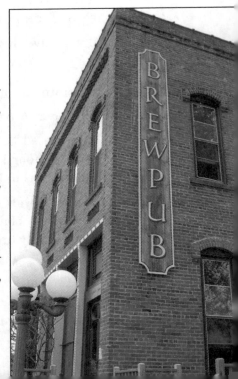

White Winter Winery

Founded: 1996
Mead Maker: Jon Hamilton
Address: 68323A Lea Street • Iron River, WI 54847
Phone: 800-697-2006
Website: www.whitewinter.com
Annual Production: 5500 cases
Number of Beers: 2 plus a lot of meads, ciders and a distillate or three

Beers:
  » Premium Oak Brackett (aged with oak chips)
  » Traditional Brackett

Mead and Distillates:
  » A wide variety of meads and a port-like fortified mead (delicious)
  » 3 varieties of Eau de Vie (Blueberry, Raspberry, Strawberry)
  » Oak aged Eau de Vie

Tours? Yes.

Samples? 3 free samples or the whole lineup for $5 (and you keep the glass)

Best Time to Go: Open Mon–Sat 10–6, Sun 11–4, but hours change seasonally, so call first or check the site. Summer Festival (mid-June), Blueberry Festival (late July) in Iron River, and Oktoberfest. Sundays in the summer often host live music. Don't miss the Labor Day Weekend Sunday "Emergency Pig-out" with live music, pig roast, and more—to benefit local emergency responders.

Where can you buy it? Bottles on site and liquor stores throughout Wisconsin, Minnesota, and Illinois.

Got food? Great fresh popcorn, baguette and cheese trays featuring locally baked bread and Wisconsin cheese.

Special Offer: 10% off any White Winter meads, bracketts or hard ciders or other products made on site.

Directions: At the west end of Iron River along the north side of US Hwy 2, look for the winery set back from the road across a parking lot.

The Beer Buzz: Jon comes from a long line of beekeepers, and though his family lived in the Minneapolis area, his father kept an empty hive out in the backyard while Jon was growing up. Jon knew of mead since middle school when he would do his term papers on honey and bees. When he was older, he decided making this ancient fermented honey concoction was easier than sneaking into the liquor store. Just off US 2 at the west end of town, his winery offers a great variety of meads and ciders all made from local ingredients, but he also has a couple types of bottled brackett. This is the missing link in the evolution of beer, you might say. Fermented honey (mead) is believed to be the happy hour drink of choice with the longest history, and the Scandinavians came up with brackett which is a cross between mead and ale by adding malted barley to the recipe. Brewmaster Bo over at South Shore Brewery in nearby Ashland helps out with this one since a winery must otherwise get another license to brew beers. Mead is associated with Winter Solstice celebrations (daylight hours start getting longer after December 21, and you are hopeful winter might actually end in May this year instead of June). The winery name comes from the legend of Old Man Winter, who is a resident in these parts for all but those two weeks of road construction in summer. Just kidding. Sort of.

Jon got his distiller's license in 2014 and is now making three varieties of *Eau de Vie*. Meaning "water of life" in French, it is a colorless brandy not aged in barrels so that the fruit essence remains. *Eau de Vie* is good as a digestif, easing your big stuffed belly after a hearty Wisconsin meal. Oak-rested varieties of *Eau de Vie* are also available.

Stumbling Distance: Pick up some fresh brats and meat sticks from *Jim's Meat Market* (68455 District Ave, 715-372-8566, jimsmeat.com). For some excellent diner fare with some very creative twists (baked puffy pancakes, baked omelets), head over to *Delta Diner* (www.deltadiner. net, 715-372-6666), southeast of Iron River on Cty Hwy H. You can't miss it—it's one of those classic shiny, aluminum-sided 1940s Silk City diners, restored and parked in the middle of the Northwoods. There are local bottled beers on hand, and dishes are also made with many local ingredients. Pick up some of Jalapeño Nina's Spicy Pickled Garlic while you're there too. *Oulu Glass* (www.ouluglass.com, 1695 W Colby Rd, Brule, 888-685-8969) eight miles west of Iron River features the amazing blown-glass work of the Jim and Sue Vojacek family from May 1 to January 5. Free demonstrations in November and December. Herbster, a town to the north, has sponsored an annual *smelt fry* every April since 1956, and it is a delicious taste of local culture. There are also many other area festivals—check with the Iron River Chamber of Commerce (www. iracc.com, 800-345-0716) for specific event dates.

Thirsty Pagan Brewing

Founded: 1996
Brewmaster: Allyson Rolf
Address: 1623 Broadway • Superior, WI 54880
Phone: 715-394-2500
Website: www.thirstypaganbrewing.com
Annual Production: 600+ barrels
Number of Beers: 16 on tap plus a beer engine

Staple Beers:
- » Burntwood Black Ale (named after a local river; cool points if you can name which one!)
- » Derailed Ale (classic American Pale Ale)
- » Indian Pagan Ale (IPA)
- » Lawn Chair Light Lager
- » North Coast Amber Ale
- » Trouble Maker Tripel
- » Velo Saison

Rotating Beers: Lots of them! Rotation is frequent, often a new beer every couple of weeks or so.
- » Oktoberfest
- » Pineapple IPA
- » Pinta Colada (cream-style stout with coconut)
- » Reinhold Berlin(er) Weisse (summer)
- » At least 2 sours on at all times, plus a barrel-aged brew
- » Also serving Hard Cider from *White Winter Winery* in Iron River

Most Popular Brew: Indian Pagan Ale

Brewmaster's Fave: "This is always that question no one really wants to answer, isn't it?" To brew, she's always been a fan of Burntwood Black Ale. To drink, it's Lawn Chair or IPAs.

Tours? Informal ones by chance or by appointment.

Samples? Yes, 3-oz pours in a house flight (up to 9 house beers) or seasonal flight (up to 9 beers) for about $12.25.

Best Time to Go: Open daily 11AM–10PM. Live music every night.

Where can you buy it? Only here and to go in growlers.

Got food? Yes, the best pizza in town and various appetizers and a kids' menu.

Special Offer: A free 10-oz glass of prune juice! No, I'm kidding—it's a beer.

Directions: Follow Hammond Ave south from the interchange with Hwy 53/I-535. Continue driving south to the first stop light, and take Broadway to the right (west). Or US Hwy 2 from the west becomes Belknap St. Take this to Ogden Ave and turn right north to Broadway where you will see the brewery on the corner of Ogden Ave and Broadway.

The Beer Buzz: In 1999, brewer Rick Sauer (now at Hudson Brewing) moved his Twin Ports Brewing to this 1910 creamery building on the corner of Broadway St and Ogden Ave. It's an unassuming place, still tiled like the creamery and all the feel of a northern town tavern. Local breweriana hangs on the walls. Steve and Susan Knauss took over and changed the name to Thirsty Pagan in 2006. Before this place, Superior hadn't had its own beer since Northern Brewing Co. emptied its tanks for the last time in the late '60s. They're serious about their beer here, but loads of fun to drink it with. The bar has expanded a bit adding space for forty more patrons. The restaurant side of the brewpub can seat larger parties.

Brewer Allyson is originally from Iowa and went to school in Mankato, but moved to Duluth in the early 2000s. She has always been a patron here and has a long history of drinking their beer. The beer inspired her to start homebrewing. She spent as much time talking to other brewers as possible and even went into a few other breweries to just sort of follow people around and pick their brains. She read a lot. Finally, she did an internship under the previous brewer, Nate McAlpine. When he left, she

stepped into the position. Her degree is in art, and while the job is not always about being creative, it's about being a maker. So whether it's a house brew that she makes the same way every time or something new, exciting and innovative, she feels happy to be producing something. She's very into sours and tries to keep 2 or 3 on at all times. She even isolated a local yeast strain. Allyson makes cider from apples in her yard and using the wild yeasts, so she knew there was a good yeast in her neighborhood in the upper east hillside in Duluth. She collected some plums, added them to some wort, and found she had some great beer. She plated out the yeast and collected a single colony that she maintains for brewing their Belgian-style beers. Allyson is one of three female head brewers in the state (see also Wisconsin Dells Brewing and Capital Brewing), but more and more women are becoming assistants and this will likely become less unusual. Guest brewers and collaborations are common. The brewery added a 7-barrel system in 2014, but still uses the previous 2-barrel system which is a fun and flexible system that they can really use to engage with a lot of people and do a lot of beer styles. All her assistants actually brew their own creations on it.

Free WiFi. Cribbage and cards. No TVs. Assistant brewer Jeredt Runion is an artist and his art adorns the walls.

Stumbling Distance: Dive into a dive at the *Anchor Bar* (413 Tower Ave, 715-394-9747) five blocks away. Burgeoning (yes, I really just used that word) with ship-themed paraphernalia, this cozy local tavern has many kinds of burgers—some weighing in at a pound—that are excellent, cheap, and inventive (*cashew* burger??). Take a growler of Burntwood Black Ale and get some fresh air at *Wisconsin Point* (Moccasin Mike Road), the world's largest freshwater spit (a sand bar with trees) with a lighthouse, Native American burial grounds, driftwood, agates, and many species of birds. History buffs shouldn't miss the *Richard I. Bong World War II Heritage Center* (www.bongheritagecenter.org, 305 Harbor View Parkway, 888-816-9944) where the ace of aces namesake is commemorated along with all the veterans of that war in an informative and sharply designed museum. A restored Lockheed P-38 Lightning fighter plane—the type of plane Bong used in his record 40 enemy kills—is on site.

South Shore Brewery

Opened: 2015
Brewmaster: Bo Bélanger
Address: 532 West Bayfield Street (WI 13) • Washburn, WI 54891
Phone: Not at this location (see Ashland)
Web Site: www.southshorebrewery.com
Annual Production: 3,300 barrels
Number of Beers: 8 taps

Staple Beers:
  » Inland Sea Pilsner
  » Northern Lights Cream Ale
  » Nut Brown Ale
  » Rhoades' Scholar Stout
  » Wisconsin Pale Ale

Rotating Beers:
  » American Pale Ale
  » Applefest Ale (with local cider direct from the orchard)
  » Belgian-styles Saison and Tripel
  » Bitter Blonde
  » Bourbon-barrel Coffee-Mint Stout
  » Bracket
  » ESB
  » Honey Double Maibock
  » Irish Milk Stout
  » Maibock
  » Porter
  » Pumpkin Beer (with maple syrup)
  » Red Lager
  » Schwarzbier
  » Street Corner 40 Malt Liquor
  » Sumac Wit
  » Weizen Eisbock (rare and amazing)
  » Wheat Doppelbock
  » …many more experimental batches at this location

Most Popular Brew: Nut Brown Ale

Brewmaster's Fave: Inland Sea Pilsner

Tours? Yes, on Saturdays; check the schedule on the website.

Samples? Yes, a rack of samplers of what's on for about $6.50

Best Time to Go: Tasting room is open Fri 3:30–7:30 and Sat 11AM–4PM. Come for Brownstone Days at the end of July. (Washburn Homecoming is every 5 years on that weekend.)

Where can you buy it? Here on tap and in growlers and six-packs to go. Bottles distributed throughout much of Wisconsin, western Upper Peninsula Michigan, North Shore of Minnesota, and Duluth Metro area.

Got food? Peanuts. Otherwise, there are area to-go menus from local restaurants, and the tasting room is food friendly.

Special Offer: Buy your first beer, get 1 free during your signature visit.

Directions: From Ashland, WI 13 passes north right through Washburn as Bayfield St. Where the road bends in downtown, watch for the brewery on the left side (not the lake side) of the street.

The Beer Buzz: See South Shore Brewery in Ashland for the full history here, but this is what happens when your beer gets popular and you run out of room to brew it: you open a separate production brewery. Brewer Bo did just that up the lakeshore a short way from where he got his start. Set in a former bowling alley, this 15-barrel brewhouse with 30-barrel fermenters is aiming to produce double of what is produced out of the basement at their location in Ashland. The tasting room, set in a 1920s bar building attached to the old bowling alley, has limited hours, but it's worth finding your way here: more experimental beers make their way on tap here than at the restaurant. Don't expect WiFi and TVs, but there may be some tunes in the background and a shuffleboard table made from an old bowling lane. Otherwise, this is all about the beer.

Stumbling Distance: *Washburn Cultural Center* (1 E Bayfield St, 715-373-5591, washburnculturalcenter.com) has a regional historical museum where you can see my grandfather in one of the old Du Pont dynamite makers photos. *Coco Artisan Breads* (146 W Bayfield St, 715-373-2253, coconorth.com) is way more than a bakery, with soups, sandwiches, and pasties plus coffee. *Good Thyme* (77180 State Highway 13, 715-373-5255, goodthymerestaurant.com) is fine dining in a casual setting just south of town. Don't miss the *South Shore Brewery* location in Ashland which is connected to *Deep Water Grille*.

Beer Festivals

Ah, there is nothing quite like a beer fest. Brat tents, music, and copious amounts of great beer. Variety is the spice of life, and a good brew festival allows you to travel through a whole lot of breweries that would have required a much longer trip.

This is only a general guideline. New beer fests pop up all the time. Specific dates change from year to year as do ticket prices. Also, some festivals sell out the same day tickets go on sale, months in advance, so plan ahead!

JANUARY

Ice Cold Beer Festival is around the second Saturday in January in Minocqua, WI. Tickets for the Wisconsin Brewers Guild event are cheaper in advance. Along with the beer from 45+ breweries, sample some gourmet cheeses and other fine foods. (wisconsinbeerloversfest.com).

Isthmus Beer & Cheese Fest is in Madison on a Saturday in January. Over 30+ brewers pair beers with about 2 dozen artisanal cheesemakers' best stuff. Bigger every year. (isthmusbeercheese.com).

FEBRUARY

Milwaukee Ale House Mid-Winter Brewfest is on a Sunday in February (www.ale-house.com) at Milwaukee Ale House and benefits the MACC Fund (Midwest Athletes Against Childhood Cancer).

Fond du Lac Brewfest got its start in 2010. This event aims to be annual and breaks up a bit of winter blues with four hours of beer pouring from Wisconsin brewers, live music, and food. Tickets are cheaper in advance or cost around $50 (facebook.com/FDLBrewfest).

Food and Froth is Milwaukee Public Museum's fundraising fest, offering samples of Midwest and import beers, plus great local food. Tickets are about $70 (cheaper for museum members) and $100 for VIP. (mpm.edu/plan-visit, click Calendar).

MARCH

Hops & Props brings in over 250 beers on a Saturday evening in early March. The event benefits the EAA AirVenture Museum in Oshkosh. VIP tickets also available. (800-236-1025, www.eaa.org).

APRIL

Superior Gitchee Gumee Brewfest (www.ggbrewfest.com) is in early April. A $25 ticket gets you access to over 120 beers from 30 brewers.

The **Dairy State Cheese and Beer Festival** (kenoshabeerfest.com) benefits the Boys and Girls Clubs of Kenosha. Watch for it in mid- to late-April at The Brat Stop right off I-94 outside Kenosha.

Milwaukee Beer Week (milwaukeebeerweek.com) is a late April series of events around the Brew City which features a passport so you can keep track of where you've been and need to go. These can also win you prizes.

MAY

Great Taste of the Midwest tickets usually go on sale May 1. The 6,000 tickets sell out in a couple hours (see August).

Madison Craft Beer Week is a 10-day (2 weekend) series of events around the city typically starting around the first week of May (or late April). Beer walks, parties, food/beer pairings, films, lectures—you name it! (madbeerweek.com).

Wisconsin Micro Beer Fest in Chilton has been running since 1992 when late founder and brewer Bob Rowland of Calumet Brewing Co. started a small event that quickly became the second largest of its kind in the state. Held in late May (Sunday before Memorial Day weekend), it features over 100 beers from more than 20 Wisconsin brewers. Sample these while enjoying good food and live music. Tickets go on sale at the end of March and sell out early. Held at the Calumet County Fair Grounds, Chestnut and Francis Streets, Chilton. Contact Rowland's Calumet Brewpub at 920-849-2534.

CRAFT BEER WEEK

The Brewers Association honors American Craft Beer Week (craftbeer.com) nationwide in the month of May. While anyone anywhere can tip back a few beers this week, several communities in Wisconsin have organized local craft beer weeks, coordinating a calendar of events that range from beer tastings and pairing dinners to lectures and presentations about beer and brewing-related topics for the general public and for hardcore beer geeks.

Kenosha Craft Beer Week

kenoshacraftbeerweek.com

In tandem with the national craft beer week, the city hosts events at about a dozen bars and restaurants, while the two breweries—Public Craft Brewing and Rustic Road Brewing—are heavily involved and even collaborate on a special beer for the event.

Madison Craft Beer Week

madbeerweek.com

Spans two weekends and includes so many venues and events that it merits its own mobile-friendly website complete with personalized calendar to help you sort it all and share your itinerary with friends. This 10-day event, organized to include all area distributors, brings in brewers from all over for tap takeovers, beer dinners, presentations, and tastings. As of 2015 it was already up to 110+ venues and 400+ events.

Milwaukee Beer Week

milwaukeebeerweek.com

Held in April rather than competing with the national event, the Milwaukee Beer Week is organized by Beechwood Distributors, and spotlights the 20+ breweries they represent for a series of tap takeovers.

Green Bay Craft Beer Week

gbcraftbeerweek.com

Green Bay had their first craft beer week in 2015, paralleling the dates of the national event. A booklet was available with the schedule of events which involved the four big breweries—Titletown, Hinterland, Stillmank and Badger State—plus many craft beer bars and notable restaurants. Establishments in De Pere, including Chatterhouse Brewing, joined the activities as well.

JUNE

Kohler Festival of Beer is a three-day fest usually held in late May/ early June and hosting craft brewers from around the country. Check akohlerexperience.com under Events for more information.

Milwaukee Beer Barons World of Beer Fest is in early June (www. beerbarons.org) and features over 250 beers from over 90 brewers. The Beer Barons also host a Monster Mash Homebrew Competition.

Door County Beer Festival on a Saturday afternoon in mid-June brings craft beer and local food together with live music, seminars, and more in Bailey's Harbor. Tickets are $35–40, plus a bit more for limited VIP tix. (doorcountybeer.com).

Great Northern Beer Festival is held in Eagle River the second Saturday in June (www.greatnorthernbeerfestival.com). Tickets typically sell out early. 30+ brewers turn up for this—many from Wisconsin but also several foreigners (from Minnesota and Michigan and the like)—and it grows a bit each year.

Rotary Brewfest is hosted by the Ketchum/Sun Valley Rotary Club and takes place mid-June. Sample beers, wines, craft liquor, and help charitable causes. Tickets are about $20. (rotarybrewfest.com).

Wisconsin Beer Lovers Festival in Glendale is hosted by the Wisconsin Brewers Guild in mid-June and features Wisconsin-only brews and their brewers, plus local chefs with foods to pair beers with. (wisconsinbeerloversfest.com).

JULY

Bacon, Brew & BBQ Fest (bbbfest.com) brings a holy trinity together for a fest with 40 brewers, nearly as many restaurants and caterers, plus bands on 2 stages. Held on a Saturday in mid-July in Sun Prairie.

Oshkosh Brews & Blues (www.oshkoshjaycees.org/bnb.htm) takes place around the second Saturday of July at the Leach Amphitheater in Oshkosh and proceeds go to local charitable causes.

Milwaukee Firkin Craft Beer Festival highlights cask-conditioned beers from over 50 breweries. Held on a Saturday in mid- to late July, tickets about $50 or $80 with VIP option. (milwaukeefirkin.com).

German Fest is a huge ethnic party at Maier Park in Milwaukee at the end of July. (germanfest.com).

Lac du Flambeau Lions Club Brewfest is held at the end of July on a Saturday in Minocqua. Over a decade old, the fest brings nearly 50 brewers together with food and live music to boot. $35–40 tickets, either ordered or at the gate. (lacduflambeaubrewfest.com)

Milwaukee Brewfest takes place in late July and features over 200 craft brews, live music, Wisconsin food for sale and sample, exhibits, games, and even the crowning of the Brewfest Queen. A great time right down by the lakeshore (milwaukeebrewfest.com, 414-321-5000).

AUGUST

Great Taste of the Midwest is sort of the big kahuna of beer fests and the second longest running craft brew festival in North America. Over 500 beers from over 150 brewers! All 6,000 tickets typically sell out in a couple hours and go on sale around May 1. The event itself is the second Saturday in August. Contact the Madison Homebrewers & Tasters Guild at mhtg. org. Tickets only in advance!

The Firemen's Catfish Festival in Potosi, home of the National Brewery Museum, serves up some the town's original beer for a massive fish fry. Also features music, truck and tractor pulls, a euchre tournament, fireworks and dance. Call 608-763-2261 for more info.

West Bend Germanfest in late August (www.downtownwestbend. com) features two stages of continuous music, authentic food, dancing, Sheepshead tournaments and daily raffles. Friday hosts a Fish Fry.

SEPTEMBER

The Fiery Foods and Beer Festival is from the same geniuses who brought you Bacon, Brew & BBQ, and takes place in Sun Prairie at Angell Park in mid-September. www.fireicefest.com

Great Lakes Brew Fest is in the middle of September, third Saturday generally, several great hours in the afternoon with the beer of over 60 brewers represented and unlimited sampling right on the shore of Lake Michigan. Lots of food is served and various forms of entertainment are provided. It gets bigger and better every year. Festival Park in Racine. About $50 plus a VIP option for more (www.greatlakesbrewfest.com).

Wisconsin Oktoberfest (wisconsinbeerloversfest.com) Held in Wausau on a Saturday in late September this is another Wisconsin Brewers Guild event with over 35 breweries and as many food vendors.

Chippewa Falls Oktoberfest (visitchippewafallswi.com) Northern Wisconsin State Fairgrounds (Hwy 124/Jefferson Ave), three days in the middle of September ($8 daily or weekend rates). Lots of song, dance, sauerkraut eating contests and Leinie's beer. Good family event.

Thirsty Troll Brewfest is around the second Saturday of September in Grundahl Park, 301 Blue Mounds St, Mt Horeb (trollway.com).

Egg Harbor Ale Fest brings 40+ brewers together on a Saturday in September, with live music, VIP early entry and a trolley shuttle for local lodging. (eggharboralefest.com)

Appleton's Octoberfest is late in September and draws over 100,000 people. www.octoberfestonline.org.

La Crosse Oktoberfest (www.oktoberfestusa.com) starts the last weekend of September (or first of October) and lasts four days.

Quivey's Grove BeerFest is at 6261 Nesbitt Rd, Fitchburg, 608-273-4900, quiveysgrove.com and takes place at the end of September or in early October. This beer fest features 45 breweries, 100 beers, and great food.

Weissgerber's Gasthaus Oktoberfest at 2720 N. Grandview Blvd., Waukesha 262-544-6960 in late September.

OCTOBER

Dallas Oktoberfest (no not Texas!) features the grilling of the colossal brat (over 160 feet long). How's that for a taste of Wisconsin? Seriously, Valkyrie Brewing Co. makes its home here. Not huge, but worth the trip! "You never know who else will be there. Or how dangerous it may become." www.valkyriebrewery.com, 715-837-1824.

New Glarus Oktoberfest is in Village Park, New Glarus the last weekend in September or the first full weekend in October. New Glarus Brewery hosts a beer tasting and there is lots of live music, food, and entertainment including kids' games (swisstown.com, 800-527-6838).

Sand Creek Brewing Oktoberfest (www.sandcreekbrewing.com, 715-284-7553) 320 Pierce St, Black River Falls, the first Saturday in October right on site in a huge tent with crafts and music all day and night.

Northeast Wisconsin Beer Festival brings in 30+ brewers in mid-October. It's indoors since this could either be beautiful weather or the

OKTOBERFEST

Oktoberfest was originally a wedding celebration. Prince Ludwig of Bavaria married Princess Therese in 1810. They hosted a horse race outside Munich and 40,000 people came to watch. The event celebrated the marriage (I imagine it was open bar) but also was a sort of harvest fest, a religious thanks for the crops and such. Each year, parades bring together floats and bands, and of course BEER. Munich may be the home of the festival, but Wisconsin provides a nice variety of them, most notably in La Crosse. And the namesake beer, which is traditionally aged from spring until this event, is often available at non-October times as well. Check with your local brewer!

eternal winter depending on the year. There is wine, food and music on hand. (craftbeerfestivalgb.com, stonecellar.com).

Wisconsin Dells is home to **Dells On Tap** in October (a weekend around the 20th), part of Autumn Harvest Fest, a family friendly festival with a craft fair, farmer's market, hayrides and more (wisdells.com).

NOVEMBER

Janesville Kiwanis Fall Fest of Ale occurs in mid–November (fallfestofale. com) with beer, food and music and benefit local charities.

DECEMBER

I got nothing here. Get yourself a growler or a few six-packs of craft brew from the local brewer or liquor store and have some friends over for the holidays. Don't forget your lederhosen. Prost!

BEER, BOATS AND BIKES

BOOZE CRUISES

Sort of the malt and hops version of the Love Boat, or Gilligan's Island without the hole in the hull. Or the big storm. Or the Professor. Or Ginger. OK, *nothing* like Gilligan's Island. Here are a few boat rides with beer:

Madison

Capital Brewery serves the beer and Ian's provides the pizza on this boat cruise around Madison's lakes with great views of the Capital, the University, and one of the finest cities in the country. Cost is about $36–40 per person, departs on Thursdays during May–October and lasts 2 hours. Reservations are required. Betty Lou Cruises (bettyloucruises.com, 608-246-3138).

Milwaukee

How about two brewery tours in one easy cruise? Sundays in Milwaukee, get on the **Brew City Queen II** or **Milwaukee Maiden II** and set sail along the Milwaukee River for a three-hour tour that includes tours of *Lakefront Brewery* and *Milwaukee Ale House*. Various tours start and end at each of the breweries. Check tour times when you make your reservation. Tickets are around $30 and include samples at the breweries and possibly on board, and an hour visit at each brewery. For information or reservations, call Brew City Queen 414-283-9999.

Or just stay on the boat to drink and eat with **Edelweiss Milwaukee River Cruise Line** which hosts various themed cruises including a **Beer and Cheese Cruise** and a **Beer and Brat Cruise**. Cruise along the Milwaukee River and Lake Michigan shoreline while drinking local beer and eating (local) Usinger brats. Tickets are about $25 and include *Milwaukee Brewing Co.* beer and unlimited bratwurst. (edelweissboats. com, 414-276-7447)

GET ON THE BUS

Think of this as the ultimate designated driver option—you and a busload of other beer enthusiasts being carted around, beer in hand, to various beer destinations. Brewery tours, beer bars, sporting events with beer. Based out of Madison, **Hop Head Tours** runs public and private group tours to small round-ups of regional breweries (plus distilleries and wineries), sporting events in Milwaukee, and more. Tickets often include samples, meals, a guest host, and a souvenir of some sort (hopheadtours.com, 608-467-5707). They also organize tours by bicycle, which have been quite popular in Madison.

Country Roads Brewery Bus Tour
New Glarus Brewing, Wisconsin Brewing Co. and Grumpy Troll Brewpub.

Brewers and Vintners Bus Tour
Wollersheim Winery, Capital Brewery, Grumpy Troll Brewpub and Fisher King Winery.

Suds and Spirits Bus Tour
Ale Asylum, Karben4 Brewing and Old Sugar Distillery

Brews, Booze, and Bees Bus Tour
House of Brews, Old Sugar Distillery and Bos Meadery

Suds and Spirits Bike Tour
Karben4 Brewing, One Barrel Brewing and Old Sugar Distillery

Madison Brewery Bike Tour
Ale Asylum, Next Door Brewing Co. and One Barrel Brewing.

Untapped Tours is a locally owned and guided bus-tour operation that takes you on a three-hour journey of Milwaukee. See the historic buildings, the Calatrava-designed art museum, North Point Lighthouse, and many other attractions, and stop for photos along the way as well as cheese samples at Clock Shadow Creamery and beer tasting at Lakefront Brewery. (414-698-8058, untappedtours.com)

BIKING FOR BEER!

Wisconsin has a large network of bike trails, many of them former railway corridors, and what better way to end a ride than with a locally made beer? Here are some options for where to ride and where to take a break.

Where required, bicyclists ages sixteen and older must purchase a State Trail Pass which costs $4/day or $20/year. Often they can be purchased at self-pay stations along state trails.

Zone 1

The Glacial Drumlin Trail (920-648-8774) starts in Cottage Grove heading east and passes south of **Lake Mills**, home to *Tyranena Brewing*

Co. and ends in Waukesha. Ambitious bikers may veer off the trail at **Delafield** for *Delafield Brewhaus* and *Water Street Lake Country*. Trail pass required. (Another trail, the Lake Country Recreation Trail, connects Waukesha and Delafield.) You may also ride bike-friendly roads west from the Glacial Drumlin trailhead to reach the *Great Dane* Eastside pub at 876 Jupiter Dr., **Madison**.

The "400" State Trail (608-337-4775, 608-524-2850) starts in **Reedsburg,** home to *Corner Pub,* and heads north where it connects to the Hillsboro, Omaha and Elroy–Sparta trails. Reedsburg is 16 miles from **Wisconsin Dells** where you'll find *Wisconsin Dells Brewing Co.* and *Port Huron Brewing Co.* Trail pass required.

Madison has over 100 miles of trails in and around the city and special lanes in some streets just for bikes. With the high number of breweries in the city and the adjoining cities of **Fitchburg** and **Middleton,** you have a lot of options here. Capital City Trail winds around Lake Monona and passes within three blocks of the *Great Dane* off the Capitol Square, a block from *One Barrel Brewing* and *Next Door Brewing* on Atwood, and within one block of the *Great Dane* Fitchburg location. Be sure to check out La Crosse's *Pearl Street Brewery* and their summer Tour de Pearl for a great way to pedal for pints and win something.

Military Ridge State Trail (608-437-7393) will take you from **Madison** (home of several brewers), through **Verona** (right past *Hop Haus Brewing* and not far from *Gray's Tied House* and *Wisconsin Brewing Co.*) and **Mount Horeb** (*The Grumpy Troll*). The trail ends at Dodgeville and provides trails to Blue Mounds and Governor Dodge state parks. Trail pass required.

Cheese Country Recreation Trail (608-776-4830) connects **Mineral Point** (*Brewery Creek*) to **Monroe** (*Minhas Craft Brewery*).

Badger State Trail (608-527-2335) stretches from **Madison** to Freeport, Illinois, via **Monroe** (*Minhas Craft Brewery*) and within a few miles of **New Glarus** (*New Glarus Brewery*) down the Sugar River Trail. Trail pass required.

Sugar River State Trail (608-527-2334) starts in **New Glarus,** home of *New Glarus Brewery,* of course. Trail pass required.

Zone 2

Interurban Trail (800-237-2874) cuts through historic **Cedarburg,** home of *Silver Creek Brewing*. The trail crosses Washington Ave in downtown just a couple blocks from the Cedarburg Mill, Silver Creek's home.

Oakleaf Trail (800-231-0903) in **Milwaukee** is an asphalt trail right through the brew city and yet somewhat peaceful and secluded as it passes along the river. You'd have to venture into the streets to get to breweries though. (Also see Glacial Drumlin Trail in Zone 1.)

You can actually *paddle* along the Milwaukee River to visit *Lakefront, Rock Bottom*, and *Milwaukee Ale House*.

Zone 3

La Crosse River State Trail (608-337-4775, 608-269-4123) connects the Elroy–Sparta Trail to the Great River State Trail and **La Crosse** is home to *City Brewery* and *Pearl Street Brewery*. Trail pass required. Be sure to check out *Pearl Street Brewery's* summer Tour de Pearl for a great way to pedal for pints and win something.

Old Abe State Trail (715-726-7880) ends in **Chippewa Falls**, home of *Leinenkugel's* and *Brewster Bros Brewing Co.* The trail ends right at the brewery. Say no more! Trail pass required.

Lucette Brewing Co. lies right alongside the Red Cedar State Trail (715-232-1242) in **Menomonie** and is about a mile away from *Real Deal Brewing* farther into town. The Red Cedar heads south 14 miles to connect to the Chippewa River State Trail which could then get you to **Eau Claire** for *Lazy Monk Brewery, The Brewing Projekt, K Point Brewing* and *Northwoods Brewpub.* Trail pass required.

Work is still in progress to connect the Chippewa River and Old Abe State Trails so that Eau Claire, Chippewa Falls, and Menomonie would all be connected by a rails-to-trails bike system.

Zone 4

Bearskin State Trail (715-453-1263) starts south from (or ends north to?) **Minocqua**, home of *Minocqua Brewing Co.* Trail pass required.

See also Mountain Bay Trail in Zone 5. By the way, *Red Eye Brewing* in **Wausau** has a great number of cyclist fans who stop by after their rides each day. Brewer Kevin Eichelberger is also an avid pedaler.

Tomorrow River State Trail (715-346-1433, co.portage.wi.us/parks) connects *O'so Brewing Co.* in Plover with *Central Waters Brewing Co.* in Amherst. See also the Central Wisconsin Craft Collective for a circle tour that adds *Kozy Yak Brewery, Stevens Point Brewery* and *Great Northern Distilling.*

Zone 5

Mountain Bay Trail (www.mountain-baytrail.org) connects **Wausau** in Zone 4 to **Green Bay**. This means *Red Eye Brewing, Bull Falls Brewery* and *The Great Dane Pub and Brewery* are connected to *Titletown, Hinterland, Badger State, Stillmank,* and *Legends* in **Green Bay**.

Wiouwash State Trail (dnr.wi.gov) passes right in front of *Bare Bones Brewing* in **Oshkosh**.

Zone 6

Osaugie Trail (800-942-5313) starts in **Superior**, home of *Thirsty Pagan*, and heads east. This connects to the Tri-County Corridor Trail (715-372-5959) which passes through **Iron River** near *White Winter Winery* and connects to **Ashland** (61 miles), home of *South Shore Brewery*. This one is pretty rough though for a biker. Mountain bike? ATV?

For up-to-date information and other state trails go to www.wiparks. net and click on Find a trail.

ROAD TRIPS FOR BEER

Maybe you've gotten signatures at all the Wisconsin breweries in this book. Or perhaps you have a cousin in Minnesota or a friend in Michigan. If you are fan of craft beer, you've got a lot more ground to cover in two more Midwestern states. As in Wisconsin, Kevin Revolinski takes you on a pils-grimage to find the locally made brews and the people who make them.

Michigan's Best Beer Guide and *Minnesota's Best Beer Guide* are available in bookstores and online, or check out Revolinski's website TheMadTraveler.com

Got a bookstore or a gift shop and think you might want to stock the latest beer guides? Contact Partners Book Distributing in Holt, Michigan. www.partners-east.com

HOMEBREWERS ASSOCIATIONS

A.L.E. Club, Appleton Libation Enthusiasts
General club meetings are the third Thursday of
even-numbered months at Stone Cellar Brewpub
1004 South Olde Oneida Street • Appleton
www.thealeclub.org

Beer Barons of Milwaukee
Meets fourth Wednesday 7:30PM, $5.00/meeting fee
10448 W. Forest Home • Hales Corners
www.beerbarons.org

Belle City Homebrewers & Vintners
www.bellecitybrew.org

Bull Falls Home Brewers of Central WI
Meets second Thursday of the month
www.bullfalls-homebrewers.org

Central Wisconsin Draught Board
Meets the second Tuesday each month.
facebook.com/CWDraughtBoard

Chippewa Valley Better Beer Brewers
www.cvbetterbrewers.org

Green Bay Rackers
www.rackers.org

Kenosha Bidal Society
kenoshabidal.com

**LUSH, Inc., Lazy Unmotivated Society of
Homebrewers (Northwoods)**
Meets second Thursday of each month
Eagle River / Minocqua area
northwoodslushinc@gmail.com

Madison Homebrewers & Tasters Guild
Meets two Wednesdays a month.
www.mhtg.org

Manty Malters
Meets the first Thursday of every month.
www.mantymalters.org

**MASH, Marshfield Area Society of
Homebrewers**
Meets the first Thursday of the month
www.mash54449.org
marshfieldhomebrewers@gmail.com

Menomonie Homebrewers Club
Meets the first Monday of the month
www.mhbrewers.com | info@mhbrewers.com

Milwaukee Beer Society
Beer appreciation club
milwaukeebeersociety.com

SOB's, Society of Oshkosh Brewers
Meets third Wednesday of the month.
www.realsob.org

UWP Homebrewing Club
University of Wisconsin Platteville
uwplatt.collegiatelink.net/organization/
homebrewingclub

HOMEBREW SHOPS

Brew & Grow
2246 Bluemound Rd Ste B | Waukesha
262-717-0666 | brewandgrow.com
1525 Williamson St | Madison
608-226-8910 | brewandgrow.com

Farmhouse Brewing Supply
3000 Milton Ave Suite 109 | Janesville
608-305-HOPS | farmhousebrewingsupply.com

The Frugal Homebrewer
238 W. Broadway | Waukesha
262-544-0894 | www.frugalhomebrewer.com

Grape Grain and Bean
816 S 8th Street | Manitowoc
920-682-8828 | www.grapegrainandbean.com

Hop to It
234 Wisconsin Avenue | Racine
262-633-8239 | www.dpwigley.com

House of Homebrew
415 Dousman Street | Green Bay
920-435-1007 | www.houseofhomebrew.com

Point Brew Supply
1816 Post Road | Plover
715-342-9535 | www.pointbrewsupply.com

Purple Foot
3167 S. 92nd Street | Milwaukee
414-654-2211 | www.purplefootusa.com

Smokin' Brew
9 S Wisconsin Street | Elkhorn
262-729-3001 | shop.smokinbrew.com

Wine & Hop Shop
1931 Monroe Street | Madison
608-257-0099 | www.wineandhop.com

GLOSSARY OF BEERS

Ale — Short answer: beer from top-fermenting yeast, fermented at warmer temperatures. Long answer: see Ales vs. Lagers in the History of Beer Section.

Altbier means "old" beer—as in a traditional recipe, not a brew that's gone bad. It's a bitter, copper-colored ale.

Amber is that funny rock-like stuff that prehistoric bugs got trapped in and now makes great hippie jewelry or that pretty girl you were sweet on in middle school. But here I think they're just talking about the color of a type of American ale that uses American hops for a bitter, malty and hoppy flavor.

American IPA is generally a term used for an IPA recipe made with American ingredients, especially the hops.

APA (American Pale Ale) is a pale ale using American hops. The hops flavor, aroma and bitterness are pronounced.

Barley wine is like precious gold wherever it's brewed. This ale jumps off the shelves or out of the tap. It is strong, sweet, a bit aged, and those who know are waiting to pounce on it.

Berliner weisse is a wheat ale made a bit tart or sour with lactic acid bacteria.

Bitter is part of the family of pale ales, cousin perhaps to the IPA. Like folks in a small Wisconsin town, all beer is related in some way, I guess. This brew has a wider range of strength, flavor and color than the IPA. See "ESB." You'll be back.

Blonde or Golden Ale is a lighter form of pale ale usually made with pilsner malt. It's a popular Belgian style and gentlemen prefer them.

Bock is a strong lager darkened a bit and brewed in the winter to be drunk in spring. Monks drank it during the Lenten fasting period because it had substance to it, you know, like liquid bread? The name comes from the medieval German village of Einbeck. So, no, it does not mean Bottom of the Keg or Beer of Copious Kraeusening. (*What IS kraeusening anyway?*) Bock means goat in German. Thus the goats on so many of the labels and the popularity of headbutting at fraternity bock parties. Brewmaster Jamie in the Dells calls it the "chili of beers."

Brackett (also called braggot) is the first form of ale and a sort of beer and mead hybrid. It was first brewed with honey and hops and later with honey and malt—with or without hops added.

Brettanomyces or "Brett" does not refer to the Green Bay Packers' Hall of Fame quarterback, but rather the genus name of a group of yeasts used to make sour beers such as lambics, wild fermented Flanders red ales, and *oud bruins*.

Cask ale or **cask-conditioned ale**: see **Real Ale**

Cream Ale is a smooth and clean, light-colored American ale similar to a pale lager. Cleaner flavor than your usual ale.

Doppelbock see "Bock" and read it twice. Seriously, just a bock with a stronger punch to it though not necessarily double.

Dunkelweiss is a dark wheat beer, a German style. "Dunkel" means dark.

Eisbock if you say it outloud is probably easier to guess. No, it's not beer on the rocks. Take a bock, freeze it, take the ice out, and you have a higher alcohol content bock. Weizen eisbock then is a wheat version of this beer and it's delicious.

ESB (Extra Special Bitter) see "Bitter" and add some more alcohol. Isn't that what makes beer special?

Gose is an unfiltered 50% malted wheat beer style still found in Leipzig, Germany. Some lactic acid and the addition of ground coriander seeds and salt make an unusual sour beer.

Gueze is a blended beer made by combining a young 1-year-old lambic with an older one of 2 or 3 years.

Gruit or **Grut** is a mixture of herbs that beer makers used to use before hops came into favor. It added bitterness and in some cases preservative qualities, and the unique blends offered a variety of flavors for beers. Some brewers might do unhopped beers and use things like juniper berries, chamomile, heather or other things that sound like lawn clippings.

Hefeweizen (German Wheat Beer) is *supposed* to be cloudy—it's unfiltered. Don't make that face, drink it. That's where all the vitamins are and stuff. See also "Weisse" et al. It's recommended not to drink beers directly from the bottle, but to use a proper glass, but especially in this case. Germans even write that on the bottle sometimes in case you forget.

Imperial Stout see "Stout." The Brits originally made this for the Russian imperial court. It had to cross water as cold as International Falls so the high alcohol content kept it from freezing. Expect roasted, chocolate, and burnt malt flavors and a strong left hook. Also called **Russian Imperial Stout.**

IPA (India Pale Ale) is what the Brits used to send to India. The long journey spoiled porters and stouts, and so this recipe calls for lots of hops. Did you read that part yet? About hops as a preservative? You can't just skip parts of the book. I'll catch you. And there will be a quiz. Don't say I didn't warn you.

Irish-style Stout is a dry version of stout, typically served under nitro for the creamy special effect. However, it's very dark and thus too difficult to dye green on St. Patty's Day.

Kölsch is just an excuse to use those little dot things—"What is an umlaut?" for those of you looking to score on *Jeopardy*—and a difficult-to-pronounce-correctly-and-still-retain-your-dignity name for a light, subtley fruity ale that originated in Cologne... the city in Germany; please don't drink your aftershave no matter how nice it smells.

Lager — Short answer: beer with bottom-fermenting yeast, fermented colder than ale. Long answer: see Ales vs. Lagers in the History of Beer Section.

Lambic — Let's just call this the Wild One. It's a Belgian ale with a bit of unmalted wheat and it uses naturally occurring yeast, the kind that's just floating around out there. The brew is tart and may have a fruit element added such as raspberries or cherries.

Low alcohol — See "Near Bear."

Maibock is not your bock and if you touch my bock, there's gonna be trouble. This is the lightest of the bocks and is traditionally brewed to be drunk in May, but we're not always hung up on tradition and it is often around whenever you want it.

Märzen takes its name from March, the month in which this lager is typically brewed so it can age in time for Oktoberfest when it magically becomes Oktoberfest beer.

Mead is honey fermented in water. It ain't beer but it's good. And there's plenty of honey in Minnesota to make it. The word "honeymoon" comes from a tradition of gifting a newlywed couple a month's worth of mead to get things off to a smooth start. From this you can guess why we say "the honeymoon's over" with such lament.

Near Beer — Let's just pretend we didn't hear this and move on, shall we?

(Nut) Brown Ale uses brown roasted malt, and a bit of hops brings some bitterness. Brown ales can be a bit malty sweet or a bit hoppy; the style varies even from London to Newcastle (malty, almost nutty) where the term originated. Originally it was simply a description of the color (of porters, stout), but it has evolved to be a style. In America they tend to be a bit hoppier and stronger. *Does not contain nuts and is not processed in a facility that uses nuts.*

Oktoberfest is Märzen after the 6–7 month wait as it ages a bit.

Pilsner is a style that comes from Plzen, a Czech version of Milwaukee. Dry and hoppy, this golden lager is hugely popular and most of the mass-produced versions fail to imitate the Czech originals. Best to try a handcrafted version at your local—or someone else's local—brewpub. Also a term I use to describe residents of Moquah, Wisconsin, which is also the Township of Pilsen where my grandparents lived. Interestingly, the first pilsner was brewed in Plzen in 1842 by Josef Groll, a brewer hired from Bavaria. The pale malt, the Saaz hops, bottom-fermenting yeast (lager), and the super soft water of Plzen created a very different brew from the (until then) top fermenting ales of Bohemia, and it quickly became a sensation.

MEASURE FOR MEASURE

A **growler** is a half-gallon jug, refillable at your local brewpub. Many brewers sell them to you full for a few dollars more than the refill.

A **howler** or **grumbler** or **squealer** is a term coined variously for a container that is half a growler.

A **crowler** is a 32-oz can fillable on demand at the taproom like a growler.

A **bomber** is a 22-oz bottle.

One **US barrel** (1 bbl) is two kegs or 31 gallons or 248 pints, so you better start early.

A **keg,** sometimes casually and inaccurately referred to as a barrel, holds 15.5 gallons—this is the legendary half-barrel of the college party fame

A **Cornelius keg** is a pub keg, similar to one of those soda syrup canisters and holds 5 gallons.

A **US pint** = 16 oz = a proper US beer. (Also defined as 1/8 of a gallon)

A **can** = 12 oz or 16 oz typically, unless you are from Australia.

A **UK or Imperial pint** = 20 oz (lucky chumps) and there are laws protecting the drinker from improperly filled pints! Look for that little white line on the pint glass.

**Ah, but wait. Imperial pints are 20 *Imperial* ounces, which are different from the American ounces. The imperial fluid ounce is 28.4130625 ml while the US fluid ounce (as opposed to the dry ounce) is 29.5735295625 ml exactly, about 4% larger than the imperial unit. And if that isn't clear, be aware that the US *also* defines a fluid ounce as exactly 30 milliliters for the purposes of labeling nutrition information.

A **firkin** is a small cask or barrel, usually the equivalent of a ¼ barrel or about 9 gallons (34 liters)

A **buttload** is a real thing. In winespeak, a butt was a large cask with the volume of four standard wine barrels, just about 480 liters. In US gallons, that would be about 126. So just over 4 barrels of beer would truly be a buttload of beer.

Getting confused yet? I gave up at "pint" and drank one. And don't even get me started on the whole metric vs. Imperial gallon vs. US gallon vs. 10-gallon hat conundrum.

Porter is not only a Wisconsin brewer (Tom at Lake Louie) but also a fine, dark ale made with roasted malt and bitter with hops. Baltic Porter (a bit stronger to be shipped across the Baltic Sea) and Robust Porter (may be stronger, more aggressive with the hops).

Rauchbier is beer made with smoked barley malt. It may be an acquired taste, but if you like bacon… Back in the day, when open fires were sometimes used to dry malt, most beers likely had some smokiness to them. Beginning in the 1600s, the use of kilns eliminated this effect. This intentional style is associated with Bamberg, Germany, where it is still done.

Real ale is another way of referring to **cask ale**. It is unfiltered and unpasteurized and completes its secondary fermentation in the cask it is served from, without the use of carbon dioxide or nitrogen pressure "pushing" it through a serving line. They are either hand-pulled (on a hand pump or "beer engine") or gravity fed.

Rye beer substitutes some malted rye for some of the malted barley. Remember in that "American Pie" song, the old men "drinking whiskey and rye?" Yeah, that's something else. This gives a distinct slight spiciness to the beer.

Sahti is an old Finnish style of beer, herbal in its ingredients, typically employing juniper berries but not always hops.

Saison is French for "season" (those people have a different word for everything it seems) and this beer was intended for farm workers at the end of summer. It's Belgian in origin and the yeast used ferments at a higher ale temperature. It's generally cloudy and often has something like orange zest or coriander in it. While it was originally a low-alcohol brew so the workers could keep working, many American revivals of the style are packing a bit of a punch.

Saké — This is more of a trivia note than anything. It's not wine or rice wine; it's actually a Japanese rice beer, technically, as it is a fermented grain.

Schwarzbier is the way they say "black beer" in Germany. This lager is black as midnight thanks to the dark roasted malt and has a full, chocolatey or coffee flavor much like a stout or porter.

Scotch Ale or Scottish-style Ale is generally maltier than other ales and sometimes more potent. The FDA insists it be labeled "Scottish-style" as it is not actually from Scotland if brewed here in Wisconsin. Fair enough.

Smash is a slang term for "single malt, single hop" referring to the brew recipe.

Sour Ale is a variety of beer that uses wild yeasts and bacteria to get a brew that makes you pucker a bit. Beer can become unintentionally and unpleasantly sour when bacteria infect it. This is different; it's intentional and when done traditionally, it's kinda risky to other nearby brewing, so steps must be taken to keep unintended infections from happening. A lambic fits this category.

Stout is made with dark roasted barley and lots of hops, and it is a black ale most smooth. It can be bitter, dry, or even sweet when it's brewed with milk sugar (lactose). On occasion brewers add oatmeal for a smoother and sweeter ale and you have to start wondering if there is something to that saying, "Beer, it's not just for breakfast anymore." Imperial Stout is a strong variation on the recipe first done up by the English exporting to the Russians in the 1800s. The real fun of it is when it is on a nitrogen tap. Look that up!

Tripel is an unfiltered Belgian ale that has a very high alcohol content. The combination of hops and large amounts of malt and candy sugar give a bittersweet taste to this powerhouse. Many brewpubs will only allow you to drink one or two glasses to make sure you can still find the door when you leave.

Wheat Beer is beer made with wheat. You didn't really just look this up, did you? Dude.

Witbier, Weisse, Weizen, Wisenheimer — three of these words are simply different ways of saying white wheat beer that originated in Belgium. They are sometimes flavored with orange peel and coriander and are mildly to majorly sweet. The fourth word describes the kind of guy that would write that Wheat Beer definition.

And what the hell IS kraeusening anyway???

And finally, *what is kraeusening?*

Brewers can add a small amount of unfermented beer and yeast to beer that is done fermenting and being put into a bottle, keg or tank. The resulting bit of fermentation produces additional carbon dioxide which dissolves into the beer giving it carbonation. So I guess you could say it's a beer belch waiting to happen.

BIBLIOGRAPHY

Akin, Ron and Reiherzer, Lee. *The Breweries of Oshkosh – Their Rise and Fall*, 2012.

Apps, Jerold. *Breweries of Wisconsin*, 2nd Ed., University of Wisconsin Press, 2005.

Glover, Brian. *The Beer Companion: An Essential Guide to Classic Beers from Around the World*, Lorenz, 1999.

Harper, Timothy and Oliver, Garrett. *The Good Beer Book: Brewing and Drinking Quality Ales and Lagers*, Berkley Books, 1997.

Kroll, Wayne. *Wisconsin's Frontier Farm Breweries*, self-published.

Smith, Gregg. *Beer: A History of Suds and Civilization from Mesopotamia to Microbreweries*, Avon Books, 1995.

Swierczynski, Duane. *The Big Book o' Beer: Everything You Ever Wanted to Know About the Greatest Beverage on Earth*, Quirk Books, 2004.

Yenne, Bill. *The American Brewery*, MBI, 2003.

INDEX

Signatures

3 Sheeps Brewing (Sheboygan)

_____Date_____

10th Street Brewery (Milwaukee)

_____Date_____

841 Brewhouse (Whitewater)

_____Date_____

Ahnapee Brewing Co. (Algoma)

_____Date_____

Ale Asylum (Madison)

_____Date_____

Alt Brew (Madison)

_____Date_____

Angry Minnow Restaurant And Brewery (Hayward)

_____Date_____

Appleton Beer Factory (Appleton)

_____Date_____

Badger State Brewing Co. (Green Bay)

_____Date_____

Bare Bones Brewing (Oshkosh)

_____Date_____

Barley John's Brewing (New Richmond)

_____Date_____

Bent Kettle Brewing (Coming soon!)

_____Date_____

Big Bay Brewing Co. (Milwaukee – Shorewood)

_____Date_____

Big Head Brewing (Wauwatosa)

_____Date_____

Biloba Brewing (Brookfield)

_____Date_____

Black Husky Brewing Co. (Pembine)

_____Date_____

Bloomer Brewing Co. (Bloomer)

_____Date_____

Blue Heron BrewPub (Marshfield)

_____Date_____

Brady's Brewhouse (New Richmond)

_____Date_____

Brenner Brewing Co. (Milwaukee)

_____Date_____

Brewery Creek Brewpub (Mineral Point)

_____Date_____

The Brewing Projekt (Eau Claire)

_____Date_____

Brewster Bros. Brewing Co. (Chippewa Falls)

_____Date_____

Bull Falls Brewery (Wausau)

_____Date_____

Capital Brewery (Middleton)

_____Date_____

Central Waters Brewing Co. (Amherst)

_____Date_____

Chatterhouse Brewing (De Pere)

_____Date_____

City Brewery (La Crosse)

_____Date_____

Common Man Brewing (Ellsworth)

_____Date_____

Company Brewing (Milwaukee)

_____Date_____

Corner Pub (Reedsburg)

_____Date_____

Courthouse Pub (Manitowoc)

_____Date_____

Dave's BrewFarm (Wilson)

_____Date_____

Delafield Brewhaus (Delafield)

_____Date_____

District 14 Brewing (Milwaukee)

_____Date_____

Door County Brewing Co. (Baileys Harbor)

_____Date_____

Driftless Brewing Co. (Soldiers Grove)

_____Date_____

Esser's Cross Plains Brewery (Cross Plains)

_____Date_____

Fixture Brewing Co. (Waukesha)

_____Date_____

Fox River Brewing Co. (Appleton)

_____Date_____

Fox River Brewing Co. (Oshkosh)

_____Date_____

Funk Factory Geuzeria (Madison)

_____Date_____

Furthermore Beer

_____Date_____

Geneva Lake Brewing Co. (Lake Geneva)

_____Date_____

Granite City Food and Brewery (Madison)

_____Date_____

Gray Brewing Co. (Janesville)

_____Date_____

Gray's Tied House (Verona)

_____Date_____

Great Dane Pub and Brewery (Fitchburg)

_____Date_____

Great Dane Pub and Brewery (Hilldale-Madison)

_____Date_____

Great Dane Pub and Brewery (Madison)

_____Date_____

Great Dane Pub and Restaurant (Wausau)

_____Date_____

Grumpy Troll Brew Pub (Mount Horeb)

_____Date_____

Hillsboro Brewing Co. (Green Hillsboro)

_____Date_____

Hinterland Brewery (Green Bay)

_____Date_____

The Hop Garden Tap Room (Paoli)

_____Date_____

Hop Haus Brewing Co. (Verona)

_____Date_____

Horny Goat Brewing Co. (Milwaukee)

_____Date_____

House of Brews (Madison)

_____Date_____

Jacob Leinenkugel Brewing (Chippewa Falls)

_____Date_____

K Point Brewing (Eau Claire)

_____Date_____

Karben4 Brewing (Madison)

_____Date_____

Kozy Yak Brewery (Rosholt)

_____Date_____

Lakefront Brewery (Milwaukee)

_____Date_____

Lake Louie Brewing (Arena)

_____Date_____

Lazy Monk Brewery (Eau Claire)

_____Date_____

Legends Brewhouse & Eatery (De Pere)

_____Date_____

Legends Brewhouse & Eatery (Green Bay)

_____Date_____

Lucette Brewing Co. (Menomonie)

_____Date_____

Miller Brewing Co. / MillerCoors (Milwaukee)

_____Date_____

Milwaukee Ale House (Milwaukee)

_____Date_____

Milwaukee Brewing Company / 2nd Street Brewery (Milwaukee)

_____Date_____

Mines Creek Brewing (Spring Valley)

_____Date_____

Minhas Craft Brewery (Monroe)

_____Date_____

Minocqua Brewing Company (Minocqua)

_____Date_____

MobCraft Beer (Milwaukee)

_____Date_____

New Glarus Brewing Co. (New Glarus)

_adam Timmers_____Date_ 10-1 _____

Next Door Brewing (Madison)

_____Date_____

Northwoods Brewpub and Grill (Eau Claire)

_____Date_____

Octopi Brewing Co. (Waunakee)

_____Date_____

Oliphant Brewing (Somerset)

_____Date_____

One Barrel Brewing (Madison)

_____Date_____

O'so Brewing Company (Plover)

_____Date_____

Pabst (Milwaukee – page 201)

_____Date_____

Parched Eagle Brewpub (Westport)

_____Date_____

Pearl Street Brewery (La Crosse)

_____Date_____

Pigeon River Brewing Co. (Marion)

_____Date_____

Pitchfork Brewing (Hudson)

_____Date_____

Plymouth Brewing Co. (Plymouth)

_____Date_____

Port Huron Brewing Co. (Wisconsin Dells)

_____Date_____

Potosi Brewing Company (Potosi)

_____Date_____

Public Craft Brewing Co. (Kenosha)

_____Date_____

Rail House Restaurant & Brewpub (Marinette)

_____Date_____

Real Deal Brewing Co. (Menomonie)

_____Date_____

Red Eye Brewing Company (Wausau)

_____Date_____

Rhinelander Brewing Co. (Rhinelander)

_____Date_____

Riverside Brewery & Restaurant (West Bend)

_____Date_____

Rock Bottom Restaurant & Brewery (Milwaukee)

_____Date_____

Rock County Brewing Co. (Janesville)

_____Date_____

Rockhound Brewing Co. (Madison)

_____Date_____

RockPere Brewing Co. (Rockland)

_____Date_____

Rocky Reef Brewing Co. (Woodruff)

_____Date_____

Rowland's Calumet Brewing (Chilton)

_____Date_____

Rush River Brewing Co. (River Falls)

_____Date_____

Rustic Road Brewing Co. (Kenosha)

_____Date_____

Sand Creek Brewing Co. (Black River Falls)

_____Date_____

Second Salem Brewing Co. (Whitewater)

_____Date_____

Shipwrecked Brew Pub (Egg Harbor)

_____Date_____

Silver Creek Brewing Co. (Cedarburg)

_____Date_____

South Shore Brewery (Ashland)

_____Date_____

South Shore Brewery (Washburn)

_____Date_____

Sprecher Brewing Co. (Glendale Milwaukee)

_____Date_____

St. Francis Brewery and Restaurant (St. Francis)

_____Date_____

Starboard Brewing Co. (Sturgeon Bay)

_____Date_____

Stevens Point Brewery (Stevens Point)

_____Date_____

Stillmank Brewing Co. (Green Bay)

_____Date_____

Stone Cellar Brewpub (Appleton)

_____Date_____

Sweet Mullets Brewing Co. (Oconomowoc)

_____Date_____

Thirsty Pagan Brewing (Superior)

_____Date_____

Titletown Brewing Co. (Green Bay)

_____Date_____

Tribute Brewing Co. (Eagle River)

_____Date_____

Turtle Stack Brewery (La Crosse)

_____Date_____

Tyranena Brewing Co. (Lake Mills)

_____Date_____

Urban Harvest Brewing (Milwaukee)

_____Date_____

Valkyrie Brewing Co. (Dallas)

_____Date_____

Viking Brew Pub (Stoughton)

_____Date_____

Vintage Brewing Co. (Madison)

_____Date_____

Water Street Brewery (Milwaukee)

_____Date_____

Water Street Grafton Brewery (Grafton)

_____Date_____

Water Street Lake Country Brewery (Delafield)

_____Date_____

Water Street Oak Creek Brewery (Oak Creek)

_____Date_____

White Winter Winery (Iron River)

_____Date_____

Wisconsin Brewing Co. (Verona)

_____Date_____

Wisconsin Dells Brewing Co. (Wisconsin Dells)

_____Date_____

Woodman Brewery (Woodman)

_____Date_____

ABOUT THE AUTHOR

Kevin Revolinski is an amateur beer snob and born-again ale drinker with a writing habit. A Wisconsin native, he has written for a variety of publications including *The New York Times*, *Chicago Tribune*, *Wisconsin State Journal* and many postcards to his grandmother. He's appeared on The Today Show and Wisconsin Public Radio talking about beer. His

PHOTOGRAPH COURTESY OF TOM RISTAU

other travel books include *Minnesota's Best Beer Guide*, *Michigan's Best Beer Guide*, *Paddling Wisconsin*, *Best in Tent Camping Wisconsin*, *Best Hikes Near Milwaukee*, *Backroads and Byways of Wisconsin*, *60 Hikes Within 60 Miles of Madison*, *Camping Michigan*, and *The Yogurt Man Cometh: Tales of an American Teacher in Turkey*. Check out his website and blog, The Mad Traveler at www.theMadTraveler.com and revtravel.com. He also contributes to the beer travel site www.Pilsgrimage.com. Look for him at your local brewpub. (It's more likely he's at one of his own local brewpubs in Madison though.)

ABOUT THE PHOTOGRAPHER

Preamtip Satasuk is originally from Bangkok, Thailand. Her work has appeared in *Chicago Tribune* and various guidebooks. She maintains a bilingual food and travel blog at TipsFoodAndTravel.com.